FEAR OF FIFTY

By Erica Jong

Fruits & Vegetables
poetry, 1971

Half-Lives
poetry, 1973

Fear of Flying
fiction, 1973

Loveroot
poetry, 1975

How to Save Your Own Life
fiction, 1977

At the Edge of the Body
poetry, 1979

Fanny: Being the True History of the Adventures of
Fanny Hackabout-Jones
fiction, 1980

Witches
nonfiction, poetry, 1981

Ordinary Miracles
poetry, 1983

Megan's Book of Divorce: A Kid's Book for Adults
fiction, 1984

Parachutes & Kisses
fiction, 1984

Serenissima: A Novel of Venice
fiction, 1987

Any Woman's Blues
fiction, 1990

Becoming Light
poetry, 1991

The Devil at Large: Erica Jong on Henry Miller
nonfiction, 1993

FEAR OF FIFTY

A MIDLIFE MEMOIR

ERICA JONG

HarperCollins*Publishers*

A leatherbound signed first edition of this book has been published by Easton Press.

HarperCollins books may be purchased for educational, business, or sales promotional use. For information, please write: Special Markets Department, HarperCollins Publishers, Inc., 10 East 53rd Street, New York, NY 10022.

FIRST EDITION

Designed by Nancy Singer

Library of Congress Cataloging-in-Publication Data
Jong, Erica.
  Fear of fifty / Erica Jong. — 1st ed.
    p. cm.
  ISBN 0-06-017739-X
  1. Jong, Erica—Biography. 2. Women authors, American—20th century—Biography. I. Title.
PS3560.O56Z468   1994
811'.54—dc20   94-10671
[B]

94 95 96 97 98 ❖/HC 10 9 8 7 6 5 4 3 2 1

For my daughter, Molly—
your turn now

Let us answer a book of ink
with a book of flesh and blood.
—Ralph Waldo Emerson

CONTENTS

ACKNOWLEDGMENTS

Special thanks to my intrepid editors: HarperCollins Vice President and Associate Publisher Gladys Justin Carr, and Tracy Devine of HarperCollins in New York; and Carmen Callil and Alison Samuel of Chatto & Windus in London. Thanks also to Ed Victor, Joni Evans, Ken Burrows, and Mari Schatz, my first readers, cheering and booing section, and unofficial editors. With my first book, I resented proposed cuts and suggestions. With this, my sixteenth, I am profoundly grateful. Nevertheless, as with my life, the faults of the book are mine alone.

PREFACE

NEVER FOLLOW A DOG ACT

"You know you're on the skids when you play yourself in the movie version of your life," my father used to warn me when I was nine. I had no idea what he was talking about.

He had come out of show business to make a killing in the tchotchke* business, and though he trafficked in ceramics and phony antique dolls, all his metaphors were drawn from that other business he had left in his twenties.

"Never follow a dog act" was his other favorite saying. I never knew what that meant either. Or how it applied to my life. But, as it happened, my life was to teach me both these lessons.

"You might as well give up, Mom," my daughter says. "You're a seventies writer." My daughter says "seventies" as a synonym for "old stone age." "The kids in my class say you write pornography—is that true?"

I explain to Molly that women who push boundaries are often treated with something less than respect, and I give her *Fear of Flying* to read. She sits absorbed by it on a train from Venice to Arezzo the summer of her thirteenth birthday. Every few minutes she looks up at me and asks, "Hey, Mom—did this really happen?" or "Who was that guy anyway?"

I tell her the truth. In the funniest way I know. About a hundred pages into the book, she loses interest and picks up *The Catcher in the Rye.*

A year later, on a publicity tour for *The Devil at Large,* my book about Henry Miller, Molly confides to Wilder Penfield III of the

---

* A delectable Yiddish word that means bauble or knickknack.

Toronto *Sunday Sun:* "I make it a policy not to read any of my mother's books because [they] really scare me. I got a hundred pages into *Fear of Flying* and I was so nervous! I kept asking her, 'Did you really do this?' I was so shocked, I had to stop reading."

She smiles with satisfaction as all her quotes are written down. She's dying to do her riff on "My Mother's Husbands"—exit, stage right, husband number 1; enter, stage left, husband number 2; et cetera—but I give her a withering look and kick her under the table.

At fourteen, Molly already knows that I'm her material, just as she sometimes has been mine. If she has to put up with a writer-mother, she'll take her revenge with words.

Molly is never at a loss for words.

Nobody could make her follow a dog act.

So here I am at fifty, whiplashed between the generations. I am reduced to a sort of missing link in the evolutionary chain. I have all this advice from my father and all these riffs from my daughter. Somehow I have to make sense of it all.

That's how this book was born.

HE'S FIFTY, SHE'S NOT

At fifty, the last thing I wanted was a public celebration. Three days before my birthday I took off for a spa in the Berkshires with Molly (then thirteen)—slept in the same bed with her, giggling before sleep, slumber party style—worked out all day (as if I were a jock, not a couch potato), learned trendy low-fat vegetarian recipes, had my blackheads expunged, my flab massaged, my muscles stretched, and thought about the second half of my life.

These thoughts alternated between terror and acceptance. Turning fifty, I thought, is like flying: hours of boredom punctuated by moments of sheer terror.

When, on the evening of my birthday, my husband (who shares the same birthday but is one year older) arrived, I had to adjust to the disruption of my woman's world. He liked the food but wisecracked about the holistic hokum. His critical-satirical male eye did not quite ruin my retreat but somehow tainted it. I was doing inner work in the guise of outer exercise, and his presence made that inner work harder.

Real men don't like spas.

The year before, when he turned fifty, I had made a party for him. I sent out invitations that read:

> HE'S FIFTY.
> SHE'S NOT.
> COME HELP CELEBRATE.

I still couldn't face fifty, so I knew I did not want him to reciprocate for my fiftieth birthday. Nor did I want to do what Gloria Steinem had done: make a public benefit, raise money for women, and rise resplendent in an evening gown, shoulders dusted with glitter—as Gloria's lovely shoulders were—and say: "This is what fifty looks like."

Who can fail to admire such brave affirmation of older women? But I veered between wanting to change the date on my *Who's Who* entry and wanting to move to Vermont and take up organic gardening in drawstring pants and Birkenstocks.

I needed something private, female, and contemplative to sort out these conflicting feelings. A spa was perfect. And my daughter was the perfect companion—despite her adolescent riffing that spares no one, her mother least of all. Still, there is something about a woman turning fifty that is female work, mother-daughter work, not to be shared with the whole male world—or even with those representatives of it whom one loves and cherishes.

My husband and I have always made much of our birthday—in part because we share it and because, having met in midlife, after the wreckage of many relationships, we treasure the synchronicity of our births during World War II, a world of ration coupons and fear of Axis invasions that we only dimly remember from twice-told family tales. One year we took our daughters to Venice—my magic city—another year we made a blast in our new apartment in New York, bought jointly—the ultimate sign of commitment in a world where marriages die like moths.

But fifty is different for a woman than it is for a man. Fifty is a more radical kind of passage to the other side of life, and this was something we could not share. Let him make fun of "new age" contemplation. I needed it, as have women back to antiquity. Venus de Milo contemplates herself turning into the Venus of Willendorf—if she doesn't watch out.

You tell yourself you ought to be beyond vanity. You read feminist books and contemplate falling in love with Alice B. Toklas. But years of brainwashing are not so easy to forget. The beauty trap is deeper than you thought. It's not so much the external pressures as the internal ones that bind. You cannot imagine yourself middle-aged—cute little you who always had "it" even when overweight.

For years I had stayed legally single, fearing both the boredom and the entrapment of something not accidentally called "wedlock"; now I thought the most difficult challenge of all was to keep my mental and spiritual independence while inside a nurturing relationship. This meant constant negotiation of priorities, constant noisy fights, constant struggles for power. If you were lucky enough to feel safe enough to fight and struggle, then you were lucky indeed. If you felt loved enough to scream and yell and exercise your power openly, the marriage had a fifty-fifty chance.

I had come to such a marriage only because I had come to a place where I was not afraid of being alone. I discovered that I liked my own company better than dating. Treasuring my solitude, secure in my ability to provide for myself and my daughter, I suddenly met a soul mate and a friend.

Famous for writing about relationships that flamed with sex then petered out, I surprised myself with this one.

Conversation ignited. The sex was at first disastrous—detumescence at inopportune moments and condoms limply abandoned on the counterpane. So much fear of commitment on both sides that ecstasy seemed irrelevant. Instead, we talked and talked. I found myself liking this person before I knew I loved him—which was in itself a new thrill. I would run away—to California, to Europe—only to call him from far-flung places. We felt our connection so strongly that it seemed we had been together all our lives.

Has anyone dared to write about the disasters of safe sex in the age of AIDS? Has anyone dared to say that most men would rather wear condoms around their necks to ward off the evil eye than put them on their cocks? Has anyone recorded the traumas of midlife lovers who have been through everything from fifties technical virginity to sixties sexual gluttony to seventies health and fitness (you met your lovers at Nautilus Clubs) to eighties decadence (long limousines and short dresses and men who impersonated Masters of the Universe) to nineties terror of AIDS warring with natural horniness?

And then there are the eternal questions of love and sex: Can there be friendship between men and women as long as the hormones rage and rule? How is sex related to love—and love to sex? Are we truly pigeonholed in our sexuality—or does society alone insist on this? What is "straight"? What is "gay"? What is "bi"? And does any of it matter deep in one's soul? Shouldn't we get rid of these labels in an attempt to be really open to ourselves and to each other?

What was happening to me in the second part of my life? I was getting myself back and I liked that self. I was getting the humor, the intensity, the balance I had known in childhood. But I was getting it back with a dividend. Call it serenity. Call it wisdom. I knew what mattered and what did not. Love mattered. Instant orgasm did not.

I look around me at fifty and see the women of my generation coping with getting older. They are perplexed, and the answer to their perplexity is not another book on hormones. The problem goes deeper than menopause, face-lifts, or whether to fuck younger men. It has to do with the whole image of self in a culture in love with youth and out of love with women as human beings. We are terrified at fifty because we do not know what on earth we can become when we are no longer young and cute. As at every stage of our lives, there are no role models for us. Twenty-five years of feminism (and backlash), then feminism again—and we still stand at the edge of an abyss. What to become now that our hormones have let us go?

It may seem that, in the last few years, there has been a spate of empowering books for midlife women, but how much have things really changed? Can we so easily undo fifty years of training for midlife self-annihilation?

I figure that if I'm confused, you are too. After all, we are the whiplash generation (patent pending):* raised to be Doris Day, yearning in our twenties to be Gloria Steinem, then doomed to raise our midlife daughters in the age of Nancy Reagan and Princess Di. Now it's Hillary Rodham Clinton, thank goddess. But sexism (like athlete's foot) still flourishes in dark, moist places.

---

* My husband, the lawyer, tells me that I am legally incorrect. "Whiplash generation" is really a "trademark," quoth he. But I have lived my life according to the principle "Don't cut funny," and *p*s are funnier than *t*s.

What a roller-coaster ride it's been! Our gender went in and out of style as hems went up and down and up and down and up again, as feminism rose and fell and rose and fell and rose again, as motherhood was blessed then damned then blessed then damned then blessed again.

Raised in the era of illegal abortion (when a high school or college pregnancy meant the end of ambition), we grew up into the Sexual Revolution—an essentially fake media event that was promptly replaced by good old-fashioned American Puritanism when the AIDS epidemic hit. The tragedy of losing a whole generation of some of the most talented among us was predictably turned into an excuse to bash the life-force and her messenger, Eros. Sex was out, was in, was out, was in, was out—a new twist on what Anthony Burgess called "the old in-out" in *A Clockwork Orange*.

The point was: We whiplashers could depend on nothing in our erotic or social lives.

Think of the advice we got growing up. Then think of the world we grew up into!

"Don't wear your heart on your sleeve!"

"Don't let men know how smart you are!"

"If he has the milk, why should he buy the cow?"

"It's as easy to love a rich man as a poor man."

"The way to a man's heart is through his stomach."

"A man chases a girl until she catches him."

"Diamonds are a girl's best friend."

If we'd been stupid enough to live the lives our mothers and grandmothers made proverbs of, we'd all be bag ladies, scavenging in garbage pails. If we'd been stupid enough to live the lives the magazines and movies of the sixties and seventies recommended, we'd all be dead of AIDS.

Raised to believe that men would protect and support us, we often found we had to protect and support them. Raised to believe we should care for our children full time (at least when they were little), we often found Donna Reed motherhood a luxury few of us could afford. Raised to believe that femininity consisted of softness and conciliation, we often found that our very survival—in divorce, in work, even in our homes—depended upon our revising those ideas of femininity and fiercely sticking up for our own needs.

We found ourselves always torn between the mothers in our heads and the women we needed to become simply to stay alive. With one foot in the past and another in the future, we hobbled through first love, motherhood, marriage, divorce, careers, menopause, widowhood—never knowing what or who we were supposed to be, staking out new emotional territory at every turn—like pioneers.

We have been pioneers in our own lives, and the price of the pioneer is eternal discomfort. The reward is the stunning sense of pride in our painfully achieved selfhood.

"I did it!" we exclaim with some shock and amazement. "I did it! You can too!"

Did men change or did women change? Or was it both? My father and grandfathers, sexists though they were, could never have abandoned their children to waltz off with younger women. They may have been pigs. Perhaps they were less than faithful. But at least they were pigs who were providers. They were in for the long haul, providing also a kind of security unknown today. Why did the generation of men who followed them have no such scruples?

Did women let them off the hook? Or did history? Or did some enormous change take place between the sexes which we still have not recognized or named?

As women grew stronger, men appeared to get weaker. Was this appearance or reality? As women got little crumbs of power, men began to act paranoid—as if we'd disabled them utterly.

Do all women have to keep silent for men to speak? Do all women have to be legless for men to walk?

The women of my generation are reaching fifty in a state of perplexity and rage. None of the things we counted on has come to pass. The ground keeps shifting under our feet. Any psychologist or psychoanalyst will tell you that the hardest thing to deal with is inconsistency. And we have known a degree of inconsistency in our personal lives that would make anyone schizophrenic. Perhaps our grandmothers were better able to cope with the expectation of oppression than we have been able to adjust to our much-vaunted freedom. And our freedom anyway is moot. Our "freedom" is still a word we can put in inverted commas to get a laugh.

For decades, we couldn't expect to take a maternity leave and get back, let alone find affordable child care. No day care, no Americans who wanted to be nannies—and yet we were (and *are*) penalized for hiring those who needed child-care jobs.

The dirty secret in America is that every working woman has had to break the law in order to find child care. I have broken the law. So have most of us. (Poor women use unlicensed day care and middle-class women find nannies without green cards.) Look for a woman who is squeaky clean and you'll end up with a woman who has no children. Or with a man.

With ascending expectations and a declining standard of living, we asked ourselves what on earth went wrong. Nothing went wrong. We were merely brought up in one culture and came of age in another. And now we are hitting fifty in a world that is grandstanding about feminism once again. But this time we have good reason to be skeptical.

The whiplash generation is, in its own way, a lost generation. Like spectators at a tennis game, we keep snapping our heads from side to side.

No wonder our necks hurt!

Perhaps every generation thinks of itself as a lost generation and perhaps every generation is right. Perhaps there were flappers of the twenties who longed for the security of their grandmother's lives. But the first wave of modern feminism at least carried its members along on a current of hope. And the second wave (of the late sixties and early seventies) made us dream that women's equality would soon be universal. So my classmates and I have seen women's expectations raised and dashed and raised and dashed and raised again in our not very long lives. The brevity of the cycles has been dizzying—and enraging.

The media still try to comfort us with bromides. Fifty is fabulous, we hear. We should wear hemorrhoid cream on our wrinkles and march off into the sunset popping Premarin. We should forget centuries of oppression in exchange for a new hat with "Fabulous Fifty" embroidered on the brim.

What about our need—women and men both—to prepare for death in a culture that mocks all spirituality as "new age" pretension? What about our need to see ourselves as part of the flow of creation? What about the deep loneliness our individualistic culture breeds? What about the dismissal of community and communal values? What about society's mockery of all activities other than getting and spending? What about our own despair in seeing liars and manipulators become rich and powerful while truth tellers are chronically outmaneuvered and fall through that porous "safety net" the liars have woven with loopholes for themselves and their children?

But most of all, what about meaning and what about spirit? These are not empty words. These are the nutrients we hunger for increasingly as we age.

"More things move," the poet Louise Bogan wrote in her last years, "than blood in the heart." As human beings, we long for some ritual that tells us we are part of a tribe, part of a species, part of a generation. Instead we are offered hormone replacement therapy or pep talks about how hip it is to be fabulously fifty.

Let's be clear: These pep talks insult our intelligence. We cannot so easily forget that we were raised in a world that mocked female maturity. We cannot instantly forget generations of hoary jokes about old bags, cows, yentas, witches, crones. "Menopause-lady painters" my artist-grandfather used to say about the women who shared a studio with him at the Art Students League. And I didn't even realize this remark was sexist and agist. I just dismissed the old bags—as he did—hardly knowing I was dismissing my own future.

Just because new shibboleths are broadcast over the airwaves, or printed on glossy pages, we cannot expect our images of self to be instantly healed. We are more than just consumers of magazines, television shows, makeup, face-lifts, clothes. We have inner scars, inner wounds, inner needs. We cannot be treated like chattel for fifty years and then suddenly be flattered into political compliance because it has been discovered (quite belatedly) that we vote.

The new hype trumpets that fifty is fab because the baby boom generation has reached that formerly dangerous age and we now run things—or rather our husbands and brothers do.

But I look around and see the best minds of my generation still bucking the system. Women directors are still begging male studio heads for money; women writers and editors are still pleading their cases to male CEOs; women actors are still scrambling for a handful of parts that truly reflect their lives; women artists are still paid and exhibited far less than their male counterparts; women conductors and composers are still seldom heard. Women everywhere are settling for half a loaf or even crumbs. Not losers, these women, but the fiercest and brightest. Not complainers, not whiners, and certainly not lazy, but still subject to a relentless double standard.

As mediocre men are promoted upward, supplied with their platinum parachutes, stock options, lemon tart wives, new families, new cars, new planes, new boats, we get older only to become less and less employable. Of course, we are spiritually strong—who ever doubted it? But spiritual strength alone does not overcome discrimination.

In a world where women work three times as hard for half as much, our achievement has been denigrated, both marriage and divorce have been turned against us, our motherhood has been used as an obstacle to our success, our passion as a trap, our empathy for others as an excuse to underpay us.

In our prime, we looked around the world and saw an epidemic of rape frequently not even reported in mainstream newspapers. In our childbearing years, we frequently met our deadlines only by giving up sleep. We began to get angry, really angry, angry for the second time in our adult lives. But now we knew the time was short.

We are finally learning to harness our anger and use it to change the world. But we have not stopped turning against each other. Until we do, sisterhood will continue to be a comforting theory rather than an everyday reality.

This is the next great taboo subject: When will women learn not to divide but to unite? And how can we learn to be allies when society still pits us against each other as tokens?

At fifty, the madwoman in the attic breaks loose, stomps down the stairs, and sets fire to the house. She won't be imprisoned anymore. The second wave of anger is purer than the first. Suddenly the divisions between women don't matter. Old or young, brown or white, gay or straight, married or un-, poor or rich—we are all discriminated against just because we are women. And we won't go back to the old world of injustice. We can't. It's too late.

The anger of midlife is a ferocious anger. In our twenties, with success and motherhood still before us, we could imagine that something would save us from second-classness—either achievement or marriage or motherhood. Now we know that nothing can save us. We have to save ourselves.

*   *   *

My books have always been written out of headlong passion. Despite the fact that I've somehow made my precarious living as a professional writer for twenty-three years, I cannot write for hire. I have to feel a deep internal pressure that says: This book doesn't yet exist; I have to make it. I always write as if my life depended upon it—because it does.

At the beginning of *Tropic of Cancer,* Henry Miller quotes Ralph Waldo Emerson: "novels will give way, by and by, to diaries or autobiographies—captivating books, if only a man knew how to choose among what he calls his experiences that which is really his experience, and how to record truth truly." Actually, women have fulfilled this prophecy more than men have. Women writers have taken up Emerson's prophecy and made a whole literature of it—a literature that has also changed the way men write books.

"Truth truly" is what I am after. And clearly we live in an age where documentary or bearing witness has the force for us that fiction used to have. The novels and memoirs we take up as guides for our lives have that quality of immediacy, of truth told truly, at the expense of false modesty, shame, or pride.

Hard as it is to tell the truth without the comfort of a mask, "an autobiography must be such that one can sue oneself for libel," as Thomas Hoving said—apparently not knowing whom he was paraphrasing. Mary McCarthy, in her *Intellectual Memoirs,* gives the source as George Orwell: "An autobiography that does not tell something bad about the author cannot be any good." McCarthy then confesses more sins than even her detractors can load her with: And we are charmed. But then she's dead—always more charming in a woman than being alive.

The fear of criticism has silenced me many times in my writing life. And the criticism has often been fierce, personal, and wounding. But criticism—as everyone from Aphra Behn to George Sand to George Eliot to Mary McCarthy knew—is one of the first things a woman writer must learn to bear. She does not write of experiences that the dominant culture applauds as "important," and, like any writer, she does not write with a guarantee. To become inured to ridicule is surely a woman writer's most important task.

Often I have tricked myself into writing with candor by telling myself I would not publish (or would publish only under a pseudonym—perhaps even a male pseudonym). Later, I might be persuaded to sign the book by the loving letters I received from readers or by the publisher's need for a brand name. But during the writing process, I could be free, could knock the censor—my mother? my grandmother?—off my shoulder only by promising myself never to let my words see publication.

I wrote *Fear of Flying* that way and many subsequent books (including this one). Writing has often been accompanied by terror, silences, and then wild bursts of private laughter that suddenly make all the dread seem worthwhile.

But the great compensation for being fifty in a culture that is not kind to older women is that you care less about criticism and you are less afraid of confrontation. In a world not made for women, criticism and ridicule follow us all the days of our lives. Usually they are indications that we are doing something right.

Is fifty too young to start an autobiography? Of course it is. But maybe eighty is too old.

Fifty is the time when time itself begins to seem short. The sense of time running out has been exacerbated lately by the AIDS epidemic and the deaths of so many friends still in their thirties, forties, and fifties. Who knows whether there will be a better time? The time is always now.

At nineteen, at twenty-nine, at thirty-nine, even—goddess help me—at forty-nine, I believed that a new man, a new love, a move, a change to another city, another country, would somehow change my inner life.

Not so now.

I know that my inner life is my own achievement whether there is a partner in my life or not. I know that another mad, passionate love affair would be only a temporary distraction—even if "temporary" means two or three years. I know that my soul is what I have to nurture and develop and that, alone or with a partner, the problems of climbing your own mountain are not so very different.

In a relationship, you still require autonomy, separateness, privacy. Outside a relationship, you still need self-love and self-esteem.

I write this book from a place of self-acceptance, cleansing anger, and raucous laughter.

I am old enough to know that laughter, not anger, is the true revelation.

I make the assumption that I am not so different from you or you.

I want to write a book about my generation. And to write about my generation and be fiercely honest, I can only start with myself.

1

FEAR OF FIFTY

When people say
"I've told you *fifty* times,"
They mean to scold, and very often do;
When poets say, "I've written *fifty* rhymes,"
They make you dread that they'll recite them too;
In gangs of *fifty*, thieves commit their crimes;
At *fifty* love for love is rare, 'tis true,
But then, no doubt, it equally as true is,
A good deal may be bought for *fifty* Louis.
　　　　　—George Gordon, Lord Byron, *Don Juan*

(Was Byron afraid of fifty? Probably. He died at thirty-six.)

When I undertook to write about myself I found that I had
embarked upon a somewhat rash adventure, easier begun than left
off. I had long wanted to set down the story of my first twenty
years; nor did I ever forget the distress signals which my adolescent self sent out to the older woman who was afterward to
absorb me, body and soul. Nothing, I feared, would survive of
that girl, not so much as a pinch of ashes. I begged her successor
to recall my youthful ghost one day from the limbo to which it
had been consigned. Perhaps the only reason for writing my books
was to make the fulfillment of this long-standing prayer possible.
When I was fifty, it seemed to me that the time had come.

　　　　　—Simone de Beauvoir, *The Prime of Life*

So there I am at the spa with Molly, facing my fiftieth birthday, and
feeling hideously depressed. I am no longer the youngest person in the

room, nor the cutest. I will never be Madonna or Tina Brown or Julia Roberts. Whoever the flavor of the month is by the time this book appears—I will never be her either. For years those were my values—whether I admitted this to myself or not—but I cannot afford such values anymore.

Every year another crop of beauties assaults me on the streets of New York. With thinner waists and blonder hair and straighter teeth, with more energy to compete (and less cynicism about the world), the class of 1994, or 1984, 1974, is inexorably replacing my class—Barnard '63—yikes! Thirty-plus years out of college. Most of my contemporaries are *grandpères,* as my daughter would say. They press baby pictures on me at parties, the offspring of offspring.

Having started late, I have no grandchildren yet, but I do have a couple of grandnephews crawling around Lebanon, Lausanne, and Litchfield County. My older sister's children are moving me closer and closer to the state of grandparenthood. I am the older generation now, and I'm not always sure I like it. The losses sometimes seem more clear-cut than the gains.

The astounding energy of postmenopausal women (promised by Margaret Mead) is here, but the optimism to fuel it is not. The world seems ever more surely in the grip of materialism and surfaces. Image, image, image is all it sees. As an image, I'm definitely getting blurry.

What has happened to our twenty-five years of protest about not wanting to be plastic Barbies? What has happened to the anger of Naomi Wolf analyzing beauty myths, or Germaine Greer fiercely celebrating cronehood, or Gloria Steinem showing us how to accept age gracefully and turning inward at last?

Is all our angst (and attempted self-transformation) just more fodder for the talk shows as the youth culture grinds on inexorably? Are we just a bunch of old broads talking to each other in the steamroom, cheering each other up?

We write and talk and empower each other, but the obsession with newness and youth (newth?) does not seem to change. Ours is a world of shifting video images more real and more potent than mere words. The television age is here, and we word people are relics of a past when the word could change the world because the word was still heard.

The image is all now. And the time of the image is always NOW. History no longer exists in this flickering light show.

These were some of my thoughts as I trooped around the spa in the Berkshires with Molly, doing step aerobics, aqua-trimming, speed-walking, and other fitness rituals, and avoiding my own image in the mirror. Molly dragged me out of bed for every class, and I lost the same few pounds I always lose (and gain back), drank water, steamed my pores, and felt restored—but the gloom still wouldn't lift. (I was facing the eternal question: to lift or not to lift—and should I do it before the next book tour?)

Worse than my despair over my inevitable physical decline (and whether or not to "fix" it) was my despair over the pessimism of midlife. Never again, I thought, would I walk into a room and meet some delicious man who would change my life. I remembered the mad affairs begun with a flash of eyes and a surge of adrenaline, and the upheavals they inevitably led to. By eschewing upheavals and embracing stability, by disowning my tendency to throw my life into a cocked hat—so to speak—every seven years, I had also becalmed myself. I wanted contemplation, not boredom; wisdom, not despair; serenity, not stasis. The sexual energy that had always called forth the next book, the adventurousness of a life that settled nowhere, had begun to seem rash and foolish at fifty. At last I had "settled down" to cultivate my garden. Now all I needed to do was figure out where my garden was and what to grow in it.

Because that, after all, is the question, isn't it? You can never really "fix" mortality and death even if you can snip back your chin flab and eye bags. You may look good in a glossy, but in life, there are still scars. The real question has to do with how to grow inner-directed in a relentlessly other-directed society; how to nurture spirituality in the midst of materialism; how to march to your own drummer when alternative rock, rap, and hip-hop are drowning her out.

Thoreau is our touchstone writer in defining the central American dilemma: "Beware of all enterprises that require new clothes." In this, contemporary women are more Thoreau's heirs than are men. Bill W.'s philosophy of AA is our touchstone spiritual philosophy (whether we are alcoholics or not), because we are always thirsting for spirit, looking for it in all the wrong places (booze, drugs, money, new clothes), and finally finding ourselves only by losing ourselves, surrendering the materialism on which we were raised.

Mortality is the question here, not face-lifts. Can we embrace our mortality, even learn to love it? Can we pass along our knowledge to our children and then pass along, knowing our passing is the proper order of things?

That is the problem I and all my contemporaries are facing at fifty. We have come smack up against the spiritual hollowness in our lives. Without spirit, it is impossible to face aging and death. And how can women find spirit in a society in which their most enduring identity is as consumers above all, where every struggle for autonomy and identity is countered by the relentless dicta of the marketplace—a marketplace that still sees us as consumers of everything from hormones to hats, from cosmetics to cosmetic surgery?

I wander around the spa with my daughter, knowing that my body is not the issue. It's whether or not I have the right to my immortal soul.

Even the phrase sounds suspect. Women? Immortal? Soul? You can just hear the cries of derision. Yet whether or not women have the right to their own souls is the whole question. It is not a matter of fad and fashion. It is not a matter of new-age or twelve-step hype. It is the essence of whether we are allowed to be fully human or not.

If you own your soul, you don't have to be afraid at fifty.

I flash back to a time exactly three years before my fiftieth birthday, when the age clock inside me was inexorably ticking.

I am on a plane, flying to Switzerland to attend the wedding of a former beau, now a friend. He's a beautiful Roman ten years younger than I, and he is about to marry a German princess ten years younger than that. I'm happy for them and, at the same time, desolate. It's not that the bridegroom and I are still in love, but just that we have talked endlessly about how we'd wind up together (because neither of us would ever marry), and now he is marrying and I am not.

I don't want to marry again, I think (at not quite forty-seven). I'm free. My freedom is such that I'm involved in a long-distance triangle with another delicious Italian, a domestic triangle with a man who can't decide to leave his wife, and I'm also seeing a variety of men who are as terrified of commitment as I've become. My life is a social circus, but I can never relax and curl up in bed with a book. Though I may deny it, I am off to this wedding, as usual, in search of the perfect man. Of course, I don't believe in the perfect man. Of course, I nevertheless hope to meet him.

The wedding takes place in the little town hall in a Swiss mountain village that looks as if it belongs on a cuckoo clock. The beautiful bride and groom sign the register, pronounce their vows—the groom saying "Sì," the bride saying "Ja"—whereupon the judge who has married them falls to the floor with a thump, his skin turning the slate blue-gray color of sudden cardiac arrest. It is absolutely clear to me that the judge is dead, *gestorben, morto.* The relatives scurry to call the EMS and frantically reassure each other. (At least the Germans are reassuring each other that the judge will be fine; the Italians, on the other hand, are muttering darkly, *"Maledizione, maledizione."*)

Pretty soon an ambulance races uselessly to the hospital with the irretrievably dead judge, and the silent, chastened wedding party wends its way up the streets of the snow-frosted town to a reception in the elegant chalet of the bride's mother. Toasts are made, champagne glasses clink. The German relatives deny that anything bad has happened, and the Italian ones keep wringing their hands and clutching their groins to ward off the evil eye.

The wedding is darkened by this event—despite everyone's denials. But the baby who emerges the requisite months later is beautiful and blond, perfect in every way. And the bride and groom are as happy as Candide and Cunégonde in this best of all possible worlds. Death has darkened life, but life goes on.

At the wedding supper, held in the very grand but sufficiently rustic hunting chateau of another of the bride's relatives, I am seated next to a handsome young playboy from Monaco, Milan, Paris, and London, who, seeing a placecard with my name, attempts this witty proposition: "You write naughty books. Will you be naughty with me?"

My heart plummets. Gloom claims me in the midst of the festivities. My reputation is a kind of dirty joke, and my best friend has just gotten married. I drink too much, dance too frantically, kiss the bride and groom, and depart into the snow on the arm of a gay friend (whose houseguest I am). I will awaken at three A.M. in his attic guest room, wringing my hands and weeping.

In the morning, the vapors are gone, banished by the sun on the snow. I drive down through the Alps with my friend, stopping in a trout restaurant to eat and talk, eventually passing Lake Como and Milan and winding up in Venice, where my lover awaits.

As always, the sex between us is a magical abolition of time, and for three days I am happy. We sit in his boat rocking on the lagoon, watching the mirages of Venice float over the waters. We make love at odd times, in odd places, avoiding his relatives. We part, promising to be together "someday." (I will buy the palazzo adjacent to his wife's, and he will visit me morning and evening—via underground tunnel, presumably.)

But my old boyfriend's new domestic bliss has changed the equation. Of course I need my own soul to face fifty, but don't I also need a partner and a friend?

Surely I could go on for another few years borrowing husbands. There are always plenty of them on loan. But that isn't the point. I may have my own houses, my own bank accounts, a wonderful daughter, and some degree of control over my future, but the truth is I feel I am adrift in the world. I can't control aging, nor the fate of my books. And I am lonely. I may not need a husband, but I sure do need a friend.

For the first time in my adult life I find myself thinking of my parents' marriage. I feel nostalgic for it as if for a marriage I once knew. My parents were friends at the end of the day—they giggled in bed and read aloud to each other from *The New Yorker*. They never seemed to tire of each other's laughter. I remember their bed covered with books and their animated arguments punctuated by S. J. Perelman riffs read aloud.

I am almost fifty and I have no one to read aloud to in bed. I have lovers and I have friends. But the friend who was also a lover has just gotten married. And that shines a spotlight on my loneliness.

Why are all the independent women I know alone? And why are all my men friends marrying younger women? I return to New York with some chink in my armor suddenly open. And when a friend wants to introduce me to a friend, I surprise myself by saying yes.

My parents' marriage, of course, is where it all begins. She was seventeen and he nineteen when they met in the Catskill Mountains. He was from Brownsville and she was from Washington Heights. His father and mother were Polish Jews with a German name: Weisman. Her father and mother were Russian Jews from England with a Russian name: Mirsky.

They fell in love over a drum. He, seeing she could paint (and thinking her foxy and hot), invited her to "paint his drum." She, seeing he was handsome and blue-eyed and a good drummer, agreed. She painted his drum and flirted with him. He ingratiated himself into her bed. By summer's end, Eda Mirsky and Samuel Nathaniel (Seymour) Weisman decided to get married. They were very young and it was the Great Depression.

Her father said: "What? Marry a *barabanchik*?" (a drummer, in Russian).

His mother said: "I think she's using you."

But pheromones are stronger than parental warnings. They got married in City Hall on March 3, 1933.

Their early years were tough. He worked all night in little boîtes—Bal Musette, Bal Tabarin—and she stayed home. Too many girl singers and too much reefer tempted him. Left alone till the wee small hours, she wondered if she had made a mistake. Her father was by now a prosperous portrait painter and commercial artist with a sprinkling of famous clients. There were Oriental rugs and bone china and a life very far from the Russian shtetl where my grandfather Mirsky was born.

Even during the Depression, my mother's parents were prosperous—though my grandfather had fled a boyhood of dire poverty in Odessa and my grandmother had, like so many grandmothers, married beneath her. She had been the daughter of a Russian forester and timber merchant, wooed and wed in Russian, in London, before the Great War. *Her* parents ran a grocery store in the East End of London until the wealth of their eldest son rescued them and they retired to his gentleman's farm in the country. So my mother's family had already begun their climb in the world when she married an impecunious musician and had to start all over again.

Plunged into the reality of being a poor troubadour's wife, my mother woke up—as my grandmother had before her. Marriage is never easy for the young. (It's even harder for the middle-aged.) My mother painted, worked in Bloomingdale's demonstrating art supplies, designed clothes and fabrics, while my father got his first job in a Broadway show—Cole Porter's *Jubilee*—where he played "Begin the Beguine" in the band on stage.

"I introduced that song," he still brags.

Success was hovering just on the horizon. But when my mother was pregnant with her first child in 1937, she gave my father an ultimatum: show business or us.

"Did I ever tell you about the time," she asks, "when Daddy brought home twenty showgirls and I was hugely pregnant with your older sister? Well, the girls were so beautiful and I was so pregnant that the next morning I got on my bicycle and rode all the way up Riverside Drive, vowing to ride and ride until I lost that baby." She laughs. "I was eight months pregnant!"

But the baby wouldn't be lost. It hung on like a barnacle, as babies do. And my father did eventually quit show business.

How can anyone choose between love and work? (Women have been forced to do that for centuries, and finally we recognize the impossibility of the choice.) I know my father would have made a success of anything he set his mind to: He has that tenacity. But my mother resented his being a traveling troubadour when she had set aside being a famous artist for motherhood, and she was to win this war.

When my older sister was born, my mother, exhausted by the unrelenting toil of raising a baby, moved back to her parents' comfortable home. My father still worked nights and my mother still had plenty of admirers.

"How did I—a married woman with an infant—have all those admirers?" she asks rhetorically. "But I did."

One was a doctor—someone with a real job. My mother contemplated divorce.

My father's brother came to take his clothes back to Brooklyn.

"Don't stay with him if you're not happy," my grandmother (who had done just that in her marriage) told my mother. "I'll help you all I can."

I was almost not to be.

But pheromones prevailed and my parents reunited. Seymour became a traveling salesman of tchotchkes. Eda got pregnant again. I was born in 1942.

"We are born and what happened before that is myth" V. S. Pritchett says in his autobiography, A Cab at the Door. In Speak, Memory, Vladimir Nabokov talks about an empty carriage on a porch, awaiting his birth. We marvel at the days before our coming to consciousness because, in truth, they predict our mortality (which it takes our whole lives to make peace with—if we ever do).

What if I were never born? What if that egg and that sperm had never met? Would it be worse than death? Or better? (I am heading toward that final annihilation of self—so I'd better decide this question soon. More time is behind me than ahead.)

I think of that hiatus in my parents' marriage as the time when I hovered, wondering whether I would be embodied at all. Called forth by their love—ambivalent like all loves—I came into the world a sickly child, with dehydrating diarrhea, a red, raised angioma on my neck, and an allergy to milk.

What time was I born? I always ask my mother, wanting to have my astrological chart done. (My birth certificate is lost. The hospital in which I was born has closed, and the records are not to be found in the city's archives.)

"Who knows?" she says. "It was the war. There were too few doctors. The nurse put an ether mask over my face to hide the fact that I had given birth before the doctor came. I bit the nurse's hand! I yelled, 'The baby's already born! Don't you dare drug me!'"

So I was born in the midst of feminist rage: My feisty mother bit the nurse's hand, refusing anesthesia.

I must have looked awful.

"Do we have to take it home?" my father is reported to have said on first seeing me. (I had either fallen out of the crib and been given that famous angioma—or else I was born with it. In any case, everyone agrees I was a mess.)

"All the babies on that ward died of infectious diarrhea," my mother says.

"All?"

"I think so. You were the only survivor—so I was determined to keep you alive."

Whether this epidemic was fatal to each and every baby or not, I am unable to verify. But the important thing is that my mother was—and is—convinced that I was the sole survivor of a baby plague.

Clearly disappointed I was not a boy, my father tried to make me into one, teaching me drums, how to shoot baskets, and contempt for all womanly limitations. For the longest time, I thought I was a boy in girl's clothing. When later various analysts hinted at something called "penis envy," I shouted them down. I thought I *had* a penis. Why be envious?

"I loved you more because I had such a struggle to keep you alive," my mother says. And then she tells again the old family tale of lactose-free milk reconnoitered on midnight runs and how I nearly "starved to death" and how she loved me despite the ugly crimson angioma—which miraculously shrank to nothing in the first two months, leaving a pink, towheaded baby girl.

"By the time you were pretty, I didn't even care," she says, "because I'd had to love you so just to keep you alive."

My older sister, Suzanna (Shoshana Miriam, nicknamed "Nana" after some baby mispronunciation), had been sheer perfection at birth:

round, auburn-haired, bright-eyed. I was the designated ugly duckling—but more loved for all that—or so the story went.

I always used to scoff at that story when I was younger, but now I believe it. The rage to keep a child alive is seismic. It overwhelms all other considerations. My mother's passion and my father's midnight milk runs kept me breathing. That—and the luck of my parents having found an iconoclastic pediatrician.

Dr. Aubrey McLean was a fierce Scotsman who dared to take on the milk lobby. Fifty years ahead of his time, he pronounced me allergic to cow's milk, and had me fed on acidophilus milk and raw scraped liver. No matter how much I shat, I was to be fed and fed: some nourishment would have to stick. Every day he came, examined me, and sat with my mother discussing babies, life, fate, and how he hated the medical establishment—which had cast him out for his radical views. He was also a drunk.

"He saved your life," my father says. "He's a big part of the story. Or maybe he was just in love with your mother." How will we ever know? Dr. McLean, wherever you are: Thanks.

Born in wartime to a big European-style family—my parents, my sister, my Russian-speaking maternal grandparents (who never taught us Russian so that they could have a secret language)—I remember early games like "running away from the Nazis" or my grandmother lathering my hands with Ivory soap to wash away "the Germans." Thus did the war enter my childhood. I remember deliberately wetting my bed at night so as to be taken to my parents' bed, to sleep between them in that safest of all places—both dividing and joining them. I remember looking up at the ceiling of their room to see kaleidoscopic light shows—"peas and carrots" I called them, meaning the fragments of green and red on the insides of my lids when I closed my eyes again in their big warm bed.

"The tempter under the eyelid," Dylan Thomas names this flickering creature. Is it that tempter who makes a poet?

My memories of early days are few, and all of them are visual. I may even remember being in a carriage, rolling through a park, and looking up at myriad green leaves fracturing the light. Never am I happier than looking up at leaves, so I imagine this relates to some early infantile euphoria. The leaves in the park, the optical illusion created by small octagonal bathroom tiles, which seemed to form a funnel into another world as I leaned over my seat on the bathroom throne and stared at their changing configurations on the floor—these are the most vivid memories I have.

By the time I was two, we lived in the apartment I re-create in all my dreams—a rambling neo-Gothic affair occupying the top three floors of a building at 44 West Seventy-seventh Street, opposite the Museum of Natural History. We moved there from Castle Village in Washington Heights in 1944, and stayed until 1959, when we moved to another prewar palazzo, the Beresford, on the north side of the museum.

My childhood memories of home are at once spooky and grand. The building on Seventy-seventh Street had been built for artists at the beginning of the century, and the studio had north light. We were always seeking north light, it seemed, like some strange plant life growing twisted to reach the sun.

The apartment I remember is probably not the apartment that exists today—now far more elegant than in my forties childhood. Lions' heads framed the living room fireplace; the dining room had dark wood paneling and Gothic moldings and faced a court; the kitchen had an ancient hooded gas stove and a zinc sink; the bedrooms were spaced along down a crooked hall; and a stony foyer, with Gothic wood trim, opened out into a stony hall where you summoned a mirrored, paneled elevator whose whorled wood looked like midnight owls half-hidden in midnight trees.

The living room ceiling was double-height and covered with something called "gold leaf." (In my child's mind, I imagined these harvested from golden trees.) Four Venetian-looking lanterns swayed from its darkened golden squares. The front windows faced the museum with its brownstone facade and green conical turrets; the back windows saw the sunny courtyard and the leafy gardens of the New-York Historical Society and the row of limestone mansions on Seventy-sixth Street. Above the living room was a balcony, its rail hung with a Balinese batik on which evil demons danced in profile. And up two flights of stairs was Papa's (my grandfather's) studio, with a trapdoor, a ceiling that pointed up like a witch's hat, and two huge windows—one facing north (that unchanging light that artists seek), the other south (too mutable, thus often darkened with double green shades manipulated by pulleys).

Papa's studio, filled with artists' accoutrements—plaster masks (of Beethoven, Keats, Voltaire), a real skull, a real skeleton, reproductions of T'ang dynasty horses—was both a place of refuge and a place of fear. It smelled deliciously of turpentine and oil paint, like some enchanted wood. But the death masks of Beethoven and Keats, and the skeleton and skull, gave the place a creepy air. You would not want to be there alone at night.

Every Halloween, the studio became the site of ghost and vampire storytelling. A candle would illuminate the skull, and the skeleton and death masks would wear white sheet shrouds like KKK members. Papa would set a painting of another skull (Yorick's perhaps?) on his old paint-encrusted easel (which had traveled with him from Edinburgh, Bristol, and London many years ago when he first migrated to the New World, again escaping the draft in England as he had the Russian draft as a teenage boy in Odessa). We think our lives so singular, but historical forces lift us up and fling us down. My grandfather (like yours and yours) fled Europe and its wars.

My mother told the story of Dracula—embellishing it bloodily—and the children shrieked in fear and pleasure to hear of the undead, of fangs, of maidens pale and anemic from their nighttime trysts.

On normal workdays, I was always welcome to paint beside my grandfather. He would prepare me a little canvas (he always proudly stretched his own), give me an extra palette filled with such mellifluous colors as alizarin crimson, rose madder, viridian, cobalt blue, chrome yellow, raw umber, Chinese white, and he would place two little metal clip-on cups, one for linseed oil and one for turpentine, in the thumb-hole of the palette. "Don't muddy the colors," Papa would say, giving me both sable and pig bristle brushes. Then I would paint away at my grandfather's side, in utter bliss, stoned on the smell of the turps and the sound of brushstrokes. Papa whistled Russian folk ballads and Red Army songs as he worked. Seventy-seventh Street might as well have been the banks of the Dnieper.

Papa was a tough taskmaster. If I "muddied colors" or failed to take my painting seriously, he would rage and chase me down the stairs with his maulstick, whipping the air. He never had to hit me. His roar was enough to terrorize me. I have read with amazement all these books about childhood incest and abuse, and I know that my grandfather's roar was abuse enough. How unstylish to have to report that no one molested me in childhood. Except psychologically. It was enough.

My grandfather had a studio, my father had an office, but my mother set up a folding easel when and where she could and resented this bitterly. My grandmother meanwhile ruled the house, chasing after our Jamaican maid, Ivy, to make sure she did things right.

Iviana Banton was the feisty West Indian woman who ran our household (when my grandmother would let her). Her hands were leathery and black on the outside and marvelously pink on the inside. I loved her accent, and West Indian speech patterns still seduce my ear.

Ivy was ugly, with a huge wen on her nose, sprouting a hair, but she was alive and strong. I learned early that being alive and strong were far more important than being beautiful.

Despite enough analysis to support a small country, I have repressed all early childhood memories of my mother. I know she both adored me and resented adoring me, and her extreme volatility had to be filtered out like poisons from a household tap. I loved her more than life and I was also terrified of her mutability. My older sister was often physically violent to me, twisting my arm till I fell to the floor writhing in pain; she also tormented me by "winning" my gold watch in fixed crap and card games, embarrassing me in front of friends. Two women tyrannized me for much of my childhood, but my memory is blank for most of it. Still, I conclude that my conciliatory temperament, my tendency to hide my anger even from myself, then explode years later, or use my pen to poison relatives, must stem from years of forgotten emotional tyranny.

No complaints. Everyone needs something to shape a complicated character. Tyranny was the force that created my love of liberty, my identification with the underdog, my passion for the rights of man— and woman.

When my sister Claudia was born in 1947, the whole family constellation shifted. Suddenly there was "the baby." Suddenly it was the postwar boom and my father was rich—or so it seemed. Suddenly my parents did things like fly to Havana or Jamaica for winter holidays or to London and Paris for summer ones. Suddenly there was a baby nurse who wouldn't let me touch the baby because I had caught ringworm from my best friend's cat.

Home from kindergarten for what seemed like an eternity, I was banished by the baby nurse from the baby's room. The little red-headed interloper—my sister—ruined my life. Everyone fussed over her. My mother lay in bed like a lady of leisure; my grandparents moved out to a nearby apartment (banished at last because my parents had now been analyzed and had outgrown such retrograde Mitteleuropa notions as extended families). Life changed dramatically. And mostly I remember standing in a tub, holding my gauze-swathed arm above my head and being hosed down by my mother, who wanted to make short work of me so she could run to "the baby." That damn baby—how Nana and I made her suffer. We bundled her in suffocating clothes and made her sit in the doll carriage. We dragged her into the linen closet, which was still our running-away-from-the-Nazis cave, because even though the war was over, it wasn't over in our heads. There, we would eat butter-and-applesauce-and-powdered-sugar sandwiches (based on a recipe in a Booth Tarkington novel my big sister was reading). There we would hide and whisper, running out to the kitchen for more supplies when the coast was clear.

Claudia smiled sweatily and put up with all our mishandling. She was "the baby." She knew her place. Today she tells me how much she resented us. That was nothing to how much we resented her merely for being born. While we went to school, she got taken to Caribbean islands in the sun. While we were left with Mama and Papa, she was with Eda and Seymour. Of the three of us, she is the only one who calls our parents Mommy and Daddy. And we also resented her for that. My parents seemed mysteriously like siblings to me and my older sister. And my grandparents seemed the real parents. Maybe that was why they had to be banished.

When I was eight, my older sister thirteen, and my younger sister three, my grandparents set sail for Paris, hoping to find the artists' Paris of Papa's youth. He had sojourned there as a poor Russian art student before he married, subsisting on bananas donated by some art-loving Jewish philanthropist—possibly a Rothschild—or so it went in family myth.

"Mirsky wanted to go without her," my father says. "He thought he could dump Mama with us."

"But I refused," my mother says. "How dare he have the delusion he could recapture his youth?"

Mama and Papa sailed on the *Mauretania*. Little black-and-white square glossies record that fateful day: Claudia and I racing around the decks in our English chesterfield coats, matching bonnets, and kid gloves; Nana a sullen, sulky, Elizabeth Taylor clone of a teenager, draping herself on assorted deck chairs and smokestacks and flaring her nostrils for the camera.

My parents must have felt as liberated as we felt bereft. And as for

Papa and Mama, what on earth could they have been thinking? How could the Paris of 1951 fail to disappoint an artist who left Montparnasse in 1901? He was no longer young, no longer single, no longer in love with bananas. The Russian-Jewish boy from Odessa had become a man of the world (or at least a man of Manhattan). How could he go back? It turned out he couldn't. He and my grandmother missed their grandchildren too much. Paris proved no substitute for us. In six months, Papa and Mama sailed back.

A donnybrook ensued. Papa and Mama wanted to move back in with us, and my parents (and their analysts) would not let them. Papa and Mama were too pre-Freudian to understand all this, and they never got over the hurt. My mother found them another West Side palace (with north light), a short walk away, but Papa and Mama refused to forgive her. Nor did they forgive Paris for having changed in fifty years. Time was supposed to stand still. Alas, it never does.

So I am fifty and Papa and Mama are dead. Tomorrow I am going to lunch with my father to see how much I got wrong in this opening chapter.

2

HOW MY PARENTS WERE AND "ALL THAT DAVID COPPERFIELD KIND OF CRAP"

If you really want to hear about it, the first thing you'll probably want to know is where I was born, and what my lousy childhood was like, and how my parents were occupied and all before they had me, and all that David Copperfield kind of crap.

—J. D. Salinger, *The Catcher in the Rye*

Fortunate are those of us who are daughters born into knowledgeable, ambitious families where no sons are born . . .

—Tillie Olsen, *Silences*

It's Thursday and I've made a date for lunch with my father to verify "all that David Copperfield kind of crap."

"Your mother doesn't remember anything," my father says, "but I do."

Now, you have to know that my father is the kind of guy who never has lunch with me alone because he thinks my mother might be jealous. If we meet during the week—which may happen every seventeen years or so—we snatch lunch at a greasy spoon like rushed adulterers. But this time history is at stake. My father takes a proprietary interest in my literary career—everything from moving books around in bookstores (so that *Fear of Flying* or *Fanny* covers the latest from Stephen King, Danielle Steel, or John Grisham), to subscribing to *Publishers Weekly* (and worriedly reporting on the latest deep-discounting trends), to wringing his hands over my nasty reviews.

"Why do they call you a pornographer, darling?" he'll ask, actually, at times, informing me of a shafting I've missed. I try to avoid reading reviews—good or bad—and my father, in his solicitude, has actually brought some of the more apoplectic ones to my attention.

Why, why, why? he questions like Job. His purgatory is to have a daughter who is castigated in the press every few years. At this point, I think it hurts him even more than it hurts me. I want to call up all the reviewers and say: "Look, my dad is eighty-one and a nice guy—give him a break." (My students at City College in the sixties and early seventies used to do that to me: "If you give me an F, my mother will have a heart attack. And besides, I'll end up in 'Nam." Special pleading. And often, it worked.)

So we are to meet in my father's showroom at 12:30. But it's pouring in New York, so the cab ride, from Sixty-ninth to Twenty-fifth Street, takes nearly forty minutes and I am, as usual, late.

My father is dancing around his showroom with great excitement and impatience, wanting all his staff to meet the famous daughter. He takes me on a tour of the "new line": "antique" dolls, ceramic tureens and teapots shaped like pumpkins and aubergines, decorative plates in the shapes of sunflowers and asparagi, roses, and onions. Years pass between visits to this showroom, and I am always astonished by what my father and brother-in-law have wrought—as curious in its way as making books out of a blank piece of paper and a pen. The way people make money in America! A Depression-era *barabanchik* can become a millionaire making "antique" dolls and selling them via the home shopping channel. What other country boasts such absurdities? In America you can change classes as fast as you can say *barabanchik*, because in America there really are no classes—but that is for a future chapter.

I admire my father's stuff and greet his staff; then we are off to lunch in the luncheonette in his building—a lunch of turkey sandwiches and Diet Cokes.

My father is blue-eyed, thin, wiry, still handsome. He looks about sixty-five. Okay, he looks seventy-five. But not eighty-one. (What does eighty-one look like?) Vitamins and exercise are his religion. He discovered vitamin C before Linus Pauling, beta carotene before Harry Demopoulos, and he tells me the secret is "to enjoy being hungry."

He has produced a document for me, aware of the gravity of my writing an autobiography, but secretly he has called my husband to say: "I'm giving Erica all this information. I hope she doesn't plan to use it." This is typical of the mixed messages that abound in my family.

I reproduce it here, verbatim.

HOSPITAL NURSERY HAD MANY FATALITIES DUE TO INFECTIONS AND DIARRHEA. AT BIRTH YOU HAD LARGE BALLOON FILLED WITH FLUID— HYGROMA, I BELIEVE. DR. AUBREY MACLEAN SAID IT WOULD BE ABSORBED AND DISAPPEAR. HOWEVER YOU COULD NOT HOLD FOOD— MOTHER FED YOU 24 HRS A DAY—KIND OF STRAINED MUSH WAS FORCED DOWN YOUR THROAT. CHOPPED RAW MEAT WAS ALSO FORCE FED. YOUR SURVIVAL WAS TOUCH & GO. DR. AUBREY MACLEAN WHO WAS FIRED FROM BABY'S HOSPITAL AT PRESBYTERIAN BECAUSE OF HIS UNORTHO-DOX TREATMENT OF SICK BABIES CAME EVERYDAY TO EXAMINE YOU. MILK WAS FORBIDDEN. HOWEVER, A NEW WALKER GORDON MILK PROD-UCT WAS OBTAINED AT THE BORDEN PLANT. (I PICKED UP A COUPLE OF BOTTLES EVERY OTHER DAY.) YOU GREW STRONGER BECAUSE FOOD INPUT WAS GREATER THAN RUNNING STOOL. APPROX. AFTER 6 MONTHS YOUR METABOLISM WAS STABILIZED AND WEIGHT INCREASED. THE FLUID IN YOUR BALLOON WAS ASSIMILATED AND VANISHED.

AT AGE TWO ON OUR WEEKLY FAMILY DRIVE TO A RESTAURANT THERE WAS A GREAT DEAL OF TALKING. YOU SHOUTED "THIS IS NOT A TALK-ING CAR, PEOPLES" AND THEN CARRIED ON A MONOLOGUE ABOUT THE SCENERY. WHEN WE PASSED A MONASTERY ON CROSS-COUNTY DRIVE, YOU CALLED IT A MONKEY.

YOUR FAVORITE GAME IN RESTAURANT WAS POURING A MOUND OF SALT ON THE TABLE, THEN VERY CAREFULLY YOU RAN YOUR FINGER IN CIRCLES AND CREATED A NEW WORK OF ART WHICH WAS CALLED AN *INBUT*. THIS CREATIVITY OCCURRED IN RESTAURANT WHEN YOU SPOT-TED A FULL SALT SHAKER.

WHEN YOUR SISTER CLAUDIA WAS ABOUT TWO YEARS OLD YOU AND NANA HID HER IN A CLOSET SCREAMING MYSTERIOUSLY, "THE GER-MANS ARE COMING!"

AT AGE SIX OR SEVEN YOU AND YOUR FRIENDS WERE PLAYING IN CEN-TRAL PARK AN AMBITIOUS PRODUCER FROM NBC SELECTED YOU AS A

CHILD BALLET DANCER, YOU APPEARED ON NBC IN A BLACK TUTU AS
PREMIER CHILD BALLERINA.

FIRST OVERSEAS TRIP ON LIBERTÉ YOU PACKED A KING SIZED VALISE
WITH EVERY COLOR LIPSTICK, POWDER, SPRAYS, OINTMENTS, HAIR
CURLERS, BULGING LIKE A HELENA RUBINSTEIN SAMPLE CASE.

I REMEMBER THE PIG'S FETUS YOU BROUGHT HOME FROM BARNARD—
SCALPEL AND ALL. THESE WERE PROMPTLY TRADED IN FOR PENCIIL AND
PAPER. IN ONE FELL SWOOP WE LOST A DOCTOR AND GAINED A WRITER.

My reaction to this? Relief that I didn't get the details too wrong.
And wonderment at why my father wrote all this if he didn't want it
used.

But I am also struck by the fact that it is all about me and not at all
about him. He made the assumption that his life was of no importance
and that all I wanted to hear about was how I rose from neonatal jeop-
ardy to the fetal pig that ended my dreams of a medical career. I had
wanted to interview him about his life. That never entered his mind.

So I begin to interview him as if he is a stranger about whom I am
assigned to write an article. My father takes easily to the game. He
likes it. He is setting the record straight.

What was Brooklyn like when you grew up?

Full of gardens and yards. People moved from the Lower East Side
as if they were moving to the country. The subways were new and
Brownsville was considered a step up.

Was everybody Jewish?

I'd say, 90 percent Jews, 10 percent Italians.

How about your parents, Max and Annie—what do you remember?

My father bringing tailoring home and standing over a pair of
pants. He worked two jobs, moonlighted. Everybody worked two jobs
or three. There were six kids! He'd do alterations to make extra
money. And my mother always stood over the soup pot and she swat-
ted us as we ran by. I remember that and her advice when I was older:
"Never spend your life in worriment." Worriment! What a word.
Every day she would threaten to jump out the window. Every day I
would talk her out of it. That was my job as number-one son. Once a

week, a letter arrived from Germany or Poland or wherever the border happened to be. My father read it aloud to my mother in Yiddish. It came from the shtetl. A place called Czkower, I think. My parents lived in two worlds—Brownsville and Czkower. I think Czkower was more real to them.

When did you get interested in music?

It was Sammy Levinson who showed me a whole other kind of life. He had music lessons, an Amati violin. He played MF—mit feeling. His family paid for him to study. My father expected me to bring money home. I had one lesson at the New York Music School—a fly-by-night place that later went out of business. One lesson! After that, we got gigs—weddings, bar mitzvahs, golden weddings. My father said: "You're already making a leeving, why waste money on lessons?" (He also hid my letter of admission to City College. Years later, I learned this and was furious.) He needed me to help support the family. He didn't see the point of college. At the golden weddings, we played all the old chestnuts: "Just a Garden in the Rain" and "Oh How We Danced on the Night We Were Wed." I decided I never wanted a golden wedding. I'd rather be dead. And Russian dances—always Russian dances—especially at the weddings. They danced the *kazatska* till they fell down.

How did you fall in love with show business?

When Sammy and I were in high school, it was still burlesque. 8 SHOWS 8 [he writes it on a napkin]. When Hershey's with the nuts inside was launched they had a gimmick. There was supposed to be a dollar in every ten bars—so we sold candy like it was going out of style. It wasn't true—of course. You never actually saw a dollar, but people are gullible for giveaways. They believed it. So we hung out at the burlesque and got fifty cents for every dollar we sold. Nice margins.

Why did you tell me never to follow a dog act?

Because in vaudeville you can't compete with dogs and little kids. Also, it's a lousy spot on the bill—in the middle. You want the last spot—or the first. Never the middle. Burlesque kept going through the twenties. The skits were unbelievably stupid by even today's television standards. But the rule held: You had skits, dogs, a magician, the strip show, the headliner. You'd never follow a dog act. Anyway, I was always in the band.

Why did you change your name?

When I was twenty, I joined the union—local 802. Seymour Mann and his orchestra sounded good—but also there was another reason. There was a crook named Izzy Weisman in the union, who'd been involved in some scandal. So Weisman was not a good name to have in local 802. I liked the ring of Seymour Mann and his band. You couldn't sound Jewish in show business then. Cohen became King. Moskowitz became Moss. Rabinowitz became Ross. Goldfish became Goldwyn. Ethnic wasn't in yet.

Where did you meet Eda?

At a place called Utopia in the Catskill Mountains. It really was called Utopia. It was a family resort near Ellenville in "The Mountains." Your mother wore a black velvet cape (in the middle of summer) and dragged it through fields of daisies and cowflop. She was an artist—very bohemian.

"What's a beautiful girl like you doing in a dump like this?" I asked, using the corniest line I knew. It worked. I thought she was easy because she was sleeping in the same room as the owner of the place. But it turned out later, he never laid a finger on her—couldn't, in fact. She was his beard. Anyway, she was painting murals, so I got her to paint my drum. We fell madly in love. After the summer, I visited her once a week, taking the subway from Brooklyn to Upper Riverside Drive. Papa and Mama always left us alone. We took chances that were unbelievable. I think I first said I loved her on the top of an open Fifth Avenue bus. Do you know that they had open Fifth Avenue buses? I was working at Paul's Rendezvous with a five-piece band and also trying somehow to go to NYU at night. At seven dollars a point, I couldn't afford it. (As I said, I never knew I got into City College.) Maxwell Bodenheim used to come into Paul's Rendezvous to recite poetry in exchange for a drink: "Death comes like jewels dropped in a velvet bag . . .," I seem to remember. We got married in 1933 because the Volstead Act was being repealed and we thought there'd be work in the clubs. Roosevelt was inaugurated in March. People were starving: apple sellers on the streets, Hooverville on the river. Our first apartment was on Twenty-second Street between Eighth and Ninth. It was a rooming house with the bathtub in the middle of the kitchen. We'd get two months concession on the rent and move out when the concession was up. We lived in a lot of places that way. At one time we were at 118th and Riverside Drive—thrilled to be on the same avenue as George Gershwin. Musicians worked from eight o'clock until unconscious. Eda would meet me and we'd walk home at night up Broadway and have breakfast at Nedick's. Romantic. She worked all day demonstrating art supplies at Bloomingdale's. She got to take home the paints, so it seemed like a good deal. We never slept. Then, when I was twenty-four, in 1935, I got my first big break. Mickey Green the agent—don't use his name, he's still alive—got me an audition with Cole Porter for *Jubilee*—and I got the job. From then on I was working.

So what happened?

Your mother hated show business. The hours, the insecurity. She'd been the best artist in art school but didn't get the Prix de Rome because they never gave it to girls. Also, there was this fierce competition with your grandfather. And she hated the musicians' union—which was crooked then and demanded kickbacks. Also, when your sister Nana was born we moved back in with Mama and Papa to have some help with your sister.

But didn't you miss show business?

I would have missed her more. We were really in love. I couldn't have done any of this without her. And your mother had a tough life. She didn't know her father till she was eight, you know, because he left the family in England when she was two and her sister Kitty was barely three. Escaping the draft in England. Jews were always escaping the draft. Why should they die for an anti-Semitic czar?

Were you ever in love before?

Oh, there was a girl in high school—but nothing serious. I was nineteen when I met your mother. Marriage was serious, a commitment. You just didn't get divorced. Don't think we didn't have *tsuris*. We did. But divorce was out of the question.

What did your parents think of her?

Mama came up to Utopia to check her out. "Watch out—that girl is using you," she said. [He laughs.]

And what did her parents think of you?

They thought I wasn't good enough, but they kept leaving us alone in the apartment.

Didn't it bother you to quit show business just when you were about to make it?

I wrote some songs that got published, but I knew I was no Cole Porter or Lorenz Hart. No Irving Berlin. No Gershwin. Those were my gods. Look—I would have sold my soul to write "Mountain Greenery" or "Isn't It Romantic?" but all that came out was "The Lonely Little Music Box."

Where did you get the confidence to go to auditions, or to be a salesman?

I always hid my fear when I went out to sell myself. I expected to feel fear, but I knew never to let that control me. Everyone feels fear. In *Jubilee,* the biggest stars would drink out of silver hip flasks before the curtain went up. They were a mess. Fear was expected, predictable. You never expected not to feel fear. But you went on anyway. When I left show business and became a salesman, I never expected not to succeed. And when I started this business and figured out how you make money, I never expected not to make it.

So what are you most proud of in your life?

I gave you what my parents couldn't give me—an education.

But what are you most proud of for yourself?

That. You can't win against powerful daughters who have their own opinion and you can't tell them who to marry—but you can make them get an education. At least that. If you wanted to go to medical school now—I'd still send you.

Thanks, Dad. But I remember the fetal pig from Barnard. I was a menace with a scalpel and the formaldehyde nearly knocked me out.

Maybe you'd feel differently about it now.

You'd still like me to be a doctor, wouldn't you?

Look, you're a terrific writer, but you need a PR agent. It's all in the PR. And you got lousy PR. Look at Madonna. She's got no talent, but great PR. Why don't you call that Della Femina guy? He'll advise you.

He's an ad man, Dad, not a PR agent. He's an old friend of mine, but PR is not his line of work.

PR is everybody's line of work today. And somebody ought to handle you. What about the movie rights? How come they never made that movie? Books are fine, but who reads anymore? You need more than books to make a career.

I don't seem to be very lucky in show business. Every time someone wants to make a movie or play of my work, I waste years of my life and wind up in some legal mess. I can't communicate with Hollywood people. They don't speak my language. Or maybe I don't speak theirs. They can't understand why I'm attached to small details in my books— like the story or the characters—and I can't understand how they make so much money for being on the telephone. It's not a match.

Nonsense, you just have the wrong PR.

So we have made the same trip we always make: from him to me. Since I am the part of him that was meant to go out and conquer show business, he is critical of me, as he would be critical of himself. I bear the burden of his dreams and so he pushes and prods, never dreaming that I feel it as criticism. Once, when one of my books seemed not to be performing as predicted, I screamed at him on the phone: "You'll just have to love me whether or not I'm on the best-seller list!" I think the message got through. Never before had my father understood that when he tried to push me, I felt criticized. But parents can't help themselves. They see so clearly what their children can be, and they are so invested. I probably do the same thing with my daughter—pushing, prodding, seeming to be discontented with her, when in truth she is everything I wanted her to be and more: outspoken where I was shy, tough where I was timid, full of my dreams and ambitions, but with her own special spin. In short, she is my arrow into eternity—but she cannot see it that way.

Dad, every time I ask about you, you wind up talking about me.

I do? Well, I always thought you would do what I didn't do—and in a way you have—all except for the PR.

How can I explain to him that the vicissitudes of my career cannot be undone by mere "PR." I have broken rules that are invisible to him because he is a man: written openly about sex, appropriated male picaresque adventures for women, poked fun at the sacred cows of our society. I have lived as I chose, married, divorced, remarried, divorced, remarried and divorced again—and, still worse, dared to write about my ex-husbands! That is the most heinous of my sins— not having done these things, but having confessed to them in print. It is for this that I am considered beyond the pale. No PR can fix this! It's nothing more or less than the fate of rebellious women. They used to stone us in the marketplace. In a way, they still do.

And he'd still send me to medical school! Should I consider that an insult or a compliment? And should I take him up on it? I might love being a doctor for the second part of my life. Writing is not an easy way to make a living.

And then it is late—3:30 almost, and we have to fly. My father pays the bill and we walk back to the showroom. I catch a cab and head uptown, with my reams of indecipherable notes and a tape recorder that, I realize, didn't pick up a word.

Very well. I will reconstruct the conversation as I always do any- way, writing fiction. It's all made up anyway. Especially the parts that sound real.

Looking back over this dialogue, I fear I may have made my father sound a bit too much like Mel Brooks's 2,000-Year-Old Man. But something else emerges, something that seems to have escaped me when I was younger. My parents each gave up an artistic ambition— his music, her painting—to create a family and a business together. And the business used both their talents—her designing and drawing and modeling and his knack for guessing trends and his salesmanship. The dolls became their joint product, like their daughters. It was a mom-and-pop operation. At the end of it all they still had each other—and nine grandchildren—and plenty of money. For kids who started out in the Depression, with parents who spoke Yiddish and Russian, that was nearly a miracle. More than that, it was their ideal of marriage: a partnership, a compromise, and, of course, a commu- nist enterprise—from each according to his or her capacities, to each according to his or her needs. Neither one felt cheated at the end. (The middle is another story.) Each took credit for the other's success. Not many people in my generation have marriages like that. I never thought I would. And getting there was the hardest battle of my life.

But I am getting ahead of the story. First, I have to tell you about my mother.

How hard it is to write about her and how necessary. And where do I begin? Then or now? And do I tell the story from my point of view or hers? We are so linked that it's hard to know the difference. I tell myself that my mother would never agree to be interviewed, that she would bitterly mock the idea. (I am to be proven wrong.) But I believe it was her frustration above all that propelled my success. Then she was both jealous of me and fiercely proud. She made me everything I am today—warts and all.

When did I first understand female limitations? From my mother. And when did I first understand I was destined in some way to become my mother? At puberty. Until then I was unfettered in my ambition and enthusiasm. I expected to be Edna St. Vincent Millay, Madame Curie, and Beatrice Webb all rolled into one. I expected to take the world by its ears and shake it until it said, Yes, Erica, yes, yes, yes, yes. And now I understand that my mother had had the same experience. But that because of the times in which she lived, she had gotten stuck in that experience as I did not—and her stuckness was one of the things that set me free.

I go back, back, back in time. I try to transcend the family myths and the communal screen memories and transport myself to a time I know chiefly through Henry Miller's life—not my parents' life—the Jazz Age, the Crash, the speakeasies, rolled stockings, and bootleg gin: 1929.

My mother was in art school at the National Academy of Design. A brunette with bobbed hair and big brown eyes and a fast mouth, she was the best draftswoman and painter in her class and she had every reason to win the top prizes—including the big traveling fellowship—the Prix de Rome. "Watch out for that Mirsky girl," her art teacher used to say to the guys: "She'll beat you all."

And my mother felt teased and tantalized by this because she knew (yet did not know) that her sex precluded her from ever being sent to Rome. When she won the bronze medal and was told—quite frankly (no one was ashamed to be sexist then)—that she hadn't won the Prix de Rome because, as a woman, she was expected to marry, bear children, and waste her gifts, she was enraged. That rage has powered my life—and also, in many ways, impeded it.

"I expected the world to beat a path to my door," she always says. "But the world never does that. You have to make them come."

Feminism was hot in my mother's time too. The twenties were a time of hope for women's rights. But those rights were never codified into law. And without law, feminism never sticks. My mother blamed herself for "her failures." She never thought to blame history. And I never wanted to be as consumed with anger as she was. I wanted the power of sunlight, not the power of night. I wanted abundance, not scarcity; love, not fear. Sometimes I think my mother made my father quit show business so he would have to make the same renunciation she had made. If children were to hobble her, they should also hobble him. She would not accept the "womanly" role of enabler. She would not let him be an artist if she could not let herself be one. So the mother-daughter dynamic is a subject I can't avoid if I am to tell "all that David Copperfield kind of crap." My mother's frustrations powered both my feminism and my writing. But much of the power came out of my anger and my competition: my desire to outdo her, my hatred of her capitulation to her femaleness, my desire to be different because I feared I was much too much like her.

Womanhood was a trap. If I was too much like her, I'd be trapped as she was. But if I rejected her example, I'd be a traitor to her love. I felt a fraud no matter which way I turned. I had to find a way to be like her and unlike her at the same time. I had to find a way to be both a girl and a boy.

In this I may be most typical of my whiplash generation. The models of motherhood we had did not serve us in the lives we led. Our mothers stayed home, but we hit the road. We were often the first female members of our families to stay in hotel rooms alone, to raise children alone, to face tax problems alone, to stare at the glass ceiling alone and wonder how to crash through. And we were guilty, and therefore ambivalent about our lives, because many of our mothers never got even that far.

When I talk to the members of my college class, the theme that comes up again and again is guilt toward our mothers.

"We are the sandwich generation," one member of my Barnard class said at a little pre-reunion dinner we had to celebrate our fiftieth birthdays. "Our generation suffered because our mothers had nothing to look forward to at fifty," said another. "We held ourselves back so as not to lose our mothers' love," said another. "Mixed messages," we all agreed. Mixed messages about competing and not competing, about making money and not making money, about assertiveness and subordination. These are the earmarks of the whiplash generation.

We held ourselves back in misplaced loyalty to our mothers, I think. Since they were not fully free to be assertive, we stayed chained to their limitations as if this bondage were a proof of love. (Often, in fact, we equated bondage with love.) In midlife, with time beating its wings at our backs, we finally snatched the courage to break free. We finally let go of that ambivalence that was our mothers' collective lot—and we crashed through the glass ceiling inside ourselves, to real freedom.

Contemporary American feminism pays a terrible price, I think, for its rejection of Freud. By labeling Freud a sexist and nothing more, and throwing out his revolutionary concept of the unconscious along with his sexism, we lose the very tools we need to understand what goes on between ourselves and our mothers. And without that understanding, it is hard to make feminism stick. A great undertow of ambivalence threatens us in all our achievements. Guilty about succeeding where our mothers failed, we sometimes unconsciously sabotage our success, just as we are about to taste its fruits. I fear that if we don't look at the generations psychologically, we are doomed to keep replaying the same old cycle of feminism and backlash in alternating generations.

In 1929, when my mother graduated art school and failed to win the prizes she deserved, the world was on a similar pivot between the newness of feminism and the old accustomed ways of male chauvinism. But ideas are only abstractions. They do not enter the body politic until they are carried along in the hearts of individual human beings. And those human beings were raised by parents of a different generation, with a different set of assumptions. Every person carries on an inner war between generations. And it is the outcome of that war that determines how and whether the world changes.

With women, this war is particularly acute. Women identify with their mothers automatically and powerfully, but they must also overthrow their mothers to become themselves. If each generation does the opposite of its mothers' generation, we shall continue to have the alternation of feminist generations and backlash generations we know so depressingly well. We shall continue on the same little toy track, never getting anywhere but going round and round.

Mothers tend to seed their daughters with their own unexpressed rebellion. As a result, rebelling generations follow quiescent ones, quiescent ones follow rebelling ones, and the world goes on as it always has. Just at the moment when women find their intellectual or artistic powers, hormones kick in, making the yearning to bear children overwhelming. If we have learned from our mothers, that childbearing defeats creativity, we will rebel by not having children or rebel by making childbearing our only creativity. Why not break this vicious cycle and become the women our mothers wanted to be? Because we feel we cannot do this without killing our mothers, and so, in retribution for the murderous wish, we kill, instead, the mother within ourselves.

In my twenties, after winning most of the writing prizes in college and even publishing a poem or two, I went through a period of excruciating blockage. I would sit at my desk trying to write and have an anxiety attack as I envisioned a man with a loaded gun standing behind me, ready to shoot me if I wrote a line. I was lucky to be in analysis with someone smart enough and patient enough to guide me until I made the association between the man with the gun and my imaginary mother, who both wanted me to write and wanted to kill me for writing. The mother in my fantasy felt I was a traitor for writing, even if my real historical mother did not. I had to fight this battle between self and soul in order to write a line. And in some way or other this battle comes back with every book I write. Each time the solution is the same: Bring the demons to consciousness and they may leave me alone long enough to let me break through the blockage and finish the book.

Creativity demands nothing less than all you have. It means revealing murderous rage, the marksman behind the writing desk, the inner demons that confound us all.

How can creativity be other than a terrifying force full of unexpected turnings? If you give your life to creativity, you give up forever the promise to be a good girl. Creativity will inevitably lead you to give away dark family secrets. It will lead you into the labyrinth to face the minotaur. You can't face the minotaur and stay a good girl. You can't look the minotaur in the eye and continue to silence the artist in yourself.

I imagine my mother at nineteen or twenty, worrying this same sad bone of female creativity. "I will defeat the dybbuks!" she must have thought. She chose a man who shared her loves. She chose a man who loved her art. But the sabotage of the world played nicely into her own self-sabotage. Art is hard. You have to be on your own side. And it is difficult for women to be on their own side when they are told they are supposed to be on everyone else's. The world reinforces all their doubts. And then comes the baby and the need to earn a living—and what unequal opportunity doesn't kill, love lays waste.

A baby is a full-time job for three adults. Nobody tells you that when you're pregnant, or you'd probably jump off a bridge. Nobody tells you how all-consuming it is to be a mother—how reading goes out the window and thinking too.

All this assumes the baby's normal and healthy. What if the baby's sickly, or starving, or what if the mother is? Every mother who ever lived has faced that fierce moment when a baby turns its milky mouth to her breast and she knows she is all it has.

My mother panicked and went home to Mama and Papa—with their clutching competition and their infantilizing care. She took the path of least resistance and hated herself for it. Harder to break with your parents when you depend on them. Harder to break with your parents when you're a parent too. The dependency of an infant links women to their mothers. So one generation gets lost in the wars of the previous one. My grandmother's struggles were passed to me by my mother. My grandmother, with her crushing marriage to my tyrannical grandfather, with her barbaric abortions on the kitchen table and her inexhaustible maternal sweetness and nurturance, admired most of all her friend who was a woman dentist. She always spoke of her with awe and pride.

"Having a friend who was a dentist somehow gave her status," my mother says. "Mama was a feminist too—and she didn't even know it."

Thus the generations of women are linked in their ambivalence. And so it goes. So it goes. So it goes.

I had waited until I was fledged as a writer before I succumbed to the seductions of motherhood. *Fear of Flying* was my emancipation proclamation—which also, by chance, gave me the material success to support the child I bore.

My mother didn't have this luck. Raised by immigrant parents who had left their own parents young and therefore needed to hold their children too close, she began her rebellion against her mother early and let it fizzle too soon. Faced with the unfairness of a world that didn't treat women artists equally, she retreated into a more

acceptable form of female creativity—as women have done throughout the ages. Then she filled her daughters with feminist rage—as
women have also done throughout the ages.

But that dynamic alone wasn't enough to fuel my ambition. My
father also needed me to be his son. My drive came from a potent
brew my parents made together. The ingredients were just right to
make a girl who thought she was allowed to be a boy. But who also
had to punish herself for this presumption.

This brew is certainly no recipe for contentment. I went out and
thrust myself into the world like a boy, and then I atoned with female
fears—fear of flying, fear of the marksman behind the writing desk,
fear of fifty. I paid for my success by making myself fat, by depriving
myself of good relationships, by depriving myself, for many years, of
the joys of mothering. I also pushed my mother away because her
example was too scary. And she pushed me away because my success
was too painful. In that mutual repulsion-attraction dance, I feel my
mother and I are all too typical of mothers and daughters of the
whiplash generation.

I try to see my mother as a separate person, and still I cannot. She
is a part of me, a part that criticizes and stings and disapproves. She
will never be satisfied because what she wants is basically impossible:
for me to be just like her and yet to succeed as she did not.

I was really the marksman behind the desk. It was not my mother
or even my imaginary mother. I wanted to kill the traitor self that
wanted to break from my mother. I knew my writing was my means
of escape, and I wanted to stay, yet go at the same time. Hence the
perfect metaphor I devised was fear of flying.

Fly I would, but never without fear. Fly I would, but always in a
state of torment—a metallic edge behind the teeth that says: You cannot dare, dare this. I flew but suffered for my hubris like Icarus. Even
my chosen symptom was half-father, half-mother. Even my chosen
symptom expressed the split in my soul.

In Isadora Wing, I invented a typical heroine of the whiplash generation. She flew and fucked and achieved in the world, but she punished herself with men. With her heart in the past and her intellect in
the future, she was doomed to suffer no matter what she did. Her self-
mockery and humor became her survival tool, because only through
irony can you say X, yet mean Y.

I think Isadora touched women of my generation because so many
of us are similarly split. We are our mothers, but we are also women of

the future. We earn our own livings, support our own children, fight for our careers in a world that still does not give us economic equality with men, but that dark undertow is pulling us back to our mothers, making us feel guilty even for the crumbs of autonomy we achieve.

Often we express our darkest ambivalence with our men and our children. Fierce competitors in the world of work, we crumble in relationships or become slaves to our children. Some of us finally give up men because it is just too tough to keep on suffering. We tend to give too much in love, so some of us decide to give nothing at all. Some of us turn to women, hoping that way to break the sadomasochistic chains that bind.

With our children, it's harder. Often we spoil them because we have no model of mothering that includes independence. We can't stay home as our mothers did, but the mothers in our heads still have the power to make us feel guilty. So we set too few limits and buy too many goodies we cannot really afford and consequently we raise children who dictate to us, all the while feeling deeply insecure.

Thinking of my mother's life, I am overcome with feeling. Talent alone is never enough. My mother had talent to burn. She could draw and paint, model clay, cut patterns, create collages from bits of silk and paper, create ballet dresses from ordinary crepe paper, embroider a green needlepoint forest without any pattern but the pattern in her head. She once turned me into a forest sprite for Halloween, covering my leotard with green and gold and orange leaves until I fluttered in the wind like a quivering autumn tree. She made me cut-outs, sewed my baby dolls Victorian bonnets and crinolines, painted tiny portraits to hang over the mantelpieces in my doll's house. There was nothing her nimble fingers could not do, nothing her visual mind could not conceive. But all this talent was not enough. She lacked the courage to follow her talent into the dark woods of any artist's destiny. She couldn't bear the world's criticism as I could. Her inner bad reviews were so sharp and biting that she could not risk a single outer one.

Or maybe her maternal urge was too strong. She couldn't stop at one child as I did. She gave birth to me and gave up struggling to be free. And how can I protest her giving birth to me?

I suffer too, and my kind of writing has never left me free of criticism, but I also have my father's mad tenacity. Rejection and criticism hurt, but I can bear them as long as I go on writing. I know that the world will not beat a path to anyone's door. I drag the world to my door by never giving up.

It was not that my mother gave up. It was just that she chose a more acceptable female path: outer capitulation, inner resentment—the old, old story. The world controls women by playing on our need for approval, for love, for relationship. If we behave ourselves, excising our unruly creative impulses, we are rewarded with "love." If we do not, "love" is withheld. The woman creator pays a fearsome price as long as she is controlled by love. Creativity is dark, is rebellious, is full of "bad" thoughts. To suppress it in the name of "femininity" is to succumb to an anger that leads to madness.

What I remember most about my mother was that she was always angry.

I wanted to undo this spell, break this cycle, so for the longest time, men and motherhood were secondary. Men were acceptable as long as they typed my poems, and motherhood frankly terrified me. It had been my mother's Waterloo, I felt, and I had no intention of taking that risk.

"No sperm could ever get through that goop," one of my husbands said about the excessive amounts of jelly I used to use with my diaphragm. I was unapologetic. I hated the idea of losing control and I knew that an abortion would certainly break my heart. My diaphragm was the guardian of my literary ambitions, and about those I had no ambivalence. I was absolutely single-minded. It was number one on the bestseller list or bust!

Now, at fifty, when it is too late, I wish I had more children. What safe nostalgia! But when I was fertile, I mostly saw motherhood as the enemy of art and an appalling loss of control. My mother was always so torn. "The drive of women to have children is stronger than anything," she used to say—somewhat ruefully, it seemed to me. I did not confront that drive until I was thirty-five, and by then, I was a writer first and a mother second. I had, like Colette, a "masculine pregnancy"—book-touring in my sixth month, finishing a chapter about an eighteenth-century masked ball as my water broke. I nursed the baby as I wrote Book II of a picaresque novel.

For years, I resolutely remained a writer first, a mother second. It took me the whole first decade of my daughter's life to learn to surrender myself to motherhood. No sooner had I learned that essential surrender than she was entering puberty and I menopause.

What do I regret? Nothing. I have raised a daughter who also recognizes no limits. And I have learned at last that my mother was right. Surrendering to motherhood means surrendering to interruption. Molly comes home from school and work stops. She claims all my attention. I become her sidekick, her buddy, her duenna, her walking credit card. I resent it, yet I also love it more than anything. She fills me up with feeling as no one can. She also has the power to drive me mad. She assumes her own primacy, as all healthy children must. If there were three of her—as my mother had—this book might never be. Would that matter? Or only matter to me? Who knows? I write because I must. I hope my books are useful for you, too. But if I did not write them, I would surely be half-alive, and half-mad.

So I have made my choices and I am mostly glad of them. The intensity of one mother–one daughter sometimes makes me wish I had a household full of noisy kids, but the truth is I know now that even I, with all my prodigious energy, can't do everything. Motherhood cannot finally be delegated. Breast-feeding may succumb to the bottle; cuddling, fondling, and pediatric visits may also be done by fathers (and surely we could make life easier for mothers than we do), but when a child needs a mother to talk to, nobody else but a mother will do. A mother is a mother is a mother, as Gertrude Stein surely would have said had she become one.

Certainly children need dozens of parental figures: mother, father, grandparents, nannies, cousins, teachers, godparents—but still, nothing substitutes for good old Mom. Am I a female chauvinist? So be it. The power of being a mother is actually quite awesome when you think about it. Who but a megalomaniac would be willing to take on such power without a backward glance?

Years after giving birth, I became a mother against my will because I saw that my daughter needed me to become one. What I really would have preferred was to remain a writer who dabbled in motherhood. That felt more comfortable, more safe. But Molly would not permit it. She needed a mother, not a dabbler. And because I love her more than I love myself, I became what she needed me to be.

"Earth to Mom: Space in. You're zoning out again," says she. Molly hates it when I wander through the house (the store, her school), writing in my head. So I space in—the hardest of all things for me to do—and I try to be present for her. Can I delegate that to anyone else? No. Would I want to? Sometimes, yes. (So I'm not a perfect mother—who is?) But I do attempt to focus on her needs above my own. And I know in my heart (as I know I will die) that Molly is more important than my writing. Any child is. That's why motherhood is so difficult for writing women. Its demands are so compelling, so clearly important, and also so profoundly satisfying.

Who can explain this to the childless? You give up your self, and finally you don't even mind. You become your child's guide to life at the expense of that swollen ego you thought so immutable. I wouldn't have missed this for anything. It humbled my ego and stretched my soul. It awakened me to eternity. It made me know my own humanity, my own mortality, my own limits. It gave me whatever crumbs of wisdom I possess today.

What do I wish for Molly? The same. Work she loves and a child to lead her to herself. Why should any of us settle for less? We know why: because the world has deliberately made things difficult for women, so that they could not have motherhood and also the life of the mind. Mine may be the first generation in which being a writer and a mother is not utterly impossible. Margaret Mead says somewhere that when she finally had her only daughter in 1939, at the age of thirty-eight, she looked at the brief biographies of famous women and discovered that most of them had no children—or only one. This has only recently begun to change.

But it is still hard. And the battles are far from over: The abortion battle, the "family values" battle, the "should mothers work outside the home?" battle—all are symptoms of an incomplete revolution. And incomplete revolutions produce passionate and angry feelings.

Those women who have given up work, art, literature, the life of the mind, for nurturance naturally resent those women who have not had to. The privilege to create is so new for women. And the privilege to create and also nurture is newer still. Those women who have given up nurturance feel resentful too. Perhaps they could have done things differently, they feel, when it is already too late. Is it possible they blame *Roe v. Wade* for the newness of choices their mothers did not have to make?

Motherhood is an awesome choice. Who would make it lightly, knowing all that it entails? Perhaps some women still feel it would be better to make a slip and not be able to undo it. Perhaps they would prefer to reach the state of motherhood by accident.

Choice is terrifying. What if you make the wrong choice? Compulsion and resentment have been the lot of women for so long that if nothing else, we are used to them. Freedom is too hard. Freedom puts responsibility squarely on our own shoulders.

And it is true that women's control of their own fertility has led men to disclaim some of their ancient responsibilities. Choice also gives men choice. Choice demystifies motherhood and takes away some of the ancient female power. For a woman who has other power, that may be wonderful, but for a woman who has only the awesome motherpower, surely there is a sense of loss. After all, it's less than a hundred years since women's lives have been transformed by aseptic childbirth and reliable control of fertility. Those two things have changed the world beyond recognition. Those two things, not merely feminist ideology, have brought a revolution in women's lives. And some women apparently still long for the past.

Is this really so strange? The past may have been bondage, yet it was familiar bondage. The equation of woman with her maternity at least gave women an unambivalent identity. As feminists we ought to understand those feelings of loss instead of mocking them. We ought to acknowledge the huge power of the motherknot and the great importance it once conferred on women. Having honored that feeling of loss, we might then insist on everybody's right to embrace motherpower or else let it go unused. Renunciation, after all, is also a form of power.

When I see angry hordes storming abortion clinics, or meditative ones standing in silent prayer-circles outside pro-choice rallies, I think we are seeing the last generation to have nostalgia for the old chthonic imperatives of human life. Why else would they shoot doctors in the name of "life"? They want to kill the very concept of choice. They want to kill it first within themselves, then within us. Our embracing freedom of choice somehow negates their lives. They are ready to kill for "life." They want to go back to a time when women could not make choices and thus would not feel eternally in the wrong. (At least this applies to some of the women who embrace that misnomer "the right to life.")

The men are another story. They want control over women. And the evangelical leaders who fan the flames of the right-to-life movement want political control. They are simply exploiting tax-free church money to lobby for political ends. We should tax their organizations as we do professional lobbyists.

Still, motherhood is not light, optional, and free of ambivalence; it is a dark, compelling force that overrides many human preferences.

We ought to understand that some women (and many men) fear any diminution of motherhood. Maybe if we open our minds to understanding this, we can combat the right-to-lifers' ideas more effectively. I suspect I understand this because of my mother, my mother who was torn always between motherhood and art, my mother who never resolved that ambivalence but passed it along, instead, to me.

What I would most like to give my daughter is freedom. And this is something that must be given by example, not by exhortation. Freedom is a loose leash, a license to be different from your mother and still be loved. Freedom is not binding your daughter's feet, not performing a symbolic clitoridectomy, not insisting that your daughter share your own limitations. Freedom also means letting your daughter reject you when she needs to and come back when she needs to. Freedom is unconditional love.

Molly, I want to release you. If you hate me or want to reject me, I understand. If you curse me, then want to atone, I also understand. I expect to be your home plate: kicked, scuffed, but always returned to. I expect to be the earth from which you spring.

But if I release you too much, what will you have to fight against?

You need my acceptance, but you may need my resistance more. I promise to stand firm while you come and go. I promise unwavering love while you experiment with hate. Hate is energy too—sometimes brighter-burning energy than love. Hate is often the precondition for freedom.

No matter how I try to disappear, I fear I cast too big a shadow. I would erase that shadow if I could. But if I erased it, how would you know your own shadow? And with no shadow, how would you ever fly?

I want to release you from the fears that bound me, yet I know you can only release yourself. I stand here wearing my catcher's padding. I pray you won't need me to catch you if you fall. But I'm here waiting anyway.

Freedom is full of fear. But fear isn't the worst thing we face. Paralysis is.

Letting go, I love you. Letting go, I hold you in my arms.

3

THE MAD LESBIAN IN THE ATTIC

> If one is not permitted to express anger or even to recognize it
> within oneself, one is, by simple extension, refused both power
> and control.
>
> —Carolyn Heilbrun, *Writing a Woman's Life*

As I write this, my aunt, my mother's only sister, is in a straitjacket in
the locked psycho ward of Lenox Hill Hospital. She is there not only
because she has senile dementia and probably Alzheimer's, but
because she is a woman alone, a lesbian displaced homemaker,
dumped by her lover of thirty years when she started acting strange,
and nobody else wants her as a full-time commitment. She has no children (except the lover's child she helped raise). She and my mother
have not spoken for years and years. The origins of the feud are as
murky as the origins of all family feuds. But the result remains: My
mother does not want her, my sisters do not want her, I do not want
her, the stepson she raised does not want her, and her lover has long
since moved on to younger pastures.

To be old and alone can happen to anyone—and for women the
statistical possibilities are overwhelming. But in the case of my Aunt
Kitty, other factors also played a part. My aunt is an artist, a lesbian
of a certain age, a homemaker and nurturer. Those are not qualities
that earn you a pension or a nest egg, those are not qualities our society rewards. My aunt also has Alzheimer's complicated by alcoholism—and being sick in America is still only for the rich. All these
things play a part in her fate. And her fate, for reasons I will presently
explain, has fallen into my lap. Meanwhile, Kitty waits at Lenox Hill,

where she was taken by a stranger (who also apparently took her wallet and used her credit cards when she collapsed at the Metropolitan Museum of Art several weeks ago).

As I deliberate about what to do—not wanting the responsibility, yet knowing that it is mine by default whether I want it or not—I am taken prisoner by some old family photographs. I have three pictures of my mother and aunt at the ages of not-yet-one and not-yet-two, seven and eight, seventeen and eighteen.

The first, stamped on the back "U.S.A. Postcard, U.S.A. Studios, London and provinces" shows two little girls—one nine months old, one a year and a half old—sitting on a Victorian settee and looking at the camera. The baby on the left is my mother: round, brown eyes (with a startlingly strong gaze), a tonsure of brownish hair, curled toes, fat fingers; and the one on the right is my Aunt Kitty, big round eyes just as blank and innocent as those she has today, a rosebud mouth, and little hands clutching a doll. The photo was not prophetic. My mother had three daughters, my aunt had no biological children. But the relationship is clear. Two little girls close as twins, inseparable growing up, are destined to become mirror images of each other and mirror enemies.

In the next photograph, they are perhaps seven and eight and wearing middy dresses, high-button shoes, and floppy hair bows. They hold hands. Eda looks straight ahead; Kitty inclines her head toward Eda's. Again this is a studio portrait, on a French-style settee, taken in England. My mother-to-be is the more assertive of the two girls, my aunt the more "feminine"—if feminine is defined (as it was for most of her life) as pliable and complaisant. It was this temperament that brought her where she is today.

The third and last photo, taken in New York before a trip to Paris (I was once told), shows two teenagers of the twenties, seventeen and eighteen years old, with bobbed hair, silk stockings, strappy silk shoes, and low-waisted, short-skirted dresses. Again the four round brown eyes, my mother's stubby fingers and my aunt's slim ones, my mother's boldness of expression and my aunt's soft diffidence. Eda touches Kitty's shoulder with one fingertip; Kitty rests her silken elbow in Eda's lap and leans toward her in warmth and closeness, the older sister seeming almost like the younger one, the younger one almost like the older.

What happened between this sequence of photographs and today? That is the mystery delivered into my hands by Kitty's crisis. It may be insoluble, but I am going to try to solve it nevertheless. Why? It's in my nature never to let a tangled skein pass through my fingers without trying to untangle it. It may untangle some part of my tangled self.

Autobiography, I am learning, is much more difficult than fiction. In fiction, the writer can impose order, if not moral meaning, on events. Of course the characters do not all obey the writer's bidding like puppets, but they certainly can be coaxed into dances that are pleasingly symmetrical and seem to have beginnings, middles, and ends, a sense of purpose, plot, motivation.

Not so with life. And especially the lives of relatives. Sometimes people go to their graves without our learning their mysteries, and certainly without any sense of purpose, plot, motivation. Fiction writer that I am, I want to give shape and symmetry to this story, but I am stuck with the facts—in all their crudeness and disorder.

The facts unfold backward, as facts often do. Tomorrow, I will meet my aunt in court to try to get the legal power to become her caretaker. Then I will try to find a place for her. Tonight, I promise myself to visit her at Lenox Hill, but I do not. I stay instead at my desk, sifting through old family photographs and wondering what they mean.

Memory is the crux of our humanity. Without memory we have no identities. That is *really* why I am committing an autobiography. And it cannot be an accident that smack in the middle of my beginning it, my aunt's loss of memory claims center stage in my life.

We meet in court, a somber columned building on Centre Street. The cast of characters are: my Aunt Kitty, who looks dazed, her dyed brown hair gone gray at the roots, a puzzled expression on her child-like old face; her former partner, Maxine (an imposing presence in frizzed red hair, orange lipstick, a coral suit, and large jewelry); a bossy young woman lawyer, who is advocating Kitty's civil rights for the City of New York; a fortyish, florid-faced, red-bow-tied male lawyer, appointed by the city to be Kitty's guardian *ad litem*; a young friend of Kitty's called Frank, who is not yet thirty and wears at least that many hoop earrings in his left ear; my father; my husband, who is acting as the family's lawyer; a Haitian nursing aide from a private agency, who is minding Kitty; and a Chinese-American judge, who takes a rather dim view of any petitioners who attempt to put their older relatives anywhere but in their own homes. (Since I was once married to a Chinese-American, I realize we have not been lucky in drawing this particular judge. The Chinese do not warehouse the old. Instead, they honor them.)

We have come to this court case because of the impossibility of our making a decision about Kitty's welfare without it. Court, in our society, is often the last resort of stubbornness.

Just about a year ago, Kitty began to give increasing warnings of her inability to live alone. She collapsed and was hospitalized God knows where, while we all tried in vain to track her down with the help of various police precincts. When at last we found her in a small hospital on East Sixteenth Street, she insisted she was fine and wanted only to be released. Though she was still good at charming everybody, the social workers and psychiatrists warned us that she had "serious memory deficits" (as they called them) and should not be left alone. A nursing home was recommended, but nobody could make Kitty enter it. I visited the home, made celebrity love to the admissions director, brought my aunt pictures of her possible room-to-be, whereupon she adamantly refused even to visit. One night she simply walked out of the hospital, returned to her loft, and informed us that she intended to stay there forever.

I was relieved. Still not ready to face the finality of a nursing home, I deluded myself about her competence. And Kitty did get by at home for a while. Frank visited her every day and Maxine took her to the Hamptons when conscience overwhelmed her. Still, Kitty's memory had so deteriorated that she could remember neither outings nor phone calls, the names of relatives nor when to take her medicine. It became clearer and clearer that this expedient would not last long.

"Don't you have an extra room for me?" she'd plaintively ask. And I wondered guiltily why I didn't. I had a room for my daughter, for my husband, for guests, but Kitty's neediness would have taken over my life, and I simply could not do it.

Alzheimer's does not stand still. Memory unravels, and people without memory seem to forget they are memoryless. One evening Kitty brought a homeless drunk up to her loft and shared her keys with him. Frank found him there, making himself quite at home. When Frank warned Kitty of the danger, she became furious and ordered him to "butt out" of her life.

This went on for a while. Things disappeared from the loft.

Friends were reluctant to go there for fear of being set upon by strangers. Kitty struggled on. She knew she was lonely, but not much else.

The street people, the drunks and drug addicts of Chelsea were her people. "They're just lonely people," she said, which was, of course, true. But when she started picking fights in various local pubs, there began to be places where she was no longer welcome. Increasingly, she was perceived as mad. (What is "mad" anyway but unpredictable, memoryless, inappropriate?) By the time she got to Lenox Hill, everyone knew another solution would have to be found. What do you do with the memoryless old in this brutal city? It's hard enough to live here *with* a memory.

A powwow was held at my apartment. Maxine agreed to bring a petition to have Kitty declared incompetent. But the weekend before the hearing, she lost her nerve. With a petition and no petitioner and Kitty in the psycho ward at Lenox Hill, Frank and I agreed to serve. We had no choice.

And so the court was called to order. I sat with Kitty, holding her hand while a psychiatrist, called as an expert witness, rattled on about the state of her memory, the diagnosis of Alzheimer's, senile dementia, and related phenomena.

"Is he talking about *me*?" Kitty asked. "And why? And where *are* we?"

She had come straight from Lenox Hill to participate in this hearing. And she was still a bit drugged with the tranquilizers they had given her for lack of any brighter ideas about her care. Dazed by the oddness of finding herself in court, she kept repeating, "Are they talking about *me*?"

It must have been a nightmare. To wake up in court with one's sanity being mooted and not to recognize anyone—this is the stuff of Kafka novels. But who can make a decision for another person—even when her memory is gone? Without memory, who are we? Kitty wasn't sure. Nor was I.

The truth is, we should have been able to care for her without such court shenanigans, but since her next of kin, my mother, would not participate, and since her former life-partner and heir would not take the responsibility for putting her in a nursing home, we had no choice but to take the matter to court. Law, clumsy as it often is, is sometimes the way people are forced to face what they otherwise refuse to face. Law at least has the advantage of bringing all the concerned parties into the same *room*. By dragging the dubious authority of the state into a family matter, sometimes the family is forced to reclaim its own authority—if only in rebellion.

And this is what happened here. The judge, being Chinese, and having a cultural bias in favor of the dignity of the aged, seemed to close his ears to the psychiatrist's testimony and to see only the tableau of a group of grasping relatives trying to incarcerate a sweet old lady.

After the psychiatrist's testimony came Maxine's. Rattled by anxiety and guilt, she kept insisting that she didn't want anything of Kitty's. These protestations made the judge suspicious. The lawyers appointed by the city were also of little help. First the preening, bow-tied male lawyer made it clear he saw Kitty as his mother and could not face her mental deterioration. And the young woman lawyer appointed to advocate Kitty's civil rights waffled and covered herself, giving no impression of the danger her client was in. Throughout all this legal folderol, I sat with Kitty, glad that she could not really hear everything being said before the bench, the reduction of those prized treasures, her selfhood and identity, to lawyers' and psychiatrists' cant. Her sole offense was having lost her memory (and therefore being presumed to have lost her mind).

Court proceedings take a long time, and judges tend to keep punctual hours. We adjourned at five sharp, and I was delegated to take Kitty back to Lenox Hill. Maxine had vanished right after her testimony, but both the court-appointed lawyers loitered about uselessly, making lawyer noises. The point was that nobody really was prepared to take on the twenty-four-hour job Kitty had become. Maxine had her real estate business; Frank had his job as a landscape architect and a lover dying of AIDS; I had a daughter and a book deadline; my husband had other cases, which, unlike this one, would pay his overhead; my father had to go home to my mother and pretend not to have been where he had in fact been because my mother, as in a time warp, still accused her sister of trying to seduce him. How amazed she might have been had she come to court! My aunt did not remember who my father *was*. She could not even put a name to this face she had known for sixty-three years.

Returning from court, I drove in a hospital van with Kitty and her private nurse.

"Can we stop and have a drink?" Kitty asked. "Can we have dinner somewhere, at least? Can I come home with you?"

In two hours I was expected at a formal dinner honoring a friend, but suddenly I wanted to bring Kitty with me or not go at all. Impossible. She was exhausted, confused, and wearing whatever odds and ends of clothes Maxine had bothered to bring (a stained silk blouse, shoes that didn't fit, torn stockings, a moth-eaten fur coat). So it was back to the hospital for the night. Tomorrow I would bring her to her loft, arrange a home health-care worker for her, and then we'd see what we would see.

Back in the ward (which Kitty didn't realize *was* a ward), I took off her shoes and rubbed her sore feet. "God bless you," she said. And then: "What's the name of this hotel?"

"Heartbreak Hotel," I said.

"What a funny name," said Kitty.

"Where's the phone?" I asked the nurse. She stared at me as if I were crazy.

"This is the psycho ward," she said impatiently.

"It just seems like a hotel room to me," Kitty said.

I was really late by now, but I just could not leave.

"Let's have a drink," Kitty kept saying over and over and over. Every time she said that, I laughed. Laughed so I would not cry. It is the repetitive demandingness of the memoryless old that makes them so difficult. We take their repetitions as insults, which is silly of us. If only we could let go of ego and live moment to moment as the very old and the very young do. Imagine existing in a state where you repeat and repeat because every second is unrelated to every other.

"Let's have a drink," Kitty said yet again. This was her evening ritual, and she hung on to it as a life raft even when all other markers were gone. No use to tell her that drink had helped *destroy* her memory. She wouldn't care—nor even remember what it was like to *have* a memory.

Dinner in the cuckoo's nest. Patients shuffle into the cafeteria to get their trays. "Hi, Kitty! How ya doin'?" blusters a lopsided, wall-eyed man in paper slippers.

"Meet my niece, the famous writer," she says to everyone and nobody in particular. My cheeks prickle with embarrassment. Even with her unraveled mind, Kitty can demand recognition for my celebrity. What a joke to invoke something as fickle as fame in the midst of all this human mutability.

Nothing saves us from growing old, I think. Not celebrity, not talent, not personal charm, not wealth, not wit. The absurdity of trading on my fame shamed me somehow. In this nuthouse, I felt fused with Kitty: Her gaffes were also mine.

God—it was late. My friend, my child, my husband, all awaited me. As usual, I was torn by conflicting demands, and felt I fulfilled none of them adequately.

In the elevator, a woman began to talk to me, as women will. "My best friend," she said, "had another attack. Tried to commit suicide again. She's back in here again."

"My aunt," I said, "has Alzheimer's." The woman nodded in sympathy. Nobody was famous here. Just two women, caring for two other women, as is often the lot of women. "Good luck," she said. "The same to you," I said.

The moon was full and ringed with light and the night was icy. I wrapped my scarf and coat around me and ran down Lexington Avenue toward my apartment.

A free woman—but for how long? Someday I would not be able to walk out of hospitals on my own either. And then, what would become of me?

I didn't want to think about it.

The court was supposed to resume Kitty's case the next day, but another case jammed the calendar. This enabled me to call for Kitty at the hospital and take her home. Plenty of people advised against it, but I found I had to keep my promise—whether Kitty remembered it or not.

It is always easier to place old people in nursing homes from the hospital than from home. So I was burdening myself by keeping this promise, but keeping promises often means burdens. By teatime, I was back in the hospital to liberate Kitty, her paperwork, her prescriptions, her ragtag possessions. I brought her home to her loft in Chelsea with a plump Haitian health-care attendant named Chloe.

The loft was a mess, the kitchen filthy, bare spots on the walls where paintings had once been. The apartment appeared to have been partially ransacked. Odds and ends of my grandparents' furniture—a Stickley bookshelf, my grandfather's paint-spattered easel—stood around the room. Kitty's giant, luminous seascapes, which once had dominated the loft, had been picked over, and many were gone. Kitty noticed none of this. She was genuinely glad to be in a place she still identified as home.

Chloe at once sprawled on the couch and turned on the TV, making it clear that she did not consider anything else her bailiwick. Just for fun, I asked her to get some prescriptions filled for Kitty and to help me clean up the kitchen. She resolutely refused. "We're not supposed to do *that*," she said. She was a babysitter—nothing more—though at rates that would make a babysitter blush. What would a Martian think if she came to earth and saw doddering old white women being "minded" by robust young black women who sat and watched TV—and the clock? What a curious way humans arrange their society! "Blow it all up and start again!" a compassionate goddess might say.

Kitty wandered tentatively about, afraid to take off her coat. I sat her down, made her put on comfortable shoes—Chinese cloth slippers—and drink a cup of tea.

Presently Maxine bustled in with Frank and his lover, Adrian, and two handsome hunks from the Hamptons.

"Hello, darling!" Maxine said to Kitty. "We have a van downstairs. We're just going to take some paintings so we can have a show for you out there." With that, the two Hamptons Hunks began carrying out canvases, portfolios, a life-size lion that had stood in Kitty's loft as long as she had lived there. (Kitty is a Leo, so this roaring lion is her talisman.)

"What are you *doing*?" she asked Maxine. "That's *my* lion."

"No, darling, it's *my* lion," Maxine said. "*I* bought it."

"You did *not*," said Kitty.

"I did too." Suddenly I remembered all the Sturm und Drang of a dozen years ago when Kitty and Maxine "broke up" and Maxine expelled Kitty from the two homes she had helped to build and renovate—one in Chelsea, one in Southampton—buying her this modest loft and pensioning her off.

"Don't take my lion!" Kitty said. "It's all I have."

"I'm only keeping it *safe* for you, darling," Maxine said, as the hunks carried out this last symbol of Kitty's selfhood.

Aghast at the blatantness of it all, I was shocked into silence.

"I know you're her heir, but I wish you'd stop acting like she's already *dead*," I wanted to say. Or, "For God's sake—this can wait, can't it?" And Maxine, who felt my disapproval, picked up a huge book of my grandfather's pen-and-ink drawings and placed it in my trembling hands.

"Take care of it," she said, "keep it safe." The book-bribe was filled with hallucinatory renderings of Papa's Odessa childhood. More memories to people my autobiography. I took it.

And the hunks carried out the lion.

Maxine bustled around, bringing groceries, announcing to Kitty that she couldn't stay because it was her birthday and she was being taken out to dinner.

Frank, Adrian, and I were left looking after Kitty, who now also wanted to be "taken out to dinner."

"I'm buying dinner," I said. "Where do you suggest?"

We agreed on a nearby Chinese restaurant, and Frank and I began dressing Kitty for the outing.

"Your hair's a mess," said Frank. "Let me color it for you tomorrow night, okay?" He lovingly brushed her hair, threaded the golden earrings he had made for her through the holes in her earlobes, helped her do her makeup. Meanwhile, I went through Kitty's clothes, looking for something that wasn't torn or soiled or tattered. I found a passable sweater and skirt, no bras at all, and no panties that weren't soiled. I left her in her comfy Chinese slippers. The first thing that goes is grooming, I thought, then laundry, then life itself. But not soon enough. Life, alas, lingers in the absence of laundry as everything winds back to infancy at the end. We have no markers, no books about these last developmental stages, and no comforting rituals. At the beginning of the journey, a baby has a loving mother thumbing through volumes of Dr. Spock for clues and cues. But in the seventh age of woman, there is no loving mother (long since dead), no designated caretaker, no books. We make this backward journey all alone, in Chinese slippers.

Kitty was dressed. Frank, Adrian, and I put on our coats.

"What about *her* dinner?" Kitty said of Chloe, who still sprawled before the TV.

"Don't worry about me, I ate already," Chloe said, the flickering TV reflected on her shiny round face.

"Aren't you hungry?" Kitty persisted, trying to caretake the caretaker—a trait that runs in my family.

"No, dear," said Chloe. "Go have your dinner."

Kitty's round brown eyes stared.

"But she should eat too," she said. "It's only fair."

"Don't worry, hon," said Frank, "she's eaten."

"Shall we bring you an egg roll?" I asked Chloe, to appease Kitty.

"Okay," said Chloe.

"What did you say?" said Kitty. "I don't need an egg roll. Why does everybody think an egg roll will make a difference?"

We trudged down Twenty-third Street in the cold. Two young men, one with AIDS and one afraid to check the results of his blood tests, and an old woman who kept saying, "It's too cold, it's too cold" and "Where are we going?" and I, in the midst of my fear of fifty.

At the Chinese restaurant, I sat opposite Frank's beloved, who told me the story of his recent life.

"What do you do?" I asked.

"I'm on disability," he said, "for AIDS."

"What did you do *before?*"

"I went to Juilliard and studied the flute, then worked as a musician and supported myself as a personal assistant to Leonard Bernstein—a difficult job," he said.

"When were you diagnosed?" I asked.

"Oh—five years ago."

"Did it change your life?"

Adrian's handsome, square-jawed young face grew pensive.

"I suppose it did," he said. "I started to think about how I really wanted to live. I quit working for Bernstein because it was just too stressful—he was very demanding—and I began to play music for myself and to think and to meditate. It did change my life. I decided love was more important than wild sex. I decided I wanted to really love someone before I died."

"Then what happened?" I asked.

"Then I met Frank," he said, smiling at his beloved.

"Who ordered this for me?" Kitty asked when her food came.

"You did, hon," said Frank.

"I did *not*," said Kitty, her argumentativeness reassuring her of her existence.

"Yes you did, hon," Frank said kindly.

"Well, I suppose I might as well eat it," said Kitty, digging into her fried dumplings.

"You might as well," I said. I was thinking how strange this scene was and how strange all gatherings in life are if you let yourself dwell on them. What a curious Last Supper this was. Two very young men with perhaps not long to live, my aunt with not much to live for, and me in the middle as always, observing and trying to figure out how to make a story of it. Would the story help someone? I hoped so. Even if that someone was only me.

"Who ordered these?" Kitty asked again.

"You did, hon," said Frank.

Later, when Kitty was tucked in bed, and Frank was reading to her, I took a cab uptown, clutching Papa's book of drawings.

"You're late," my daughter said. "Was it horrible?"

"Actually, it was less horrible than staying home and thinking about Kitty and doing nothing. She's still a person. But her memory is threadbare in places, like the knees of your jeans."

"Ugh—depressing," said Molly. "I'm glad I didn't go."

"That's the way you feel at fourteen—but not at fifty," I said.

"You're not fifty," said Molly. "You're thirty-five and holding. Yeah—that's right. I was born when you were twenty-one."

I hug her very tight, hoping she never has to do for me what I am doing for Kitty.

My best friend and I have a plan. We will take handfuls of sleeping pills, then trudge out into the snow near her ranch in Carbondale, Colorado. While the elk and caribou stalk the pure white snow, while Venus rises over Mount Sopris, we'll make snow angels and quietly expire of hypothermia, sparing our children the mess and fuss of caring for us. Planets and stars will twinkle in the crystalline Colorado air as we peacefully and painlessly freeze to death.

But will we *really*? Who knows? By then we may forget how much trouble we are. Memory is the most transient of all possessions. And when it goes, it leaves as few traces as stars that have disappeared.

At midnight, my husband finds me in my study, looking through the book of Papa's drawings.

Here is his mother, my great-grandmother, laid out after her death from typhus. Her bier turns into ripples on the ocean; caught in its waves are the faces of her children, her grandchildren, and her great-grandchildren. The matriarch is going back into the sea—a sort of reverse Venus. Next come a series of India ink sketches of the galloping horses that always obsessed my grandfather's pen. Some are galloping into the sea; some are being attacked by wild dogs; some are spurred on by Cossacks wearing huge fur hats, who brandish thunderous cudgels at wretches cowering beneath the horses' hooves.

This was the rough Russia my grandfather crossed on foot as a boy of fourteen. He walked across Europe when Europe was much larger than it is now. And he braved its harshness to make a soft life for us all in America. His mother had just died of typhus when he set out across Russia and Europe. Unsparing as Goya or Hogarth in his willingness to confront human inhumanity, my grandfather was always sketching his past as he lived his present. That was the legacy he left to me. Just keep sketching. Try not to ask why. There may not be an answer.

"What a wonderful artist he was," Ken says, looking over my shoulder. I feel Papa's presence in the room as I riffle through his sketches. He is also the reason I am taking care of Kitty. He guards my life somehow, so I also guard the lives that mattered most to him.

"Kittinka," he would have said. "Poor Kittinka. Look out for her now that she's too foolish to look out for herself."

"Let's go to bed," I say. And Ken hugs me.

"You had a rough day," he says.

"Watching the lion being carried out was the roughest part somehow. I'd rather not have seen that."

"You'll write about it," he says.

"Does that redeem it? Does it make any difference to the pain?"

"It makes it bearable," he says, "the way Papa's sketches made his life bearable."

I close the book of memory. It comforts me to know it is there to be reopened.

When we wake up the next morning, the city is in the grip of a storm that threatens to make Manhattan an island again. Pelting rain and gale-force winds, flooded subways, and tidal waves in the streets.

Ken and I make our way to court somehow, but we are the only ones who do. Kitty and Frank get soaked and turn back. Maxine begs off. And the other two lawyers arrive so late that there is no time to resume the hearing. Again my testimony has to be postponed. Another date is chosen.

Leaving the courthouse in the furious rain, Ken and I see crowds of huddled people with torn umbrellas waiting at bus stops. The subways are stopped; the city has come to a halt. Offices are closing early. New York has the feel of disaster—as if the ultimate tsunami has arrived and all the soaring skyscrapers are about to be felled by flood.

"A cab!" Ken screams. Is it a mirage or is it really a yellow cab down at the bottom of the courthouse steps? We clatter down the flooded stairs. Just as we reach the cab, another couple attacks the opposite set of doors. Suddenly Ken is fencing with his umbrella, trying to get rid of the interlopers.

"I ain't taking *none* of youse!" the driver shouts, emerging from the cab. He shoves Ken down into the flooded gutter.

"I'm writing down your license number," Ken screams, scrambling up and trying to enter this madman's taxi.

"Are you insane?" I say. "I'd rather walk."

But Ken drags me into the taxi and we ride a block or two, with the driver cursing at us.

"Take us to the police station," Ken shouts.

The driver is swerving all over the streets and cursing like a maniac. At the first red light, I open the door and pull Ken out.

"I don't know what got into me," Ken says.

"The storm—and Kitty."

"How about a noodle shop in Chinatown?" asks Ken, and we set out in search of Hong Fat. The wind howls, the rain pelts down. All nature is out of joint, sympathizing with Kitty.

Stranded in New York for the first weekend in years, we watch the storm reduce Manhattan to a floating spar in an engulfing sea. As the storm grows, Kitty grows worse too.

With the tranquilizers wearing off, she turns bellicose. She throws Chloe out of her loft, rages at Frank when he comes to dye her hair, and refuses to let the nitroglycerin patch on her chest do its work. She keeps forgetting *why* it is there and tearing it off in a fury. "What's this? What's this?" She picks at her chest.

The storm rages and so does our Lear.

My younger sister and I visit by turns. Finally we persuade the agency to send another home-care worker. What on earth can we do while the court case drags on? Kitty is not fit to be home even *with* someone to attend her. We will have to find a nursing home for her and persuade her to enter it. The judge won't be happy, but at least Kitty will be alive.

I didn't need to be told that most nursing homes were bone-chilling. I had seen them. But there was one, friends said, that was exceptional. It was a model facility—clean, beautiful, full of art. But the waiting list was long: to get a place would take forever, I was told. The application process was like trying to get your kid into a fancy private school. Only pull and connections could even get you an application. Pull and connections were what my father-in-law liked best. He was down in Florida, running the Jewish philanthropic underground by phone and fax. He was the head of the Palm Beach Stern Gang.

"Get me the board of directors list, darling," he said. And two days later I was being picked up in a chauffeured car by the white-haired director of the Hebrew Home for the Aged.

"Maestro," I said, when the door to the car opened. For Jacob Reingold, the director, looks like the conductor of a European symphony. A shock of white hair, a weather-beaten mountain climber's face, a warm smile, a conversational style spiced with *mamaloschen*.* We talked about music, art, Europe, Japan, mountains, seas—everything but Kitty. It was a courtship. The object was a bed for Kitty, but I would be the dowry.

The Hebrew Home for the Aged is crammed with modern masterpieces (donated by eager relatives who want to dump their grannies), full of inventions—sinks and tubs that levitate—designed especially for the infirm old. There are beautiful views of the Hudson, hair salons, gyms, art studios. This is the next stop after the spa! Except that here we do not hope that fitness will make for a future of wellness. This is the end of the line. This is the place you come to if you are rich enough or famous enough to merit state-of-the-art senility.

"Get out of here, you big black thing!" screams a woman shuffling along after her walker in the Early Dementia unit. The attendant in question has a faraway look, as if concentrating on lunch, or remembering last night's loving. She has been trained to ignore these ravings.

"She doesn't know where she is," says the maestro. "A lot of them don't."

Only the great and near great are welcome here—or so it seemed to me on that visit. This is a holding camp for all the ex-moguls and ex-movers and ex-shakers whose relatives don't want them.

---

* Yiddish; the mother tongue.

There are the mad uncles of media barons, the sisters of movie stars, the mothers of famous diplomats. Rudolf Bing is in Early Dementia and Nat Holman in Regular—the unit for people whose only disease is old age. Is it better than snow angels in Carbondale? Who knows? By the time you get here, you can't say.

"Promise me you'll shoot me, darling," says the maestro, "before you have to put me here."

And yet the residents seem happy—depending on how you define the word. On the Alzheimer's unit, an old lady with a blue beret, a staring man with a checked shirt and disheveled hair, a sullen old woman with a jutting chin, sit at a table in a room that synthesizes a homey sitcom kitchen. But none of them interact with one another. This is not even parallel playpen play. Blue beret rummages with old clothes. ("You see, they use up their energy that way," says the maestro. "It's therapy.") Checked shirt picks at the food on his tray. Jutting chin mutters—to no one in particular—"I'll see that you get in trouble! I'll call the governor. He knows me! I run a very *major* company! I'm worth millions! I'm no one's fool!"

Sometimes old age strips away the veneer of civility, leaving only the hostile and aggressive residue of human nature; sometimes it leaves the social graces intact until someone gets served food first or takes away your hat. ("That's *my* hat!" says another resident, snatching at the blue beret. "It is *not*!") This reminds me of watching two-year-olds in the sandbox—except that two-year-olds are much cuter. Chubby cheeks and pink fingers go a long way toward softening our view of aggressive behavior. When a face is full of wens and sprouting hairs, even the most enlightened of us find it less than adorable. Snow angels seem a better solution. All these well-heeled ancients are using up resources that could feed and educate whole cities. Is *that* a good decision for the human race? Easy to *ask* such a question but harder to answer it. I only know I am not about to float Kitty out on an ice floe or push her down in the snow. Perhaps this place exists to salve the consciences of rich and powerful relatives, but it nevertheless remains a marvel. The Warhols and Picassos and Ertés are testimonies to our guilt.

And the director is our stand-in, our surrogate.

"You know why I could never have a love affair?" he asks, rhetorically. "I'd be checking into the motel and someone would see me and say, 'Hey, Jake—how's my mom?'"

The youngest of a brood of children, the maestro is a born care-taker, the designated nurturer in his family. Nobody gets a job like this by accident. He is a virtuoso of caretaking, conducting that vast symphony of guilt, denial, and fund-raising that makes a place like this exist.

"Most of them are incontinent," he says, "yet there's no smell of urine. How do we do that? We scrub *all* the time, that's how."

And, indeed, the place smells fresh and clean, the smell of money. Like Daisy Buchanan's voice, the Hebrew Home for the Aged is a testament to all that money can do. Delighted as I am that such a place exists, I am also troubled. Even in doddering old age, there is no equality. Especially not then.

I go home with a letter from the nursing home, promising that Kitty will be admitted.

Mission almost accomplished. But there's still the Chinese judge to convince.

What do I remember about Aunt Kitty before her life came to this peculiar pass?

I was never allowed to see her much because of the mysterious enmity between her and my mother. But still, I remember certain things.

I remember going to her sun-flooded apartment facing West End Avenue and looking through her things: her little armatures for modeling in clay, her African masks and carved amulets, her library of fascinating books.

It was Kitty who introduced me to Colette, giving me *Chéri* and *The Last of Chéri* to read when I was fifteen and much too young to understand the passion of a forty-nine-year-old woman for a beautiful man in his twenties. Like a lot of people who have no biological children, Kitty didn't really understand kids. But that was also freeing. She treated me like an adult—unjudgmentally and without the protective prudishness of a parent. Years later, when I was in my forties and suffering over the love of a very young man, I reread the copy of *Chéri* and *The Last of Chéri* that Kitty had given me. At last, I was grateful for the gift. It had to wait a long time on my shelf for my life to catch up with it, but somehow Kitty must have known that too.

On Fire Island, in East Hampton, in the houses Kitty shared with her friend Maxine, there was always an antic spirit. It wasn't just the nudity or the fact that the two women slept in the same bed. There was plenty of nudity in the home I grew up in too, but what was more liberating in Kitty's house was the omnisexuality all around. Couples came in all flavors. My mother muttered darkly of "bad influences," but I found my first taste of freedom in that house. It was a world not governed by the rules of bourgeois life, a world where men flirted with men and women flirted with women, a world where life was somehow richer and more full of possibility. It was an eccentric summer camp for grown-ups—and it smacked of freedom for me: freedom from convention, freedom from family ties. That antic spirit gave me a part of myself, confirmed me in my anarchism—sexual and otherwise.

I never let myself love Kitty openly, because my mother made it clear that she considered it disloyal. Still, Kitty's way of life was a part of my education. Her way of life told me there were alternate universes, other voices, other rooms.

In some sense, I think my mother hated Kitty for the freedom she permitted herself. My mother too had started out a bohemian, and then was captured by bourgeois life. How much of her old feud with her sister was homophobia? And how much was love gone sour? My mother had adored Kitty once, and her virulent hate was too fierce not to be passion gone awry.

We live in a world divided into "gay" and "straight." We have balkanized our sexual culture. But why? Is it all a question of politics? And doesn't politics conflict with our humanity? Clearly, gay people cannot claim their civil rights unless they organize as groups. Clearly, they need the same rights to inheritance, marriage, health care, and child custody as everyone else. But this division of worlds into "gay" and "straight" goes against what I know of human nature. There may be homosexual loves, but does that mean there are homosexual *people*? Does love necessarily have a gender? The greatest loves change gender. The greatest lovers take turns being male and female. And what do "male" and "female" mean? Aren't they *qualities* rather than people?

Only when I was young and brainwashed and knew myself badly did I imagine the penis was the only instrument of love. The men I have loved best in my life have always had a nurturing quality about them, and the women I have loved best have always been fighters.

In a sane society, women and men would try on genders and loves as simply as they try on clothes. It was Kitty who taught me all this somehow, and my mother's rejection of her taught me about the existence of a puritanism I never wanted to be mine.

Kitty's road was different from my mother's. Yet, in many ways, she was as marked by her sexual choices as my mother was by hers. She may have loved women, but she also loved *like* a woman. She gave up power for the life of the homemaker and artist, and when she was old and sick, no one was there to take care of her. No one but me—imperfect as my care was. I had come halfway along in my life to discover that I could find room for both writing and caretaking.

It's more important to be a human being than to be a writer. Or should I say that writing matters only if it somehow ripens your humanity?

About a month after Kitty is admitted to the Hebrew Home for the Aged, I make a visit to her. The court case is still on hold, thus unresolved. Kitty looks as well as I have seen her in years. Her cheeks are rosy, her hair cut and coiffed.

"This is my best friend, Pearl," she says, "my roommate."

She introduces me to a thin white-haired lady with blue eyes who pushes a walker.

"That's my best friend, Kitty," Pearl says. "I love her."

Kitty and I go to sit down in a lounge overlooking the river. The Hudson sparkles in the winter light.

"I came to visit one day and I liked the food, so I stayed," Kitty says. "But I worry about my apartment."

"Don't worry, Kitty, I'll check on it."

"I have to leave one of these days, but for some reason that makes me upset."

"You look awfully well."

"I'm sleeping well here. And the people are nice. What time is it, honey? I don't want to miss my supper."

I look at my watch. It's almost 4:30. Supper here begins at teatime, as in the nursery.

I walk Kitty to the dining room and sit down with her.

This is the Early Dementia unit, and the residents are at different stages of memorylessness.

We sit down at a table for four with a woman named Blanche who keeps licking her lips, and a woman named Brenda whose chin meets her nose.

"Meet my relative," says Kitty, probably not remembering my name. "Isn't it nice that she came?"

"You're the big-shot here," says Blanche.

"I am *not*," says Kitty.

"Yes, you are," says Blanche.

"There's a cabaret tonight," says Brenda.

"Can you stay for the cabaret?"

"I don't think so," I say.

"That's too bad," says Kitty.

Meals are starting to be served to the residents. I am offered juice, which comes promptly. I look around at the autistic old who seem sunk into themselves. One woman is wearing a huge black hat with an ostrich feather. Another is wandering from table to table staring with great fixity at nothing in particular, inspecting the other residents' meals. Now she staggers over and reaches for my cup of juice.

"What are you doing *that* for?" says Kitty. "Don't take my niece's juice!"

And the woman turns robotically and limps away.

On the wall is a sign with the residents' birthdays that occur in January. Below that is a poster in which WINTER has been spelled out in cotton balls. Below is a cotton ball snowman. This is a kindergarten for the very old. But they seem contented here. And my aunt seems secure and happy. I have never seen her so peaceful, waiting for her tray of food.

"I like the food here," she says. "Do you want some?"

"No, thanks," I say. "I have to go out to dinner."

Am I afraid to eat for fear that, like Persephone in Hades, I will then have to stay?

By 5:30, I am racing out of there, promising, of course, to return soon.

4

HOW I GOT TO BE JEWISH

To be a Jew in the twentieth century
Is to be offered a gift.

—Muriel Rukeyser, "Letter to the Front"

News of America travelled quickly around the European shtetls.
Word was that even if the streets of the "Golden Land" weren't
paved with gold, at least a Jew had a chance.

—Jeff Kisseloff, *You Must Remember This*

The older we get, the more Jewish we become in my family. My mother's father declared himself an atheist in his communist youth, so we never belonged to a synagogue or had bat mitzvahs. But we wind up in Hebrew homes for the aged and in cemeteries with Hebrew letters over the gates. Thus does our heritage claim us—even in America, our promised land. In my family, if you're still protesting that you're Unitarian, you're just not *old* enough. (I refer, of course, to one of my ex-husbands, who, having married a shiksa, worships at the local Unitarian church. That will change, I predict.)

My father, on the other hand, sends money to Israel and carries around a card that supposedly will expedite his admission to Mount Sinai Hospital and, after that, heaven, identifying him as a Big Donor. This is the sort of thing he would have done riffs on in his vaudeville days. Now Molly does those riffs. The young are cruel. They *have* to be to supplant the old. The old are such a burden, so territorial, so inclined to hold on to their money. The young have to be tough to grow up at all.

After all, what does the ritual of circumcision say to a Jewish son? *"Watch out. Next time I'll cut off the whole thing."* So Jewish boys are horny, but also full of fear about whether their cocks will survive their horniness. Alexander Portnoy is the archetypal good Jewish boy. The good Jewish boy and the bad Jewish boy inhabit the same skin— if not the same foreskin. Jewish girls are luckier. Their sexuality is less damaged—whatever those jokes about dropping emery boards may imply. Girls are allowed to be sexual as long as they keep it inside the family. Marriage is sacred as long as you marry an Oedipal stand-in. Jewish adultery is an oxymoron. We read Updike for that. Jewish men who cheat end up like Sol Wachtler or Woody Allen. In big trouble. Even Jewish lesbians are required to have silverware and bone china from Tiffany's. Jewish lesbians are required to fall in love with women who remind them of their mothers. And, in today's feminist times, are doctors or lawyers.

How did I get to be Jewish? I with no religious training? Jews are made by the existence of anti-Semitism—or so said Jean-Paul Sartre, who knew. And despite myths to the contrary, there is *plenty* of anti-Semitism in America (otherwise we'd be saying "Next year in Oyster Bay" or "Grosse Pointe" instead of "Next year in Jerusalem"). But American anti-Semitism takes the clever form of class snobbery. Let me show you what I mean.

We say that America is a classless society, but really it is not. It's just that our class distinctions are so much subtler than those of other countries that sometimes we don't even see them as class distinctions. They are uniquely American class distinctions and they follow us all our lives. We go happily into the Hebrew Home for the Aged, having learned that where aging and death are concerned, only our own kind *want* us. When we're young and cute, we can hang out with goyim— but as the sun goes down, we revert to knishes and *knaydlach*. We do mitzvahs—of the sort that I have done by getting my aunt into the Hebrew Home. We suddenly remember that—like "community service" in high school—we have to rack up 613 mitzvahs to be considered good Jews. At fifty, we take those mitzvahs seriously—unlike community service in high school. How much time, after all, do we have? Not much. Better get busy—women especially. We're not exactly shoo-ins. The Orthodox rabbis still won't let us pray at the Wailing Wall, so why do we assume they'll let us into that obscure heaven of the Jews? If men need 613 mitzvahs, I figure women need 1,839.

When I was growing up in a New York that seemed dominated by Jews whose parents or grandparents had fled from Europe, I never consciously thought about Jewishness. Or about class. And yet invisible barriers ruled my life—barriers that still stand.

Even in childhood I knew that my best friend, Glenda Glascock, who was Episcopalian and went to private school, was considered classier than me. We lived in the same gloomy Gothic apartment house near Central Park West. We both had parents who were artists. But Glenda's name ended with *cock* and mine did not. I knew that names ending in *cock* were intrinsically classier.

What was my name anyway?

My father was born Weisman and became Mann. My mother was called Yehuda by her Russian Jewish parents when she was born in England, but the intransigent Englishman in the registry office had changed it first to Judith and then to Edith ("good English names")—leaving the resultant impression that Jews were not even allowed to keep their own names. The dominant culture around our (mental) ghetto required names that did not *sound* Jewish or foreign. That left a strong impression too.

There were categories of Americans in our supposedly egalitarian country, and I did not belong to the better (as in "better dresses") category. Glenda did. Her last name bespoke this. Even her nickname—Jewish girls did not have nicknames like Glenni then—bespoke this. And yet we were close as twins, best buddies, in and out of each other's apartments—until we took a bath together one day and she accused me of making peepee in the bathwater because that was "what Jews did." I was outraged, having done no such thing. (Unless my memory censors.)

"Who says they do that?"

"My mother," said Glenni confidently.

So I reported this conversation to my parents and grandparents, and mysteriously my friendship with Glenni cooled.

She went off to private school. I did not. I was in some "Intellectually Gifted Program" at P.S. 87, at Seventy-seventh Street and Amsterdam Avenue—a great Victorian pile in those days, with girls' and boys' entrances. There I discovered other class stratifications. The closer you lived to Central Park West and the "better" your building, the more classy you were. Now I had status. Below me were poorer Jewish kids whose parents had fled the Holocaust and who lived in lesser buildings further west, Irish kids who lived in tenements on side streets, and the first sprinkling of Puerto Rican kids to arrive in New York. They lived in other tenements, on West Side Storyish side streets. In the forties, New York was far from being racially integrated. I did not meet black kids from Harlem until I went to the High School of Music and Art, where talent, not neighborhood, was the qualification. The only African-Americans we met—called Negroes then—were servants. In childhood, my world was Jewish, Irish, Hispanic—with Jews lording it over everyone else.

The WASP kids were, by this time, off in private school, meeting their own kind so they could go to Yale, run the CIA, and rule the world (like George and Barbara Bush). Jewish kids did not go to private school in *that* New York—unless they were superrich, had disciplinary problems, or were Orthodox.

I figured out pretty soon that in my school I was high class, but that in the world I was not. The kids on television shows and in reading primers did not have names like Weisman, Rabinowitz, Plotkin, Ratner, or Kisselgoff. Certainly not Gonzales or O'Shea. There was another America out there in televisionland and we were not part of it. In that other America, girls were named things like Gidget and boys were named things like Beaver Cleaver. Our world was not represented—except when the credits rolled by.

Kept out of this *proper* America, we learned to control it by reinventing it (or representing it—as in agent). Some of our parents already did this as actors, producers, or writers, so we knew this was a possible path for us. Others were businessmen, or artists turned businessmen—like my father. The point was we were outsiders longing to be insiders. In those days, we knew that Princeton and Yale might not want us—unless we were rich enough to buy the school. We knew our initials were MCA, not CIA. We knew we were not born into the ruling class, so we invented our own ruling class. Mike Ovitz, not George Bush. Swifty Lazar, not Bill Clinton. Mort Janklow, not Al Gore.

How much the world has changed since the forties! And how *little*! Except for Henry Kissinger, who has changed these laws of class and caste? Not even Mike Ovitz. What you see your parents do is what you think *you* can do. So are we defined, designed. Since my father was a songwriter-musician turned importer, my grandfather a portrait painter, my mother a housewife and portrait painter, I just *assumed* that I would do something creative. I also just *assumed* that I would graduate from college, and live in a "good building" forever. I also assumed that I would never turn out to be anything like those American families I saw on TV.

My family was fiercely proud to be Jewish, but not religious— unless our religion was buying new English Mary Janes at Saks and English leather leggings and velvet-collared chesterfield coats at De Pinna. We were dressed like little English princesses, and I understood that this was the class to which we aspired.

Dress tells you everything about aspiration. I hated the damned leather leggings but had to wear them because Princesses Elizabeth and Margaret did. How did *they* get to be princesses of the Jews? Better not ask. It was tacitly understood, just as it was understood that Glascock was a better name than Weisman (or even Mann).

I smile writing all this. I am trying (clumsily, I fear) to reenter that world of 1940s New York with its "air-cooled" movie palaces (complete with towering matrons and wrapper-strewn children's sections), its striped awnings on apartment buildings in summer, its dime bus fares, its telephone exchanges (I was ENdicott 2), its candy stores and soda fountains, its marble lunch counters that sold the most delicious bacon, lettuce, and tomato sandwiches and fresh-dipped ice cream cones.

Gone, gone forever. But just as sunlight on a series of paving stones or the taste of tea-soaked cake returned Proust* to his halcyon childhood, I sometimes stop on a street corner in New York and am taken back to the forties. The smells do it. The mouths of the subway stations still, on occasion, blow a blast of cotton candy–bubble gum breath, mixed with sweat and popcorn, with piss and (its precursor) beer, and, inhaling deeply, I am taken back to being six years old, standing in the subway, staring at a forest of knees. In childhood, you feel you'll never grow up. And the world will always be incomprehensible. First you are all mouth, then you have a name, then you are a member of a family, then you begin to ask the hard questions about better/worse that are the beginning of class consciousness. Human beings are naturally hierarchical beasts. Democracy is not their native religion.

---

* Note to reviewer: I'm not comparing myself to Proust, but am I allowed to have read him?

It was in junior high that my world opened up beyond Seventy-seventh Street and the West Side. Because my parents and I were both terrified of the violence of the local junior high, I went to private school—a deliciously comic place where the paying students were mostly Park Avenue Jews and the scholarship students mostly WASPs from Washington Heights whose parents were professors, clergy, missionaries.

The teachers were genteel and WASPy, like the scholarship students, and they had proper American-sounding names like the TV people. The school had been started by two redoubtable New England ladies named Miss Birch and Miss Wathen, who were probably lovers—but in those days we called them spinsters. One of them looked like Gertrude Stein, the other like Alice B. Toklas. They pronounced "shirt" as if it had three *i*'s in the middle, and they pronounced "poetry" as if it were poy-et-try (*poy* rhyming with *goy*). I knew this was classy. I knew this was WASP.

At Birch-Wathen, most of the Jewish kids were wealthier than I. They lived on the East Side in apartments hung with expensive art and some of them had German names. They went to Temple Emanu-El—my nephews now call it Temple Episco-Pal—and took dancing and deportment (what an old-fashioned word!) at Viola Wolf's. Again my sense of class was up for grabs. With my Russian grandparents and my West Side bohemian home, I didn't fit in with these kids either. And the scholarship kids all stuck together. I thought them snotty—though now I realize they must have been scared to death. The paying students got bigger allowances—and some of them came to school in chauffeured Cadillacs, Lincolns, or Rollses. That must have seemed daunting to kids who rode the subway. It seemed daunting to me.

Cliques splintered us. The Park Avenue kids stuck with their own kind. The scholarship kids did the same.

I floated between the two groups, never knowing where I belonged, now shoplifting at Saks with the rich kids (the richer the kids, I learned, the more they shoplifted), now wandering up to Columbia with the scholarship kids (whose parents were professors). I felt I belonged nowhere. Ashamed that my father was a businessman, I used to wish he were a professor. If you couldn't have a name that ended with *cock,* or an apartment on Fifth or Park, you ought to have a Ph.D. at least.

When high school began, I joined still another new world—a world that was racially mixed and full of kids from the ghetto. (We called it Harlem then.) Chosen for their talent to draw or sing or play an instrument, these kids were the most diverse group I'd ever met. Their class was talent. And like all insecure people, they shoved it in your face.

It was in high school that I began to find my true class. Here the competition was not about money or color or neighborhood but about how well you drew or played. At Music and Art, new hierarchies were created, hierarchies of virtuosity. Was your painting in the semiannual exhibition? Were you tapped to perform in the orchestra or on WQXR? By now, we all knew we did not belong in television-land America—and we were *proud* of it. Being outsiders was a badge of merit. We had no teams, no cheerleaders, and the cool class uniform was early beatnik: black stockings, handmade sandals, and black lipstick for the girls; black turtlenecks, black jeans, black leather jackets for the boys. Stringy hair was requisite for both sexes. We experimented with dope. We cruised the Village hoping to be mistaken for hipsters. We carried books by Kafka, Genet, Sartre, Allen Ginsberg. We stared existentially into our cappuccino at Rienzi's or the Peacock. We wanted to seduce black jazz musicians, but were afraid to. We had found our class at last.

Many of us rose to the top of it. I count among my high school classmates pop singers, television producers, directors, actors, painters, novelists. Many are household names. A few earn tens of millions of dollars a year. Most of us went to college—but it was not finally a B.A. or a Ph.D. that defined our status. It was whether or not we stayed hot, were racing up the charts with a bullet, were going into syndication, on the bestseller list, into twenty-five foreign languages. Even the professors envied *this* status: Money and name recognition level all classes in America. Hence the obsession with celebrity. Even in Europe you can pass into the "best" circles, though the rules of class are quite different there.

Having done my time with the Eurotrash set, I'm always amazed at how an aristocratic name still covers a multitude of sins in Europe. In England, in Germany, a lord or ladyship, a *Graf* or *Gräfin*, a *von* or *zu*, still carries weight. Italians are more cynical about titles. The classiest friends I have in Italy may be *contesse, marchesi,* or *principi,* but they're too cool to advertise it. They'd rather be famous for a hit record, or a big book. But go to the chic watering spots—St. Moritz, for example—and membership in the best clubs still goes by family, not by individual achievement. Walk into the Corviglia Club and say you're Ice-T or Madonna. Honey—you won't get in, while any old Niarchos or von Ribbentrop will.

Many of my European friends still inhabit a world where a name and old money can become a positive *bar* to achievement. There is so much *more* to do than merely work. If you have to be in Florence in June, in Paris in July, in Tuscany in August, in Venice in September, in Sologne in October, in New York in November, in St. Bart's in December and January, in St. Moritz in February, in New York in March, in Greece in April, in Prague in May—how on earth can you take (let alone hold) a job? And the fittings. And the balls. And the spas. And the dryings out! As a husband of Barbara Hutton's once asked: "When would I have *time* to work?" True class means never even having to *talk* about it. (Work, I mean.)

Americans are intrinsically unclassy—so the Jews *almost* fit in. All we talk about is our work. All we want to do is make our first names so recognized we don't even *need* a last (Ms. Ciccione is the ultimate American here). We believe in change as fervently as Europeans believe in the status quo. We believe that money will buy us into heaven (with heaven defined as toned muscles, no flab at the chin, interest on interest, and a name that cows maître d's). Once that's accomplished, we can start to save the world: plow some money into AIDS research, the rain forest, political candidates. Maybe we can even run for office ourselves! (Witness Mr. Perot.) In a society where pop name recognition means everything, celebrities are more equal than everyone else. But celebrity status is hell to keep in shape (just like an aging body). It needs a host of trainers, PR experts, publishers, media consultants. Plus you have to keep turning out new product—and possibly even new scandal. (Witness Woody Allen.) Maybe the reason celebrities marry so often is simply to keep their names in the news. And maybe—whether they intend it or not—they create scandal to hype their movies. (Again, witness Woody Allen, né Allen Konigsberg.)

Ah—we are back to the question of Jews and names. Can we keep our names? As long as we keep them *hot*. Otherwise, we also have to change them. We may have, as political theorist Benjamin Barber says, "an aristocracy of everyone," but not everyone can be hot at once.

Thus, the drive for class becomes as relentless and chronic in America as the diet. No matter how hot you are, you're always in danger of growing cold.

It's a lot like mortality, isn't it? No wonder Carpe Diem is our motto. This is what makes America such a restless country and its top-class celebrities so insecure.

Ah, friends, I long to be born into a membership in the Corviglia Club. But I suspect I never would have written any books.

Did you ever wonder why Jews are such relentless scribes? You may have thought it was because we are people of the book. You may have thought it was because we come from homes where reading is stressed. You may have thought it was repressed sexuality. All that is true. But I submit the *real* reason is our need constantly to define our class. By writing, we reinvent ourselves. By writing, we create pedigrees. Some of my fictional heroines are West Side New York Jewish girls like me. But the heroines I love the best—Fanny in *Fanny Hackabout-Jones,* and Jessica in *Serenissima*—are to the manor born, good little equestriennes, and you can bet they have high cheekbones.

Fanny grew up at Lymeworth, Lord Bellars's country seat. Jessica grew up on the Upper East Side of Manhattan, in the Golden Rectangle. Her pedigree was very gin and country club. Why does a West Side kid like me invent such heroines? Am I trying to escape from my *schmearer-klezmer** class? Interestingly enough, my heroines always escape too. Fanny runs away from her aristocratic upbringing, becomes a highwaywoman, a whore in a brothel, and a pirate queen. Jessica leaves the Upper East Side for Hollywood! And both of them come to regret it, and find their final happinesses back in their own backyards.

The heroines who are *apparently* more like me—Isadora Wing and Leila Sand—change their status, or else establish it, through creative work. I guess my writing tells me something that I didn't even consciously know about myself: I write to give myself a class, to invent my name, and then to leave myself a country seat.

I suspect the process is not so different with other writers—however uninvolved with class their books may seem. Saul Bellow's heroes start out as drifters and end up professors. But his very best picaresque hero, Henderson the Rain King, is a WASP to the manor born who

_____
* Artist-musician, but with a spin.

goes to Africa and embraces his multiculturalism, thereby finding his true identity. Philip Roth's heroes are equally concerned with both questions of class and questions of Jewishness. Though they themselves are almost always Jewish, they aspire to fuck their way into WASPdom—a familiar gambit for American Jewish (male) creators. We could call it the Annie Hall syndrome. Surely Woody Allen defined it forever when his autobiographical hero, sitting at Annie Hall's family's midwestern dinner table, amid the WASPs, suddenly sprouts *payess** and a big black hat.

The archetypical Jewish-American fear! If we eat *trayfe,*† we may suddenly grow *payess*! Perhaps the reason Jews in America have adopted Thanksgiving as their own special holiday is that we hope that by claiming the Pilgrims as our fathers, we will fool the rest of America too!

My former father-in-law Howard Fast is a perfect example here. His books about the American Revolution—*April Morning, Citizen Tom Paine,* and *The Hessian*—testify to his nostalgia for the Mayflower Society or the men's auxiliary of the Colonial Dames of America. He has written of ancient Rome (*Spartacus*) and gold rush San Francisco (*The Immigrants*), but it is the founding of America that calls to him again and again. In his heart, Howard Fast yearns for the pedigree of Gore Vidal.

A Jew may wander from Egypt to Germany to America to Israel, picking up different languages and hair and eye color, but nevertheless remains a Jew. And what is a Jew? A Jew is a person who is safe *nowhere* (i.e., always in danger of growing *payess* at inopportune times). A Jew is a person who can convert to Christianity from now to Doomsday, and still be killed by Hitler if his or her mother was Jewish. This explains why Jews are likely to be obsessed with matters of identity. Our survival depends upon it.

Americans, too, are obsessed with defining identity. In a melting pot culture, where aristocratic titles are considered laughable (witness Count Dracula, or Count Chocula, as kids are introduced to him—a breakfast cereal), we must constantly test the limits of identity. Andy Warhol's remark that in the future everyone will be famous for fifteen minutes delineates the quintessential American dilemma. We can

---

* Side curls worn by Orthodox Jews.

† Forbidden (i.e., unkosher) foods.

become famous, but perhaps not *stay* famous. And once having known that fame, how will we live out the rest of our lives? More to the point, how will we ever get into the Hebrew Home for the Aged?

Many American lives seem doomed by Warhol's definition. Remember George Bush struggling to stay president against the historical tide? Or Stephen King aspiring to top all three bestseller lists at once? Or Bill Clinton wiring the White House to become its own media network? Americans can never rest. They can never join the Corviglia Club and amuse themselves skiing down into the picture-book village. The grace of their skiing is *never* in itself enough. They must always climb back on the chairlift and do it again, do it again, do it again.

I see that the Corviglia Club has become my symbol of aristocratic *sprezzatura*—a lovely Italian word that means the art of making the difficult look easy. Perhaps I select that image because it evokes a world of blessed people who do not have to *do* anything but only have to *be*. I long for such status as only an American Jew can. How nice to have an entrée into the world that cannot ever be revoked. How nice to be *born* into an identity.

My yearning is real even though I know dozens of people born into such identities who use them as excuses to become drug addicts and drifters. I know it is not easy to be noble and rich. Yet, like F. Scott Fitzgerald's characters, something in me insists that the very rich "are different from you and me." Fitzgerald tested that hypothesis in *Gatsby*, showing the carelessness of the very rich to life, limb, and love. And yet the longing *remains* in American writers. Perhaps that's why this rather slight, beautifully written novel has become a classic. It embodies the American dream of identity and class.

The jumped-up bootlegger, Jay Gatz, dreams of a world where he wouldn't have to *work* to be Gatsby. And that is still the primal American dream. Even lotteries play to it, promising houses and yachts. Rootless by definition, we dream of roots.

American novelists are usually good examples of this. The first thing they do after a bestseller is buy a house and land. Alex Haley bought a farm in the South. Gore Vidal settled in a villa in Ravello fit for an Italian aristocrat. Arthur Miller bought a Connecticut farm for a Connecticut Yankee. So did Philip Roth.

I'm no different. After *Fear of Flying*, I bought a house in New

England. Believing that when writers died and went to heaven, heaven was Connecticut, I bought a piece of that literary state. To a writer, used to making up the world with ink and a blank piece of paper, roots and gentrification are the same thing. And you get them both with *words*. Rootless people often gravitate to those fields of endeavor where class has to be repeatedly self-created. Perhaps that's also why creativity flowers during periods of great social turmoil and often among former underclasses. Perhaps that's what draws Jews to the word and the image. If you think of the vitality of Jewish-American writing in the fifties and sixties, the vitality of women's writing in the seventies and eighties and nineties, the vitality of African-American writing in the seventies, eighties, and nineties, you see that there is a clear connection between change of status and productivity. As a group becomes restless and angry, it produces writers.

I may dream of what I would have done with my life if I had been born on a plantation with plenty of coupons to clip, but probably my literary ambitions would never have blossomed. Perhaps I would have written inscrutable poetry, readable only by advanced graduate students. But most likely the anxiety and aggression needed to finish a whole book would have been denied me. For writing is not just a question of talent with words, but one of drive and ambition, of restlessness and rage. Writing is hard. The applause never comes at the end of the paragraph. The rotten tomatoes often come at publication time. And, given the hours put in, the money isn't all that good. Counting taxation and time spent, most writers make less than dental hygienists.

But we don't do it for the money. We do it to give ourselves a class.

When I finished college at Barnard, I went on to graduate school, simply because I couldn't think of what *else* to do. I knew I wanted to be a writer, but I wasn't yet sure I had the *sitzfleish* to sit down and write a whole book. While I waited to mature a little, I studied English literature. Somehow I knew it would come in handy.

But the period I studied—the rollicking eighteenth century engraved by Hogarth—was the one that saw the birth of America, of women's rights, and of the novel. The novel started as a low-class form, supposedly fit only to be read by serving maids, and it is the only literary form where women distinguished themselves so early and with such excellence that even the rampant misogyny of literary history cannot erase them. Ever wonder about women and the novel? Women, like any underclass, depend for their survival on self-definition. The novel permitted this—and pages could still be hidden under the embroidery hoop.

From the writer's mind to the reader's there was only the intervention of printing presses. You could stay at home, yet send your book abroad to London—the perfect situation for women.

In a world where women are still the second sex, many still dream of becoming writers so they can work at home, make their own hours, nurse the baby. Writing still seems to fit into the interstices of a woman's life. Through the medium of words, we have hopes of changing our class. Perhaps the pen will not always be equated with the penis. In a world of computers, our swift fingers may yet win us the world. One of these days we'll have class. And so we write as feverishly as only the dispossessed can. We write to come into our own, to build our houses and plant our gardens, to give ourselves names and histories, inventing ourselves as we go along.

5

HOW I GOT TO BE THE SECOND SEX

We had a vague impression that authoresses are liable to be looked on with prejudice.

—Charlotte Brontë, excerpt from a diary

But how impossible it must have been for them not to budge either to the right or to the left. What genius, what integrity it must have required in face of all that criticism, in the midst of that purely patriarchal society, to hold fast to the thing as they saw it without shrinking. Only Jane Austen did it and Emily Brontë. It is another feather, perhaps the finest in their caps. They wrote as women write, not as men write.

—Virginia Woolf, *A Room of One's Own*

What makes it possible for women to achieve in a world where we are still the second sex? Tillie Olsen, that epic poet of female silences, says that we are fortunate to be born into families with no sons. But my sisters claim they never felt even the ambivalent freedom to achieve that I felt. And my mother, also a second sister, was clearly more conflicted than I.

What made the difference in my life? Surely that is one of the reasons I am writing this book. I mean to understand the things that propelled me and the things that held me back. What made my life different from my mother's? And what made it the same?

I don't remember a time when I didn't assume I would *do* something with my life. *What* it would be I did not know. Writing, painting, medicine, all captured my imagination for a time. I assumed that there would be leisure, there would be money enough, there would be a place for me in the world, and I used to make Nobel Prize acceptance speeches before the mirror at the age of eight or nine. What the prize was *for* I did not know—or care. The main thing was: I *assumed* I was a winner. I had survived a whole nursery of shitting babies! Such grandiosity is probably the prelude to achievement, and as long as girls are routinely discouraged from being grandiose, they will have trouble achieving. Nobody ever discouraged me at home—even though the models for women I saw were not as free as those of men (i.e., my mother with her folding easel). I somehow always knew that other women would hate and envy me for that freedom.

"Everyone thinks you're so sweet because you're *blonde*," my sister Nana used to say. "But I know what a bitch you are."

In the fifties, the dichotomy between blonde and brunette was a yawning chasm. It was Debbie Reynolds versus Elizabeth Taylor. And the dark sultry siren was doomed everlastingly to be the bad girl. The blonde was presumed good as gold. I did not know then that the opposition between dark- and light-haired sisters had a hoary literary history. But how these ancient categories stuck! My older sister hated me both for being blonde and for being confident. Boy-girl disguised as Debbie Reynolds, feeling no limitations because both my father and my mother were inside me, loving me, I burst into the world and was amazed to discover that girls were less equal out there.

That recognition dawned in adolescence. I still remember the time a prep school boy asked me if I planned to be a secretary and I replied, "A secretary! I'm going to be a doctor *and* a famous writer— like Chekhov!" I showed *him* (whose name I do not even remember) by never even learning to *type*! To this day I make my books by hand like needlepoint or embroidery. Oh, I have half a dozen computers, but have never learned to use any of them. They become obsolete waiting for me to learn. I fiddle for a while with that alternate universe and then return to my pen—phallic symbol that it is. I have no apologies to make for penis envy. What ambitious woman *wouldn't* have penis envy in a world where that unreliable scepter confers authority?

Sometimes I wonder why it took me so long to realize that I was supposed to be the second sex? What insulated me when my sisters were not similarly insulated? I always felt like the designated heir. But heir to what? Heir to my father's show business ambitions and my mother's art? Heir to my grandfather's easel and my mother's fierce feminism? "*Do as I say, not as I did,*" she somehow communicated. And "*I got gypped, but you can have it all.*"

I actually remember her saying: "If you have fame, you'll have your pick of beautiful men."

"I *never* said that," my mother protests.

But she did.

Or else I heard it. (I was not to learn the complications of that imperative until much later.)

No sons.* A family with no sons. In a family of daughters, one daughter may become the son. Is that the devil's bargain we make? I only know that somehow I became the weary carrier of most of the parental and grandparental ambitions. And what a heavy load it was. Somehow I had to be at once an artist, a vaudevillian, and an earner of big money. I wanted to be that oxymoron: a bestselling poet. I wanted to be a millionaire artist. My ambitions were so impossible that I felt like a failure no matter what I achieved. I still do.

But where did I pick up the message that I was the second sex? In school. We learn at home and we learn at school. And of the two forms of learning, perhaps school is the most damaging. We look to school for the world's authority. We look to school to tell us whether what we learned at home was right or wrong. And school too often reinforces the worst prejudices of our culture: a tendency to mindlessly rank us as if intelligence were quantifiable, a tendency to stereotype the sexes, to see male and female as separate opposed beings instead of qualities we all possess, a tendency to teach us by rote and exclusion instead of by freedom and expansion.

When I was in high school, I already called myself a feminist, and I carried a copy of *The Second Sex* as proof. I don't remember whether I read it. I didn't need to. I knew that women had to eat a lot of shit. I knew that boys were arrogant and that women learned to appease them to survive. I didn't question there was a problem. I only questioned how to *solve* it.

Although I read and wrote all the time, and reading and writing were the things I liked to do best, I told most people I was going to be

---

* "Woe to the father whose children are girls," says the Talmud. I bless my father for having had the courage to flout this.

a doctor. It was not just that I was drawn to healing—still am—but that I was looking for a profession where women were not trod upon. From my adolescent vantage point, medicine seemed to be it.

This is not a chapter about whether or not women are equal in medicine. This is a chapter about learning to be unequal, and most of that learning takes place in adolescence.

The boys snap the back of your bra. You live in terror of your Kotex bleeding through. Your body suddenly becomes an encumbrance, a source of ridicule. It's not just the unwieldiness of all bodies, but the particular vulnerability of a female body, which can bleed so unexpectedly and which marks you inevitably as a potential victim.

Of course it doesn't help that women are still raped everywhere, that one in three women is injured by the man she lives with and calls husband or lover. Even if the world were safe, adolescence would mean vulnerability for girls. Suddenly you become a sexual prey and suddenly you know it. Suddenly the long, sunny afternoons of reading Nancy Drew mysteries on the beach are over. You enter a new world—a world of menace.

When I started at Music and Art, my family lived at Eighty-first Street and Central Park West. Every morning at eight, I had to go down into the roaring subway and travel to 135th Street and Convent Avenue. The train was mostly deserted—all the traffic went the other way. Often I would see exhibitionists in the subway—old men with open flies and exposed cocks fondling themselves and whispering to me to come, come, come. Sometimes I looked. Sometimes I was afraid to look. Sometimes I bolted down to the next car, my heart thudding in my chest.

"Oh, exhibitionists never *do* anything. They're afraid of their own shadows," my mother used to tell me. This was about as comforting as being told that when we die we go back into the earth and become tomatoes. Even for a kid from a pretty sheltered childhood, it was terrifying. Nobody molested me at home, but by the time I was thirteen, nobody could *protect* me. Maleness was out there—an anarchic, unchecked force. Women didn't expose themselves in subways. I learned that women were trustworthy and men were not.

Now, when I send my daughter to school in a New York grown twenty times as violent as when I was a kid, I send her on a private bus. If somebody raped her, I would kill him and expect to be acquitted. Though she's five foot seven and towers over me, she's a vulnerable little girl at heart. I still tuck her in bed with a teddy bear. I send her off to school with trepidation. "You are surrounded by a shield of white light," I say, as I once said, "Goddess Bless and Goddess Keep" over her crib. I turn to witchcraft and the mother goddess at moments like these because I want to summon the primal forces of the universe. I need Kali and Isis, Inanna and Mary, to shield my daughter.

A society that can't protect its young women is a doomed society. Male aggression has existed throughout history, but always it has been channeled, ritualized into jousts and quests, contained. Not now. Why do we care so little for our daughters?

My mother's response to the exhibitionists was a collaborationist's response—however much she may have believed it herself. The male world teaches women what to believe about men. And about women. It teaches them valuelessness. It teaches them secondary status. It pooh-poohs the danger of rape.

In the fifties and sixties, when I was in high school and college, we hadn't publicly named the problem yet. Feminism was quiescent. The problem, as Betty Friedan said, had no name. The feminism of Virginia Woolf's day, of Emma Goldman's day, of Mary Wollstonecraft's day, of Aphra Behn's day, had been buried. In a patriarchal culture, feminism keeps getting buried. It always has to be rediscovered as if for the first time.

Even at Barnard, a women's college, founded by feminists and steeped in the tradition of female excellence, we did not study women poets and novelists. The atmosphere was full of encouragement for young women, but we felt we had been born, like Venus, from the foam. There were no role models. (How could we know our role models had been deliberately erased?) George Sand and Colette were out of print. Women poets were not taught. The poets I had discovered on my own in my high school days, Edna St. Vincent Millay and Dorothy Parker, were looked down upon. We studied to become surrogate men. We studied the penis-power poets—Eliot, Pound, Yeats—and tried to write like them. And did. Our professors doted on us, of course, and our brains were nimble, but the context in which we grew was blindly sexist. How can we even assess the stunting effect this may have had on our imaginations? We had to liberate ourselves even to *begin*.

But the sexism was not overt. Only in my senior year, when I went to my interview for a Woodrow Wilson Fellowship, would I be asked (I swear it), "Why does a pretty girl like you want to be in a dusty library?" With something of a shock, I realized that the whole world was not a women's college. The shock became more intense at Columbia Graduate School, where I encountered the chilling maleness of sexist academe. Like my mother's Russian grandfather, Lionel Trilling— then playing God at Columbia—did not pay attention to *girls*. Look to the right of you, look to the left of you, one of you will not get tenure: the one without a cock.

I wish I could say it has all changed in thirty years. But the number of women with tenure is still pathetically low. The reason can only be discrimination: We are better at reading and writing at age ten, but starting at adolescence thousands of obstacles are put in our path. Our lives become (as Germaine Greer called it in her book about women painters) *The Obstacle Race*.

From the vantage point of age fifty, the discriminatory cycle is utterly clear. That's the difference between a woman of fifty and one of twenty. At twenty we think we can beat the system. At fifty we know we have reasons for despair. We become, as Gloria Steinem says, more radical with age.

Suddenly we realize how, all our lives, we have been trained to appease and flatter men, *not* to confront them. At an Authors Guild meeting, at a party, at a business meeting, I smile and flirt and flatter and make nice. Perhaps I want to tell the truth to the men around me—but I *know* they can't take it. My very presence already offends some of them. The sexuality of my writing, my inability to grovel, my determination to confront—at least *here*—these things *automatically* offend. They go against the grain. There's only one man I tell the whole truth to—the one I live with—and even there I sometimes hedge and waffle, probably more than I know.

The truth is I *don't* blame individual men for this system. They carry it on mostly unknowingly. And women carry it on unknowingly too. But more and more I wonder how it can ever be changed. I look around and see two armed camps: the women who believe men and sex are the collective enemy, and the women who don't want to challenge the existence of sexism, who are happy to collaborate—as long as they get their little crumbs of power. And then there are all the men who benefit by being the first sex and don't even know it. They feel vulnerable and lost too. They wonder why women are so tough on them—so they go out and fuck a woman half their age.

I believe the world is full of men who are truly as perplexed and hurt by women's anger as women are perplexed by sexism, who only want to be loved and nurtured, who cannot understand why these simple desires have suddenly become so hard to fulfill. How can we blame the men we live with for a world they didn't make? We can't, yet sometimes, with the best will in the world, we do. The problem of sexism is so intractable that we are frustrated. We are sick of talking about the problem, of writing about the problem, of polluting relationships with the problem. We want it solved.

The problem of sexism is great for *all* women, but for Jewish women it is perhaps even greater because of the hidden bigotry of that pervasive anti-Semitism that masquerades as class snobbery. Sexism is practiced perhaps most fiercely by Jewish intellectual men who chronically suffer from the Annie Hall syndrome. And, curiously, the literary discrimination against Jewish women has gotten worse, not better, in the last few decades. At the beginning of the century and all through the thirties, the Jewish woman was associated with radicalism, reform, intellect, idealism. Emma Goldman, the radical author; Emma Lazarus, the poet; Annie Nathan Meyer, one of the founders of Barnard College; Rose Schneiderman, the union organizer (who popularized the phrase "we want bread and roses too" and was one of the founders of the International Ladies Garment Workers Union), were far more typical of the image of the Jewish woman than Mrs. Portnoy or Marjorie Morningstar. The more assimilated Jews became in the United States, the worse the Jewish male writer treated his mother (in print, at least). To Henry Roth in *Call It Sleep* (1934), she was a heroine of survival and female strength. To Philip Roth in *Portnoy's Complaint* (1969), she was a castrating harpy with witchy powers.

With the films of Woody Allen, the status of the Jewish woman deteriorated still further. In fact Jewish male creators prove the theory that members of a minority group tend to act out their aggression against each other rather than against their oppressors. They hate Jewish women as they hate themselves. More, in fact. They project all their self-loathing onto Jewish women. The trouble is: We remind them of their strong mothers. And they would rather have the Monkey, or Diane Keaton, or Mia Farrow, or Soon-Yi, than *any-*

one resembling mother. Our strength is too close, too threatening, too reminiscent of that primal minicastration when the Jewish mother stood passively by while the Jewish men cut off that teenie weenie piece of that teenie weenie cock of that teenie weenie future cocksman.

That, of course, is what these Jewish men will never forgive us for. We get blamed for the bris. On our heads are the sins of the fathers. So if we dare the presumption of the pen, they retaliate by cutting it off in our hands—phallic symbol that it is.

Thus, the Jewish woman writer is twice marginalized, twice discriminated against. She is discriminated against both as a woman and as a Jew. She is discriminated against by Gentiles—who see her as loud, overweight, demanding—and by Jews—who see her as the ferocious sacrificing incarnation of the mother goddess. She is discriminated against first as a woman, then as an aging woman, then as an aging *Jewish* woman. Marginalization is, of course, painful, but in certain ways it is a blessing too.

Members of the club are often afraid to write honestly about themselves. They have too much to lose. We aging Jewish women writers, on the other hand, have nothing to lose. We are already at the bottom of the barrel. Thought suitable only for fund-raising and social-climbing, we are already relegated to caretaking elderly relatives, nursing our men through midlife crises, and schlepping our teenagers to college interviews. There's no place to go but up. We have no status. We're not even a trendy minority to fulfill a quota. For some odd reason, Jews in America are no longer even considered victims of discrimination. So my generation of Jewish women has had the dubious distinction of being discriminated against by Jewish men (professors, employers, lovers) when we were young, only to be discriminated against in midlife for being "white." The mind not only boggles—it does the hora.

When my last book was published, some middle-aged reviewer called me a middle-aged writer. She stopped short of calling me "a middle-aged Jewish woman writer" though she was one herself. I thought a lot about the use of the epithet "middle-aged" and why it bothered me so. After all, this was a publishing season filled with books about the hipness of midlife—I wondered what was presumed to be wrong with being "middle-aged"? For my generation of women writers, "middle-aged" ought to be a term of honor.

Who, after all, were our role models? Sylvia Plath, Anne Sexton, Virginia Woolf—all of whom killed themselves before or during middle age. Who were our literary heroines? Charlotte Brontë, who died in pregnancy; Mary Wollstonecraft, who died in childbirth; Simone de Beauvoir and Emily Dickinson, who forswore children. Only George Sand and Colette among them had both love and art. And only Colette wrote about growing old with love. But she was *French*. French women are allowed to get older. They are even allowed to have young lovers. And write about them. (Though even Colette was kept out of the Académie Française.)

But most of our literary mentors never got to be middle-aged. We ought to be proud, not ashamed, to have made it. Yet the sexist stereotyping is so deep that a middle-aged woman reviewer calls another woman "middle-aged" and expects to have cast a blow for— what? Feminism? No—collaboration. For the woman reviewer knows she is there on sufferance. And to keep her own job, she is *expected* to trash other women—particularly famous uppity other women. Thus the culture makes capos of us all.

Those of us who protest collaboration will be punished in various ways: not fairly reviewed, not given prestigious grants and awards, not elected into academies. The rules are at once subtle and blatant. If women who practice journalism still call each other "middle-aged," how dare we blame men for the lack of greater feminist progress?

The diminution of women by women is taught everywhere— school, jobs, journalism. Women are not born knowing how to trash other women; they are carefully taught. They are taught there is only room for one token, one teacher's pet, one capo whose job it will be to show the nonexistence of discrimination. She made it against the odds. She is there to prove that anybody can.

Given my history, I should have become the capo. Wherever I went I was the token woman—Phi Beta Kappa, Woodrow Wilson Fellow, good at footnotes, research papers, good at charming elderly male professors. In short, I was good at being the good daughter. That had been my role at home. My older sister was the rebel; my younger sister the sheltered baby. My grandfather and my father adored me, and I went out into the world with long blonde hair and miniskirt, expecting to meet my grandfather and my father everywhere.

And, of course, I did. But somehow I knew that all these seductions to become the token woman were lies, betrayals of my mothers and grandmothers. I thought of my talented mother—the mad wife in the attic—and her talented sister—the mad lesbian. One went with men and the other went with women, yet both were equally discriminated against just because they were women. And I carried these two mothers in my heart. The world could not hear their cries, but I could hear little else. So when I was offered the role of token, I refused. I studied to become the voice of the madwoman in the attic. I knew her fate could just as easily have been mine.

At Barnard, I fell in love with Blake, with Byron, with Keats, with Shakespeare, with Chaucer, with Pope, with Boswell, with Fielding, with Twain, with Yeats, with Roethke, with Auden. I loved being in a place where words were valued, where poetry mattered, and I began to shape and revise my own poems. I had a poetry teacher—a poet himself—who recognized that I was a word person, not a doctor, and rescued me from pre-med and the dreaded dissection of the fetal pig.

I fell gratefully under his tutelage and followed his directives to learn to write sonnets and sestinas before I attempted "free" verse. At last there was guidance in learning the craft of poetry. At last somebody cared enough to teach me. I will always be grateful to Bob Pack for bringing rigorousness to the study of poetry.

"Learn to write a Shakespearean sonnet," Bob (I called him Mr. Pack then) said, "and after that you can fly."

I remember breaking my brains over my father's old rhyming dictionary (from his song-writing days), learning how hard it is to rhyme in English, and I remember bringing my efforts to Bob with trepidation. The first poem of mine he pronounced a success was this one, written about sending my boyfriend a lock of my hair:

ON SENDING YOU A LOCK OF MY HAIR

There is a white wood house near Hampstead Heath
in whose garden the nightingale still sings.
Though Keats is dead, the bird who sang of death
returns with melodies, on easeful wings.

A lock of hair the poet's love received
remains in the room where first it was shorn;

An heirloom, its history half-believed,
its strands now faded and its ribbon worn.

On polished floors, through squares of summer sun
I felt his footsteps move, as if the elf—
deceiving elf, he called her—had not done
with making mischief to amuse herself.

I saw him clip that tousled lock of hair
and though he did not offer it to me,
I felt that I was privileged, standing there,
and took his gesture for my legacy.

The poem tells me who I was at seventeen—a girl in love with poetic gestures, trying to relate her life to the lives of dead white English Romantic poets, not yet even beginning to confront the issues Virginia Woolf poses in *A Room of One's Own*:

> It is useless to go to the great men writers for help, however much one may go to them for pleasure. Lamb, Browne, Thackeray, Newman, Sterne, Dickens, De Quincey—whoever it may be— never helped a woman yet, though she may have learnt a few tricks of them and adapted them to her use. The weight, the pace, the stride of a man's mind are too unlike her own for her to lift anything substantial from him successfully. The ape is too distant to be sedulous. Perhaps the first thing she would find, setting pen to paper, was that there was no common sentence ready for her use.

In college, I did not find this to be so. Perhaps my search for identity was too retarded. I imitated Shakespeare, Keats, and Byron, wrote a novella in the style of Fielding (my preparation for writing *Fanny Hackabout-Jones*), and was extraordinarily grateful to be nurtured in a cloister where, for four blissful years, I could devote myself to verbal explorations. The subject of feminism did not re-rear its head in the years 1959 to 1963. Virginia Woolf, Emma Goldman, Gertrude Stein, Simone de Beauvoir, Colette, Muriel Rukeyser, Edna St. Vincent Millay, Dorothy Parker, H.D., Antonia White, Jean Rhys, Doris Lessing, Rebecca West were not taught at Barnard in my time—so how could one even know there *was* a female tradition? How could one know that one had not been born from the very foam of the wave? Virginia Woolf got it right:

> Indeed, since freedom and fullness of expression are of the essence of the art, such a lack of tradition, such a scarcity and inadequacy of tools, must have told enormously upon the writing of women. Moreover, a book is not made of sentences laid end to end, but of sentences built, if an image helps, into arcades or domes. And this shape too has been made by men out of their own needs for their own uses. There is no reason to think that the form of the epic or of the poetic play suits a woman any more than the sentence suits her. But all the older forms of literature were hardened and set by the time she became a writer. The novel alone was young enough to be soft in her hands—another reason, perhaps, why she wrote novels.

The lack of a woman's tradition (or, indeed, the deliberate *ignoring* of a tradition that, despite all odds, existed) was an issue not dealt with at Barnard when I was so happily immersed in learning the male tradition, winning A's and poetry prizes, feeling myself lucky to be the darling of my male professors. The lack of self-consciousness about feminism seems like innocence, looking back. I did not feel cheated then by the absence of women in the curriculum. Rather, I felt that a whole world of riches was there to plunder and that I was blessed to be allowed that opportunity. My poetry teacher was young, handsome, rather too flirtatious to stay at spinsterish Barnard (especially after he married one of his students), and undoubtedly a sexist pig. But he changed my life, turning me toward words forever. He flirted madly with me, but did not fuck me. The yearning fantasies I had for him surely fueled my verse. (There is so much talk these days of banishing sexuality from academe, but the fire of learning inevitably has something sexual in it. This does not mean that it should be used as a power play against adolescent girls or expressed literally. But sexuality must be there as a mythic fire, even when it goes unfulfilled in the flesh. Or is this too subtle a flame for mortal men to tend? Can't we keep our sexuality but sublimate it into poems?)

Another teacher I adored was Jim Clifford, the Johnsonian, an editor of the Boswell papers, who had the gift—rare in academe—of teaching literature as if it were part of life. A tall midwesterner who began as an opera singer, he was an instinctive feminist who encouraged us to read Fanny Burney, Mary Astell, and Lady Mary Wortley Montagu and to think hard about the conditions of women's lives in the eighteenth century: their lack of financial independence, their lack of the vote, their lack of birth control. It was his belief that you could not understand people and how they thought unless you understood their plumbing fixtures (or lack thereof) and their patent medicines. Surely this is true for women above all. How can we appreciate their art if we do not understand their underclothes—whalebone, crinolines—their birth control or its absence, their menstrual bandages, washbowls, and privies? The extraordinary woman depends on the ordinary woman, Virginia Woolf famously wrote. By stressing the physicality of London life in the eighteenth century, Jim Clifford made us consider the conditions of being a woman in that era. It was a great gift.

Inspired by Jim Clifford's teaching, I wrote a mock epic in the style of Alexander Pope and then a novella in the style of Henry Fielding. I learned more about the eighteenth century by inhabiting its end-stopped couplets and its Latinate sentences than I ever learned from the books about books about books I was later required to read in graduate school. For the tenor of any age lingers in its verbal cadences. By inhabiting its style, you inhabit the age—almost as though you were trying on eighteenth-century petticoats and panniers.

Maristella de Panizza Lorch—a tiny Italian mother of three who had her last baby, Donatella (now a reporter for the *New York Times*), while I was her Italian literature student—was the third of this trio of Barnard mentors and undoubtedly the most important. A Greek and Latin scholar and an expert on Italian Renaissance literature, Maristella was to become my lifelong role model and friend. She changed my life simply by being herself: a passionate scholar who was simultaneously a passionate mother.

In those days most of the women professors at Barnard harked back to another tradition of female excellence. They were unmarried (to our eyes anyway) and had deep voices and shingled hair. Of course there was sexuality in their lives, but their students were the last to know it. They wore mannish suits—like Miss Birch and Miss Wathen—or else Greek togas and suede dancing sandals. They seemed to me as distant as the moon.

But Maristella was someone I could *become*. Reciting Dante and nursing Donatella, by her very *existence* at Barnard she struck a blow for freedom.

Looking back, I thinks it's pathetic that I was so grateful to have one teacher like Maristella. There should have been dozens! But the truth is, mother scholars were very few. I'm grateful that my daughter will be going to college in a time when there are many. So many as to be almost unremarkable.

Adolescence is such a tumultuous time. Suddenly vulnerable, suddenly sexual, we look at the world to tell us what on earth to do with our bodies and minds, and the world seems to be saying: *You have to choose.*

The current passion for political correctness has not made this better. Far from receiving more choices, women are still being dictated orthodoxies. Certain women writers are kosher—Gertrude Stein, Virginia Woolf, Adrienne Rich, Toni Morrison—and others are not. As if to correct centuries of neglect, writers of color and lesbian writers are being touted whether they are good or not. This hardly creates diversity and pride in the female heritage. In the long run, nobody will be fooled, uplifted, or inspired if a bad writer is celebrated because of her sexual orientation or the color of her skin. But in academe today, good and bad do not apply. "Great" is a forbidden word. Only social and political relativism are acceptable in discussing works of literature. Our misplaced American populism has at last summoned the temerity to undermine "great literature" by asserting that the very term is a bigoted construct. I hope this will change. Feminism cannot become an excuse for know-nothingism. Ethnic cleansing in the curriculum to get rid of "dead white males" is a purely retaliatory move that has no place in combating sexism and racism. The worthy goal of creating a more diverse curriculum will backfire if it ends up depriving women, people of color, and poor people of the joys of what used to be called "a classical education." Yes—we were "oppressed" at Barnard, but at least we learned the tradition so we could parody it. And enter it. That has to be better than being left out altogether.

At Barnard, I reinvented myself and became a preppy fashion plate—perhaps in rebellion against the school's grungy image—or perhaps in rebellion against my Music and Art black-stockinged days. I wore three-inch heels that stuck in Columbia's red brick paths (and often lost their lifts), tight straight skirts, cashmere twin sets with pearls. I changed my nail polish every day. I never went out without a full mask of makeup—and a new pair of stockings and a bottle of Chanel No. 5 in my bag.

Were Barnard girls supposed to be grinds and drudges? I'd show them. I'd be a secret drudge who looked like the cover of *Seventeen*.

I met my boyfriend the first month of school, deliberately planned to lose my virginity three months later, and was grateful to get rid of it. Michael and I "went steady" for four years. I found it convenient. Monogamy kept me pure for my work—monogamy with someone who typed my poems.

Michael was short, had flashing brown eyes, close-cropped brown hair, and a brilliant gift for words. All my life, I have fallen for the same qualities in men: bravado, blarney, verbal brilliance, and musical virtuosity. Also, bookishness. Michael recited Shakespeare by the folio and knew more about classical literature, medieval history, and modern poetry than any boy I'd ever met. He was funny; he was smart; he was full of wild energy. He had the touch of the poet I have always found irresistible.

"Great wits are sure to madness near allied,/And thin partitions do their bounds divide," Dryden wrote. This is the story of my life— or at least my love life.

How could I know that a year after we married, Michael would be hospitalized at Mount Sinai for a schizophrenic episode and sedated with thousands of milligrams of Thorazine?

I have told the story of Michael's breakdown—or a fictionalized version of it—in *Fear of Flying*, so, like most writers, I can no longer remember what really happened. My memories have vanished into the fictional narrative. I remember only bits and pieces: his disappearance (he was rowing on Central Park Lake); his reappearance (he tried to lead me out the window to prove to me we both could fly); his hospitalization (he called me Judas and quoted Dante in Italian to prove it).

Michael had quit law school and had been working for a mad market research genius who was computerizing America's buying habits and selling the results to advertising agencies. Michael's boss became rich but Michael went crazy. And who wouldn't have gone crazy spending night after night watching those huge computers of the sixties spew out news of Tide, Clorox, and Ivory Snow and how soap-suds correlated with educational status and TV watching? Michael hated himself for the work he was doing. But he was captured by the promise of lucre beyond his wildest dreams. Alas, he cracked up before the gold rolled in.

I became a daily visitor to the psycho ward at Mount Sinai during the long, hot summer of 1964, when Harlem burned. The city was teetering on the edge of apocalypse, and so were we. Dazed, enraged, Michael berated me and tried to get me to help him escape. I was torn between my loyalty to him and my desire to go on with my studies, my writing, my life.

His parents—his mother a tiny brunette with a wife-of-Bathish gap between her front teeth, a penchant for wearing three-inch open-toed mules, and a three-pack-a-day cigarette habit, his father a tall, bewildered, yet belligerent bald man—appeared from California and promptly decided *I* had driven their son crazy. *It was all my fault.* After all, I was the wife. Michael's mother, a Jewish princess from West Hartford, Connecticut, had married beneath her (like all Jewish princesses) and wound up a navy wife in San Francisco. She took out all the disappointments of her marriage on my parents' seeming wealth. Michael's parents had struggled to put a lanai on the house and pizza on the table. My parents found them hopelessly déclassé. Michael's parents, in turn, found my parents hopelessly snobbish. (All four of them were right, of course.) All four of them could agree on nothing but the necessity of breaking up our marriage.

They succeeded. When Michael's health insurance expired, his parents and my parents made a deal: *Take him back to California.* I was enlisted as the nurse. My father and I flew out to San Francisco with Michael and a psychiatrist in tow. Michael was heavily sedated in order to be allowed on the plane at all.

What a flight! The blind leading the drugged! Later, living in Germany with Allan, I tried to evoke that time in a poem: The chilling details of being in love with someone who suddenly opts out of the assumptions that constitute what the world calls "sanity" are evoked in "Flying You Home." Michael's brilliance had ratcheted up several notches and turned into madness. The world we walked through was painted by a surrealist. We thought we could climb down into rain puddles and talk to apples. At first, I was more attracted than repelled by all of this. There turned out to be more than a touch of madness in me, too.

FLYING YOU HOME

1

"I bite into an apple & then get bored
before the second bite," you said.
You were also Samson. I had cut
your hair & locked you up.
Besides your room was bugged.
A former inmate left his muse
spread-eagled on the picture window.
In the glinting late-day sun
we saw her huge & cross-eyed breasts appear
diamond-etched
against the slums of Harlem.
You tongued your pills & cursed the residents.
You called me Judas.
You forgot I was a girl.

2

Your hands weren't birds. To call
them birds would be too easy.
They drew circles around your ideas
& your ideas were sometimes parabolas.
That sudden Sunday you awoke
& found yourself behind the looking glass,
your hands perched on the breakfast table
waiting for a sign.
I had nothing to tell them.
They conversed with the eggs.

3

We walked.
Your automatic umbrella snapped
into place above your head
like a black halo.
We thought of climbing down rain puddles
as if they were manholes.
You said the reflected buildings

led to hell.
Trees danced for us,
cut-out people turned sideways
& disappeared into their voices.
The cities in our glasses took us in.
You stood on a scale, heard the penny drop—
but the needle was standing still!
It proved that you were God.

    4

The elevator opens & reveals me
holding African violets.
An hour later I vanish
into a chasm whose dimensions
are 23 hours.
Tranquilized, brittle,
you strut the corridors
among the dapper young psychiatrists,
the girls who weave rugs all day,
unravel them all night,
the obesity cases lost in themselves.
You hum. You say you hate me.
I would like to shake you.
Remember how it happened?
You were standing at the window
speaking about flying.
Your hands flew to my throat.
When they came they found
our arms strewn around the floor
like broken toys.
We both were crying.

    5

You stick. Somewhere in a cellar of my mind,
you stick. Fruit spoke to you
before it spoke to me. Apples cried
when you peeled them.
Tangerines jabbered in Japanese.
You stared into an oyster

& sucked out God.
You were the hollow man,
with Milton entering your left foot.

        6
My first husband!—God—
you've become an abstraction,
a kind of idea. I can't even hear
your voice anymore. Only the black hair
curled on your belly makes you real—
I draw black curls on all the men I write.
I don't even look anymore.

        7
I thought of you in Istanbul.
Your Byzantine face,
thin lips & hollow cheeks,
the fanatical melting brown eyes.
In Hagia Sophia they're stripping down
the Moslem plaster
to find mosaics underneath.
The pieces fit in place.
You'd have been a saint.

        8
I'm good at interiors.
Gossip, sharpening edges, kitchen poems—
& have no luck at all with maps.
It's because of being a woman
& having everything inside.
I decorated the cave,
hung it with animal skins & woolens,
such soft floors,
that when you fell
you thought you fell on me.
You had a perfect sense of bearings
to the end,
were always pointing North.

9

Flying you home—
good Christ—flying you home,
you were terrified.
You held my hand, I held
my father's hand & he
filched pills from the psychiatrist
who'd come along for you.
The psychiatrist was 26 & scared.
He hoped I'd keep you calm.
& so we flew.
Hand in hand in hand in hand we flew.

Almost immediately upon arrival in California, the shrink, my father, and I enrolled Michael in a Southern California clinic that looked a lot like a health spa but was a funny farm. This was to be Michael's postgraduate training: Thorazine 101. ("Exit husband number one," as my daughter says—given any opportunity.)

Michael, of course, accused me of being Judas and selling him out for twenty pieces of silver. I wept. My father led me away like Eurydice out of the underworld. Unlike Orpheus, my dad did not look back. I escaped. A handy family lawyer annulled our marriage as if it had never been. I never saw Michael again. He did call me once or twice hinting at money after *Fear of Flying* was published. I remember being disappointed. For one brief summer, after all, we'd both thought he was Christ.

We should have lived together for a while and never gotten married at all. But it was 1963, and in 1963, you married the first guy you slept with. (My daughter finds this funny.) Sex was permitted only as long as you were in love. Love led, inexorably, to marriage.

Back in New York the following fall, I taught English at City College and "made Ph.D. noises" at Columbia Graduate School. My best friend that year was a greengrocer's son from Blackburn, in Lancashire, England, named Russell Harty. Fresh from the Giggleswick School in Yorkshire and, before that, Oxford, Russell was vamping until ready for prime time. He was later to become one of Britain's most famous chat-show hosts.

Thrilled to be in New York and out of Giggleswick, Russell fell in love with me and my West Side bohemian Jewish family, who were everything his family was not.

"You taught where?" I asked.

"Giggleswick."

"You made that up," I said.

"I wish I *had*," he told me.

I had a crush on Russell, but he would never kiss me. He adored me, of course, and we had worlds of wit in common, but eventually, I realized he liked boys.

We were destined to be lifelong friends, even, at times, lusting after the same men. ("If you bring dishy guys like that to London with you," he said once at a dinner for four at Langan's, "I refuse to be responsible for my behavior.") Russell later became not only famous but notorious. His North Country accent deepened. He became the London celebrity the tabloids loved to hate. Inevitably, he interviewed me on the telly.

By then his days of marking blue books in a City College cubicle were far behind him, as were mine. We were also destined to have the same kind of fame: famous for being famous, famous for sex, drugs, and rock and roll, famous for our nasty reviews. The irony of it was we had both started out rather donnishly. Russell had studied at Oxford with Nevill Coghill, when I was studying at Columbia with James Clifford. Defrocked dons was what we both became.

He died of AIDS, of course—one of the bumper deathcrop of the early eighties. In those days, people simply disappeared and months later you'd learn they were dead. I lost many friends that silent way: Russell Harty; Tom Victor, the photographer; David Kalstone, the literary scholar and writer; Paul Woerner, the theatrical lawyer. One day we were laughing in New York or London or Venice, and the next day they seemed to vanish. After a deadly pause, a mysterious obit would run in the newspaper: "After a long illness," it would say—with no mention of AIDS in the early days, or of the partner left behind to mourn. These friends seemed to crawl off into holes to die, long before AIDS or HIV was an acceptable diagnosis.

Recently I told my daughter Molly about these deaths at the unacknowledged beginning of the plague years.

"They simply disappeared," I said, "ashamed to be ill, afraid no one would understand. Some of them went home to their families, and you never heard from them again. Some had companions to nurse them, but unless you were part of their community, they didn't keep you informed. There was so much *shame*—"

"Write about it, Mommy," said Molly, "so my friends will know. We were all just little kids then."

If I close my eyes, I can still see Russell's buckteeth, the part in his reddish-brown hair, and his big brown eyes. I can still hear him saying: "Me muther wunders why I never married you—and the bluddy thing is—it's too bluddy late to tell 'er."

I imagine Russell chatting everyone up in that great bathhouse in the sky that is gay heaven. I hope he's having fun with Oscar Wilde, Marcel Proust, William Shakespeare, Michelangelo Buonarotti, and the rest of the chorus line. It must be crowded there.

So I taught at CCNY, where my students use to threaten that I was sending them to 'Nam if I flunked them, and I wrote my unreadable master's thesis: "Women in the Poems of Alexander Pope"—a proto-feminist document if ever there was one. (In those days, women scholars used to write about male poets in "the canon," but we usually tried to prove that they were really women under their periwigs!)

I dated. It was 1965 and I had long blonde hair and lots of pheromones. There were always men. I didn't like any of them as well as Russell, but I assumed unthinkingly—good girl of the fifties that I was—that you *had* to have a man whether you liked him or not.

I went through a series of male chauvinist piggy graduate students who thought women should be their research assistants. Then I fell in love with a very well hung but otherwise remote and chilly musician, with whom I went to Europe as a camp-follower at music festivals. When it became clear that he wanted to split to see an old girlfriend in London, I took off for Italy, land of my dreams, where I vengefully fucked a married Italian (the first in a long line of those).

"Eat it like gelato, baby!" Paolo or Gino or Franco or Sandro raved in bed. I laughed so hard, I thought I'd swallow his *pisello*.

Being single was always tricky for me because I was the girl who couldn't say no. I liked men a lot, and I liked a lot of different men. When I wasn't near the guy I loved, I loved the guy I was near—to paraphrase Yip Harburg. Marriage was therefore refuge, a way of concentrating on work.

In the autumn of 1965, I met and was ferociously moved by a Chinese-American Freudian psychoanalyst whose last name I still bear. He was handsome, sexy, nonverbal ("He communicates like a telegram," my grandfather said, "as if the words cost money"), but he had the magic ingredient—shrinkdom. Being a priest of the unconscious, he was the antidote to Michael's craziness—or so I hoped.

"You have always lived your life by a violent alternation of extremes," my present husband says. "Oh, yeah?" I bristle. But I know he's right. The only thing I don't know is which extreme *he* represents.

Allan and I met and married in two months. Marry in haste, repent at leisure, the proverb goes. My impulsiveness in marrying Dr. Jong shows me how traumatized I'd been by Michael's breakdown. I doubt that I loved him, but love didn't seem to be the point of marriage. I knew I wanted to get away from my family. I knew I hated graduate school. I knew I needed to be analyzed. I knew I needed to write. And I knew I was afraid to do these things alone.

The truth is: I was *afraid* to be without a man. Afraid because, for reasons unknown to me, I attracted men like a honeypot and had no natural netting. With a gloomy psychiatrist husband, who supposedly knew the secrets of the unconscious, I assumed I'd be safe. I turned out to be right and wrong about that. Besides, being married to Allan at that time was a lot like being in solitary confinement. And solitary confinement is *great* for writing.

We shipped off to Germany in February of 1966. Allan had been drafted at the age of thirty-two and had chosen Germany for three years to rule out any possibility of being sent to Vietnam. He was sure that in Vietnam he'd be killed for his Chinese face and his American uniform. In Germany, Allan went into a three-year funk about the Vietnam War (which he opposed), being drafted out of his private practice (which he was powerless over), missing his analyst (which he was powerless over). We soon discovered how essentially unsuited we were. I loved to laugh and talk. He loved not to. I had found myself a Chinese torturer. If hell is other people, as Sartre said, then I was in hell. And I was too proud to admit I'd made another mistake.

So I locked myself in a room and wrote. Perhaps that was the purpose of it all. Perhaps he was my version of Colette's Willy. I developed a convenient theory that every woman writer needed a man to lock her in a room far from her mother so she could write.

We lived just a short trolley ride from Heidelberg, in a place called Holbeinring, where our neighbors were career army officers and their "dependents." I taught some courses at the University of Maryland's Overseas Division—where the GIs called me "Sir"—and I wrote a column on wine festivals and restaurants for a freebie magazine called *Heidelberg Diese Woche.* Mostly I locked myself in the second bedroom of our hideous army-issue apartment and wrote poems and stories.

I lived in a world of my own devising, which is, of course, how any writer must begin. I read the poetry quarterlies—*Sewanee Review, Poetry, Southern Review*—which arrived months late by sea mail. And

I worshiped at the shrine of *The New Yorker*. I would compare my own fledgling poems to those that appeared in print. My voice was too floridly female, I decided, so I attempted to emulate the cool, neutered voice I thought of as male and therefore pleasing to editors.

But to no avail. I could not really neuter my voice and become a *New Yorker* poet of the sixties. Nor could I even approximate the poems I found in the *Sewanee Review*. Just as in college I had often tried to write inscrutable poetry and despaired when my poems came out clear, I tried in Heidelberg to mold myself to what I imagined was the taste of the times. I am happy to say I failed miserably. Knowing that to be female was infinitely undesirable, I wanted to find a way to become something—anything—else. But what that something else was, I did not know.

What, I wonder, would my poetry have been like if I had studied Muriel Rukeyser at Barnard as well as Wallace Stevens? "Breathe in experience, breathe out poetry," she writes in *Theory of Flight*. I was struggling with the same female fear of growing wings, but I had no way of knowing I was not alone in this. How would my work have been different if I had known I was part of a tradition? But Rukeyser was as neglected as Ruth Stone, Edna St. Vincent Millay, Anna Wickham, H.D., Laura Riding, Marina Tsvetayevna. They might as well have written in invisible ink.

This was a pretty typical dilemma for a woman poet in the mid-sixties. Having had no women's studies courses in college, no *Norton Anthology of Literature by Women*, no professors Showalter, Stimson, Gilbert, and Gubar, we were the generation that had to name the problem and create the courses that didn't yet exist.

As I sat there in my second bedroom near the Black Forest, I had to find a way to be a woman poet in a time when "woman poet" was a term of mockery. The whole history of English poetry—which, alas, I knew so well—stressed man as creator and woman as nature. From Shakespeare to Wordsworth to Yeats and Graves, male poets plowed female Nature into androgynous fruition. The female was the muse— and muses were supposed to be mute.

"Who shall measure the heat and violence of the poet's heart when caught and tangled in a woman's body?" Virginia Woolf asked, spinning her tale of Shakespeare's imaginary sister (now the name for an English rock band). And who can measure the damage done to generations of would-be women poets by such discouraging mythologies and paradigms?

One day in 1966, a friend of my sister's in New York sent me a book of poems called *Ariel*. The author, a woman named Sylvia Plath, was already dead, but the poems were ferociously alive. And what astonishing poems they were! They dared to claim an ordinary woman's life as subject matter. They dared an openness about anger that had been forbidden to my generation of women. They dared to write of the hiss of the kitchen, the stink of baby crap, the thrill of a cut thumb, the sacred Sunday lamb in its fat.

The creator of these fierce poems had died when I was halfway through my senior year at Barnard. The winter of her death, there had been a page of her poems in *The New Yorker*. I'd read them, but I was not yet ready to absorb them. Still imitating Keats, Pope, and Fielding, still mimicking the male poets of my Barnard and Columbia education, I did not yet realize how much I hungered for those poems.

When the poet is ready, the muse appears.

In Germany, I was ready. Plath's poems cut me open. Blood spurted onto the page.

Suddenly I realized that I could abandon my neutered poems about Italian fountains and the graves of English poets and write about the life that claimed my days—the life of a "dep. wife" (as the army styled it)—the life of the market, the kitchen, the marriage bed. I could write poems about apples and onions, poems in which the daily objects of my life became doors into my inner life as a woman.

Sylvia Plath took me to Anne Sexton. *To Bedlam and Part Way Back* had been published in 1960, *All My Pretty Ones* in 1962, and *Live or Die* was just out in 1966. Poems like "Menstruation at Forty" and "Her Kind" suddenly conferred validity on my struggle to find the possessed witch in myself, the singer with a bleeding womb, the chronicler of love's "red disease."

What caused the stirring that suddenly allowed poets like Sexton or Plath to be heard? Was it the civil rights movement that marked our college years and taught us how unjust our society was? Was it the Kennedy assassination that marked our early twenties and taught us never to believe what we read in the papers? Was it the Vietnam War that marked our mid-twenties and taught us never to believe our leaders? Authority was male and it was deeply fallible.

Betty Friedan published *The Feminine Mystique* the year I graduated from Barnard. I listened to my older sister arguing about it with my mother. My sister was excited—my mother less so, having seen the feminist movement of her youth eradicated as if it had never been.

Even though I was still stuck in the eighteenth century, pretending Alexander Pope was a woman poet, feminism was in the air again, and I inevitably inhaled it. It gave permission to write out of a woman's consciousness.

My whole education at Columbia was a renunciation of such stirrings, and perhaps that was why I found Columbia increasingly intolerable. I wanted to write my own books, not the books about books about books about books that would have gotten me tenure. So I married Allan as my ticket to Europe and my escape from the sexist Columbia of my professors and the Manhattan of my parents. I needed to be far away, I knew, even to *attempt* to write the truth.

Poetry is the inner life of a culture, its nervous system, its deepest way of imagining the world. A culture that ignores its poets, chokes off its nervous system, and becomes mortally ill. That was the case with America then. (One could argue that the situation is worse now.) All those polite male *New Yorker* poets of the sixties (writing poems about their dogs and mistresses) were ignoring almost everything that was happening in the world. Reality was howling outside. Allen Ginsberg, Gregory Corso, and Lawrence Ferlinghetti were surely closer to what was happening in the sixties. But nowhere visible was a clearing in the woods for women poets—until Plath and Sexton came along, attracting our macabre fascination with their gaudy deaths. We followed in their footsteps (in tennis shoes—as Dorothy Parker said of her own stalking of Edna St. Vincent Millay in the twenties). We had to make a place for ourselves somehow. And somehow, we did.

My poetry preceded my fiction and showed me the way into my own heart. My fiction was still following (in mirrored sneakers) the elitist male footsteps of Vladimir Nabokov, who was my favorite novelist when I was in college and graduate school. It was as an homage to him that I attempted an abortive (and aborted) novel tentatively titled *The Man Who Murdered Poets*. I pretended to be a Nabokovian male madman going off to murder his equally mad doppelgänger. The book was destined never to work. I struggled with it for years, only to abandon it when *Fear of Flying* bubbled up. Neither mad nor a man, I was supremely blocked. Unconsciously I assumed only a man could narrate a novel. But my first husband was the madman, not I.

In the poems, meanwhile, a woman's voice was beginning to assert itself. It described the world as a ravenous, devouring mouth. It was full of the menace of being a woman. It was full of the frustration of being a smart woman. It was full of the absurdity of being a woman who had too many pheromones for her own good.

THE TEACHER

The teacher stands before the class.
She's talking of Chaucer.
But the students aren't hungry for Chaucer.
They want to devour her.
They are eating her knees, her toes, her breasts, her eyes
& spitting out
her words.
What do they want with words?
They want a real lesson!

She is naked before them.
Psalms are written on her thighs.
When she walks, sonnets divide
into octaves & sestets.
Couplets fall into place
when her fingers nervously toy
with the chalk.

But the words don't clothe her.
No amount of poetry can save her now.
There's no volume big enough to hide in.
No unabridged Webster, no OED.

The students aren't dumb.
They want a lesson.
Once they might have taken life
by the scruff of its neck
in a neat couplet.
But now
they need blood.

They have left Chaucer alone
& have eaten the teacher.

She's gone now.
Nothing remains
but a page of print.
She's past our helping.
Perhaps she's part of her students.
(Don't ask how.)

Eat this poem.

Living in the heart of Germany and becoming aware of my
Jewishness was also a critical part of this development. I was spending
my days exploring the half-obliterated traces of the Third Reich, por-
ing over blacked-out de-Nazified books in the library, and even discovering an abandoned Nazi amphitheater in the woods. Anne Frank
came into me. I imagined myself the ghost of a Jewish child murdered
on the day I was born. I understood that only a trick of history had let
me live.

The Plath poems and my own Holocaust of the mind came
together to create my new sense of identity as a Jew and a woman.
My first manuscript of poems, *Near the Black Forest,* was full of
images of Heidelberg after the Third Reich, the "Jewless world without men" that resulted from the twin disasters of the Holocaust and
the war.

A woman poet *is* a hunted Jew, eternally the outsider. She is asked
at first to disguise her sex, change her name, blend into the approved
poetry of male supremacy. People who suffer discrimination make up
new names, bleach their skin, bob their noses, deny who they are in
order to survive. That was, I realized, what I had done in college and
graduate school. Suddenly I found I could no longer. This proved to
be the beginning of teaching myself to write.

THE HEIDELBERG LANDLADY

Because she lost her father
in the First World War,

her husband in the Second,
we don't dispute
"There's no *Gemütlichkeit* in America."

We're winning her heart
with filter cigarettes.
Puffing, she says,
"You can't judge a country
by just twelve years."

Gray days,
the wind hobbling down sidestreets,
I'm walking in a thirties photograph,
the prehistoric age
before my birth.

This town was never bombed.
Old ladies still wear funny shoes,
long, seedy furs.
They smell of camphor and camomile,
old photographs.

Nothing much happened here.
A few jewelry shops changed hands.
A brewery. Banks.
The university put up a swastika, took it down.
The students now chant HO CHI MINH & hate Americans
on principle.
Daddy wears a flyer's cap
& never grew old.
He's on the table with the teacakes.
Mother & grandma are widows.

They take care of things.
It rains nearly every day;
every day, they wash the windows.
They cultivate jungles in the front parlors,
lush tropics

framed by lacy white curtains.
They coax the earth with plant food, scrub the leaves.
Each plant shines like a fat child.
They hope for the sun,
living in a Jewless world without men.

The Germans got their wish, I realized: They obliterated their Jews and their men at the same time. And the women went on. Alone, bitter, yet supremely in control, they scrubbed the plants and the floors. Amazons in frumpy hats and moth-eaten furs, they raised the children, tended the gardens, and gave birth to the next Germany, the Germany we know today. Now there is another generation of German men. Now trouble is brewing again.

Virginia Woolf, who understood the problems of women's creativity perhaps better than any writer, speaks of

> the accumulation of unrecorded life . . . the women at the street corners with their arms akimbo, and the rings embedded in their fat swollen fingers, talking with a gesticulation like the swing of Shakespeare's words; or from the violet-sellers and match-sellers and old crones stationed under doorways; or from drifting girls whose faces, like waves in sun and cloud, signal the coming of men and women and the flickering lights of shop windows. All that you will have to explore . . .

She is conjuring the huge part of women's lives untouched by intercourse with men. This part—and it is the greater part—is presumed to be unimportant, no fit subject for literature. As long as men set the literary agenda, this will continue to be the case. Only love—whether romance or adultery—will be thought to be fit matter for literature.

Why? Because men are at the *center* of it, and men do not like to be reminded that there is *any* part of a woman's life they are not central to. As a consequence, many women still make literature in the mode that men consider important. Hence the literary focus on "love."

What would happen if we wrote of our *own* lives, without reference to the male sex? Can we even imagine such heresies? Think of the derision that has greeted Violette le Duc, Monique Wittig, Anaïs Nin, May Sarton. After "love" is through with you, there is plenty of life left, says Colette, stating the central heresy. She was also punished for stating it—refused the funeral she deserved (the funeral that any man of her stature would have had), and the rosettes, ribbons, and medals. I doubt she cared.

Happy solitude, the happiness of two women who live together as friends or lovers, the happiness of a mother and a daughter, sharing a bed, talking all night; the happiness of two sisters when their husbands are gone, dead, away; the happiness of work; of gardening; of caring for children; of shopping; of walking; of running a house—all these are heresies.

Most of our lives occur alone, or with other women, yet we are asked to shine a spotlight on the narrow part of our lives shared with men. It is not as if female life is all darkness except for that, but we are asked to pretend it is and write of love, love, love—until it bores even us.

This is what it *really* means to be the second sex. All your pleasures and pains are considered secondary to those you share with the other sex.

Are men really so interesting? To *themselves* they are. Yet, lately, I find women *far* more interesting. I have lived for men so much of my life that this comes as something of a shock to me. Have I been so bound by the conventions that I, the supposed rebel, am as conventional as any woman of my time? Or have I been transfixed by sex because I always knew it was the primary way to seduce the muse? If I am to be honest with myself, I must answer this question.

6

SEX

Feminine sexual excitement can reach an intensity unknown to man. Male sexual excitement is keen but localized, and—except perhaps at the moment of orgasm—it leaves a man quite in possession of himself; woman, on the contrary, really loses her mind; for many this effect marks the definite and voluptuous moment of the love-affair, but it also has a magical and fearsome quality.

—Simone de Beauvoir, *The Second Sex*

Either we were a million perverts clutching our grimy handbooks in shame, or these sexual fantasies were as normal as apple pie.

—Susie Bright, *Sexual Reality: A Virtual Sex World Reader*

Women of any sense know better, after all these centuries, than to interrupt when men start telling them how they feel about sex.

—Doris Lessing, *The Golden Notebook*

"I had a dream, which was not all a dream," Byron said. And I, too, lived an idyll one perfect summer in my life. When people say "eros," I know what they mean—though they may not. And when I need a fantasy to evoke the most passion a woman can bear, this is my reference point.

I was unmarried at the time—somewhere between my third and fourth marriage—and I had fallen in love with a man who looked to me like Pan, smelled brownly of summer and sex, and sailed his sloop in the lagoon of Venice and on the Adriatic Sea.

Our affair had begun a year before—we fell in love on his boat, waited a full year in anticipation, and then, when I came back to Venice the following summer, snatched perfect hours in the house he shared with the woman of his life. We continued by phone and fax for years after that, meeting as often as we could. I wore two watches so I always knew what time it was in Venice, and we had lovers' phone dates, when we put each other to sleep describing what we would do, had done, to each other.

"I am exploding, full of stars . . . " he would say (in Italian), coming. Everything was planetary metaphor. Sex was cosmic—by optical fiber.

I would go to Venice and stay in a beautiful suite in the Gritti (where the water rippled on the ceiling) and he would come to visit morning and evening.

But one summer (was it the second or the third? I can't remember), I decided to rent the *piano nobile* of a palazzo for three months—to give us unlimited time to explore this connection and see if it could become permanent. What I learned was that eros is never permanent, or rather the conditions of its permanence are impermanence.

I arrived alone at the end of June, settled into my rented palazzo— with its windows overlooking the Giudecca canal, ships with Cyrillic lettering sliding past, its walled garden filled with old roses and one amazingly fruitful pear tree (*pero)* in the center, which was heavy with ripening pears.

Piero (let us call him) came at eleven o'clock the first morning to say hello (*per salutarti*), he said. He said hello to my nipples, my neck, my lips, my tongue, took me by the hand and walked me into the bedroom, where he uncovered my body slowly, exclaiming at the beauty of each part, and entered me on the bed, holding firm inside me for what seemed like forever, while I filled with juice like the pears on the pear tree and began to throb as if a storm were shaking them onto the ground.

Filled by his smell, his words, his tongue, his incredibly unhurried penis, all of me rose up to him as if the cells of my body were being taken apart and put back together. It was a sort of transubstantiation— blood and body becoming bread and wine instead of the other way around. I looked up at his faunlike brown eyes, his curly reddish-gold hair, and said, "*Mio dio del bosco*"—my forest god—for that was how it felt. It was like being possessed by a very gentle grandmaster of the coven, a stagman, a horned god, the god of the witches, the greenman. It was like being possessed by all of nature, giving up my intellectuality, my will, my separateness, to the green fuse that drives the flower.

The sun shone in squares on the bed, the canal water rippled on the painted ceiling (with its figures of Hera, Venus, Persephone, and assorted sibyls), motorboats puttered by, and in the wake of my oneness with the forest and the sea, I saw clearly what the life of a man and a woman was meant to be like, two halves fitting into each other, out of time, for eternity. I knew that people took drugs trying to simulate this, pursued money and power for this, tried to destroy it in others when they could not have it themselves. It was a very simple gift—but no less elusive for its simplicity—and most people had never known it. All their thrashing around was in its pursuit.

"I must go," he said, and I followed him into the bathroom—laughing, literally jumping for joy—while he washed under his arms and his crotch, put on his clothes, and fluttered a kiss between my breasts.

"I will call for you at five," he said.

And I sat down to the day's writing, with his sap between my thighs, and his smell on my fingers and mouth.

I wrote till three, dressed in a bathing suit under a sundress, and walked the length of the Fondamenta to the swimming pool, where I swam laps in the sunlight, feeling my limbs heavy as water, bright as the air. Then I had something to eat and walked back down the Fondamenta, seeming to float over the stones.

At five he called. "*Siete sola?*" (Are you alone?) he asked.

Of course I was alone. And then we were back in bed, with the afternoon light, not the morning light, playing on the ceiling, with his rod and staff comforting me, with his salty kisses turning my mouth into the lagoon drowning the fiery pink sun.

Sometimes we'd walk together on the Fondamenta or stop for a glass of wine at Harry's Dolci—and then he was gone to his other life and I to my dinners with friends, concerts, operas, long walks in the city.

Sometimes, I'd see him puttering through the lagoon, squiring his other lady. Sometimes, I'd wonder where he was. But always with pleasure, not pain.

This went on for eight days. And on the evening of the eighth day he vanished without a word. He was at sea with people I did not know. He was gone, and I had no idea if he would ever return.

The days grew long. A suitor from home showed up and, later, one from Paris. They failed to banish him from my bed. Eventually my daughter came and my assistant, and I crammed the day with motherhood and work.

I was enraged with Piero, not for going, but for going without a word, and I vowed never to see him again. The summer dragged on, hot, humid, useless. Venice was like a cruise ship where I knew and was bored by all the people. Eventually my daughter had to see her father and my assistant had to see her lover. Friends arrived and took me on an endless round of parties—and then one morning, he rang as if nothing had happened.

"*Siete sola?*" he asked.

"*Cretino!*" I shouted. "Idiot!"

"I have to go to Murano in the boat—will you come?"

I flew out of the house to tear his eyes out.

In the boat, I hammered my fists at his chest.

"How could you leave me when I came here to be with you?"

"I had no choice—I *had* to."

And his mouth was on my mouth, silencing me.

In a little while, we were parked behind a mud bank, thick with rushes, making love. And the boat rocked with us and the sun shone.

My houseguests were amused as I cursed him, then ran to him, then cursed him again. We would meet in the secret little studio near my walled garden, whose roses were over but whose pear tree still dropped fruit. We would make love morning and night, and then he would flee.

I forgave him because I had to. When he entered me, I felt complete. Yet when he left, I did not trust him to return.

There is no end to this story. If he appeared here today and touched me I would be drawn back into that forest, that lagoon, that whirling sabbath dance.

The sense of impermanence made his hold on me permanent, and his unreality also made him real. Some nights I go to sleep thinking I will wake up in that other country with that other husband. He is my husband on the moon, and when it is full, I think of him. He populates my dreams.

When people say "sex," I think of him.

What would have happened if I joined my life with his?

I can only speculate. He claims he does not make love with the lady he lives with, and maybe this is true, maybe not. I only know that

I would rather be the one he runs to than the one he escapes from, and somehow I have insured that situation by not sticking around. I would rather keep sex alive in my fantasy life than kill it by marrying it. But maybe I am deluding myself. Could I have lived with the god of the woods? Only part time. He was not willing to be there *except* part time. And I accepted his conditions and went on with my life.

When I was a little girl I loved the fairy tale of the Twelve Dancing Princesses. The princesses went to sleep in their beds like good girls, but in the morning their shoe leather was all worn out because they had danced all night. My writing is like that. I may lead the most straitlaced life, but my books betray worn shoe leather, sun, sea, pear trees, sap between the thighs. I lived that way one summer—or rather two weeks out of one summer. I would live that way always, but I fear it is impossible.

The perfect fit, even when you find it, may not be the perfect companion. Passion has to stay untangled from ordinary life to stay passion. And ordinary life tends to take over and banish passion. Ordinary life is the toughest weed of all.

I first discovered sex in my dreams when I was thirteen. I lusted for a tall redheaded boy (whose name I never knew) who ran—wearing a Harvard scarf—to the subway station next to the Museum of Natural History on Central Park West. When he appeared in my dreams, my face would flush, my thighs grow damp, and my heart beat a fast double step. When I glimpsed him at a distance, these things happened again. I never learned his name, but I loved him anyway. He awakened my sexuality.

After freshman year in high school, I never even saw him again until once, in Bath, England, where I was doing research for *Fanny Hackabout-Jones,* my mock-eighteenth-century novel, a curly red-headed eighteenth-century bandit with slanting green eyes came into my four-poster bed and made perfect love to me. Was he a dream, a dybbuk, a prowler? I never knew. But I transformed him into Fanny's love, Lancelot, and made him the hero of my book.

Sex is something I have always fought. It works so strongly on me that I have to battle it to keep my life my own. When I was a teenager and discovered masturbation I would say to myself: "I am keeping myself free from *men.*"

I wanted men sexually but I did not want them to have *power* over me. This was something men could not accept. Most men like power better than they like sex, and if you give them one without the other, they eventually rebel.

That is why the greatest lovers tend to disappear. They don't want to be at your beck and call. They don't want to be predictable. As soon as you find your lunar mate, prepare to lose him. He doesn't like the heat of the sun.

There are all kinds of other loves—satisfying in all kinds of other ways. There is talking love, cuddling love, cooking love—and some of these are accompanied by great thumping orgasms. That's not the point.

In every woman's heart, there's a god of the woods. And this god is not available for marriage, or for home improvement, or for parenthood.

Men, no doubt, have the equivalent: Lilith, not Eve. But there have been enough books about men. I don't need to add to the literature. The point is: You're always a bigamist. Married to one in your heart and another in your womb. Sometimes the heart and the womb come together for a night or two. Then they separate again.

My fantasy is a ménage à trois: moon-husband, sun-husband, and me. I haven't yet figured how we can live together. But when I get it worked out, I'll tell you. I know that plenty of women long for this too. And only fear and compulsion toward useless niceness make them claim that they don't.

In all the books that have been poured out about love and sex, there is seldom any sense of that mystery. Sometimes, at night, switching channels, I come upon the sex shows. Dial 1-900-BOOBS or 1-900-STUDS or 1-900-BALLS. The men look cynical and crude and the women all talk with Bronx accents. The men are in love with themselves and have no room for anyone else. These are not my fantasies.

Once, my third husband and I went to Plato's Retreat. We went as sexual reporters, with little spiral notebooks. We kept our clothes on at first, and then we took them off, wanting verisimilitude.

We wandered from the spa room (scummy water, pimply bodies) to the snack room (peanut butter and jelly, bologna and mustard—as at some very déclassé kids' party), to the mat room (dentists from New Jersey hydraulically screwing their hygienists). Finally, detumescence set in and we went home. Again the fantasy wasn't mine. My fantasy would have included Beluga, not bologna, but that wasn't all.

I wanted an orgy that approximated those dreams that haunt you through the day. Plato's Retreat was not my dream.

Oh, the things that have been done in Plato's name! Chaste love has come to be called "Platonic love." But it is really *ideal* love that we seek—like the courtly lovers of the Provençal south. Physical consummation is the least important thing here. It is the ideal of *yearning*—the lover who can never be possessed—that makes for Provençal perfection.

Perhaps the lover can never be possessed because he runs away. Perhaps he can never be possessed because time intrudes on timelessness. Or perhaps the rest of our life is promised to another. And only in dreams can we participate in this ménage à trois.

Impossibility is part of its essence. Impossibility alone makes it possible. Or maybe I only tell myself this because I am a coward. Maybe I don't want to risk the limits of experience.

The tall redheaded boy and I never touched. But when I was fourteen or fifteen, I was chosen as an *inamorata* by a someone less immaterial: His name was Robbie and he was tall and brown haired, with a bumpy, slightly lopsided nose and a big beautiful cock.

"Maybe someday you'll take it in your mouth," he said tentatively, knowing it was against the "rules." And did we have rules in 1955! Outside or inside the bra, outside or inside the panties, inside or outside the jockey shorts. If writing rhymed poetry is tennis *with* a net (to paraphrase Robert Frost), then "making out" in 1955 was a tournament with its own elaborate rules. One false move and you could be *out*. Until then, you delicately went as far as you could—avoiding, of course, penetration of either the oral or the vaginal kind.

The excuse then was babies. Pregnancy was an irreversible condition. Or was perceived as such—as AIDS is today. The lust to break the taboo was not nearly as strong as the need to have a safety net. So we invented all kinds of expedients: finger fucking, jerking off with various handy lubricants, dry humping. You wanted to have your cake and eat it too. You wanted "technical virginity." Later in my life, in an unhappy marriage, I would allow myself adultery with a condom—so no skins or fluids touched. Or have oral sex, but stop short of intercourse. These limitations *mattered*. Human beings are always bigger on form than content.

The melting pleasure I experienced with Robbie had its dues. I got anorexic from my guilt and literally stopped eating, stopped even drinking water. Symbolically, I must have thought all my orifices were one.

So if I could stop taking things in my mouth, perhaps it would make up for what I had taken in my vagina. I remember the terror and obsession, the passion to undo what I had done! *What* had I done? I didn't even have a name for it! I thought we had invented it!

Will there ever be a Trobriand Island adolescence where sex is free and children can refrain from such doing and undoing? I don't anticipate it.

The sex we have in books, in movies, and on television is so devoid of mystery that it frightens me. Mystery is the essence of our humanity. It is what makes us who we are.

Sometime in my forties, a famous poet about a decade older fell madly in love with me. We had lunch in my house in New York and kissed and cuddled somewhat tentatively. Then he went home to Ireland and I went to my house in Connecticut for the summer. The letters flew across the Atlantic. They were full of black garter belts, black silk stockings, lines of poetry, double entendres. They were the beginning of an erotic novel.

We waited for each other's letters. Then we answered as cleverly as we could.

After a couple of months of this, I flew to Venice, planning to meet him in London a few weeks later. In Venice, there was a complication. I remet Piero and we began our fierce love affair.

Suddenly the Irish poet went cold for me. Yet he had moved heaven and earth with the lady of his life to come and meet me in London.

He came to my posh hotel with a pasteboard suitcase and two cartons of cigarettes (he really planned to stay!). He looked around my oval suite overlooking the park and said snidely: "Your books must be doing well."

His hands were shaking and he lit cigarette after cigarette and paced. At last, he said, "Let's read poetry to each other, because it's through poetry that we met."

We tried. This did not calm us either.

Finally, we went out to dinner at a greasy pub where he felt comfortable. He tried to drink himself silly, but he remained every bit as nervous. I found the plonk he'd ordered unpotable.

Back at the hotel, I wondered how to get rid of him. The last train to the unfashionable shire where he was staying had already left. I hadn't the heart to make him sleep in some awful station hotel. I vanished into the bathroom, as I often do when perplexed.

When I came out I found him installed in my bed, smoking his twenty-eighth cigarette.

"We might as well sleep together for *warmth*," he said, and smiled a snaggle-toothed smile. His letters had been far more appealing.

Reader: I put a rubber on him and fucked him. Then I went out to the living room and slept on the couch, wrapped in a satin comforter.

In the morning I gave him a wonderful breakfast, which he mocked for its elegance, before he went his way. I had discovered he was vain, snobbish, anti-Semitic, and not very nice.

But I still have the letters. Sometimes, I take them out and read them, pretending I don't know the ending. The story is better without it.

Sex, by definition, is something you have with someone other than a spouse—which doesn't mean the other isn't good. It's simply in another category. Call it *conjugal* anything and the mystery withers. Sex has mystery, magic, a hint of the forbidden.

It isn't practical. It has nothing to do with money. That's why those 900 numbers couldn't get me off even if they *did* click with my fantasies. Pay for it and you are out of the realm of mystery. It becomes a transaction, a part of the gross national product, something to enter our anesthetizing national dialogue about whether or not porn is good for women's equality. We are out of the realm of money and politics here. We are into the realm of myth, fairy tale, and dream.

In another myth I loved as a child, Princess Langwidere of Oz had thirty heads, one for every day of the month. Some were good and some were bad, but she could never remember which until she wore them—and by then, it was too late.

The good girl could not be blamed for being bad. The bad girl was really a good girl with her heads mixed up!

In my fantasy, I am Princess Langwidere with my simple flowing white chiffon dress and the ruby key I wear at my wrist to open the cupboards where my heads are kept. I open the cupboard, put on the tousled, Medusa-like black head, and suddenly I am screaming at the Irish poet: "Get out! How dare you bring that pasteboard suitcase in my room!"

I do not fuck him. I send him home to his long-suffering wife and luxuriate in my big hotel bed alone.

The enemy is niceness, manners, trying to be good.

Whenever I feel that way, I say to myself: *Change heads!*

Good daughter, good sister, good niece, good wife, good mother— and the only place I am honest is in the adulterous bed. Forbidden sex gives us ourselves because selfhood is still forbidden to women. Sex is the root of all this, sex is the key. Sex is the catalyst for metamorphosis. That is why we cannot give it up.

And so I sit in the palazzo watching the boats go by.

The telephone is about to ring.

Of course I will say yes.

There is nothing more discouraging than a woman who has given up sex. She reminds you of Oscar Wilde's line: "Twenty years of romance make a woman look like a ruin; but twenty years of marriage make her look like a public monument."

Here is the difference between Oscar Wilde and me. For all the tortures he suffered, for all the ugliness of being punished for loving men, nobody read his lines and asked him: "What does your husband think of that?" Jail, exile—these were his lot. But never "What does your husband think?"

Women may have the vote, but they are not free as long as that reaction erupts. Even those *without* husbands are judged as if they had offended them merely by writing the truth.

So immovable is the wall around a woman's freedom that she can't do a thing without being asked to think of its effect upon some man who is presumed to be more important than she.

So it is with women's sexuality. It is always put at the disposal of the species. For this reason, it is hard even to *locate* your fantasy—let alone express it. Even the dream world is hedged about with prohibitions.

I am a method writer. I need to experience the things I write about. Are they horrific? So much the better. Deep into *Any Woman's*

Blues, my novel about an artist in eighties New York, I decided that sadomasochism was a part of my story. I knew nothing about its official side—bondage parlors, chains, whips—all I knew about sadomasochism came from my family. But I decided to learn. I used the journalist's ploy. I went to "interview" a dominatrix.

She was thrilled to be interviewed. She had only one request: that I use her real name in anything I wrote. That was the one request I couldn't fulfill. Was this the beginning of our sadomasochistic relationship?

Of course she opened her "studio" to me and let me observe. And of course she told me everything about herself. But there was more she wanted. She wanted me involved in her life.

"I am sending my personal slave to get you and bring you to my studio," she said on the phone one day.

And sure enough, a smiling girl in black tights and a black sweater arrived in a black radio cab to take me to the mirrored midtown highrise where Madame X worked. I had never been with a "personal slave" before, and I wondered what the etiquette was.

The girl's body language said, "Abuse me." She cowered. She was a girl, not a woman. How I knew this I cannot say.

At the studio—a three-bedroom apartment on the thirty-ninth floor—there were three mistresses ready for action. One was model-slim, red-haired, and wore a black rubber jumpsuit, one was blonde and elegant, with razor cheekbones and a red velvet dress that unzipped everywhere, and one was black-haired, with a gamine face and legs, in black velvet boots, that went on forever. All of them were students. One was getting a Ph.D. in English.

Disguised in a rubber face mask with zippered mouth, I had free run of the fantasies. I wandered at my will from room to room.

How clichéd they all were! Enemas, racks, nooses, stocks. And how repetitive were the postures of subjugation. Flat on your back, on your belly, or kneeling like a submissive shoe salesman. The main thing was—nobody touched. The main thing was—to be out of control.

If you are chained and subjected to sexual fantasies against your will, you have both pleasure and a total absence of responsibility. It is a little like my twelve dancing princesses. You are doing it in a dream, therefore you are not doing it.

Is my waiting at the palazzo a version of the same thing? I, too, am out of control. I, too, long for the lover who may let me just kiss his shoe.

It is a game of abstinence: You are teaching yourself to live on air. It is minimalist sex. You get so little that you think you've had enough.

I had had enough of S&M from this visit, but Madame X had not. She wanted me back for more. She wanted to introduce me to friends in Paris, in Milan, in Rome, who did Black Sabbaths and were looking for new blood. The world of S&M was international. Its denizens had frequent-flyer miles.

In Paris, I met the wife of a famous opera singer who was reputed to be the founder of a celebrated dungeon of love. We sat in the Crillon lobby at teatime and talked about Proust. The lady was so demure. I didn't even believe she had a body, let alone a body in bondage. She was off to a music festival in Prague. She did not give me the key to her love-dungeon.

I admit my research has not been very deep, but I have not been awed by the S&M I've seen.

"My" dominatrix wants fame more than she wants sex. She has hired a flack. Open any glossy magazine and you will see her picture. She has blown her secret to the world. Once that happens, she can never evoke forbiddenness again. She can only have call-in shows like Dr. Ruth, advertise condoms, douches, and eventually adult diapers on TV. She has joined the world of commerce, and when you do that, Pan deserts you. All the rubber suits in the world cannot save you then.

My heart flies into my mouth when I hear a motorboat on a canal. My erotic gear are: sailboats, the Mediterranean sun, a lover I would never in a million years take as a husband.

I don't believe you can standardize fantasy. By its nature, fantasy is unique. I have thumbed through books of fantasies, looking for my own, and I cannot find them. Madame X says she will set up "scenes" for me in foreign cities. It is not because of AIDS that I refuse or even because of what my husband might think. I refuse because I am afraid of the loneliness. When you exit the S&M studio and go out into the blinding sunlight, having seen what you have seen, you are more alone than ever. That's the terrible secret O* knew.

Boats are erotic, so are cars, so are trains. On a rocking train, going through a mountain tunnel, you can make love to the man

---

* The eponymous heroine of *Story of O*.

opposite you, part, then rearrange your clothes as if nothing has happened. In the wink of an eye, you are taken and given back. This is the lightning flash of sex under the eyelid. Is it the tempter who tempts you, that dybbuk, yourself?

Why won't the Royals give us some royal sex? It's nice to think of queens and princesses without knickers, but must they cavort with such moldering, moth-eaten men? And must they always pretend to need them for *other* reasons? *Financial advisor? Groom?* Wouldn't it be better to say Groom of Her Majesty's Pudenda?

If I were queen, I would have as many beautiful men as I wanted. Kill or castrate them later—or even marry them off. For centuries *men* did these things, and their cast-off consorts (Anne Boleyn, Catherine Howard) went to their bloody deaths singing the king's praises. Let women so much as say they won't do the dishes—and we are called bitches or whores. But admit to a fantasy like this and all hell breaks loose. Say it, ladies: You want to fuck them, then kill them, having had your way.

Unnatural monsters. Goneril, Regan, Lady Macbeth. What are they but women with the primal rage put back? And without that primal rage there *is* no sex. My personal slave would have to be male.

Years ago, there used to be a book in paperback racks called *The Power of Sexual Surrender.* What a démodé title by today's standards. Never having read the book, I can't comment on the contents. It was supposedly written by "Marie Robinson, M.D." Important to have M.D.s involved with sex books then. In actual fact, it was penned by a male writer and his psychiatrist wife. I met that writer later, when he married a poet friend of mine.

She was in love. She had surrendered. She told me that all of sex was surrender. She pointed to the title of the book. It was true, she said. She'd lived it and she knew.

Now, there are surrenders and surrenders. Surrendering to someone who embodies your fantasy is one thing. But surrendering to a rapist is another.

The possibility of sex is the possibility of surrender. Some people need costumes, faraway places, different languages, chains—and some people can get there quicker and with less fuss—but the fact of surrender is the same. *Story of O* works for me as no other book of erotica does because it captures that surrender. It doesn't tell you how to lead your life. It acknowledges that eros is something *apart* from, maybe even antithetical to life. So naturally it is condemned by those who want practical handbooks above all else. America has no place for fantasy. Books have to be didactic here—or else.

But fantasy can't be kept down completely. It will surface in romance novels, in horror, in thrillers.

Take us away, make us surrender! we cry. Give us a place where all bets are off. Give us a place where we can just relax! For centuries men have had brothels, but has there ever been a *women's* brothel? A cross between a health club and a beauty parlor, but staffed with beautiful, compliant men? (They would be AIDS-tested, of course.) You could go there for two hours between the office and home. No snitching to husbands. No snitching to kids. No good works. No fund-raising or volunteering. No career benefits. No networking. No interviews with Oprah or Sally Jessy. Why does this fantasy seem suspect?

Because some woman who saw you there and fancied your husband would blow the whistle on you, and the place would be raided.

Women don't protect each other's pleasures. They have so few of their own, they want other women to suffer too.

And then there is the question of *transport*. And I don't mean wheels. A woman in love nearly loses her mind. She cannot compartmentalize her sexuality in a *place*. After a while she would blow the system up. Just to prove the explosiveness of love. Women in groups tend to become puritanical. You won't find the Bacchae at your country club, the garden club, the wedding shower, the Girl Scouts! Even whores become puritanical in groups. What is more controlling and controlled than a harem?

What is this urge toward puritanism in women? Sex means too much to us. We lose ourselves. For generations, this was *literally* true: death in childbirth, death in compulsory pregnancy, and all the other travails of women's lot. We still have a racial memory of that lostness. We still are too much stirred by sex to let it be free.

That is why it is so hard to take male sexual fantasies and apply them to women. They just don't seem to fit. The anatomy is different, but so is the *context* of sex. A man compartmentalizes his cock. A woman's cunt is a metaphor for her being. She *wants* to be taken. She *wants* to be carried away.

For a number of years I was in group therapy. The members all were stars—artists, writers, actors, dancers. Some were straight, some gay, some bi—and all had sexual problems with their mate.

Not always. Sometimes. The more they loved, the more elusive sex became. It was not the lack of love that made for this, but the overabundance of it. And the fear of abandonment that overabundance wrought.

One man loved his wife too much to fuck her. When she went out of town, he always called his ex-girlfriend, the one he *hadn't* married. He would get hard just dialing her number. When he arrived at her apartment, his cock would be erect and there would be a wet spot on the front of his jeans.

One of the group members was an older gay man who had chosen to be celibate. He would bring home beautiful boys to befriend and mentor. While they slept in his son's room (the son had left for college), he'd fantasize about them and jerk off explosively. He never touched any of these boys, nor his wife, who was his best friend.

So it went around the circle. The actor became impotent with his wife when she had a hit movie and he didn't. The artist left his wife and moved to the mountains of Colorado with a ski instructor. Sex seemed a conundrum to one and all—mated sex, that is. Yet mating was what they all longed for—especially when single.

The therapist was a woman who believed in marriage. Her husband was the other therapist, who drowsed through the sessions, drowsed through all her brilliant interpretations.

As the evidence piled up that mated sex is an oxymoron, she analyzed and analyzed, analyzing this sexual anesthesia as fear.

At the time of the group, I was single. I was spreading my sexual life among three suitors, including Piero, and though it was often anarchic and not always satisfying, it was never dull.

Why did these people get married, I wondered, if marriage banished sex? They pitied me my single state. I was contemptuous of their married state. Yet I was also jealous. I longed for a mate, a partner, a best friend. I knew that marriage was a search for that.

Some members of the group parted from their mates, had affairs, remarried, got restless again. I eventually remarried too, finding great comfort in being able to blossom rooted in one place, great comfort in having that one best friend.

And yet the wildness doesn't go away. And the yearning doesn't go away. In dreams, in fantasies, it surfaces, provoking our most passionate thoughts.

We need a bacchanal, a Mardi Gras, a witches' sabbath, far more than we need all these divorces and remarriages. We need a place to dream, a place to meet the tempter under the eyelid. Video games won't do it. Not even virtual reality suits. They only condemn us to replay the video artist's cartoonish fantasies over and over again. We need corporeal fantasies, not fantasies embodied in film and chip. But we have outgrown the ancient mysteries of the vestal virgins, the corn goddess—or have we?

Last night, in the middle of this chapter, I went to sleep and dreamed. I dreamed I had a call from an old boyfriend named Laurence. He met me in Connecticut, near my house in the hemlock woods, and walked me through the underbrush and over the rock ledges. There in the New England woods was a formal garden I had known nothing of: arches, terraces, pastures, boxwood hedges in cunning Elizabethan forms—hearts, foxes, canopy beds. Through the garden we walked, looking for a private labyrinth in which to lie down.

Our families were pursuing us. There were shouts and giggles outside the hedges. But we pressed on, looking for sanctuary.

Then the scene shifted. I was walking up the stairs to a massage room high above the woods. Two women awaited me. One put special lenses inside my eyes to darken the room. Another took off my stockings and my bra. I was wearing no panties, but only a garter belt over my moist center. They laid me down on the table and began to lick me—therapeutically, of course. One licked my labia and sucked my clit while the other massaged my neck, my arms, my head, and licked my lips. The phone kept ringing, but I disregarded it. Laurence and Piero and my husband were all outside, knocking importunately on the door. Drowsily, I muttered, "Go away."

I woke up with the dew of the dream still between my legs.

Always in my dreams, I am journeying, searching for some fulfillment that never comes. The dream is the quest and the quest is the dream. If there is orgasm in the dream, it is usually incomplete. What is fulfilled does not provoke our dreams. The best marriage is usually like dreamless sleep: unconflicted, innocent.

I wake up to a big, bearded man who hugs me and brings me orange juice. My thighs are wet with dream longings. Is this a paradox? No more than life is.

"Tell me your fantasy," he says, "tell me." He reaches down between my legs. "You're so wet," he says.

"I was writing in my sleep," I say.

As this chapter has unfolded on my desk—these fantasies, reveries, memories—my waking life with my husband has become more and more sexual. We find ourselves making love every night, laughing and kissing in the morning. I find myself telling him my dreams and fantasies, reading him pages which excite him, teasing him like a new lover. We have gone into a domestic idyll.

This astonishes me. Each day I write that married sex is impossible. Each night I disprove it.

Perhaps the truth is that it is the sharing of fantasy honestly that makes sex possible and that mating in captivity is usually antithetical to this honesty. We fall into marital roles. We impersonate our parents. We forget the dreams and fairy tales that heated our adolescence. We allow anger to build its Berlin Wall.

And then the sex is gone. In America, we divorce and remarry. In Europe, we stay married and have "adventures." Nowhere do we confront the problem.

Marriage can only be free and sexual when it is not captivity. Marriage can only be sexual when the fantasy includes not being married. To be free in a marriage is perhaps the hardest challenge. We do not own each other's fantasies. All our closeness—sexual and otherwise—depends upon our knowing that.

Nor are we naturally monogamous. Whether we choose to act out our nonmonogamy or not, it resides in us and we eradicate it at our peril. A liberated woman is one who knows her own mind, and does not hide it. Her fantasies belong to her. She can share them if she chooses.

I know that sex in marriage comes and goes. Sometimes we bring our fantasies along and sometimes not. Sometimes we act out childish petulance, distance the person we depend on most, go to sleep and dream of others. That is only human. We are big-brained babies who have too much gray matter to be consistent. We would be happier if our frontal lobes were less busy—but we would also be less human. Humans are apes and angels both at the same time. That is why our sexuality is so complex. We dream things that are beyond our ken. We dream disturbing dreams.

Last night, I saw a film based on a friend's novel. In it, a man throws his whole life away for a few minutes of passion with a strangely beautiful, strangely sad girl who needs to disturb lives, inching them toward tragedy.

The audience tittered at the obsessive sex scenes. There was palpable discomfort in the air. They did not want to know that fantasies could invade our lives and turn them toward darkness. They did not want to believe in the destructive, obsessional power of sex.

And yet we all live balanced on a beam above chaos. We try to keep our lives in order, but chaos calls to us through sex, through illness, through death. AIDS and cancer lurk under our pleasures. The skull leers beneath the skin.

At nineteen, I went to Italy for the first time and stayed in a Florentine villa overlooking the Arno from the hill of Bellosguardo.

There, having gone to study Italian, I studied Italians instead, learning what so many American girls learned, that sex was better in a foreign tongue because guilt could be left at home.

In the somewhat ramshackle garden of the villa, between the boxwood hedges, and overlooking the twinkling city, I and my classmates learned the old approach-avoidance dance of passion.

Under the crickets' recitative, in the blue moonlight, I felt for the first time the sweet danger of sex.

I wrote a poem that summer as sharp as any poem I have since written. Even today, I do not know how I knew what I knew.

"When did the summer censor choiring things?" the poem asked. And it answered its own question.

"We know the blood is brutal—though it sings."

Where does politics enter in all this?

Some women I know have given up men because they cannot stand the pain.

What pain?

The pain of seeing fifty-year-old men going out with twenty-eight-year-old "stepdaughters," the pain of waiting for telephone calls that never come, the pain of needing too much, wanting too much, the pain of being sick of needing too much, and so deciding, once and for all, to stop wanting men.

You can train yourself to this. You can be like the man who trains his horse to need less and less food, and who is astonished when at last the horse dies. You can live without hugs, without fucks. You can seal off your skin, your eyes, your mouth.

But sooner or later love will come to claim you. You will dry up like a brittle flower and a breath of wind will blow your pale powder away.

I would rather stay open to love even though love means disorder, possibly pain. How many times have I redone the curtains and bookshelves? How many times have I undone my life?

I hate the chaos, but it has also kept me young. Anarchy is the sacred fount of life, and sex breeds anarchy. The pagans understood this better than we do. They made spaces in their ordered lives for anarchy. All we have left of this is Mardi Gras.

I hate the American way of sex. One decade we pretend to fuck everyone, the next decade we pretend to be celibate. Never do we balance sex and celibacy. Never do we acknowledge the search for Pan and the search for solitude—the two poles of a woman's life. Never do we acknowledge that life itself is a mixture of sweets and bitters.

Feminists can be the worst puritans of all. Since maleness is a force for disorder, let's get rid of maleness altogether, some would say. Only impotent men pass muster. Only gay men are thought to be pure. Women today find themselves in a tautological trap. Bad boys turn us on, but bad boys are politically incorrect. Does this mean that being *turned on* is politically incorrect? To some, it does.

I have also run from sex at times in my life. I can be a puritan too. But I know it is important to *fight* my own puritanism. I know that the mouth of Bacchus is full of purple intoxication. His mouth may also be full of pointed teeth—but beauty lives there. Beauty is always intimate with danger. Beauty is always intimate with death.

7

SEDUCING THE MUSE

Think you, if Laura had been Petrarch's wife,
He would have written sonnets all his life?

—George Gordon, Lord Byron, *Don Juan*

A more important form of optimism concerns your attitude to
your work. . . . Try to get away from that "succeed or fail" attitude . . . get *absorbed* in it, as you are in a window box or an
interesting conversation or redecorating a room . . .

—Antonia White, *Diaries 1926–57*

When did I first discover that sex and creativity were allied? It was
1969 and I was twenty-seven. I'd had three and a half years of analysis in Germany—an analysis that focused on my writing blocks and on
my marriage. If it did not make me wholly free, at least it gave me a
taste for freedom.

Nineteen sixty-nine was the year sex was discovered. (Philip
Larkin says it was 1963.) It was the year of the moon shot, of male
astronauts walking on the female moon and planting their spikes in
what was called "One small step for a man, one giant leap for
mankind."

Womankind was not much thought of in all that phallic blasting,
phallic thrusting. We were an afterthought, born out of rebel ribs, but
the times they were a-changin'. With the Beatles romancing the radio,
with astronauts seducing space, with civil rights marchers fucking the

Old Confederacy, with campus protesters screwing the Vietnam War, it wouldn't be long before feminism reared its Medusa's head.

After a sojourn in my own Third Reich, I was primed for protest. On August 26, 1970, I marched through Central Park with my sisters, celebrating women's rights, decrying women's wrongs. Hope was rampant. We expected nothing less than to change the world. Instantly.

By the time my first book of poems, *Fruits & Vegetables,* came out in 1971, the second wave of feminism was crashing on our shores. Women were in again—and sex was in again. But not for long.

I had come back from gray and rainy Germany to a brilliant world I hardly recognized. On the streets of New York: afros, bell-bottoms, dashikis, Nehru jackets, tie-dye, platform shoes, Zuñi jewelry, the scent of marijuana, headbands to hold in blitzed brains.... The world had gone *wild* while I was in Heidelberg learning to write. I wanted to go wild with it.

Sartorial madness was something I knew from my mother's taste in clothes—clothes that could double as costumes for her portrait sitters. And wildness was incipient in my Music and Art days. I dressed like a beatnik *then*, but I had made the decision to turn preppy in college. Because my parents had been Provincetown bohemians in the thirties, my early rebellion was to be square. I had become a "good wife" (who cooked steamed rice for her Chinese-American husband). I had repressed my rebellion. Now I wanted more than anything to be bad!

There had been previews of my *fin de sixties* madness in Heidelberg. I'd smoked hashish at student parties and wished to God I weren't married. I'd watched the students hurling cobblestones, mimicking their Parisian counterparts, as they chanted *Ho Ho Ho Chi Minh, Ho Ho Ho Chi Minh, Ho Ho Ho Chi Minh* (with German accents) down the Hauptstrasse. But it was not my culture, and by New York standards, Heidelberg was as provincial as Schenectady.

The German students of the sixties were protesting their Nazi parents; the American students were protesting *their* World War II daddies (who'd really believed that Vietnam was the same as the Land of the Rising Sun). A generational war was raging. It hardly mattered whether your parents had been Nazis or not; it was enough that they were *parents*. And parents had to be crushed.

We called *their* country *Amerika*. What was our country? Woodstock? Haight-Ashbury? Beatlemania? *The Whole Earth Catalog?*

The Forest of Arden—with love beads? Marijuana was our weapon; so was long hair; so was sex. Had our parents settled down to have babies after their war? Well then, we would *never* settle down. We would have sex, sex, sex, and refuse to grow up! We followed our leaders—or at least our lead singers: *All you need is love, love, love . . .*

In 1969–70, I went back to Columbia, this time to the School of the Arts, to study poetry. I also taught at City College again, as a lowly instructor, then as a lowly assistant professor—sans health insurance, sans job security, sans everything. I grew to love my students. I was moved to lie down on the streets of the West Side with them to protest the Kent State massacre. Eyes to the sky, we stretched out on the blacktop of Amsterdam Avenue outside the Riverside Funeral Home. Corpses dying to get buried, and we were holding up the hearses. I will never forget the policemen circling and the street lights flashing green then red then green then red as we kept that silent vigil outside the funeral parlor. Even death stopped for us.

I had just encountered the brave new world of open enrollment at City College. Bright students whom no one had ever bothered to teach to read and write, not-so-bright students who proved ultimately ineducable, were thrown at us to rescue. Remedial teaching at the college level infuriated the tenured staff—which was odd because they didn't have to *do* it. They had *us* for that.

Sometimes it was exhilarating; sometimes it was impossible. My best times were always with my older students: the housewives and office workers who'd come back to school at night. They *got* it when Othello killed Desdemona in a jealous rage, or when Lady Macbeth egged Macbeth on to bloody his hands. They'd seen plenty of Othellos and Lady Macbeths by this time. They could easily relate Shakespeare to life in the ghetto. These students were survivors. Learning turned them on.

"Miss Mann," they'd say, "does all *littershure* have so much sex in it?"

The bourgeois day students from the Bronx couldn't be bothered to ask.

At the Columbia School of the Arts, I promptly fell for both my poetry teachers—Stanley Kunitz (another literary grandfather) and Mark Strand (a beautiful bad boy, the only poet in America who is a dead ringer for Clint Eastwood). I used to stare at Mark in class—his perfect, chiseled profile, his chilly, cynical eyes, and begin poems to him that would turn out never to be about him.

If he's my dream he will fold back into my body
His breath writes letters of mist on the glass of my cheeks
I wrap myself around him like the darkness
I breathe into his mouth
& make him real

"The Man Under the Bed" (described in that stanza) became the universal bogeyman, vampire, night crawler every girl hears breathing under her bed, waiting to entrap her—she hopes. Mark was that fantasy man. He was also Gulliver striding through Lilliput, aloof to all us scurrying Lilliputians. We frantically threw tiny ropes around his huge legs.

I want to understand the steep thing
that climbs ladders in your throat
I can't make sense of you.
Everywhere I look you're there—
a vast landmark, a volcano
poking its head through the clouds
Gulliver sprawled across Lilliput.

Mark taught in a chilly, almost disdainful way—as if students were hardly worth bothering about. But he turned us on to Pablo Neruda and Rafael Alberti, and he freed me from compulsive rhyming, encouraged me to try prose poems and to jump into my images. He also excited me—which taught me more about poetry than anything. I would go home and write poems to the impossible he—the he of my dreams—Adonis, father, grandfather, with Clint Eastwood and the exhibitionist on the subway thrown in. What we fear we also desire, and what we desire we fear. Masculine menace was in those early poems, but also a real yearning for an unknown lover. Allan and I fucked, but we had long since ceased to be lovers—if a lover is defined as someone you yearn for. I was writing poetry and madly yearning. Those yearning poems went into *Fruits & Vegetables* and *Half-Lives*.

The more I yearned, the more I wrote. Yearning is an essential emotion for a poet.

Is the yearning spiritual or sexual? Who's to say the two are not the same? Rumi and Kabir and most of the Persian poets see them as aspects of the same force—but then, of course, the Persians invented love. Héloïse and Abélard discovered how close the two were—to their infinite regret. Only Protestant puritanism has built a wall between physical yearning and the yearning for God.

In Mark's class, I yearned for God in man, and in Stanley's class for man in God. I was less terrified of Stanley than I was of Mark. Stanley was cuddly; Mark was aloof. At twenty-seven, I found aloof sexier. Even my then-husband was chilly and distant. I couldn't imagine a lover who was not like my husband—a more frequent occurrence than we care to admit.

That first year, back from Germany, I worshipped weekly at the 92nd Street Y. The poetry flavor of the week had my undivided attention. I also haunted poetry festivals, poetry cafés, poetry bars.

In love with poetry, I thought I could live on air. In love with poetry, I thought I could live with Allan.

When Yehuda Amichai, the Israeli poet, came to New York, we read poetry together at Dr. Generosity's, passed the hat, and collected $121—mostly in silver. We split it, both agreeing it was the best money either of us had ever earned. It still is.

Dr. Generosity's was dark, beery, full of sawdust and peanut shells. Poets, wannabes, and sad sacks turned out. Also crazies. Poetry readings were always well-supplied with crazies. One such threatened to shoot me before one of my first readings in Philadelphia. He had written me a yearning letter that I had failed to answer. His blood boiled and he vowed revenge. It can't have been fatal attraction: I'm still here.

The truth is: Nobody *bothers* to kill poets in America. It's enough to bury them in universities. Undead.

It was a time of festivals for women poets. Carolyn Kizer and I met en route to one. We were seated right behind the driver. Carolyn began a wonderful monologue about her life as a woman poet. I was proud to be her confidante.

"Then I woke up, with Norman Mailer sitting on my face!" she said at the end of a long tale.

The bus nearly swerved off the road.

I met the dashing, sinister Ted Hughes after his reading at the

92nd Street Y. In my copy of *Crow* he wrote: "To a beautiful surprise, Erica Poetica." Then he filled the half-title page with a phallic snake curling through a new poem about Crow.

"In lapidary inscriptions a man is not upon oath," Dr. Johnson said. But poets often pimp with book inscriptions.

I went to dinner with Ted (and his entourage) and we flashed eyes at each other all night. In those days, Ted Hughes had a reputation in feminist circles for being a lady-killer, or indeed the devil incarnate. This only made him more exciting. I grew wet, imagining the handsome hulking author of *Crow* in bed. Then I fled in a taxi—fighting my own fantasies. Sylvia Plath and Assia Gutmann floated before my eyes like Shakespearean ghosts, warning me. I knew I wanted to write and live, not write and die.

Why was it always the fate of women poets to *die*? Were we punishing ourselves for the presumption of the pen? Were we trying to undo our lives to undo that presumption? Had we internalized the punitive rules of the game? (For even then I did not believe that Sylvia Plath's suicide was anyone's choice, finally, but her own.) Still, I understood how hard it was to be a woman poet in a literary world in which the rules were made by men.

In Chicago for a celebration of *Poetry* magazine, I collided with a beautiful young Southern poet (whom I will not name in the unlikely event that he is still with his wife). This poet wrote about his search for himself, his thwarted hankering for love, the many frustrations of his interminable marriage, his endless and unappeasable yearning.

Yearning was my middle name. So we went back to the Lake Shore Drive apartment of one of the moneybags behind the poetry festival (the poets were all put up in maids' rooms of these glorious mansions in the air), crept stealthily past the Jasper Johnses, the Motherwells, the Rothkos, the Frankenthalers, the Nevelsons, the Calders, the Rosenquists, the Dines, through the kitchen into the maid's room, where we made tender love all night. At dawn, we woke (as if to an explosion) and walked along Lake Michigan. We had not really felt welcome with the rich folks anyway. And we were suddenly seized with guilt about our spouses.

At home, I wrote poems to him—or whomever he represented—and he wrote poems to me—or whomever I represented. We corresponded for a while. We still send each other sweetly autographed books.

These encounters somehow fueled my first two volumes of poems. They also led ineluctably to *Fear of Flying*. "The muse screws," I used to joke. Flippant but true. In *The White Goddess,* Robert Graves says that true poetry springs from the relationship between the muse (the White Goddess) and the poet. It relies on the poet's erotic knowledge of her, embodied in an earthly woman. Graves followed his own theory with increased desperation as he aged. Eventually, he became a parody of his younger self. Henry Miller did likewise—if only in the area of "love." When he wasn't being a sage, he was being an old goat—wisdom side by side with low burlesque. Many aging poets find they have to crank up poetry with "love." What comes naturally in youth becomes the ultimate self-deception of age.

The muse, for a woman poet, has historically been a male adventurer: Adonis, Orpheus, Odysseus. Since a woman poet also discovers inspiration through her solar plexus, the prohibition against women's sexuality has hurt us creatively as much as it has hurt our pleasures.

There were quite a lot of muses in those days. I usually kept them sacred by never "knowing" them in the flesh. And those I fucked, I quickly fled, turning them into pen pals.

I was seeking inspiration, not relationships—whatever they may be. All I could deal with were relation-dinghies or relation-surfboards. I had to get home *fast* and write it all down. That was, after all, the point. Besides, I didn't want to be disappointed by a mortal man. I wanted a muse, who, by definition, only appears in moments of ecstasy and is never given the chance to disappoint. He is the prince who may revert to a frog if you take him in, the Odysseus who may revert to a pig. If you don't linger, you'll never know. And you'll have the poem.

Every time I have set out to achieve something in my life, it has been total immersion. At that time, poetry was my element. It was bread and breath to me, husband, lover, child. Allan was just a shadowy companion, a crow sitting in a tree.

Poetry remains my solace still. I actually *read* other people's poems. Poetry refills the well when I am empty. Poetry finds me when I am lost. The temporary trauma of a painful relationship, the career disappointments, the pains of motherhood, the deaths of friends, are healed by poetry. If I let myself surrender to poetry, eventually it will bring me to the next novel, predicting its themes.

Novices in the arts think you have to start with inspiration to write or paint or compose. In fact, you only have to *start*. Inspiration comes if you *continue*. Make the commitment to sit still in solitude several hours a day and inevitably your muse will visit. "I write fifty pages until I hear the fetal heartbeat," Henry Miller used to say.

The very mechanical act of sitting down in privacy, turning off the phone, giving yourself the time to play and make mistakes, being non-judgmental with yourself, knocking the censors off your shoulders, is enough to get anyone going. *It's not etched in stone,* I tell myself. *You can always edit and rewrite later. You don't even have to publish if you don't want to. This is just for you.*

I write as if for *samizdat,* not above-ground publication. All my writer friends from the Eastern Bloc tell me that *samizdat* gave a more intimate tone to books. They felt they were writing for friends, not enemies. They felt they were writing letters—letters to themselves.

The permission to fail, plus certain artificial goals—*I will write ten handwritten pages, then stop*—often works. It also defeats the habitual self-flagellation that accompanies the writer at work. If you dare to play, you can risk everything on the page.

Submitting poems for scrutiny was another matter. At first it was impossible for me. My anxiety was so great that I heard jeers of derision when I even *thought* about sliding a sheaf of poems into an envelope. I solved this pragmatically. In Heidelberg, I bought myself a three-by-five-inch plastic box and named it: POEMS SENT OUT. On each card was a date, a list of poems, the magazine sent to, and the date of acceptance or rejection. This was simply a way of fooling my fear. If I couldn't lose the fear, at least I could contain it in a plastic box.

"I will know I'm a terrible poet when this box is filled," I told myself. I had published a book of poems before the box was even partly full.

Was my threat to myself hollow? Poets are not made by editors' approval but by their own *self-approval,* as the fates of Emily Dickinson and Walt Whitman remind us.

When the plastic box is full of rejections, the real poet will simply say: "If the second box is full, or the third, or the fourth . . . " but she will keep sending her poems out—if only to toughen her hide.

Was I a real writer or was I only a hound for approval? I became famous so young that I could hardly know. I only learned the truth later when the approval stopped and I went on writing anyway.

Sooner or later, *every* artist encounters rejection—even the most famous. If you persevere a lifetime with your work, it *must* go through periods of being out of sync with the politics or literary theories of your time. And you must work *past* that, even if it means rejection. Politics change. But the time to work can never be brought back.

Nabokov would be astonished to see his work in print all over Russia. He predicted that would never come to pass.

Rejection from outside is always better than inwardly rejecting your writer-self. Your writer-self is all you have to deal with. If you deprive yourself of that, you will never come to know how ultimately unimportant outer rejection is. But if you ally yourself with the forces of rejection, you will have committed creative suicide. The bastards will not only have got you down, they will have killed you, with your own enthusiastic complicity.

My poetry mania led me annually to assemble collections and send them to contests that promised publication of a first book. Each year from 1967 to 1970, I collected what I thought were my best poems (some revised within an inch of their lives), arranged them by theme, gave them titles and half titles, and sent them off to University Press X, University Press Y, and University Press Z—each of which had a literary lottery. I had no notion of how to contact a commercial publisher, and anyhow a university press seemed more elegant to me, with my graduate school snobbery (or fear of rejection in disguise). Even then New York publishers were phasing out poetry, but it hadn't quite reached the final solution stage yet.

The first collection I submitted was *Near the Black Forest*. Weighted with poems about my discovering my Jewishness in Germany, it contains things I still read with an occasional intake of breath, wondering *how did this little pisher know that?* The following collection, called *The Tempter Under the Eyelid*, contained the best of the Heidelberg poems, plus a sheaf of new ones about seducing the muse, marrying poetry, chasing after love in fruit and vegetable form. The third collection, *Fruits & Vegetables*, took this tendency even further. It was full of ironic poems about the poet in the kitchen, the poet as housewife, sex, love, feminism, and whiplash womanhood. Freer than the first two—in both form and content—the collection still (mostly) pleases me. I was peeling the onion of myself, and finding in that pungent vegetable my own endlessly shedding soul.

By the time I came to assemble *Fruits & Vegetables*, I was furiously impatient for publication. It seemed that only a published book of poems could give me what I lacked. Little magazines and poetry quarterlies no longer satisfied. I was hungry to be heard by my contemporaries. I believed a volume of poems would change my life. I was fretting to become one of the unacknowledged legislators of womankind, to reach the huge audience of poetry lovers I believed was out there, to lash the world with poetry and bring it to its senses.

How entirely mad these assumptions seem now! I lived for poetry, so I assumed the world did. By now my duo of poetry mentors had become a triumvirate. Louis Untermeyer, that defiant Old Red and indefatigable anthologist, had joined Mark Strand and Stanley Kunitz in my personal pantheon. Louis had seen one of my poems in a dismal quarterly and had written me a letter: "What are you doing in that mass of mediocrity?" It was the literary equivalent of "What's a nice girl like you doing in a place like this?" Soon after, he invited me to his Connecticut house for dinner, and we fell immediately in love—as only a poet of twentysomething can fall in love with an anthologist of eightysomething (and vice versa).

There followed many other literary dinners—dinners with Arthur Miller and Inge Morath, Howard and Bette Fast, Muriel Rukeyser, Robert Anderson and Teresa Wright, Arvin and Joyce Brown, Martha Clarke, and any number of other poets, playwrights, novelists, actors, dancers, directors, and Old Reds.

Because of Louis and his wife, Bryna, I believed that Connecticut was a low-key New England version of Mount Olympus. Because of Louis and Bryna, I met the Fasts, who introduced me to my daughter's father. Because of Louis and Bryna, I revised the poetry book yet again.

So I sent the *new* collection to X, Y, and Z. Through a fluke of fate, which really turned out to be a major synchronistic miracle, I also sent it to Holt, in those days called Holt, Rinehart & Winston.

I had come home from Germany the summer before our "tour of duty" ended, to find my grandmother dying. She languished on her real linen sheets, gazing out her sunny West Side window. She was altering her clothes to make them smaller—"so I will have something to wear when I go out again." But she never went out again. The pancreatic cancer killed her faster than AIDS killed my friend Russell. But we were both denying cancer. Neither of us mentioned the word.

She asked me weakly what I was doing. "Working on my poems," I said tentatively. Not tentatively at all, she admonished me: "Go see Gracela, Gracie, Grace." (My grandmother always tripled or quintupled names, often calling me "Erica, Claudia, Nana, Edichka, Kittinka.")

"Gracela, Gracie, Grace" was the daughter of an old friend of my grandparents', an indomitable Russian lady named Bessie Golding.

Grace and I later discovered that Bessie had been my grandfather's lover while my grandmother was waiting in London to be summoned to the Golden Land. This only took eight years.

When Mama arrived in New York, Papa immediately found a proper communist husband for Bessie. Ever after, he described her as "an anarchist, a follower of Emma Goldman, a believer in free love." In short, the opposite of my proper grandmother, who believed in real pearls, creamy kid gloves with pearl buttons, real linen sheets, real linen tablecloths with monogrammed napkins, duvets with embroidered covers. She also believed in fresh-squeezed orange juice, cod liver oil, soft-boiled eggs with toast "soldiers" (strips to dunk), and English chesterfield coats with velvet collars for little girls. She also believed in leather leggings. But not free love. She definitely did not believe in that.

So off I went with my poems to Gracela, Gracie, Grace (the product of Bessie and the proper communist my grandfather had fixed her up with). I had my three consecutive manuscripts of poems in a tough black morocco spring binder.

The crosstown bus took me near Park and Sixty-eighth, where Grace (who had spent her life in publishing) now worked for *Foreign Affairs* magazine.

With its band of limestone nautilus and scallop shells, its imposing limestone facade, Roy Cohn's limousine (RMC-NY) double-parked across the street, the Council on Foreign Relations, which published *Foreign Affairs*, was an awesome place. A nest of WASPs, a covey of Calvinists, a hutch of Harvard men, the Council emitted rumors of CIA manipulations. You could imagine James Bond being dispatched from there. And secret staircases, bookcases that revolved to reveal secret *oubliettes* for unnameably evil foreign agents, or man-eating sharks swimming in piss-warm pools sunk into the bedrock cellar floor.

I walked in boldly, concealing my timidity with my usual bullshit bravado. (More than afraid of *being* scared, I am afraid of *looking* scared—a legacy from my father.) I mounted the graceful curved stairs to Grace's office.

This office was a cave of books and flowers, of colorful prints and paintings. It was a pregnant sanctuary presided over by an incarnation of the great mother goddess: Grace. In those days, she was pudgy, with close-cropped pepper and salt hair and the flowing clothes fatties used to wear to disguise themselves from themselves.

I plopped myself down in the deep green leather chair next to her desk, crossed my legs under my red pleated miniskirt, adjusted my red linen vest and red flowered blouse. Crossing my legs in red platform sandals, I felt fashionable but powerless.

"How can I help you?" Grace asked, trying to make it easy. But it wasn't easy. I looked into Grace's soft brown eyes and could hardly speak.

"Mama says you write poetry," Grace said gently.

"I guess so, but it's probably not any good," I lied. I knew it was better than "not any good." That was my protective spell to blind all the evil eyes lurking in the walls.

"May I see?" The black morocco binder was wet from my sweaty palms.

"Do you really want to?"

"Or I wouldn't ask."

She took the book, flipped open to the title page, which by now read *Fruits & Vegetables*, opened to the first poem, and said quickly, "Poetry is so special; somebody's whole life framed in these wide white margins."

Then, silently, she began to read.

I fretted.

She's hating them, I thought, being polite to get rid of me, doing Mama a useless mitzvah because Mama's dying.

For about twenty minutes, she read, engrossed, not looking up.

Then she declared, "You're going to be the most famous woman poet of your generation."

It was as if an ocean wave had knocked me over. I was breathless.

But I said, "Thank you very much."

Then I dismissed her as a pushover.

"No—I mean it," she said. "These are wonderful poems. They have their own voice, their own humor, their own imagery. I want to send them to a friend at Holt."

"They're not ready. They have to be revised," I said.

"You can revise forever as a way of not risking publication," Grace said, knowing my games without even knowing me.

So I was pressed into leaving *Fruits & Vegetables* (already submitted to X, Y, and Z) with Gracela, Gracie, Grace. Unbeknown to me, she passed it on to Robin Little Kyriakis at Holt, who passed it on to Aaron Asher, the publisher.

Weeks went by. A book of poems always seems a rose petal fluttering down the Grand Canyon, but this seemed a daisy petal drifting into a time warp.

"They love me, they love me not," I told myself, preparing for the blow that would surely fall.

About two months later, I got a letter from X, offering publication, a letter from Y, offering publication, a letter from Z, saying I was first alternate. (Would I please submit again next year?)

The next day a letter from Holt arrived, unmistakably offering to publish *Fruits & Vegetables*.

Was I happy? I was too terrified to be happy.

Sheer panic claimed me, then guilt, then shame. I had broken the rule—quadruple-submitted—and now I would be exposed as a fraud. I had lied to *publishers at august university presses!* I had not disclosed my evil plan. I was desolate. Certainly nobody could protect me now. In less than thirty seconds, I had turned success into failure.

"The poets will hate me," I thought, tossing sleeplessly beside Allan. "I have done an immoral thing!"

How could I know that the poets would hate me *anyway* after *Fear of Flying*? And how could I know that I had absolutely no control over that?

I went to lunch with Aaron Asher and promptly fell in love with him. Blue eyes, wry humor, a fabled history of publishing Saul Bellow and Philip Roth. If he liked me, I *must* be good. The same spring *Fruits & Vegetables* came out, he published another unknown writer, called Toni Morrison. Her first novel, *The Bluest Eye*, had been turned down elsewhere because who would care about an ugly black kid called Pecola having her father's baby? In those days, black people were presumed not to read, and white people were presumed not to want to read about black people. Aaron had taste—and, perhaps more important, guts.

"Tell them you have to come to Holt because you also plan to write novels," Aaron said, scheming for a novel with poetry as lure. (How antique this now seems!) "Tell them *I'm* your publisher for everything!"

Thrilled that my work provoked such possessiveness, I went on agonizing. I tried to write the "Thanks but no thanks" letters to those university presses, but I was blocked. A big-time poet with a New York publisher? Me? A potential (poetential) novelist?

"Go write a novel," Aaron had said, "in the gutsy voice of those poems."

I refused to believe he meant it. And I continued to flagellate myself for this first little burst of success. It was too big for my mother's failures, my grandfather's failures. After all my painstaking work to reach this first rung, I could think of nothing but to sabotage my climb and fall back into my neurotic family.

This pattern has followed me all my writing life. I have hesitated, rewriting and rewriting books I should have launched into the world. The source of my fear? My family's anger. Exposure to their mockery—as unforgiving as my own.

When I moved West after *Fear of Flying* hit, I bought an inexpensive car, a Pacer, rather than my fantasy Rolls-Royce Corniche. What was I thinking? That a cheap car would let me be loved? I wanted to be loved much more than I wanted a Rolls. Until I stopped worrying about this, I couldn't work in peace.

Whether you are loved or not depends more on others than on anything *you* do. Talent is not finite. There's more than enough of it to go around. Talented people know they can use your achievement as inspiration. But stingy souls think that by tearing you down and also tearing down your work, they will prosper. They are wrong, of course, but all of this is out of your hands. You can only do the work. "The rest," as T. S. Eliot says in *Four Quartets,* "is not our business."

I finally found the courage to inform those patient university presses that I was engaged, or at least pinned. Then I signed with Holt as I was meant to do. Having sold the book myself, I now hired an agent to take a piece of it. An agent conferred credibility. I liked saying "my agent" to my parents and friends. My advance on *Fruits & Vegetables* was munificent for poetry: $1,200. The agent received $120, my abject gratitude, and the option on a novel called *Fear of Flying.*

Watch out, world. Another poet was about to vanish down the Grand Canyon.

But first I had to have a name.

I'd begun to publish under my maiden name, Erica Mann, which, after all, had always been my name. But when my Freudian husband said ominously, "The poet has no husband," I was wracked with useless guilt.

Instead of lobbing back, "Of course not! Poets are married to their muses!" I let him browbeat me into using his name.

To be fair, he would have been satisfied with "Erica Mann Jong." It was *I* who was fearful of being mocked as "a three-name lady poet." I toyed with "E. M. Jong" (to disguise my second-class sex), then with "Erica Orlando," after my favorite novel, then with "Erica Mann Jong," after my father and husband. I finally settled on Erica Jong because it sounded enigmatic, punchy, and had four beats, like my maiden name.

The decision to drop my maiden name was a decision to defy sexist mockery, but I fell into a sexist trap all the same. In my twenties I didn't yet know that *anything* women do—use three names, drop their maiden names, persist in being "Lucy Stoners" (women who keep their maiden names on principle)—they will be in the wrong simply because their choices are not faced by men. Eventually they will be mocked—like Hillary Rodham Clinton: damned if she does and damned if she doesn't, but evoking a secret shout of joy in all our hearts.

What's in a name? My father's disappointment that my name does not shine directly on his; my daughter's bewilderment at bearing the name of someone she's never met. (We called her Molly Miranda Jong-Fast. Molly so she would bloom and Miranda so all tempests would blow her home, Jong for my *nom de plume* and Fast for her father and his family.)

But a name also confers a legend. If it is taken with resentment to undo patriarchal black magic, then the bearer forever resents her own name.

My name was a dodge, a dodge of Allan's disapproval, a dodge of sexist gibes at "three-name lady poets," a dodge of Erika Mann, Thomas Mann's writing daughter, who inspired my name.

Fear is not a good reason for a name. A name should be taken as an act of liberation, of celebration, of intention. A name should be a magical invocation to the muse. A name should be a self-blessing.

Unfortunately "Erica Orlando" would have suggested Disney World and Florida to more people than it would have suggested Virginia Woolf to. And "Erica Porchia," after a South American poet I loved, would have eventually been made into a joke about my weight. I thought of calling myself "E. M. J. Parra" after Nicanor Parra, another favorite poet of mine, but that would have proved baffling, eventually even to me. And the made-up names I temporarily craved all sounded silly in the sunlight: E. M. Brontë, E. M. Bloomsbury, Erick de Jong. Besides, they were dishonest names for someone whose whole struggle was to be honest.

If I was a woman and a poet, so be it. I went with Erica Jong and made it lucky by inhabiting it. Now I would like to Rodhamize, with thanks to Hillary, and maybe I shall.

But Erica Mann Jong is, alas, just as patriarchal as Erica Jong. When Thomas Mann's daughter, Erika, was alive, the confusion of names bothered me. My parents had met and admired Thomas Mann. They loved his daughter's name and wished creativity upon me. *Erica* means white flower in German, and queen in old Scandinavian, but to them, it meant *writer.*

By now I am used to Jong, which rhymes with Viet Cong, dong, Ping-Pong, Hai Phong, song, tong, long, wrong, among, and young. I get mail from readers under "Dear Erika de Jong," "Dear Erica Mann Jong," "Dear Erica Mann Jong Fast Burrows," "Dear Asian-American Writer," and "Listen you kike commie porno bitch—Hitler should have finished the last of you!"

So what's in a name? Everything and nothing. Sometimes I just want to be Erica—as Colette (who first signed herself "Willy," then "Colette Willy," then "Colette Willy de Jouvenel") eventually became Colette. But "Colette" was, after all, her father's surname. It served as both first and last name for someone who would have otherwise wound up as Sidonie Gabrielle Colette Willy de Jouvenel Goudeket.

In names for women, I believe in self-invention: a name that embodies desire. It should be taken when you commit yourself to your life's work. Nothing should part you from it.

Is it too late for me? My writing name has already curiously fused with my essence. Perhaps I'll restore my maiden name (which is only, after all, my father's *nom de théâtre*: Mann). For twenty-three years, I was defiantly a "Mann." Then I submitted to Freudian marriage.

Perhaps when this book is finished, the author will appear.

Odd that it took me so long to find my name, because in Heidelberg I was lucky to have that rare sort of analysis that lays the groundwork for a writer's life.

My analysis could only have happened through the intervention of the angels of analysis. If the process works, it is usually because of them. They hover over consulting rooms on three continents, blowing analysands along like swollen-cheeked bearded winds on antique maps.

Stranded in Heidelberg with a husband I couldn't talk to, I found, through a shrink in New York, a certain Professor Herr Dr. Alexander

Mitscherlich. He was said to speak English. He happened to practice in Heidelberg.

The referring doctor was one I had consulted about my marriage-panic—my fear that marriage would enslave me to household duties, that it would interfere with writing.

"Nonsense," this analyst had said. "Men work at home too. They do the lawn, they fix things around the house, they take out the garbage. It's an equal responsibility, don't you think?"

I didn't. But I didn't have the feminist facts to prove it then. The problem still had no name. I thought *I* must be crazy.

Unlike the New York doctor who referred him, Dr. Mitscherlich was no sexist. Nor did he think in clichés. He'd fled Germany during twelve years of Nazi rule to live and practice in Switzerland and England. He had waited out the war. That didn't keep me—in my ignorance—from calling him a Nazi from the couch, which always made him deathly quiet.

It was October of our first year in Germany when I first took the trolley to his office. I entered the cobbled courtyard of a nineteenth-century clinic with high yellow walls. Tall, tilted windows winked down at me.

I climbed three steep flights. Dr. Mitscherlich lurked in his book-lined office. Oriental rugs were unfurled this way and that on the wooden floor. An old-fashioned analytic couch threatened me, and I refused to lie down.

"Sit opposite me then," the doctor said.

I obeyed.

He was athletic and tall, in his sixties. A long face, serious intense eyes of blue gray, thick glasses glittering as squarish oblongs, a quality of total attention.

He was wearing a white clinician's coat, a purple woven woolen tie, crepe-soled shoes that squeaked faintly as he walked. His white coat seemed a sort of *Engelhemd,* or "angel shirt" (as Germans call hospital gowns). Indeed, it seemed to angelize him. When I talked, his eyes belonged entirely to me.

Why had I come?

I was blocked in my writing, blocked in my marriage, homesick for New York, glad to be away from my family. I needed my husband. I hated my husband. I was bored with my husband. I wanted to write. I couldn't write. I couldn't send work out because I was forever revising it. I stood in my own way. I knew that I didn't want to end up blocked and bitter.

From the first session on, he took me seriously, took my poetry seriously—even before he had much reason to.

I soon surrendered to the couch, from which I could scan the book titles in English, German, Hungarian, Czech, French, Italian, Spanish. I remembered my dreams and related them.

Meandering from dreams to memories, to my life in Heidelberg, I simply "taught the unhappy present to recite the past," until sooner or later "it faltered at the line where/Long ago the accusations had begun"—as Auden describes the process in his poem about Freud. There the needle stuck in the groove, pricking my heart until I said what the pain was.

Analysis is surrender—and who *wants* to surrender? No one. We fight till we have no other option, till the pain is so great we must. The ego wants brute power—and health be damned. The ego prefers death to surrender. But life keeps trying to assert itself. We keep stumbling over the same blocks until one day, after some trivial unraveling, the floor seems clear enough for us to walk a little way without tripping.

So it goes—Monday after Monday, Tuesday after Tuesday, Wednesday after Wednesday, Thursday after Thursday, Friday after Friday. It gets easier for a while, then it gets harder. It gets boring, then bearable, then impossible again. We keep on as if inching along on a novel we have come to hate. Only the discipline of finishing carries us through. And somewhere toward the end, the light shines again, as if through a clerestory window.

Dr. Mitscherlich's Heidelberg office had clerestory windows. Those remain my metaphor for the way analysis began to shed light on my pain. Gray days followed one another endlessly; it rained and rained, as it always does in Germany. One day, the rays of sun were pouring in.

At the end of my first year of analysis, Dr. Mitscherlich moved his office to Frankfurt. From my gloomy army apartment, it was a fifteen-minute car ride to the Heidelberg Bahnhof, a one-hour train ride to Frankfurt, a twenty-minute trolley ride to the Sigmund Freud Institute.

I rarely missed a session.

I had just stopped calling Dr. M. a Nazi—having learned that his silence concealed his reputation as an anti-Nazi, as an author, as a researcher into the conditions that had made Nazism thrive. The *fatherless society* was the term he coined. He had become famous for his theories of the underlying causes of Nazism. He was a star and I hadn't even known it. More important, he always treated *me* like a star long before I was one. His belief in me made my whole creative life possible.

I commuted from Heidelberg to Frankfurt as if my life depended on it. It did.

I'd leave the house at 7:20, arrive at the Heidelberg station at 7:35, park my old Volkswagen Beetle (or "Beatle" as I liked to call it), catch the 7:50 train to Frankfurt/Darmstadt, arrive at Frankfurt Bahnhof at 8:52, wait for the 9:07 trolley (in any weather), then walk several blocks to be in Dr. M.'s waiting room at the institute by 9:40. My hour began at ten o'clock sharp.

I've never made such complicated arrangements and kept them, except when in love.

I suppose I was.

Four days a week, I took the same long journey back, running to catch the twelve-something train, reaching my apartment in Heidelberg by 1:30 or 2:00.

There was grocery shopping to do, three hours to write, dinner to cook. There were army shindigs at night that officers and their *Frauen had* to attend. The shlepping to Frankfurt never stopped seeming worthwhile. There were only two days when I sabotaged the schedule and missed the train. On both occasions I was standing on the platform and staring after it.

The train became my life. I read, wrote in my notebook, scribbled poems and stories. The rocking motion soothed me and erotic fantasies came. I scrawled them down, made fables of them, explored them with Dr. M.

Fear of Flying somehow emerged from those train rides. On trains you can dream that the man opposite you will take off his thick glasses, strip to his savage loincloth, and make passionate love to you in an endless tunnel, then disappear like a vampire into the sunlight. The train rocks you back and forth on your wettest dreams; it merges the moist divide between inner and outer. I have come on trains without touching myself. It is only a matter of concentration. The impossible he (or she) comes *into* me. The fantasy takes over. Time stops as the train rocks. Suddenly my lap is full of stars.

After three years, I parted from Dr. M., promising to write. And I did: letters, poems, novels.

He had shown me how. He had taught me to find the courage to climb down into myself. The unconscious is full of darkness, Oedipal stand-ins, broken legends, half-told tales. A shaky ladder with rotten rungs descends into it. Another golden ladder may take you to the stars. But first you must find yourself in the dark. If you don't know yourself, how can you find anything?

"How can I receive the seeds of freedom," asks Thomas Merton, "if I am in love with slavery and how can I cherish the desire of God if I am filled with another and an opposite desire? God cannot plant his liberty in me because I am a prisoner and I do not even desire to be free."

The analytic journey had at least made me *desire* to be free.

"The only true joy on earth is to escape from the prison of our own false self"—Merton again. He was describing the search for the contemplative life. But writing also requires the contemplative life.

Psychoanalysis is dismissed today as elitist, sexist, and self-indulgent. I disagree. How can you love yourself as a woman if you are looking at yourself through a wall of knives? And how can you love your sister if you think those knives are made of steel rather than of your own fear? As women we need to know ourselves more than ever. We need the truths of the unconscious more than our mothers and grandmothers did. Cynicism and despair seduce us. We are afraid to let love in. We prefer "the rotten luxury of knowing [ourselves] to be lost," as Thomas Merton calls it.

Analysis can crack despair. It can be prayer and meditation both. But it requires a strong desire for change.

When I left Germany, I was writing fluently. I still flagellated myself, but not to the point of utter paralysis. I still trapped myself in despair, but at least I knew my despair was a flight from change.

I went back to the States with my poetry manuscripts. And I went home really slim. This had not been a goal of analysis, but suddenly I had fewer reasons to hide.

At twenty-seven, I had decided to be a writer. I thought I was *old* compared to Neruda, who published at nineteen, *old* compared to Edna St. Vincent Millay, who wrote "Renascence" at twenty, *old* compared to Margaret Mead, who was already world-famous at twenty-seven. So I gave myself until thirty to make it, believing that once a book of poems was published, I would be happy forever. Hope was my jet-propellant.

How could I know that a published writer is hardly the happiest creature alive? "Ingrown toenails" Henry Miller called us. We sit and stew for years, picking lint out of our navels, only to experience that anticlimax, publication—which often confirms our worst fears, putting into print things only our most bitter enemies would say about us.

For a woman, the profession is doubly precarious. Sooner or later women writers come up against the problem that a woman who wields the pen is forever an outsider.

Women writers are expected to be girl guides through the swamps of heterosexual love. We are allowed to be pop novelists (coddled by the money men who run the congloms), but dismissed by the lit crit crowd as trashmeisters. We are allowed to write fleshly fables to be used as anodynes by other women, bromides to content them with their horrid lot. When we don't, but give vent instead to satire or the creation of perverse imaginary worlds, we are faulted not for our books but for our imperfect *womanhood,* since womanhood is, by definition, a fault.

Why? Because it is not manhood.

But what would my life have been like had I been born a man? My husband tries to convince me that given *my* family, I would have been forced into servitude in the tchotchke business and would never have become a writer at all.

"You only *escaped* by being born a woman," he says. "Had you been the son, you would have spent your life peddling giftware."

Perhaps he's right, but I see another picture. I see myself having been given the automatic entitlement of the male creator: A man who writes is not automatically considered a usurper.

A male writer surely has to find his voice, but does he also have to first convince the world that he has the *right* to find his voice? A woman writer must not only invent the wheel, she must grow the tree and chop it down, whittle it round, and learn to make it roll. Then she must clear a path for herself (over the catcalls of the kibitzers).

Even today, when one woman's book is reviewed for three men's books, it is considered uncool to mention the percentages. It's not ladylike to remember that, but for our obstinate uncoolness, we'd still be one out of twelve.

I always identified with the male heroes in the books of my bookish childhood, so eventually I tried to write picaresque novels for women. At first I did this unconsciously *(Fear of Flying, How to Save Your Own Life).* Later I did it deliberately, mocking the picaresque form itself in *Fanny: Being the True History of the Adventures of Fanny Hackabout-Jones.* Virginia Woolf's question "What if Shakespeare had a sister?" had led me to wonder "What if Tom Jones had been a woman?" and to apply my love for the eighteenth century to my investigation of one eighteenth-century woman's fate.

By then I knew that I was consciously adapting a male heroic form to a woman's unheroic life. That was the fun of it.

Women have been allowed few heroic stories. The archetypes of wolf or moon goddess have only recently been revived. Under patriarchy, women's stories have invariably ended in marriage or death. All the other alternatives were deemed unfit for telling.

As a beginning writer in Heidelberg, I puzzled over these limitations and decided to write my first novel from a male point of view. I called the novel *The Man Who Murdered Poets*, and went as far with it as my imitation of Nabokov's mirror worlds could take me. Not far enough. Since I could not know what a man felt in his physical being, I halted, leaving the book unfinished.

Today perhaps I *could* write from a man's point of view. I have lived with enough men to know their feelings as if from the inside. But now I also know how *much* women need their own stories to be told.

Every writer, someone said, is either a man or a woman. But for a man, there is a mold to break or follow, for a woman, there is a beckoning void. Writers usually build on each other's foundations. I think of Byblos, of Split, of Istanbul. One civilization's rubble is remade into the architecture of another. Women writers have consistently hungered for this rich creative rubble. Doomed always to start from scratch, we have begun our civilization's records by fits and starts. Our matriarchs have been invisibilized, our myths obliterated. It seems we're always listening to famous male writers telling us what we're *not*.

In the past few years, we have invented some new forms and unearthed some old traditions. But our permission to be creators is still so unaccustomed that we tend to be ungenerous with each other. We prefer to denounce each other rather than denounce the self-appointed gurus who set us up as rivals.

As feminists, we ask literature to do more than literature ever can: fight the revolution, bury the dead, erect statues to our favorite heroines. That is hardly the way to stimulate a literature that mirrors life. Life is messier than politics usually allow, and less predictably pat. Life is merely *what happened next* and *to whom*. In asking life to be so purposefully political, we thwart our need to dream, to play, to invent.

In the name of feminism, some of us have forbidden women to be playful creators. Our pioneers—Mary Wollstonecraft, Mary Shelley, Jane Austen, Emily Dickinson, the Brontës, George Sand, Colette, Virginia Woolf, Simone de Beauvoir, Doris Lessing—would be horrified to see us banishing play and freedom from our art. Play is the ultimate source of freedom. If we become artists of agitprop, we might as well have been born in Mussolini's Italy, Hitler's Germany, or in Stalin's Soviet Union. Feminists above all must fight for freedom of expression, because otherwise we will be doomed to silence—with "decency" as the excuse.

But I hardly knew these things when *Fruits & Vegetables* was published in 1971.

It came out the same spring as Germaine Greer's *The Female Eunuch*. With a new burst of feminism in the air, it was warmly received. For a book of poems, that is.

My publisher made a party at a fancy fruit and vegetable stand, a place called Winter's Market on Third Avenue. The bright bins of fruit stepped out onto the sidewalk. The lemons and oranges gleamed in the sunlight.

I wore purple lace hotpants and a matching shirt with pockets strategically placed over the nipples. With purple granny glasses and purple shoes, I hoped I looked properly improper—as was de rigueur in 1971.

Poets and publishers milled about, eating fruit kabobs and skewering one another with their witticisms.

I sat on a crate of oranges, reading a poem about an onion:

I am thinking of the onion again, with its two O
mouths, like the gaping holes in nobody. Of the
outer skin, pinkish brown, peeled to reveal a
greenish sphere, bald as a dead planet, glib as
glass, & an odor almost animal. I consider its
ability to draw tears, its capacity for self-scrutiny,
flaying itself away, layer on layer, in search of its
heart which is simply another region of skin, but
deeper & greener. I remember Peer Gynt. I consider its sometimes double heart . . .

The party noises drowned out my peelings. Karen Mender, the pretty young publicist who had organized the party, had amazingly succeeded in getting an evening news team to come. (A slow day in Vietnam, I guess.)

I was videotaped on the crate of oranges, mouthing inaudible lines about onions. My thighs were showcased. So were my high-heeled fuck-me sandals.

"It could only happen in New York," said the voice-over, "a book party in a fruit and vegetable market."

"What do you think of poetry?" a reporter asked the butcher.

He chomped a big cigar and said: "Frankly, I prefer *meat.*"

"Is that so?" asked the reporter, egging him on.

"Fruit is nice, but you can't beat a good brisket."

When the choice is between meat and poetry, meat always has the last word.

The evening news ran the piece twice, failing to mention the name of the book, the publisher's name, or the author's name.

The poems went out into the world anyway, bringing back their own news. I began getting letters, invitations, reviews, Polaroids of naked men, baskets of fruit, of onions, of eggplants. Readings were proposed, poetry awards proffered. Little magazines that had formerly snubbed me now *invited* me to submit. I was asked to teach poetry at my shrine, the 92nd Street Y.

My students and I met around my dining room table in the West Side apartment I shared with Allan Jong. Poems were begun, poems rewritten, love affairs blossomed, marriages died. My students taught me about poetry and life.

I collected my new poems into a volume called *Half-Lives.*

"Where's the novel?" Aaron asked.

"Coming," I swore. But I was still noodling over *The Man Who Murdered Poets* and I knew I couldn't show him *that.* (Eventually he did me the great favor of rejecting it, encouraging me to write a novel in the voice my poems had discovered.)

In July of 1971, Allan and I took off for a congress of psychoanalysts in Vienna—the first time analysts had returned to Vienna since Freud had fled the Nazis in 1939. Anna Freud would be there; so would Bruno Bettelheim, Erik Erikson, and Alexander Mitscherlich.

A handsome young shrink from England arrived wearing love beads and an Indian *kurta.* I fell for him like a ton of psychiatric books.

He was to become the muse of my first novel.

8

FEAR OF FAME

Ambition was my idol, which was broken,
Before the shrines of sorrow and of pleasure . . .
　　　　　　　—George Gordon, Lord Byron, *Don Juan*

If my books had been any worse, I should not have been invited to
Hollywood, and if they had been any better, I should not have
come.
　　　—Raymond Chandler, *Selected Letters of Raymond Chandler,*
　　　　　　　　　　　　　　　　edited by Frank MacShane

Beware of what you wish for in youth because you will get it in
middle life.
　　　　　　　　　　　　　　　　　　　　　—Goethe

Vienna was a dip into the Nazi past again. And *going to Europe* had
always been my family's excuse for diving into the primal ooze of their
creation. They were all great travelers and great malcontents. Europe
was the place for the culling of memory, for rekindling dreams, ideals,
stories, sex. My grandfather had dreamed of turn-of-the-century Paris
his whole New York life; my mother had dreamed of the 1931 Paris
Exposition with its models of Angkor Wat, and of the handsome boys
who chased her in her rolled silk stockings and cute cloche hat. She and
my aunt raved on about the *Bremen* (later called the *Liberté,* the first

tub I also crossed the ocean on), where Nazi boys with patent leather hair and violet-smelling cologne pursued them through Deco lounges, not knowing they were *Jewesses.* (My mother had the most admirers always.) From *Bremen* to *Liberté,* we followed in their sea-steps.

It was a family tradition: Europe was sex to us—the place where guilt retired, can-can dancers flashed, and boys you kissed under bridges melted into the Seine, or Thames, or Arno, with no consequences. Europe was one-night stands with guys who barely spoke your language and therefore could not tell. Europe was poetry and Bacchic flings and wine and cheese and the land of the twelve dancing princesses. Nothing counted there. After all, we had got out in time. The Holocaust did not consume us. But we played with danger at the edge of the flame, licking at sex, the invitation to the conflagration. The fact of having narrowly escaped the greatest pogrom in history made Europe sexier for American baby boom Jews. God made only two forces—love and death—and wherever they were closest the heat was greatest.

Asked, "Don't you want to go to Europe, Nana?" my present husband's hundred-and-one-year-old grandmother replied (as she had for years), "I been."

But my family *never* turned its back on the old country. The summer I was thirteen, I went to Europe on the *Liberté* with my parents, lugging a makeup case filled with fifteen lipsticks, twenty nail polish colors, through the Grosvenor House, the George V, and the Trianon Palace Hotel in Versailles. I flirted with all those midget elevator operators in their ascending golden cages. I danced with pursers and called them "pursuers." The summer I was nineteen, I was packed off to the Torre de Bellosguardo in Florence to study Italian, and the summer I was twenty-three, I went back to do the same without the feeble excuse of summer school.

I fell in love with Italy as if it were a man—a man with many *campanili.* Forever after, Italy was the country of love. It still is—even though plastic bottles and condoms wash up on the tarnished shores and VIP now means *visite in prigione.*

Willkommen in Wien, the sign said. This was not Italy, but it was *close.* Right across the Alps lay the Land of Fuck, a furiously dancing boot, kicking Sicily into an azure sea. And Vienna was enchanting even if it *was* crammed with Nazis and analysts and even if I *was* with my husband.

I soon took care of that, laying eyes on and simultaneously falling in love with a properly unsuitable protagonist—a radical Langian hippie shrink with gorgeous green eyes (one of them wall), shaggy blond hair, and abundant pheromones. I only wanted a fling to ease the boredom of marriage, but I had picked myself a psychopath who liked nothing better than to mess with lives—and other analysts' wives.

His real name was so absurd that I couldn't possibly use it in a book. I called him "Goodlove" instead—hoping to evoke Clarissa's Mr. Lovelace. Otherwise I have got him mostly skewered. Falling instantly in lust leads to skewering. Being out of control leads the lover to play darts with the object of her emotional chaos. Darts go with love. Even Cupid used them. Stabbed through the heart, I retaliated in kind.

At all the public functions—dinners on the Danube, banquets at the Rathaus, conferences of luminous analytic stars in headsets—we flaunted our flirtation. Everyone noticed. They were meant to. It gave us the needed kick. We didn't so much want to fuck each other as to fuck with everyone else's head—particularly my husband's and my analyst's. But my analyst wasn't watching. Only my husband was.

After a preliminary poke in the Wiener boardinghouse where all the Brits stayed, I knew he was unreliable in bed. I was nuts for him anyway. His talk seduced me. He wanted nothing less than to take me to the bottom of myself. And I was tempted. He was the tempter I had been looking for.

My first book of poems had come out that spring and I was looking for my reward. Publishing a book has always made me hungry for chaos. A book orders and puts an end to one section of a life. That phase is over; another is about to begin. I look for a raft to help me cross the Rubicon. The raft has always been a man.

I came, I saw, I was conquered. My knack for turning a slave into a master did not fail me. My heart and my cunt pounded that old tattoo: *Take me, take me, take me or I'll die.*

My husband and I stayed up all night analyzing the attraction. This was meant to quash it, but it only made it more keen. Since every book is a peeling away of skin, I was raw now. I wanted to grow new flesh to cover the blood.

A love affair does that—grows new wrapping, if only scar tissue. Love doesn't even have to be involved. The man was beautiful only to me. But he provoked me, and provocation felt like love.

After two weeks of this, we took off together in his MG, having no destination. A brazen act, an act of regicide. Allan was king, and I was the assassin. I wanted to kill the king inside my head. Chess would not do. The man had to be flesh. And he had to talk, to philosophize, to challenge, not just to fuck. Like all my lovers, he had to rouse the daredevil in my breast. He said, "You won't, you can't." I said, "I can! I will!"

What a fool way to start a journey! We took off for the Alps and zigzagged through alpine passes. Salzburg, St. Gilgen, Berchtesgaden, Hitler's nest. We stopped in modest bed and breakfasts. We were destined never to like each other again as much as that first day we met.

Panic set in. To appease it, I told the story of my life. "Adrian Goodlove" egged me on, provoked me into candor. By the time we came to Paris, I'd heard my own story—though it had been a Scheherazade act to keep him interested. Of course, I embellished, exaggerated, and invented extra relatives. That's what storytellers do.

He dumped me in Paris without a car. He was going to meet his girlfriend and kids. I raged. I bit his lips. I bit his neck. He laughed and asked for an autographed poetry book. After a Left Bank descent into Hades à la Miller, Orwell, Hemingway, and other fallen idols, I reclaimed my soul, and reclaimed my husband shortly after.

The hippie shrink and I met again in London, on Hampstead Heath. We sat in Keats's garden and waited for the nightingale to sing. Adrian, my muse, gave me a kick to start the book: "Write it," he said. "You won't be sorry."

"And after that?" I asked.

"You'll write another and another one," he said.

"That's all?"

"That's all there is. You finish and then you start again."

"What if it's not successful?"

"What's that to do with you? You're the writer, not the critic of your book."

"What if I can't do it?"

"You can. You know you can conquer your fears. That's what a writer is—a conqueror of fears."

So I went home and began. Whenever I faltered, I'd play a recording of his voice. Made on the Autobahn outside Munich, it sounded like trucks whizzing and horns blasting. But under the roar of traffic, I heard his voice provoking me.

I can still hear it. It got me on my way. I wrote the story like a vagabond in flight. My Scheherazade act was the frame. Every day, every night, I wrote with a thudding heart. It was half-confession, half-defiance. I wrote it because I thought I couldn't. I was driven by the power of fear.

I began the book in September and had a draft—but for the ending—in June. The ending cost me more pain than all my other books combined. I knew that *whatever* I had my heroine do at the end, it would be wrong for *someone*'s politics. So I left her in the bathtub, being reborn.

Rebirth is the real point. Divorce, marriage, death can all lead there or not. Novels today usually favor divorce. In the last century, they favored marriage. Neither ending matters as much as the heroine's rebirth. Because so many heroines had died, I wanted mine reborn.

When I had four hundred pages or so, I dashed into my publisher's office and dumped it on the desk. Perhaps he had come to feel there was no novel. I flew out the door and left for Cape Cod, where the shrinks summered.

When Aaron called me to tell me how he loved the book, I was far away and almost afraid to listen. I dimly remember his saying, "It's got everything—feminism, sex, satire, ambivalence, it tells the story from a unique point of view." Could this be *my* book? Then I plunged into the six-month process of dealing with the ending.

What I remember most is wanting to take back the book from the printers. I had terrors and night sweats as I anticipated my doom. I knew this book was an emancipation proclamation. But I didn't know whether I would know *how* to be free.

The nights I lay awake wanting to tear up the contract, to commit the book to a locked desk drawer, to incinerate it on the beach! Sheer defiance made me persevere. I no longer knew whom I was defying. Myself? My husband? My family? The tradition that dooms uppity women to death? I knew yet did not know all I was doing.

Writing blocks came back. I had written the book in a rush to outwit the blocks, but the last fifty pages took as long to write as the preceding four hundred. The outtakes are illustrative. In one, Isadora writes long letters, à la Herzog, to Freud, to Colette, to Simone de Beauvoir, to Doris Lessing, to Emily Dickinson. In another, she dies of a botched abortion. In another, she blows off Bennett and goes to

Walden Pond to live alone in the woods. In another, she promises eternal slavery, and he takes her back.

None of these would do. The ending of a book is a magic amulet for its author as much as for its reader. We *know* that books cause things to happen, so we hold back, wanting to unhappen them. I went back to what I knew I must do: make the ending consistent with the character. She was on her way. But she was not there yet. She would not grovel, but she would not yet fly away. She would change her head, but not the desk at which she wrote. Not yet. She wasn't quite ready. She had another mountain pass to cross.

When the book started circulating in its pale-green-covered original galleys, there was a buzz. I didn't understand this. Enthusiasm and denunciation both at once. Galleys were stolen and passed around. They disappeared.

My panic intensified as success beckoned. I knew I wanted success, but did I want it *this* way? The nakedness of the book terrified me. I had written on my skin and stood before the world like a naked tattooed lady. The heat was on.

The first summer at the Cape, I had dreamed of unwriting the book; the second summer at the Cape, it was in galleys. I agonized over the ending, over the copyediting (even reading the dialogue into a tape recorder to hear if it sounded real). I had already *doven*ed over the manuscript with a Liquid Paper brush in my hand until I was stoned on the fumes.

Publication day loomed in November like the day they roll the guillotine into the town square. If I could have stuck my head into it and put myself out of my misery, I would have.

A certain skinlessness goes with the ability to observe and describe feelings. This does not make for blithe unconsciousness. Writers are doubters, compulsives, self-flagellants. The torture only stops for brief moments.

So the book went out into the world, making its own way, having its own fate. Its fate was not predictable. No child's fate is, and the parent just stands there, biting her cuticles and praying.

Two years later I found myself famous, with a paperback atop the bestseller list for the better part of a year.

But my fame was hardly the sort a Ph.D. candidate in literature might have lusted after. Talk shows and cover stories, photographers in the dune grass outside my rented shack in Malibu, movie deals gone sour, Hollywood heroics, and the frazzled fallout of drugs. But also requests for my underwear (unwashed if possible), notes in bottles from marooned Crusoes who wanted shipwrecked me to rescue them. Answered prayers are always harder than unanswered ones. I came up against my own compulsion for self-destruction. I had got what I wanted; now I couldn't wait to throw it away.

When the student is ready, the teacher appears. Julia Phillips was my teacher in self-destruction. She was way ahead of me in that specialty. When I met her—that one-hundred-pound bundle of nerves with hair that gave off sparks like firecrackers—I fell in love. Her energy was manic; she talked nonstop; she had a child, an Oscar, an obedient husband. She was running the world from the Sherry-Netherland Hotel. In 1974, that wasn't usual for women.

One of Edna O'Brien's heroines says somewhere that movie people are possessed by demons, but a very *low* form of demons.

But a demon was once a daemon—a creative force—and Julia was also that. She gave off energy, ideas, a kind of charisma. I was awed by her before I hated her.

She wooed me for the movie rights to *Fear of Flying* and eventually bought them for a modest option, no reversion clause, and $50,000.

Even in 1974, that was not a good deal. The deal dragged on, magically changing clauses in her lawyer's computer for at least a year. Meanwhile, I was writing my first screenplay, having endless story conferences in the Sherry-Netherland with my role model, and saying good-bye to my marriage one day at a time. And the book was out there getting famous. The first sign of this was truckloads of mail.

By the time I got to California in the fall, with my first-draft screenplay under my arm, Julia had gone to another level of drug use. But knowing nothing about cocaine, I thought she was merely rude and abusive.

I'd wait in a hotel room—the Beverly Hills—and she'd call to say, "There's a wreck on the San Diego Freeway. I'll be an hour late."

An hour later her secretary would call with a report of another wreck, an emergency meeting, or a child-care disaster. As the hours went from one to two to six, I'd start feeling victimized and enraged. She alienated directors and actresses the same way, and she dismissed her own behavior with a kind of brass and bravado that was alternately inspiring and depressing.

Shit disturbers can be thrilling. We all hate the hypocrisy of the world and want to call the world on it, but when the shit disturber becomes a hypocrite, it is a more distressing betrayal than any other. As W. H. Auden says, "It is morally less confusing to be goosed by a travelling salesman than a bishop." Julia was no bishop, but I had made her my high priestess of shit-disturbing; the rebel's rebel. When she proved to be just a front for the embezzling David Begelman, I was confused. *Who then was the potter and who was the pot?*

Between meetings that never happened and a deluge of book publicity, I was busy meeting and falling in love with Jonathan Fast, whose parents had become my friends through the Untermeyers' dinner parties. Julia meanwhile was busy alienating everybody in the movie business with her bad habits.

When directors like Hal Ashby and John Schlesinger and actresses like Goldie Hawn and Barbra Streisand had all been driven away by Julia's craziness, Julia decided to direct the movie herself.

That was when I crashed. Notwithstanding her brief course in directing at the American Film Institute, Julia was a novice—and a grandiose novice at that. (So, of course, was I, but I wasn't planning to direct the movie.)

By then, Jonathan and I were living together in Malibu and I was trying to extricate myself from my marriage to Dr. Jong.

Our house in Malibu had a waterbed overlooking the Pacific, a hot tub overlooking the Pacific, and a central jungle atrium open to the elements. Garter snakes and lizards played in it. I once came home to find a snake in the living room—and not the usual kind you find in Malibu living rooms.

The house was one of those slapped-together-by-a-studio-carpenter playhouses for midweek, midafternoon producer-starlet sex.

We were happy. We were in love. But we were also traumatized. *Newsweek* was doing a cover story on me and planting photographers in the ice plant and bougainvillea. Jonathan was trying to launch his career as a screenwriter and suffering the usual torments of rejection. I was trying to shut out the world and write a second novel—though writer friends assured me there was no point since *anything* I did after *Fear of Flying* was likely to be damned, and there were no second acts (or second chances) in American lives.

"Write screenplays," Mario Puzo said. "There's more money in it."

Little graduate school snot that I was, I looked around Malibu—

with its sullen multimillionaire hyphenates running on the beach, growing ever richer and more grizzled, and thought only of *Literature* with a capital *L*.

"If I don't write the second, how can I write the third?" I asked Mario. "If I don't write the third, how can I write the fourth, if I don't write the fourth, how can I write the fifth . . . " Et cetera.

I wanted to be Ivy Compton-Burnett or Simone de Beauvoir, not Robert Towne.

"Fools die," muttered Mario Puzo.

Or maybe he only said, "Schmuck."

Was I in Hollywood? Well, then, I would be Isherwood, Huxley, or Thomas Mann—certainly not the Marx brothers. My elevated notions of Literature have always done me in.

Or maybe it's my father's show biz entrepreneurism gone wrong.

Somewhere around the time Julia put her hand on a rock and declared herself *director* and I anointed myself the Mistress of Literature, I met a certain man. Someone brought him to a party at our beach house. It could have been anyone. A number of unsavory characters flocked to our house in Malibu the year I was *really* famous.

"Meet my close personal friend," the matchmaker said, using that adjectival expression that denotes an utter obliviousness to the meaning of the word "friendship." The close personal friend's means of livelihood was not clear. How *could* he be a business manager, a personal manager, a producer, and a lion tamer all at the same time?

He could. This was Hollywood.

It is no news to anybody (except snobbish, literary me in 1974) that Hollywood is and was crawling with characters who have laundered their pasts to resemble character actors' résumés.

Financial skulduggery was omitted. Failures were erased and successes were claimed, no matter how remote the association. Dropped famous names littered the floor like autumn leaves.

Mr. "Manager" had twinkly green eyes and shaggy gray hair. I seem to remember him wearing Zuñi jewelry and linen tunics that resembled Roman togas—but surely this must be wrong. He claimed to have been a boy preacher in Christian carny shows in his youth. He claimed to have been a sinner turned penitent and have seen the light, hallelujah. He reminded me of an ancient Christian orating before being thrown to the lions. I reminded him, apparently, of the same.

This gentleman and I started talking out near the hot tub before

the flaming backdrop of the Pacific sunset (which we both congratulated ourselves for having wound up silhouetted against). He had been
following the trials of *Fear of Flying* in the gossip columns. He was
outraged on my behalf.

"She says she's a director now and she can't even get along with
an actor for more than one meeting. I know it's none of my business,
but if you ever want to do something about that deal, I can get the
rights back for you. You were screwed. You were offered a *rock*-bot-
tom deal. And the agents conspired to make you take it."

The hook was set. My brain was ticking like a bomb. My shit disturber was up and prowling like a lion. My shit detector had broken
down.

In a few days, Jonathan and I were invited to meet our new
friend's lions.

Kept in a secret canyon in the desert, they roamed an environment
tarted up to look like the African veldt.

Jon and I were invited to cuddle them, sprawl around them, on
them, between their paws. We posed for Polaroids to take home to
Howard and Bette Fast in Beverly Hills, knowing that they would
make appropriately Jewish parental clucking noises.

Our tamer leapt among the lions, roaring at them to prove he
could roar at anyone. He lofted stools, chairs, whips. His wife, a
beautiful actress who now seldom worked, seemed equally passionate
about them. So did his exquisite teenage stepdaughter, a child star.

"You'd better get out of the cage," he said ominously. "This could
be hairy."

We stood outside to watch as our tamer put his hand inside the
bocca di leone, then smiled. How could I know he was demonstrating
my role in this whole affair?

From lions' dens, we drifted into lawyers' offices. Mr.
"Manager" explained to me why suing Julia, Columbia Pictures, and
ICM was utterly safe and riskless. I thought he was talking about
me; he was, of course, talking about himself. He provided his own
lawyer, offered himself as producer, and lion-tamed me into the
nightmare of my life (complete with agents testifying, holding up
telephone logs with enormous holes like Swiss cheese). He promised,
of course, to take all costs upon himself, but his promises were a
carny preacher's promises.

If someone ever promises you a "free" lawsuit or that you'll never have to pay taxes again, run for cover. The tax trick was done to me too, at about the same time in my life, and I have been paying ever since. These two disastrous errors of judgment became a way to destroy myself and my fame in one convenient package.

Raised on movies in which the little guy wins against the system, I had no more idea about court than a mouse does about a cheese-judging contest.

Any fool could have known that suing a movie company in the town of Burbank was about as smart as walking into a lions' den in a canyon in the desert. My new advisor expected a quick capitulation and instant victory. He proved to be even more out of touch with reality than I was.

The suit was announced in the press, garnered the sort of hideous publicity these things garner, and dragged on endlessly. It was hard enough to write a second novel, after all that hoopla. (Fear of Flying had seemed an apprentice work to me when I wrote it, and now it was to be my tombstone, or at least "Zipless Fuck" was to be my epitaph.) But writing a second novel while waging a lawsuit was just the obstacle course I needed to make me feel as rotten as I needed to feel after all that success. Everyone advised me against it. Instead I got into the spirit of it, decided that I, not my then father-in-law, was Thomas Paine and Spartacus rolled into one.

It blasted two years of my life that should have been fun. It wound up, as any sane person could have predicted, in a total legal rout, huge bills, and no movie. I moved back to New York, promoted How to Save Your Own Life around the world, and was only ever asked about "the zipless fuck" and the lawsuit. Back in New York I began a third novel, about an ancient Christian fed to the lions, but soon abandoned it and plunged back into my old security blanket from Barnard, the safely retrospective eighteenth century. I began to research a picaresque tale about an orphaned girl who becomes a poet, a witch, a highwaywoman, a prostitute, and finally the mother of a lovely daughter, thereby triumphing over all mischance—the perfect heroine to redeem my post-fame life.

During the five years I labored on this eighteenth-century tale, I was uniquely happy, and at the denouement of the plot, I also had a baby. I wrote about her through Fanny's eyes:

I marvell'd then at the tiny turn'd-up Nose (crusted with the Blood of the Womb), at the tiny Hands groping for they knew not what Hands to hold, at the tiny Mouth sucking blindly for it knew not what Breasts, at the tiny Feet that knew not what Paths they would walk in what Continents yet to be discover'd, in what Countries yet to be born.

"Welcome, little Stranger," I said betwixt my Tears. "Welcome, welcome." And then the salty Sea of my Tears o'ertook me and I wept in great Tidal Waves of Brine. O I cried until my Tears themselves washt a Portion of the cak'd blood from the Infant's Cheaks and show'd me her translucent Skin, the Colour of Summer Dawn.

When I entered the hospital I wasn't sure whether my heroine or I was having that baby. Consequently, Molly's birth certificate at first read "Belinda"—the name of Fanny's daughter. I caught my mistake, then lay about in bed inventing names for my beautiful child. Glissanda, Ozma, Rosalba, Rosamund, Justina, Boadicea . . . I doodled on a pad. Then Molly Miranda came into my head. And Jon agreed.

"Good thing you came to, Mom," Molly says.

Molly's birth redeemed everything, and *Fanny* did the rest. I suppose I like *Fanny* better than any of my other novels (so far) because its unique challenges gave me deep satisfaction. The challenge of recreating eighteenth-century language and plot, of turning male picaresque upside down. It made me wholly happy in a way I have not been since I was six—and so did my marriage to Jon, till it didn't.

It's easier to write about pain than about joy. Joy is wordless. After that spasm of life in orbit, I was delighted to be obscure, hiding in the country.

We contemplated moving to Princeton for the library, to the Berkshires for the scenery, to Key West for the light, to Colorado for the mountains, but wound up in Weston, Connecticut (within driving distance of both the Beinecke Library and Manhattan), leading an almost idyllic life: writing, yoga, dogs, and cooking. The only mistake we made was letting *People* magazine photograph us for a happy couples piece. Those pieces make divorce inevitable, just as surely as *Time* cover stories lead to death, bankruptcy, and the kidnapping of beloved babies.

Fanny made me happy because it let me live with the *Oxford English Dictionary* always open on my desk—and what can be happier than that? Jon made me happy because of his humor and his sense that nothing could be better than writing and doing yoga. And

Molly made me happy because she was my ordinary miracle, produced somehow by God, while my mind was on other things—the ori-
gin of the word "fichu," for example.

But *fame* never made me happy, though that, of course, did not
mean I wanted to give it up. Fame is the great test of character. Do
you lose or find yourself as a result of it? Most of us lose ourselves at
least for a while. Some of us come back. Most do not. At that time, I
wanted to get lost in the woods of Connecticut, nursing my baby,
looking up words in the OED, and reading Smollett or Fielding or
Swift every morning to get the cadence of the period in my head. Fame
terrified and perplexed me. In three years it had picked me up and
tossed me into the briar patch. I wanted to get as far away from those
painful memories as I could. The reign of Queen Anne was perfect. I
had died, but I was about to be reborn as a redhead in a riding habit.

I had at least survived. So would she.

Reading back, I notice that this chapter contains nothing about
Henry Miller. Perhaps that's because I am writing here of my hunger
for self-sabotage and Henry was the reverse of that: He gave me
lessons in how to live.

Curiously, I met Henry Miller on the same day I met Jonathan
Fast—a golden California day in October 1974.

I had taken my rented Buick down Sunset Boulevard to Pacific
Palisades and spent the afternoon with an astonishing old-young
Brooklyn boy of eighty-three, who had been writing me sprightly letters for six months and now appeared in his wrecked flesh with a
spirit younger than mine.

Mostly wheelchair ridden, blind in one eye, dressed in pajamas
and a tattered terrycloth robe, with a face like an ancient Chinese
sage, Henry Miller roused himself from bed to meet me and used his
walker, with great difficulty, rather than seem passive in a chair.

He was to become my clear eye in the midst of the hurricane.

American writers tend to be drunks and melancholics whose main
relation to their young aspirants seems to be, "Tell me one good reason I *shouldn't commit suicide.*" If you go to meet and admire them,
bring gin or an AA meeting book and prepare to do a lot of cheering
up. But Henry was, as he himself put it, "always merry and bright."
His temperament was his gift and also his gift to all.

Had I met him when he was a young man, he would have been
more hurricane, more chaos. But the fact of his having survived what I

was going through, and having kept his center, was the whole point. Branded the "king of smut," he went on writing what he had to write. Having been given every reason to close himself to humanity, he remained open and passed that gift along.

Whoever pushes America's sex button must be prepared for sirens and alarms. Whatever else we do in our lives will be drowned out by them.

"Why don't you take it as a joke?" Henry asked when I was troubled by fan letters requesting soiled knickers. I still ask myself this question twenty times a day. And my ability to answer it at any given moment is still the index of my mental health.

I drove back up Sunset Boulevard, laden with watercolors, books, prints. Henry was not a person who let you leave empty-handed.

All these goodies were on the bed when Jonathan and I (having just met at his parents' party) returned to it late that night or early the next morning. We had sat for an hour on Mulholland Drive, watching the lights of Los Angeles twinkle through smog, speaking of the possibility of real marriages of the minds and hearts, and realizing we were falling in love.

I was thirty-two and he was twenty-six, but in some ways, we both had just been hatched. We pledged our lives to each other that first night, and because of Molly, they will always be joined.

In later times, we hurt each other horribly, did angry things, were irresponsible lovers and parents, blinded by pride, jealousy, and rage. It is not my business to be his scourge—though I was just that in a few books, showing only that I still thought blaming others would make me free.

I need to make this amend to him and Molly: I wish I had known myself better and hurt you less. I wish I had known then what I know now: that it is useless to blame husbands or children for your own deficiencies, that it only delays facing them yourself. And it only delays change. Until you accept responsibility for that, there is no peace.

Fame turns out to be a powerful instrument of grace because it humbles its chosen victims in a hurry. You sail into it, your canvas swelled with grandiosity, and when your fifteen minutes are over and you are becalmed, you realize that grandiosity cannot take you where you need to go.

Only then do you learn to row like hell, asking God for the strength to stay afloat.

Writing, which had begun for me as a seduction of the muse and of the public's love, now came to have a very different function in my life. It went back to being the solace it was in my childhood—a means of self-pleasuring, of self-knowledge. Several wise writers, Robert Penn Warren among them, have said that it is only when you abandon ambition that you really begin to write.

I returned again and again to poetry after each novel because poetry was guaranteed to be obscure, thus ambition-proof, so it was possible to write it with little thought for the outside world.

A society is impoverished, I think, by its scarcity of outlets for ambitionless activity. Meditation, athletics, poetry, watercolor painting, journal writing, prayer, are only as enriching as they are *without* hope of outer adulation. When the ambition imp creeps into the activity, it is tainted. But it's hard for the ambition imp to creep into poetry, because nobody *wants* poetry for money, for fame, for bestsellers, so poetry must be done for yourself if it is to be done at all.

Fame, on the other hand, is a prisoner of marketing and demands that you do the same thing over and over again—at least if you want to feed the baby. *Fanny* had reminded people of my literary roots, had collected serious notices, and worldwide bestsellerdom, but somehow my most enduring fame was still as Ms. Lonely Cunts, the spokesperson for American womanhood's darkest urges.

However deep I might go into my poetry, and however many poetry books I produced, the fame imp wanted me back in center stage as the coiner of "the zipless fuck"—a symbol of my generation's hunger for female freedom through sexual pleasure.

You don't get to choose what you get famous for and you don't get to control which of your life's many struggles gets to stand for you. The best you can do is work at not caring too much about the outer symbols and continuing to do whatever it is that centers you and makes you remember your true self.

Poetry has remained that for me.

If the goal of our brief existence is to make us accept ourselves, turn the future over to our children, and make peace—however grudging—with our mortality, poetry remains the perfect means.

Mortality is poetry's main obsession—seconded by love, mortality's handmaiden. She strews the roses; he gathers them back to his bony bosom.

9

BABY, BABY, BABY

It is neither wise nor good to start a child with too much thought.
—Colette, *The Evening Star: Recollections*

Motherhood is supposed to be a part of Nature—timeless, immutable, a kind of female Rock of Ages. In truth, nothing is more mutable than motherhood—ringed round with the conventions and pretensions of the society in which it appears. Everything about motherhood changes with our ideologies: breast-feeding and swaddling, wet-nursing and baby farming, anesthesia or the eschewal of anesthesia, mother-infant bonding or mother-infant separation, birthing standing or sitting or lying down, birthing alone or with kin, midwife, or obstetrician. There's probably not one thing about giving birth that cannot be changed by culture except for the fact that it can only be done by a woman! Even the feelings the mother supposes she is supposed to have can be changed.

How we mothers hate to hear that. We would probably prefer to believe that childbirth and its paraphernalia are made by the Mother Goddess herself and mutate not at all from historic moment to historic moment. The hormonal ritual may be the same, the ontogeny of the fetus the same (as it recapitulates phylogeny—according to our high school biology teachers), but how we respond to labor, childbirth, the gushing of milk at the baby's cry, is infinitely mutable.

We whiplashers were as jerked around by theories of motherhood as we were about sex, about femininity, about success, about money, about idealism, about men, and about everything else in our chronically bipolar lives.

We grew up amid images of Betty Crocker mothers proving their womanliness by *baking*. (A Ceres myth recycled for the fifties?) The magazines we read in doctors' waiting rooms assured us that leaving the kids and going to work would stunt their psychological growth and blast our peace of mind. Male doctors dictated to us and we seldom suspected (nor in fact did they) that there was a political agenda behind their words.

In graduate school, married for the first time, I was warned by my parents' internist that at twenty-two, I was well into my chief childbearing years.

"Better not wait too long," he cautioned.

"At thirty, you'll be an elderly prima gravida."

Elderly prima gravida. What a terrifying term. Elderly at thirty? (Two hundred years ago, childbearing women were mostly dead at thirty!) Reproduction hardly requires that we live till fifty—much less the thirty or forty *extra* years we all expect as our due.

I had absolutely no intention of listening to that internist (my older sister was the earth mother; I was the artist), but the fear seed he planted bore fruit every month. Whenever the blood sheeted down, I saw a miniature dead baby in the flow. It might be my last. I mourned every egg, wrote poems to them, feeling both abject and relieved.

My whole struggle to learn to write and go to graduate school was carried out as if under a looming threat. Perhaps, by using my diaphragm so faithfully, I was committing my life to emptiness and despair. My physical revulsion against babies was so great then that seeing another Barnard classmate pushing a white antique wicker pram down West End Avenue, I felt *nauseous*. Either I yearned for pregnancy so much that I had become allergic to my own yearnings, or I was determined never to lose control. I hated and pitied the classmate who had succumbed to female weakness and was cooing and making funny faces at the blob in the pram. *She would never do anything with her life,* I thought contemptuously.

My heroines were Simone de Beauvoir, Virginia Woolf, Elizabeth I of England—childless queens of literature and power. It was clear to me that the renunciation of weak female indulgence in the muck of maternity was the price of intellectual excellence. My diaphragm was the keeper of my flame, of my brain, my independence.

If the choices I had were Betty Crocker or Elizabeth I, I wasted no time whatever about which to choose. Maternity was a trap, had been for my mother, my grandmother, women throughout history. Even before Mary McCarthy's *The Group* came out, I had been to the Margaret Sanger Clinic for my diaphragm. It was a freshman year initiation ritual at Barnard. The only uncertainty seemed to be about whether or not you first had to go to Woolworth's for a wedding ring. I selected the option of wearing white kid gloves—as if I were being confirmed.

When my first husband proved schizophrenic, I congratulated myself for my prescience in not getting pregnant. But the pregnancy terror rarely let me rest. Every month was the pit and the pendulum. I noted my periods in my Week-at-a-Glance and went crazy if I was one day late. Control, control, control. It was a woman's only way to stay in charge.

Allan and I had never discussed babies before we were married. And after we married we never discussed *anything*. But soon after we arrived in Germany, I began to believe he was an alien creature. I could never breach the wall that separated us—so I could never imagine making a baby with him. I failed to *conceive* it, thus failed to conceive—a thing some women can do with only certain men, not others. I don't think we even tried until the end, when I knew I was leaving and, in a spasm of guilt, wanted to entrap myself. By then, I was already out the door.

But Jon always felt like flesh of my flesh. We were destined to have Molly. I saw her hovering over the L.A. smog the night we met at his parents' house and talked all night on Mulholland Drive.

"Do it, Mom," she said. "Here I come!"

"Wait a bit—whoever you are," we said.

Three years later, we welcomed her.

How did someone with such a fear of losing control manage to get pregnant?

The way was paved with stray dogs.

By then, we had moved to Connecticut, bought a house with five bedrooms, and moved in with our New York ficus tree and our store-bought bichon frise, acquired on Lexington Avenue, near Bloomingdale's, before we became animal welfare converts. Or before I did.

I got animal welfarism by osmosis (or brainwashing) from our friendship with June Havoc. Yes—she's still *alive,* darling Baby June,

Gypsy Rose Lee's sister, she of the perfect Norwegian nose (modified by forties Hollywood), living in the perfect Miss Havisham Connecticut house with a menagerie of one-eyed, lame, and crippled dogs, three-legged cats, arthritic donkeys, pigs with diabetes, and swans with broken wings.

She calls them "the kids," calls her lair for them the Old Actors' Home—and takes care of them with such devotion that they may indeed stand up on their hind legs and start reciting *Hamlet* at any moment. June, whom we had met on one of those "free" cruises (which turns out not to be so free since fans chase you around B Deck with nephews' manuscripts, and elderly parties who are translating Omar Khayyám into Urdu or redoing the Oz books in end-stopped couplets and consequently need "a good New York agent" accost you in the neon discotheque at 3:00 A.M. to discuss "the New York publishing scene").

June was aboard—along with a host of other new or slightly used celebrities.

Jon and I confided in her that we had been househunting all over the United States this bicentennial year—from Lake Tahoe to Wyoming to Santa Fe to Islamorada to Key West to the Berkshires—and we were so fed up that we were about to move back to California, to Big Sur this time, or Napa, or even Berkeley.

June's eyes lit up!

"Come to Weston," she said. "I'll find you a house."

And she did. And helped to populate it. Because of June, I was forever running off to nearby animal shelters when the call came that euthanasia day was drawing near. June and I would do local TV (when local TV showed up) to advertise the adorable doomed animals, and when local TV did not show up, we'd usually go home with abandoned animals ourselves.

On one such jaunt, Jon and I fell in love with Buffy—or rather, Buffy fell in love with Jon. The big red mutt—who looked like Little Orphan Annie's dog, Sandy—followed him everywhere around that doggie Auschwitz, and when he refused to take her, began howling like a coyote at the full moon.

"Darling," said June, "I promise you'll never regret it. If she doesn't work out for you, I'll take her to the Old Actors' Home, I promise." And so we took Buffy home.

She even *looked* like an Auschwitz dog—skin and bones draped in mangy red fur, huge brown eyes that seemed to have all human misery from the beginning of time reflected in their doggy depths, a tendency to knock over garbage cans and eat the contents, not to mention worms of incredible length living in her intestines and the resultant uncontrollable diarrhea.

After she bit his hand when he inspected her teeth, the first vet we took her to said: "This will never be a pet. She ought to be put down."

This only made us more determined. We took Buffy back home, wormed and fumigated her, flea-bathed her, did her hair with chamomile shampoo and cream rinse, and began feeding her steaks, vitamin E capsules, rice, and carrots. She still growled at us, shat in the corners of the house, and tried to chase the garbage truck up the driveway. But little by little, she calmed down.

In a couple of months, she looked like Annie's Sandy—after she was adopted by Daddy Warbucks and had a long-running hit show on Broadway—a big red mutt with spindly legs and a tuft of reddish brush on her lovely long narrow head. We renamed her Virginia Woof (to go with Poochkin, aka Aleksandr Pushkin, the bichon), but her pound name still somehow stuck. Buffy, Buffoon, Scruffoon, Ms. Woof were her aliases. She became a model pet—beautifully trained by someone more stalwart than I, to heel, to bark at strangers, and to never "make mistakes" indoors—which was more than we could say for Poochkin, who would mark his territory outdoors or in and masturbate the couch pillows until they were stiff.

The two of them had been uneasy housemates at first, but now they mirrored each other's positions at the hearth or sat like bookends on either side of the front door. Buffy was in love with Jon and Poochkin with me. Each of us had a canine sidekick in our his-and-hers studies. But Buffy was the dog of deeper soul. She had been abandoned, after all, and saved from death row. Both dogs and people are nicer after hitting bottom.

If I can turn this dog around, I thought, there's nothing I can't do. Even have a baby—even though I am a writer?

But I hesitated, still fearing the eternal Waterloo of women. By the summer I was thirty-five, I was romancing stray dogs in supermarket parking lots, crying over dogs killed by cars, writing poems about the intelligence and intuitiveness of dogs.

Looking at Buffoon one day, I thought, A baby could never be as much trouble. And look at her now—the perfect pet. What I didn't know was that the analogy between dogs and babies only lasts a year or so. After that they are cussed little creatures of their own will, until about the age of twelve, when they become dybbuks or incubi— depending on your religious persuasion.

But it really *was* Buffoon, Scruffoon, Spittoon, the very distinguished Ms. Woof, who got me ready to have a baby. It was another kind of surrender. Once a dog inhabits your heart, it's not hard to open it to a baby.

Poochkin had been my walker, my muse, my protection on the New York streets, my son, my lover. But Poochkin came to me as a healthy, perfect, baby bichon. Buffy was meant to be loved for all her trouble. I guess I knew that trouble was part of motherhood and that if you can be a woman who loves a dog too much, you can do the same with a baby or a man. (This could be a bestseller: *Women Who Run with the Dogs and Love Them Too Much*.)

A baby! A baby! We started playing musical diaphragms. We started thinking about names. We started a vegetable garden and bought a jeep (not quite the perfect car for pregnancy but domestic nonetheless).

Molly was as much Buffy's daughter as she was mine. Buffy's devotion and Jon's were fixed. Mine wavered. That was why I needed both the canine and the man. I know that women are supposed to be able to commit parthenogenesis and never look back. But I needed the security of a man and a dog. Could I train Buffy to be like Nana in *Peter Pan*? That was crucial. In my mind I was roving around Wiltshire, London, the Ivory Coast, and the Caribbean; in my body, I was getting ready to make a baby.

I have always wanted to write a book that captures the quintessential oddness of a writer's life: living one extravagant imaginary life in your study, in your notebooks, in the library stacks, while another quotidian, domestic life revolves around it. How these lives interweave each other is part of the story. How can you be writing *this* one morning . . .

> There were but five Rogues, led by a Boy of Ten, who slobber'd and shook like a Half-Wit, and who continually scream'd, "Vile Witch! She cast a Spell on me!" pointing a crooked Finger at each of my Sister Witches.
>
> In the Centre of the circle two Men held the beauteous Maiden of the Coven to the cold Ground, whilst the others rav-

ish'd her in turn, with as great Brutality as they could muster; and less, it seem'd, for whate'er Pleasure an unreasoning Beast might find in so forced an Act of Passion than for showing off their Brutality to their Brute Brothers. She was violated perhaps ten, perhaps twelve Times; and whereas at first she whimper'd and fought, after a while she seem'd to lye still, her glaz'd Eyes staring Heavenward, her mouth mutt'ring, "Gracious Goddess, have Mercy." Whereupon the Brute who then was tormenting her with his swollen red Organ, grew inflam'd by her piety and, pulling his ugly Truncheon out of her poor abus'd Cunnikin (which now spill'd o'er with dark Blood), he thrust it violently into her Mouth, saying, "This'll teach thee to pray to Devils" and he ramm'd his Organ so far back in her Throat that she turn'd red and chok'd and seem'd on the very Point of Death. Whereupon he withdrew it, and each of the Men ravish'd her Mouth in turn, until it bled as horribly as her poor Nether Lips. When I thought I had seen the worst and could bear to look no more, one of the ugliest of the Lot, a Rogue with a Strawberry nose and the slitty Eyes of a Pig, extracted his Scimitar from its Scabbard, and, ignoring her most piteous Screams and the Pleadings of the other Members of the Coven, carv'd a Cross into the Flesh of her Forehead, and carv'd it so deep that her whole Face ran red with Blood, and soon she swoon'd in his Arms and expir'd . . .

And then sit down to lunch with your family? You can.

And the exoticism of the writing is somehow fueled by the domesticity of daily life.

But what about those moments when your daily life seems to bleed into the book, when you don't know whether you are Erica or Fanny, when you don't know whether Fanny is pregnant or you are?

This book, this pregnancy, were destined to feed each other, each fattened and transformed by the other's fate.

I had taken Fanny from being the Cinderella of a great family in Wiltshire, to being raped by her stepfather, to running away "to seek her fortune," to falling in with a coven of mother-goddess-worshipping witches, to joining a band of Robin Hood–like thieves called, after his, "the Merry Men," to being cast adrift in London to earn her living as a whore in Mother Coxstart's notorious brothel, when suddenly the book was interrupted by a trip to Paris to promote my second novel, *How to Save Your Own Life,* or, as it was called in French, *La planche de salut.*

Jon and I were staying in a small hotel near St. Sulpice. We fell into bed one night exhausted, jet-lagged, and full of good wine, both wanting to sleep, but instead we reached for each other, and made love endlessly as if in a trance.

After, I lay awake as he slept. My womb felt full of light. It seemed a huge red planet glowed inside me. I felt that throbbing two inches below the navel which makes you experience yourself as a Möbius strip bringing the cosmos within.

In the morning, I was having my picture taken for some glossy magazine against the rampant lions in a fountain—when my French translator asked me why I had such mischief in my eyes.

"We made a baby last night," I said flippantly—not even sure it was true.

"And what about the next *book*?" she asked, believing me.

"What about it?" I said blithely, with that utter euphoria that in fact presages pregnancy.

Hortense Chabrier was a small chain-smoking redhead who took it upon herself to be my literary protector. She had two children of her own and was involved in a very civilized ménage à trois with my other French translator, Georges Belmont. I had met Georges and Hortense through Henry Miller. Henry and Georges were great old friends from the thirties and Hortense was a brilliant young editor who worked for Robert Laffont. Henry had discovered *Fear of Flying* and sent it to them, only to discover that it had been turned down by Laffont with the excuse: "French women don't need psychoanalysts." (Probably because they have French *men.*)

Georges and Hortense reopened the question of *Fear of Flying,* translated the book as *Le complexe d'Icare,* and discovered that French women liked it as well as American women—and for the same reasons. In the process, we all became great friends.

Blithe as I was about my first day of pregnancy, I later panicked.

I had so accepted the bluestocking either-or (the baby *or* the book) that I flew into paroxysms of doubt about how I could ever do this amazing balancing act.

Luckily the baby had no doubts, nor did Jon, nor did Buffy and Poochkin. They slept on me at night as in a love pile, and in the morning, I went up to the attic to continue the further adventures of Fanny, who, astonishingly, had also discovered she was pregnant.

> The expectation of a babe, for a Woman who is without Dowery, Husband, or i'faith without loving Relations, creates, above all, an immense capacity for hard Work.
>
> Ladies with Child who languish in the Country whilst their Husbands pursue Whoring and Gaming in Town, may indeed be curst with ev'ry Ailment of the Female Flesh; but Ladies who must work to put Bread into their own Mouths are, i'faith, too busy to suffer from Faintings or the Spleen, from Lethargy or Megrim, Sciatica or Vomiting. Idleness itself creates the Spleen, but good hard Work cures all these Maladies better than the costliest Physician.
>
> My work was hard—hard upon my Body and harder still upon my Mind, for 'tis no easy Thing to be put to Bed with Gentlemen for whom one has nought but Dread and Loathing. Picture to yourself a young Girl, still in love with Love itself, being forced to frolick betwixt the Bedsheets with cadav'rous old Men, bandy-legg'd actors, pockmarkt Booksellers, and young Merchant Apprentices still with Pustules upon their boyish Cheaks.

All the feelings of pregnancy—terror, confidence, bliss—went into Fanny and were translated into eighteenth-century terms.

I contemplated undoing the pregnancy and did nothing. Fanny went to an outlaw apothecary, Mrs. Skynner, with thoughts of aborting the babe, but she could not muster the courage. I wondered how I would ever make a living if I didn't finish this book. Fanny, on the other hand, schemed to have herself set up as a kept woman, masked from her patron, who turned out to be her own stepfather, Lord Bellars, and the father of the babe. My own child slept safe from harm in her white wicker bassinet. Fanny's child, on the other hand, was kidnapped by a wicked wet nurse and she had to run away to sea to save her. Each tumultuous surge of early motherhood was translated into another plot twist in the book. Thus do writers make books out of flesh.

"Shall we go to the health food store?" your mate asks. And you are drawn out of a bustling London street (bordered by canals full of sewage, fishheads, rotting fruit, and dead animals). "Coming in a minute!" you call downstairs. And you scribble in a few extra fish-heads and dead cats in the eighteenth century before you rush out to buy bean curd in the twentieth.

"A sort of life," Graham Greene called it—and no one has yet improved on the phrase. But it is also richer than most lives, because it is always lived in two places, two centuries, two time-continua at once.

Imagine straddling the cosmos, clinging to the tails of comets, knowing that time does not exist. That is the writer's life. It is the purest connection to the universe a mortal can have. It is also a kind of prayer.

A novel in which those two levels of life become one, in which the emerging book turns out to *determine* the emerging life, would be thrilling if it were to be written on the deepest level. But most writers use the dream-reality conceit cheaply. Many books *start* in "reality" and venture into the mirror world of fantasy, only to return to "reality" at the end. Usually the "real world" is used as a frame or a launching pad. Sometimes the characters bring ordinary objects back from the dream world to prove where they have been: the worn shoe leather of the Twelve Dancing Princesses; the child's scarf left in the Royal Doulton plate in *Mary Poppins Comes Back*. Because it is our daily experience of life to be dreaming half the time and waking half the time, it is natural for us to invent stories that embody our confusion about which world is the actual one. Perhaps we only *seem* to sleep here while we are awake elsewhere? Is it possible that we meld opposing lives in one seemingly whole personality? These questions fascinate us because our lives are forever split between fantasy and reality. A writer is merely one who makes use of that fissure as the compost heap of stories.

Pregnant with Molly, I was happier than I have ever been at any other time in my life. I was one becoming two, or two becoming one. My moods were smooth. I felt radiant, purposeful, full of life. And I wrote without any of the doubts that had paralyzed me in the past. I had the perfect integration of mind and body. My muse was inside me; centering me. My mind could roam. My body knew what it had to do without my interference.

That was the most curious thing about pregnancy. I didn't *have* to be in control. I could let go. A higher power was running this. What a blessed state for someone who always thought she had to control everything.

When I was three months pregnant, Jon and I were secretly married in our house in Connecticut. We kept it from our parents, our friends, and the media because I had written an article for *Vogue* stating that I didn't believe in marriage. How could I recant? Also, I felt my life had been too public. I wanted to take back the power secrecy imparts.

Howard and Bette nudged us for months about getting hitched. My parents pretended indifference. Just before Molly was born we relented and told both sets of parents that the baby was legal.

I, who had dreaded pregnancy, was astonished to find myself loving it. I, who had denounced marriage, was astonished to find myself happy. I possessed a calm I scarcely recognized as mine. Perhaps it belonged to the baby. Pregnancy was such a magical transformation that I understood why my older sister had six children, my mother three, and my younger sister two. Earth mothering abounds in my family. I am the aberration.

The pregnancy seemed so easy that everyone from my obstetrician to my Lamaze coach agreed: "That baby's going to pop right out."

Yoga headstands in the sixth month and forward bends in the seventh had convinced the world (Jon and our mutual yoga teacher) that the delivery would be easy. A book tour in my sixth month convinced *me*. Only one interviewer dared ask whether I was pregnant under my smock.

"You're the first to ask," I said. "The others probably just thought I was fat."

My energy remained abundant almost till the eighth month—and even then, dragging a belly like a dinosaur egg, *I* thought I looked gorgeous. The narcissism of pregnancy made me pose for photographs romancing my own belly. Demi Moore was probably in grade school, and nobody would have printed them on magazine covers in 1978, but surely I would have posed for them if I could have. Whenever possible, I wore transparent dresses that showed my belly.

I remember Jerzy Kosinski stroking it at a cocktail party. "I would give anything to experience childbirth once," he said.

But the baby did not "pop right out." Due on the first of August, she hung in there, pressing on my bladder until the end of the month. It was August 18 before she decided to budge. I was reading an eighteenth-century book on "masques and ridottos" in the Pequot Library when suddenly I was soaked. Calmly I returned the books to the librarian and drove home.

Jon and I phoned the doctor and waited for contractions to begin. Nothing happened.

I went into the kitchen and made an immense steak sandwich with homegrown beefsteak tomatoes. As soon as I had wolfed the whole thing down, the contractions began.

Calls from prospective grandparents every five minutes were more annoying than the contractions. Howard was *insisting* we go to the hospital. It was *his* grandchild after all! Rather than argue, we went. I had called my Lamaze instructor, packed my copies of *Immaculate Deception* and *Leaves of Grass*. I was determined to have this baby naturally—whatever *that* meant.

As with every other passage of my life, I was about to give birth in a hotly politicized time. Anesthesia was then considered uncool and antifeminist. Only sissies got spinal blocks. No Amazon-mother-woman would succumb to knock-out drops! So I labored in hideous pain nine whole hours, until my strength was gone.

And when my doctor suggested a cesarean, I fought him, citing feminist texts. Only the slowing of the baby's heartbeat changed my mind.

Fanny would have died. The babe would have been scarred by forceps, dismembered, or stillborn. Off in a Demerol dream of the eighteenth century, how could I know that a gnarl in a broken coccyx (from an old riding accident) had blocked my daughter's way into the world and that a cesarean was the *only* option.

"Don't kill me, I'm halfway through the best book of my career!" I shouted to David Weinstein, my beloved obstetrician, as we got stuck in the elevator on the way to the operating room. Rescued by an angelic maintenance man in a grasshopper green suit (and invisible wings), we raced out of the elevator—the doctor pushing the litter and me raving—down the hall to the OR.

Jonathan was not allowed into the OR. I barely was myself. This was a sacred circle of medical men. A spinal block was administered and my legs grew numb. I could feel cutting but no pain.

A bloody lump was lifted high for me to see.

"Is that the placenta?" I asked.

"It's your daughter," said David, putting a little creature covered in iron-ore-colored blood into my arms. She was wearing a hastily wrapped pink blanket and fluttering her blood-caked lids. Her eyes of undersea blue met mine.

"Welcome, little stranger," I said, weeping and washing her face with my tears.

Born of a sudden notion mooted between two fated lovers on a smog-filled cloud above a California canyon, she had come all this way to us, patiently traveling on feet that never touched the ground (as Colette said of *her* daughter). She was mine and not-mine all at once. She was the most beautiful thing I had ever seen and the most terrifying. God had dropped into my life wearing Molly's face. Or else God's hostage. My life henceforth would not belong to me alone.

Exhausted, elated, I waited for her to be brought to my room. A hosed-down baby, with the same inky eyes, and a tuft of reddish hair done into a shiny pink bow, arrived in a clear lucite box like a Valentine's gift. I took her to my breast, wondering if this was how to do it. It worked. She suckled. And I couldn't stop staring at her as if she were an apparition that would vanish as quickly as it had come.

Then I collapsed. A day or night of drugged dreams and then I awakened to the pink face and inky eyes and auburn tuft again. What was our fate—hers and mine? What miracle had made her? How could such a miracle be both so ordinary and so extraordinary? Molly's birth made a believer of this agnostic.

> O what a Miracle is a Newborn Babe! Snatch'd from the Void, barely alive nine Months, yet it arrives with its Fingers and Toes fully form'd, its Lips tender as the Petals of the Rose, its Eyes unfathomably blue as the Sea (and almost as blind), its Tongue pinker than the inside of a Shell, and curling and squirming like a garden Worm in sodden Spring.
>
> Almost three Decades have pass'd since I first beheld you, my own Belinda, but I will ne'er forget my Feelings as I feasted my bleary Eyes upon your flesh-hatch'd Face. The Pains of Travail may fade (ah, fade they do!) but the Wonder of that Miracle—that most ordinary Miracle—of the Newborn Babe is a Tale told and told again where'er the Race of womankind survives!

Those were the lines I wrote for Fanny when the experience was new and fresh in my mind.

I kept every scrap of paper from the hospital (the woozy list of names), every photograph (including the sonogram at ten weeks), both identification bracelets—hers and mine. With these mementos I made books for her—books for baby days, books for every little-girl birthday, and a special book for her passage into adolescence at thirteen. I was a writer before I was a mother, and it was the writer who was more formed. Motherhood is an acquired taste. You learn it humbled on your knees. Becoming a writer *about* motherhood is the easy part.

So we took her home, but at first my canine babies were not so delighted to have a sibling. Buffy howled when I breast-fed her, and Poochkin left turds of outrage in the corners of every room.

A horrid baby nurse came from an agency in Greenwich and proceeded to do what baby nurses do best: make the parents feel like idiots. She ate for two as if she were a wet nurse. She secreted the baby in her room and brought her to me every few hours, only to deliver that classic baby-nurse line: "Missus Fast, your milk's not rich enough." On the nurse's day off, I wheeled the carriage next to my bed and greedily cooed over my baby all day and night—when I wasn't madly breastfeeding or madly photographing. She held my attention like a fiery constellation. Her eyes bewitched me. Her first smile caused me and Jon to waltz around the room with the baby between us. We were besotted with her, the first parents in history.

But I was also determined to finish my novel on time. Every morning I'd march up to my study on the third floor, intent on making my deadline. The publishers had given me the sort of money women didn't usually make. If I missed the deadline, they'd take it all back. It never occurred to me to take a day off. I simply tripled my workload and pressed on. The baby was fed all night and the book all day. I produced more pages, not fewer. Perhaps I was afraid my talent would evaporate into motherhood. I tested this hypothesis daily.

Like other members of the whiplash generation, I had too much to prove—to myself, to my mother, to all the men who said it couldn't be done. I needed to prove my mother wrong. Women *could* do it all. "We have won the right to be eternally exhausted," I used to joke.

But wasn't that better than not being allowed to publish books at all?

Do I regret my drivenness? How can I? I was on trial for my life. Women's right to create both life and art was still questioned everywhere. In many ways, it still is.

"Family leave" never even occurred to me. I felt so lucky to be a woman and *allowed* to work that I had no intention of rocking the boat. They'd throw me overboard without a line.

When Molly was basket-sized, I'd sometimes bring her to my study to sleep on the floor under my desk as I wrote. But she was soon too big and hungry for that. The La Leche League somehow neglects to tell you that big babies like to suckle every hour or so. She was trying to sit up, look around, grab for things, monologue. The baby nurse went and Lula took her place. Lula was everybody's dream of a nanny.

Lula was a former numbers runner who had sinned and loved many sinners before she came to Christ, but by the time I met her, she was a God-fearing church lady, whose pastor was the center of her life—she played me his take-home tapes—and who had a great knack for sweet-potato pies, pigs' feet, collard greens, and babies. She sang to Molly, rocked her, greased her with Vaseline to ward off flu—"Colds don't *like* grease," Lula said—and took her to church in Harlem "to have her blessed." My mother found out and was not amused. But I figured you could never be blessed *enough*.

"Dat baby clap hands and praise Jesus," Lula said. "Dat baby shout 'Hallelujah.'"

"I know, I know, Lula," I said, "but my mother worries."

"What *she* got to worry about?" Lula asked.

"She doesn't *need* anything," I said.

"You Jewish people is crazy," Lula said.

"You said it," I agreed.

Lula could send headaches "back to the pit," cure colds with lemon juice and Vicks, and pray books up the bestseller list. She was a triple-threat, all-purpose household goddess. With Lula around, you never felt scared. If Vicks couldn't cure it, Jesus could.

Lula came and I finished my novel. By the time it was published, Molly was two.

One blessing of writing an eighteenth-century novel while having a baby was the gratitude it gave me for merely being alive. If I were *really* Fanny and had my obstetrical history, I'd be dead and Molly would be, too. Whatever science has done to destroy the world, it has unquestionably saved the lives of women and their babies. Nature is *not* gentle with us when left to her own devices. Now we survive childbirth and face the dilemma of turning fifty. Mary Wollstonecraft never trod this path.

Greedy for more and more life, we seldom appreciate what we have. Many of my friends have become mothers in their forties and their babies are beautiful and smart. We have extended the limits of life, yet we dare to rage at growing old.

It seems damned ungrateful. But then we baby boomers are a

damned ungrateful bunch. Nobody gave us limits. So we are good at squandering and complaining, bad at gratitude. And when we discover life *has* limits, we try to wreck ourselves in anger before we learn the importance of surrender. We are the AA kids, the qualification generation. We have to be hurled to the bottom again and again before we come to understand that life is *about* surrender. And if the bottom doesn't rise to meet us, we dive into it, carrying our loved ones with us.

Only a lucky few swim back up to air and light.

10

DIVORCE AND AFTER

Everything changes but the human heart, say the old sages, but they are wrong.

—Denis de Rougemont, *Love in the Western World*

This is a chapter I don't want to write. But it has to be a part of *Fear of Fifty,* because divorce is my generation's coming of age ceremony—a ritual scarring that makes anything that happens afterward seem bearable.

It surely has to do with how long we live. All those women who died in childbirth didn't *get* to have more than one husband, and all those men, if they didn't die of smallpox or fever or gout or shipwreck or rum, got to marry over and over again guiltlessly and with no alimony.

We marry as if our lives were theirs, but by thirty or forty or fifty, when they would have been dead, we find ourselves different people. Our values have shifted: Our pleasures seem sweeter, our pains seem sharper, but also less neurotic. We now want different lives with different loves. We outgrow mates as eighteenth-century people outgrew their families' graveplots. We were never *meant* to live this long.

At thirty-eight, with a baby and a new bestseller, having delivered the eighteenth-century female in myself, I felt I could do *anything.* Jon, who was thirty-two, felt uncertain about his career, one-upped by the baby.

"I am always *third* in this house," he said. "First the baby, then the book, and where do *I* fit in?"

Where indeed? He couldn't nurse the baby or support us. He wasn't publishing bestselling books. I must have been disdainful of his uselessness, but so was he. This was a time to nurture and reassure *him*—but I had an infant and a deadline, and for all my bravado, I couldn't do it all. We were both so thrown by the demands of the baby that we had little time to help each other. So we started doing the hurtful things desperate people do, both feeling burdened and misunderstood and alone.

More than ever we had a reason to be together; more than ever we drifted apart.

By the time Molly was three, we had accumulated enough grievances against each other to both feel righteous. The baby was the innocent bystander in all this.

I had been proud of being the main breadwinner; now I resented it. The pressure was too great. Jon had felt proud of being a nurturer; now he felt unmanned by it—or so it sometimes seemed. A baby throws all the parental roles you know from childhood back in your face. I wanted to be "taken care of"—whatever that means. He wanted to be "free" to fly away.

At a party for my thirty-eighth birthday (when Molly was one), the tension and exhaustion led me to play Russian roulette with my life. It was a Mexican party, so I drank dozens of margaritas and was already staggering when a "friend" came and offered me little blue pills as a birthday present. I took two and presently passed out.

The rest I can only reconstruct from rumor.

My pulse plummeted and I grew cold. I was immobilized on the bathroom floor and later on the bed. A doctor friend walked me and fed me coffee and vitamin C. I threw up, drank more coffee, and threw up again. A night of twisted dreams, and images of the Sahara in my throat.

When I finally awoke in the morning, the guests were gone. I was humiliated and sick. I had missed my own birthday. The end of the world loomed as a row of empty tequila bottles. The shame was immense.

Incredibly, the baby was fine. I suddenly thought of what might have happened to her and had a belated panic attack. I was in deeper trouble than I knew. The joy of having it all had turned to the exhaustion of having it all. I was *so* tired. The stress of wanting to give the baby what she needed, give Jon what he needed, and give myself what

I needed, had brought me to this precipice. My addiction kicked in, wanting to be fed. My addiction turns to food or booze or work-aholism with equal enthusiasm. Just when I start to understand her, she switches gear.

The addiction is also a part of the story I don't want to tell—and not only because so many have told it and boasted of finding "the Answer." Partly from them, I have come to honor the power of not using words for everything. The soul can only hear in silence. Facing yourself cannot be done in public. And announcing your recovery is a sure way to lose it. There's an old witch saying, "Power shared is power lost." In the matter of addiction, this is especially true.

Addiction is the disease of our age. It is cunning and powerful. It proceeds from our chronic spiritual hunger and is nourished by our focus on getting and spending, and on news and gossip outside our-selves. Everything we need is happening within us. The focus on reports of others is only a distraction from the needs of our own spirit. Addiction grows fat from our chronic quashing of the inner life. We believe the spiritual does not exist because we have made insufficient space for it to manifest in our lives. A self-fulfilling tautology.

We also give our marriages too little space for pleasure. The result is that we flee from them, searching for ourselves. We think we have lost our souls. And we have. But we probably could find them together—if only we knew how.

Regret is the most bitter pill of all. No wonder Dante made it the chief punishment in hell. I now regret my failure to make that mar-riage work—even though it was not within my power.

The summer Molly was about to turn three, I ran away from Jon to Europe, hoping he'd follow me. I went to my French translator's country house in Mayenne. But Jon did not come. Instead, he took off on his own odyssey, westward. We fought bitterly on the transatlantic telephone. During one of these fights, not meaning it, I angrily said, "Get out."

He did. I came home to the wreckage of a broken household, with Jon moving out.

I had come to my senses and wanted him back. He didn't want to hear about it. He wanted to be kicked out. It gave him permission to be "free." He had been in a deep depression almost since the baby was born. He'd felt displaced, abandoned, unloved. Surely I can under-stand that now. But *then,* the burdens on me were too great. I had no room for empathy except for Molly (and *Fanny*). I didn't even have empathy for myself.

'It went on like that for a few months. He came home, went away, came home, went away, collecting grievances and meeting his next wife.

We had killed the trust between us. After that, everything became impossible.

The legal part of the divorce was over much too soon. I asked nothing. He asked nothing. We walked away as if there weren't a child between us. So we still have unfinished business. And since we have it, Molly has it too.

What happens when your partner and best friend becomes your enemy? You scream and hang up the phone in the middle of the night; throw yourself at cars and at men; drink too much; sue and get sued, discharging money—and rage.

You can't skip all that—even though it all seems so useless at the end. Unlike childbirth, it only ends in emptiness. As with war, you are happy simply to come out alive.

How I got through those blind bitter days of pain I have no idea. I stumbled through them with a fierce headache.

I remember going to teach at Breadloaf Writers' Conference, being given the honor of Robert Frost's white clapboard farmhouse to live and write in, and feeling nothing but despair. I dragged myself to classes (leaving Molly with Frost's ghost and an English au pair). I dragged myself back. I seemed to think that alcohol would help, and I was in the perfect place for it, because in those days you could *major* in alcohol at Breadloaf. The faculty meetings were exclusively about how to mark your bottles. The whole mountain needed a Twelve Step Program. Even the trees had wet brains. They bent and swayed. The maples were turning red with shame. There was alcohol on the Adirondack chairs, alcohol in the barn, alcohol in the faculty lounge. The sky was streaked with alcohol at dusk. The cycle was fixed: alcohol till unconscious (as my father used to say of the thirties music business), and sleep and coffee to get over it. Block out those bad thoughts at all cost. But then what do you have? Unconsciousness.

I called Jon from phone booths all over Vermont, hoping for a reprieve, but none was forthcoming. I wept until my eyes turned red. Then I wept some more.

Most people were at Breadloaf to get away from their spouses. I was wanting to get back. There was the usual drunkenness and bed-hopping with the noble excuse of Literature. There was the usual chaos masquerading as lust.

Time magazine was lurking, doing a cover story on John Irving, who was about to publish the novel after *Garp*. John Gardner was blithely riding the motorcycle that would soon kill him. Hilma and Meg Wolitzer—that talented mother-daughter act—were both unfailingly kind to me in my messy grief.

A rumor reached me that *Time* was going to run a gossip item on my shattered marriage. I blew up at a lurking journalist, unwittingly confirming the rumor.

I began a harmless flirtation with a nice, married writer. We went to an inn one night and were both relieved he was impotent. He was thinking of his wife, who, at that very moment, was racing to Vermont to catch him. I was thinking of Jon, who wasn't. He kept reaching over her phantom body to touch me. I kept reaching over Jon's phantom body to touch him. After a while, we renounced our abortive attempts at sex, having at least validated each other's attractiveness. We became friends.

Sex remains a dilemma. Much as we need it, we can't just have it without feeling. Feeling always gets in the way, dammit.

After Breadloaf, things got worse.

The emptiness at home was terrible.

I was single again at thirty-nine, but this time with a child and a whole new set of circumstances to get used to. Dating rituals were different. The world of sex had changed *again*. Now it seemed you were *expected* to fuck everyone and think nothing of it.

Single at seventeen, I had wanted to get hitched and shut out all sexual distraction. Single at twenty-two, I had had a year or two of freedom, then panicked and got married to Allan. At thirty, I went from that marriage directly to the next romantic adventure, with Jon. But now, at thirty-nine, I could *live* my fantasies if I chose. Yet the prospect seemed suddenly bleak. Only to the married do fantasies seem like solutions.

In Greenwich, there lived a married friend who was the high priestess of adultery. She was the perfect exemplar of Southern womanhood moved North. Her husband was a chilly surgeon who did only high-profile sports medicine. He was never home. She appeared to be *always* home. She seemed to spend the day antiquing furniture, restoring antique quilts, and keeping creative house à la Martha Stewart—the woman who earned her freedom by glorifying the slavery of Home.

In reality, the surgeon's wife spent many weekdays from eleven to four in a hotel room in Stamford with a variety of swains half her age. She was adept at keeping adultery neat and separate—as you must when it is your "lifestyle." She was blonde, but she drove to Stamford wearing a pepper and salt wig. She always brought her own vintage champagne, Beluga caviar, home-baked pumpernickel, home-cured capers, homegrown shallots and onions—chopped. The napkins were linen, the flowers fresh from her cutting garden. Ms. Stewart would have approved.

She kept a file of special résumés for friends newly widowed or divorced. She graded them from A to E for bed skills, coded the skills according to the first letter of *her* term for them—C, F, H, B, which turned out to mean cunnilingus, fucking, hugging, and backrub.

That tells you something about her priorities.

I got seven résumés with pictures attached (head not cock shots), clear descriptions of the man and his body, and cautionary words about never meeting him at home. Rubbers were suggested, but, in 1982, still optional.

Two of these guys tided me over for a couple of months. One was a trucker, another a disk jockey. In *Parachutes & Kisses,* I called him my "Dick-Jockey," making fun, as usual, of my own pain. But each proved hard to get rid of.

Men say they want sex only, but when women *give* only that, it turns out they want more. Possession. Marriage. Community property.

When *you* want sex without home phone numbers given, they often get huffy and don't want to put out. Sometimes, they wilt.

This is another reason men and women will never work: power. A woman wanting sex only has all the power, and many men prefer to detumesce rather than have a woman dominate. She's too much like Mommy. The men who are exceptions to this rule often turn out to be utterly dependent and almost incapable of blowing their own noses. Eventually you send them packing because they're much more work than babies. Or dogs.

Role playing is a different story. A man may love playing little bedwetter, little beggar, little badboy with a paid dominatrix. Men understand such bargains. The power game is clear. But to be dominated by a woman he shares a life with is disturbing. When role playing turns to reality, the problems start.

Is this an absolute rule? No rules are absolute. But it's a general enough condition to be worth noting.

Many men prefer strong women but they must nonetheless assert *some* area of control. Without it, sex is impossible and his eyes wander.

As a single breadwinner-mother I was about to learn all the things my fifties girlhood had failed to teach me. This was the most critical period of my life—the years in which all my body and brain cells changed and I became the mistress—not to say dominatrix—of my fate.

But before I could move into myself after divorce, my body had to shed its toxins. The years of dependency on parents, on grandparents, on men, manifested themselves in one colossal headache that was to last six months. Nothing got rid of it—not aspirin, not codeine, not Tofranil, not Nardil, not booze, not pot, not men.

For sleeping with men I didn't like enough to sleep with, there was pot. For hanging out with friends who weren't friends, there was booze. For the mornings, there was aspirin. For the night, there was Valium and codeine. My head rebelled. It throbbed like a pulsar in space. Every anodyne made it more determined to ache. It *needed* to feel this pain. That was the cosmic message. As long as I failed to listen, it beat invisible drums on my skull.

The body is wiser than its inhabitant. The body *is* the soul. We ignore its aches, its pains, its eruptions, because we fear the truth.

The body is God's messenger.

I found a young medical student with a splendid appendage and a refrigerator full of magic mushrooms. With him, I dived into the salad days I'd never had in school. The salads were black and fungoid, bitter to the tongue. But they brought oblivion. I had missed the sixties. This was my way of recapturing my youth.

But the medical student, sweet as he was, couldn't cure my headache. It was bigger than I was. It was Gogol's nose—a metaphysical headache. It was the headache of my destiny. It was the headache my life had become.

The headache was a sign of blocked self-knowledge. Where was Dr. Mitscherlich now? Too far away to help me. Ill in Germany. Soon to be dead.

My head was bursting; did someone want to be born? Was Athena getting ready to burst forth? Or was it Pandora? Was I to be a warrior woman or only the bearer of a box of ills?

Perhaps depression in women is an unacknowledged passion for rebirth. Something is pressing to appear. It is not the baby; it can only be the mother.

Motherhood stimulates all our old fears of abandonment. When motherhood leads to divorce, abandonment is proved not merely a fear but the deepest truth we know. Spelunking through the primal caves of myself, I found a crying infant. It was not my daughter. It was me.

So the odyssey began—a seven-year cycle of death, resurrection, and birth. The last seven-year cycle had produced Molly. The next produced me.

At thirty-nine, I learned how to change a tire, how to shovel snow, how to stack wood. I learned how to meet a deadline without a shoulder to whine on. I became obsessed with firewood. If only there was always a fire in the fireplace, I knew that everything would be all right.

Prometheus must have been a woman. I reverted to my ancient nature: inventing fire all day, having my liver plucked out all night.

Before departing, Jon had fired Lula. He fired her because he knew my work depended on her. Two writers in one house is hardly comfortable. When one is a man and the other a woman, the nanny, as well as the child, becomes a pawn.

The nannies came and went. They didn't like being stranded in the country any more than I did. They didn't care whether I finished a book or not. They had come to America to find husbands or get degrees or green cards or stoned—the young ones anyway. The older ones were either as bizarre as recently released mental patients or else were chronically depressed. The rest left if you refused to pay them cash.

W. H. Auden once wrote that in his utopia, all the public statues would be of defunct chefs rather than condottieri. In my utopia, the public statues will be of women who led both public and private lives with equal zeal: Harriet Beecher Stowe, Margaret Mead, Hillary Rodham Clinton. (Zoë Baird is the Joan of Arc of having it all. She found child care, but the *wrong* child care. The only wonder is she found *any*.)

Of course, I suffered over paying another woman to watch my

child—but how was I to feed us if I didn't work? I had become both my father *and* my mother. And both parents warred with each other inside my head.

All this is mundane: merely the ordinary experience of my whiplash generation. Caught between our mothers (who stayed home) and the next generation (who took the right to achieve for granted), we suffered all the transitions of women's history inside our skulls. *Whatever* we did felt wrong. And whatever we did was fiercely criticized.

A woman's ability to achieve depends on childlessness or child care. In America, where we don't believe in an underclass to do "women's work," women themselves become the underclass. For love.

Nobody doubts the love is real. It's for our children. But we are supposed to do it invisibly and never mention it. Alfred North Whitehead, who wasn't a woman, after all, said that the truth of a society is what cannot be said. And women's work still cannot be said. It's called *whining*—even by other women. It's called *self-indulgence*—even by other women. Perhaps women writers are hated because abstraction makes oppression possible and we *refuse* to be abstract. How can we be? Our struggles are concrete: food, fire, babies, a room of one's own. These basics are rare—even for the privileged. It is nothing short of a miracle every time a woman with a child finishes a book.

Our lives—from the baby to the writing desk—are the lives of the majority of humanity: never enough time to think, eternal exhaustion. The cared-for male elite, with female slaves to tend their bodily needs, can hardly credit our difficulties as "real." "Real" is the deficit, oil wars in the Middle East, or how much of our children's milk the Pentagon shall get.

This is the true division in the world today: between those who carelessly say "Third World" believing themselves part of the "First," and those who know they *are* the Third World—wherever they live.

Women everywhere are the "Third World." In my country, where most women do not think themselves part of it, they are mostly third, trapped in the myth of being "first."

Before I had a child I was trapped in that myth as well. I took my privilege for granted. Only after Molly's birth did I know it for the myth it was. Only then did I merge with my mother.

After Lula, there were several nannies I would not leave my daughter with, and then came Mary Poppins, aka Bridget-from-

Brighton. Bridget-from-Brighton had big boobs, black hair, red lips, and a pretty heart-shaped face. She soon fell in love with the electrician who was helping to build my treehouse study. Soon after, they left for New Hampshire with his six-packs, his truck, his tools, her recipes for tomato quiche, lemon curd, and flan, and her willingness to serve (if not me) a man. Her boyfriend was jealous of Molly; *he* wanted a nanny.

How else could these two fairly responsible young people have left my baby sitting in the bathtub and gone downstairs to load a truck? With that maternal sixth sense that lives in the adrenals, I raced out of my study to find my daughter gurgling and cooing at the bubbles in her bath. What if I had found her under them? As the nanny and the electrician departed, they ran over my beloved Poochkin—my first child, my familiar. Yelping like a lost soul, he died on the vet's table. I hardly knew if he had died or I had.

Poochkin was gone, but Molly got older, as children do. I learned to write from dawn to dawn on her weekends with her dad. I changed my hours of tranced concentration by sheer will. (Like George Sand, like all writer-mothers, I wrote all night and collapsed on the divan at dawn.) I stopped sleeping. But what is sleep when your bichon's ghost whimpers at the door through long, rainy nights? Buffy had departed with Jon; Poochkin died under the wheels of the babysitter's boyfriend's van (to be replaced—but of course never really replaced—by Emily Doggenson, a champion bichon bitch, and Poochini, the sweet runt of her litter). Of course, you can't really replace dogs any more than you can people; each one has its own special personality and smell. No wonder our deepest losses are always heralded by dogs. We make them into poems and we go on.

BEST FRIENDS

We made them
in the image of our fears
to cry at doors,
at partings—even brief,
to beg for food at table,
& to look at us with those big
aching eyes,

& stay beside us
when our children flee,
& sleep upon our beds
on darkest nights,
& cringe at thunder
as in our own
childhood
frights.

We made them sad-eyed,
loving, loyal, scared
of life without us.
We nurtured their dependency
& grief.
We keep them as reminders of our fear.
We love them
as the unacknowledged hosts
of our own terror
of the grave—abandonment.

Hold my paw
for I am dying.
Sleep upon my coffin;
wait for me,
sad-eyed
in the middle of the drive
that curves beyond the cemetery wall.

I hear your bark,
I hear your mournful howl—
oh may all dogs that I have ever loved
carry my coffin,
howl at the moonless sky,
& lie down with me sleeping
when I die.

    And then the Mother Goddess—oddly absent for a time—
returned, relented, and sent me Margaret.

She came, I later discovered, because her daughter, who is psychic, had seen an ad in the *Bridgeport Post*. "I think that's for you, Mom," she said.

"A nanny?" said Margaret. "I have no training as a nanny."

"But you raised four children, Mom, and you love to read."

Apparently the agency had run an ad with "famous writer" in the lead. Kim and her mother perhaps expected a man. Or maybe not. The vibes were right. Kim foresaw some light for us all in the next few years. Molly would grow. I would write. No dogs would die.

When I met Margaret I knew she was for real and I was blessed. She had clear blue eyes that instantly met mine. Widowed almost a year, having nursed "my Bob" through Lou Gehrig's disease, Margaret needed a child to raise as much as I needed a Margaret. Her husband had fallen ill almost as soon as he retired. Two years of degeneration followed, then his drawn-out dying.

Depressed and lonely in Florida, Margaret was deep in grief when I met her. She went to Al-Anon meetings to learn how to stop raging at God. She learned how to affirm, not deny.

As the wife of a long-distance trucker who drove an eighteen-wheeler, she was used to running everything and making quick decisions. She had lost one baby and kept four others. She had surrendered to her life as I had not. She was sent to teach me how.

When I met Margaret, she was plump from grieving: a small round woman with intense eyes and graying hair. She came to live with me and Molly for a decade. Molly was five when she arrived, fifteen when Margaret retired for good. (In between there had been one other retirement, which didn't last.)

Margaret was not a servant—unless she was a servant of God. She needed to be needed. To overcome death, she needed to make things grow. "I would not do this for anyone but you," she always said. She was my teacher, my sponsor of self-respect, as well as Molly's nanny. She introduced me to daily meditations, to taking care of my own soul, to living one day at a time. Living with Margaret was like getting a second chance at childhood. I had had a neurotic Jewish childhood. Now I was getting the other kind.

A baby's mother also needs a mother. Molly, Margaret, and I reconstructed the primitive tribe. Our Connecticut commune might have been the caves of Lascaux. Margaret gave me the uninterrupted five hours a day I needed to write. She also helped me keep the hearth aflame.

Hers was the most precious gift I've received—after the birth of Molly and my parents' acidophilus milk. My parents gave me life. Molly gave that life meaning. Margaret helped me keep that life alive.

I hope I gave her as much as she gave me. Without her, motherhood would have swallowed my writing whole.

Molly, Margaret, and I traveled all over the world. We coddled, then bounced, numerous men. Margaret fed my swains homemade chicken soup, faithfully informed them I was "in the shower" when they called while I was in bed with another, and was there for Molly when I was not. She taught me that motherhood is a shared responsibility. She also taught me how to listen to my child. Eventually she let go and I took over. When Molly demanded me and not my stand-in, Margaret retreated into the role of executive housekeeper.

In early adolescence, Molly was lucky enough to have two live-in mothers to rebel against. She had enough wisecracks for both of us. And enough rage. Every girl needs at least two mothers to denounce.

How much our world has diminished the lives of women! The Egyptian peasant digging the alluvial mud of the Nile at least has sisters and cousins to help her. Poor and illiterate she may be, but hardly as alone as we in our fancy bathrooms. I imagine the "privileged" American woman in a palatial bathroom with a toddler peering between her legs as she sits on the throne. She has gadgets galore but never the extra pair of hands she needs most. Women in America may have the best bathrooms to clean. But they often have no one to share their children with.

Women in America read "lifestyle" pages that are really glorifications of shopping. They teach us we must veil ourselves in makeup to be loved. And we willingly take the veil, thinking ourselves *freed* by it. Makeup is no more optional for us than the veil is for Arab women: It is our Western version of the chador.

At thirty-nine, I had a three-year-old daughter, all the responsibilities of a man, and all the liabilities of a woman. I made my living by saying so—and women are supposed to do the opposite. I suddenly understood things about the discrimination against women that my earlier life had shielded me from. Without child support, I had no choice but to go on writing—it was the only way of making a living I knew—yet my writing always put me in the midst of the crossfire between the sexes. I wanted a serene life, but I had no notion of how to get one. I was living out the typical experience of my generation, and at a level of privilege most of my generation does not begin to have. Privileged or not, it was enormously stressful. I had been raised to take my place in a world that no longer existed.

If I had to live like a man, I thought I would assert my right to a man's pleasures: nubile concubines.

My fortieth birthday was imminent and I was looking for the ultimate birthday present. Didn't I deserve it for all my hard work? For keeping the fire and the baby alive?

Imagine, if you will, a blue-eyed twenty-five-year-old. He is six foot two, has a perfect ski jump nose, pearly teeth, dazzling smile, brawny chest, muscled arms, biceps, and calves. As if that weren't enough, he also has a love of poetry, a literary bent, and a cock that also has a literary bent. It curves upward like a burnished scimitar.

How did I meet him? Not through a newsletter advertising men with large appendages (though my fans send me those regularly), but in a health club, through a friend. He was sweating on a Nautilus machine—a very seventies-turning-eighties way of meeting.

Will Wadsworth Oates III was the verdant limb on a rotting family tree. He came for tea one wintry night and never left—except to buy new barbells and old Harleys.

"Horizontally speaking," as Lorenz Hart wrote of Pal Joey, "he's at his very best." But vertically, he was pretty good too. He knew how to wear a tux. He had family training in knowing which fork to use. He would never confuse the contents of a finger bowl with consommé. He also looked good in a hat, the sign of a lady's man—or an actor. He could sail, swim, sing, and strip in seconds. He was also sweet. My gay male friends adored him. My women friends sniffed the air and called him a gigolo behind my back. (But an intellectual gigolo, as the phrase goes.) He was a librophilic, a romantic, a picaresque hero. He liked hard books and soft women.

Love feeds on likeness or imagined likeness. When it is blasted, we become enraged. Why? Because we have deceived ourselves about our twin.

How could I know that Will (or Oatsie, as his old friends called him) would proposition most of my women friends, hit on my men friends for auditions, and always be "borrowing" money?

I thought I knew the rules: I got him a credit card. I didn't know them all: The limit was too high.

I bought him gorgeous clothes, gave him a car (but, being practical, neglected to put it in his name). Summers, I took him to the Cipriani in Venice as if he were a starlet. As he swam laps in the pool, he was admired by ladies and gents alike. Will was so eager to please that he could make anyone fall in love with him. All his acting went into his life.

But Jewish girls and guns don't mix, and Will kept loaded guns in my house. When I discovered this—five years too late—I threw him out. Perhaps I was ready to anyway. In the beginning, I thought the guns weren't loaded ("a likely story, ma'am") because he swore he kept the ammo separate.

When I remember him now, he merges in my mind with Colette's Chéri. I think I see him trying on my pearls in bed. He had the playfulness of the born gigolo, and every liberated woman *needs* a gigolo from time to time. The connotation of the word betrays our disapproval of pleasure itself. But living for sensation and pleasure need not always be a bad thing. Will was my Bacchus—beautiful, androgynous, full of juice.

We object to the gigolo because he is paid for love, but we do not object to the mercenary who is paid for killing. Our statues are to condottieri, not *cavalieri serventi*. Our world would be better if it were the other way around.

Gay men do this gig far better than women. Perhaps they understand the bargain better. They sometimes adopt their lovers, recognizing this relationship as a species of parental role playing. But eventually even they get fed up. When the bargain shifts, they become enraged. Then they throw the bastards out.

Will was essentially kind—though the hustler in him sometimes got the upper hand. He loved performances, as much in daily life as on the stage. Will used to lift barbells on the lawn when Jon came to pick up Molly. He was hoping to seem dangerous enough to protect me. I was touched.

He would press me to marry him and I would procrastinate. It was not only that I liked being legally unhitched, but that I knew I could never marry Will. Any day, my life might change, without the intervention of lawyers. So I didn't say yes and I didn't say no. And he got angry.

I always thought Molly liked him. Later she told me she was afraid of him. I shudder when I remember the hidden guns. Will always swore the guns were out of reach. But how could he have known this when his normal condition was *stoned*? Bands of angels must have been watching over us. Margaret must have flown in with them.

When things began to get chronically awful in our lives, I realized how much we were drinking. A lot. I dragged Will to AA, thinking *he* needed to get sober. Another grandiose self-delusion. Like many addicts, I needed his addiction to face my own.

We started to go to meetings together. At first, they terrified me and I used to cry all through them. I did not know why. I hated the jargon and the slogans, made fun of the straitlaced way AA converts spoke the lingo of the Program: Easy Does It, One Day at a Time, Take That Off the Worry List, Let Go, Let God. Then I began to see that AA was the only place in my world where I was welcomed unjudgmentally. I fell in love with AA—a blessed alternative to the nature "red in tooth and claw" that characterizes the rest of our society. AA people are kind *on principle*. They know they have to serve others to serve themselves.

Will stayed sober for a year. I did for two. That taste of sobriety got me started, and it also broke us up. I began my still-unfinished trek down the long and winding road of surrender. I am still willful and afraid, but at least I *know* I am.

As Will was moving out, I found a lump in my left breast. While I waited for the outcome of a biopsy, Will and I were reconciled briefly by mortal fear. The day the lump proved benign, he moved out. The lump lingered for a while, then disappeared as if it had never been.

I dreamed of him endlessly. Sometimes I still do. In dreams, he can still make me come. When I am alone in a hotel room or settling into a rented house anywhere in the world, he immediately arrives.

I have heard many people say that they still love all their old loves somewhere in some synapse or other. The same is true for me. Memory clouds the love as it is meant to do, but beneath the fog of forgetting, the love remains. I still love them all—Jon, Will, Michael, Allan. I even love them *better* than I did when we were together, because now I have more empathy. They probably don't want my love, but there it is anyway. I cannot lose it. It returns in my dreams.

I seem to have skated over the divorce as over thick, unrippled ice. It was hardly like that: It was like falling through. Down through the black water, submerged in ink, but unable to write with it (no quill, no paper), unable to read, unable to breathe, unable to stand on the mucky bottom. Some incidents shimmer through the blackness, bringing back the sadness of it all.

One morning, I awake in the waterbed in Connecticut with Will. The doorbell shrills. It is a process-server out of Dickens with a rough red face and a thatch of yellow hair.

I stagger out, wrapping a damp terrycloth robe around my nakedness.

"Excuse me," he says, with the icy politeness of the secret police in Nabokov's Zembla.

"Are you Missus *Yong*?"

"I am."

"This is for you."

And he hands me a thick envelope, then quickly turns and runs down the icy path and drives away.

I tear open the papers at the door, shivering. I've never seen a process-server before. Nor have I seen a piece of paper like this. It seems to say that if I move away from Fairfield County, I will be prosecuted "to the full extent of the law" and lose custody of Molly ("the issue of that union") unless I remain "domiciled" in one of the following four towns: Westport, Weston, Fairfield, or Redding.

A very confusing suit, possibly unconstitutional and unwinnable, but a needle in the heart. After all, I already feel myself to be forever a "bad mother," because I must work to support her. I have somehow accepted the lack of child support, the random cruelties (like turning off the phone and letting the machine pick up so that I cannot check in on my two-year-old), but this is the ultimate sabotage: They will take my child in trade for my rebellious books. This betrayal cuts to the bone. (At that time I had no way of knowing that custody suits had become my generation's cruel and usual punishment for daring motherhood and a career at the same time.)

Two years and several thousands of dollars later, Jon and I are sitting in a social worker's lair in the basement of the Stamford Court House. The social workers, one male, one female, ask us in social-worker lingo: "What seems to be your area of disagreement?"

Somehow, my lawyer has kept Molly out of court, has prepared me with psychological affidavits attesting to her mental health, and has had the custody case thrown out and sent us instead for "mediation"—a therapy that relieves no one really but the judge. In mediation the fair person gives in and the crazy person gets to make the decision—usually by yelling.

We have been waiting for two hours in a basement hallway full of teenage black parents from the ghetto, battered Latina women, and others so poor they can't *afford* to get divorced.

Asked to state our problem, we find we cannot even *formulate* it. Finally, Jon blurts out, "My ex-wife wants our daughter to go to Ethical Culture—and I think she should go to Dalton."

"Well—she would be *better* at Ethical, because she is . . . " I trail off.

The two social workers are looking at us as if we have both farted.

"Surely we can resolve that," the woman says, in a choked voice.

And a "compromise" is struck. I will send Molly to Dalton (Jon's former school) and he will drop the suit. I weigh Molly's inquietude over the lawsuit against sending her to a school I think is wrong for her, and I decide on the lesser of two evils. Jon shrugs and drops the suit. He is sick of it. So am I.

A year later, I am about to publish *Molly's Book of Divorce,* an illustrated children's book about a little girl who goes back and forth between Mommy's and Daddy's house. The book is ironic, but it's also a Valentine to kids and parents suffering divorce. I wrote it as a bedtime story to help Molly deal with a life in which she is always leaving socks, underpants, teddy bears at another house. I also wrote it for myself. It ends with a party in which the divorced spouses and their new partners all kiss and make up. Wishful thinking. The book is on press—when suddenly a lawyer's letter stops everything.

Jon's lawyer threatens that unless the child's name is changed, he will use every means to get an injunction against the book.

Alice in Wonderland's father never did this, nor did Christopher Robin's (of course *he* was the author), but it is useless to go to court to prove that children's books are traditionally named after real children. The publisher has already been thrown into a panic. I am summoned into his office and ordered to comply with the demand.

To avoid a lawsuit, I change the little girl's name to Megan and the presses once again roll. I am billed for the scrapped printings. Endless meetings with lawyers take place to reassure the publisher, but somehow the energy is lost. The tabloid press has picked up the story and made its usual hash of it. All the reviews of the book speak of "the scandal" and not the book. What scandal?

There was no lawsuit, no injunction, only a lawyer's letter, harsh words, and endless meetings. But the book is tainted anyway. The publisher edges away from it. And the parents who might find it comforting to their children never find it in bookstores. But, like a damaged child, I refuse to give up on it. Determined to get the book out in another form, I put the pieces for a television show together: Loretta Swit as the mommy, Keri Houlihan as the little girl, Allan Katz to do the pilot. The pilot is terrific. But it never goes to series.

"Divorce is a downer" say the network executives.

"Loretta's too *old*," say the network executives (who, six months before, insisted on her being cast). She gave a wonderful performance too, spookily stealing some of my mannerisms as actresses do. With her unique combination of grit and sweetness, she might have been an inspiration to mothers raising kids alone. But the series was inspired by women and nixed by men—as usual. Between "Loretta's too old" and "Divorce is a downer," the series was dead. It aired as a busted pilot, got better reviews than most of my books. Then it vanished into video limbo.

Half the families in America are getting divorced in 1986, but not on television sitcoms. "Divorce" is still a dirty word in network TV. A few years later, there's a stampede to make such programs.

"You must have been prophetic," television executives now tell me. "You were years ahead of your time."

Megan is out of print. Therapists for children discover it and buy it in out-of-print bookstores to help counsel kids in the midst of divorce. I send them whatever remaindered copies I have. But mostly the book cannot be found—another casualty of the divorce.

After that sabotage, I go slightly nuts and sue Jon for harassment, citing my loss of livelihood and the interruptions to my work. The harassment is real enough, but the law was not made for this—nor for the remedy of heartbreak. This absurd new lawsuit drags on expensively for a while, further interrupting my work.

Finally, I find that I cannot stay enraged enough at Molly's father to go on suing him. I still feel tenderness for him. I dream of our being friends someday. And I want to get on with my life.

Jon and I have pushed each other away, hurt each other, hurt our child. Now Molly is starting first grade at Dalton. It's time to learn to be parents if not yet friends. I am settled, weekdays at least, in a beautiful apartment overlooking the East River in Manhattan. A little distance has been put between us and our pain. The scar tissue has begun to form. It is constantly ripped off, but, little by little, we are learning to share. Weekends, Jon and I meet in Connecticut. I keep the house in Connecticut for Molly to be near her dad. Besides, the house is my writing haven.

My new apartment in New York proves to be located in one of those antediluvian buildings where Jews are encouraged to grow foreskins in order to pass as WASPs. They know they are there on sufferance because the building was formerly "restricted," so they become enforcers, keeping out other Jews.

As at the Maidstone Club in the Hamptons, where the founding fathers never planned to open the neighborhood to "fags, show business types, or Jews," the inhabitants of this stuffy building now find themselves surrounded.

They sold the apartment to me—though I was the epitome of everything they had fled all their lives. When Will moves in—with his Harley, black leather jacket, spiked wristlets, and boarding school accent—I become the Joan of Arc of Gracie Square.

It's whispered in the building that we "squeak the bed springs at night," that Will smokes—or sells—dope in Carl Schurz Park, and that the little redheaded five-year-old and the kindly white-haired nanny are practicing pagans who worship the Horned God right there on East End Avenue.

The co-op board suddenly decides to send a committee to inspect my apartment. Do we or do we not have enough carpeting? That is the question.

A bed springs committee is formed. This august body—composed of one reconstructed-foreskin Jew (a lawyer), one unrecovered alcoholic WASP (also a lawyer), and one perfectly coiffed Chanel-yenta with a lambskin bag covered with interlocking Cs (a decorator *married* to a lawyer)—solemnly inspects my apartment. The gray-mauve carpets match the river. The walls are mirrored to reflect it. The waterbed is disguised in an Amish quilt and brass headboard to look like a cuddly *letto matrimoniale* in a New England bed and breakfast.

I hold my breath as the committee walks through the bedroom. Every inch of the house is carpeted except for the tiny mirrored foyer. The waterbed is, of course, illegal—that I know. But fortunately my inspector-generals are too prudish to *touch* the surface of the bed, which would have rippled under its antique star quilt, giving me away. Having had their kicks, they depart, not a little puzzled by my seeming adherence to the rules.

Now a harassment campaign begins in earnest. There are hang-up calls each night at three A.M. and anonymous poison pen letters left under our front door. On one occasion, Molly is yelled at in the elevator for my supposed sins.

Will and I consult lawyers. They tell us nothing and want fat retainers. They promise to negotiate with the co-op board. I have a sudden flash: This is another problem the law can't solve! And what am I doing in such a building anyway? I belong on the West Side, where I grew up. It turns out that the apartment I grew up in is on the market. An enterprising realtor calls, asking do I want to see it? I do—until I hear the price. Two million? When my parents lived there, the rent was $200 a month. Thomas Wolfe was right: You can't go home again.

Will, Molly, Margaret, and I rent an apartment in Venice for three months that summer and quietly put the Gracie Square apartment on the market. One afternoon Will and I are lying in bed, watching the canal water make its magical ripples on the ceiling, when my business manager calls with the news that someone wants to buy the New York apartment.

"Sell it!" I say. Will and I fuck our brains out, then dance around the room, giggling.

Fags, show business types, and Jews unite! You have nothing to lose but your real estate! Unmarried Jewish mothers with young lovers cannot live in "good" buildings in New York. My mistake was *wanting* to live in a "good" building. Better stick to my own kind.

So we sell Foreskin Towers and set about looking for a brownstone. No more East Side co-ops. We need turf of our own to call home.

We find a narrowish row house on Ninety-fourth Street between Park and Lexington, which is inhabited by a nice psychiatrist, his bouncy wife, and three very clever children. They are hoping to move to Paris. Over the shrink's bed is a sign: MENTAL HEALTH IS OUR GREATEST WEALTH. I find this an excellent omen, so I buy the house at once.

It needs *everything*—a new roof, new kitchen, laundry, boiler, baths. I do what I always do with houses—spend till the money runs out, then go back to work to finish the book.

Sooner or later I run screaming from the renovation, crying, "*Cash flow*." Three of the four floors are inviting, even if the garden and ground floor remain unfinished. By then, the walls are covered with William Morris wallpaper of the same Victorian vintage as the house; the stairwells are purple and the chandeliers Venetian. My father tells me it looks like a whorehouse.

"How would you know?" I ask.

Good-bye Foreskin Towers. *Nobody* can tell me who to live with in my own brownstone. But the house is never quite practical. Since it has always been owned by doctors, the basement is full of spooky old medical equipment, X-rays of rib cages, pelvises, skulls. Former patients, speaking various Spanish dialects, still arrive in the middle of the night wanting succor. Even in daylight, the house is dark, as row houses tend to be, and for security's sake, all the members of my commune—except Poochini (successor to Poochkin)—are obliged to wear panic buttons to activate the alarm system if we take out the garbage or answer the door.

The brownstone solves our housing problems for a while. It also gives Will something to do and me something to be grateful to him for. But it turns out to be haunted by my old headache. Ghosts of previous tenants and their patients are in residence. I have the wrong dreams in that house—dreams that must belong to the patients of one of the former doctor owners. Or else the ghosts go back to a much earlier vintage.

Was the body of the Ruppert Brewery manager (for whom the house was built) buried in the vault under the sidewalk? Had some outraged husband murdered his faithless wife? I engaged a psychic healer (who was reputed to have helped Margaret Mead in her final year) to exorcise the place. She promised she would do so, but only if I became her patient first. I used to go to her "studio" on York Avenue, lie on a table nude, and have her talk to my unreliable thyroid gland, palpate my healthy liver, and describe the astral visits she would make to my brownstone at five in the morning. ("I came in the early morning, didn't you see me?") Then I would pay her in cash.

She always stressed how she hated exorcisms (*cleanings,* she called them), how they gave her a colossal headache. But she must have worked wonders, because I sold the place for a profit just before the real estate market crashed.

And so I moved again. When I met Ken, he was living in a building that *specialized* in "fags, show business types, and Jews." We bought a bigger apartment in that building and stayed on. I was delighted to be on the twenty-seventh floor after years of darkness.

And I was delighted to be among my own kind. The building I live in is also a major dog and cat building. Apparently fags, show business types, and Jews like animals.

Molly transferred to the Day School, where the mothers do not wear the Krupp diamond to Field Day and kids do not get picked up in limousines. (Lots of New York private school kids went to school in limousines in the eighties—before their daddies went to jail.)

I was always either flush or broke, but somehow I was able to pay the bills and raise my daughter. I even learned how to be a decent mother. Eventually Jon and I stopped suing each other and began to talk. Sometimes we even reminisce about old times and remember *why* we loved each other. And Molly's face lights up as if with a thousand candles.

I can't wait for her to tell *her* side of the story, even though I know it won't be soft on me. Until she makes sense of it all, the real story will go untold. It's hers to tell, not mine.

Everything about the divorce is at once so common and so unique. Two writers—facing fame, rejection, money worries, and their own pain—try to raise a child. The child they raise turns out to be like both of them, yet like herself most of all: wildly funny, cynical, a killer with words. She *has* to be to survive her parents.

My generation is strewn with divorces. Looking back, we often wonder why. What did we gain by *not* staying together for the sake of the children? Did we gain anything at all?

We were the generation that was going to live forever. And we've turned fifty like everyone else. We're not going to beat the *malach hamovis** after all.

Sometimes it seems both our kids and our parents were smarter than we were. We fell somewhere between our parents' thirties idealism and our kids' eighties cynicism. Somewhere deep down we *still* believe that *all we need is love, love, love.* Somewhere deep down we question how we got gray hair. How on earth did *we* get to be the grown-ups? The wonder is that our kids are growing up—despite all we did to destroy them.

---

* Angel of death.

11

DOÑA JUANA GETS SMART, OR A GOOD GIRL'S GUIDE TO BAD BOYS

If you lack Freedom, you cannot give it to others.

—Arabic proverb

Do you know, the older I grow the more sure do I become that the only man one can really love is the man one does not respect.

—Marie Dorval, quoted by André Maurois in *Lélia, The Life of George Sand*

I was raised to be a good girl of the fifties, to believe that "love and marriage go together like a horse and carriage." The first time I got married it was 1963, the second time 1966, the third time 1978, the fourth time 1989. My life, then, has proved a microcosm of love and sex for my generation. Every time I got unhitched, I felt like Margaret Mead among the Manus or the Mundugumor. Mating and dating had all "changed, changed utterly," and a "terrible beauty" was born.

Of all these fathomless Dark Ages, the eighties were the worst. The problem was that men all thought they had to be Masters of the Universe and women believed they were losers unless they captured men who could buy them emeralds as big as the Ritz. Somewhere during that mad epoch I must have decided to attempt a guidebook that would be a summation of all I'd learned about men in my much-too-long love life.

My working title was *Beauty and the Beast: A Good Girl's Guide to Bad Boys*. I knew that women wanted rules. How did I know this? I wanted them myself. So I gave them to myself:

A DOZEN PHALLACIES WOMEN BUY

Phallacy 1

If he loves me, he'll be faithful forever.

Truth

His loving you has nothing to do with his being faithful. Some men are monogamous. Most aren't. The sexy ones usually aren't. Monogamy lasts three days, three weeks, three months, or at best three years with most men. Often it lasts just about long enough to get you pregnant. Nature has a reason for this. Men are programmed to spread their seed as widely as possible and women to raise live, healthy babies. Human babies take a long time to grow to self-sufficiency—as you may have noticed. Some men lie better than others, but lying is endemic in the species. Some few paragons of maleness are faithful. Most others cheat. The question is: Can you stand it? If the cheating is not blatant and disrespectful and you get a lot out of the relationship in other ways (a friend, a lover, a father to your kids, an economic partner), then consider these alternatives: You can accept his cheating gracefully, and at the same time extract emotional and financial benefits from his guilt. You can cheat discreetly yourself—*if* (and only if) you *enjoy* it (not for spite). You can realize it has nothing to do with you. He does it *for* his manhood, not against your womanhood.

Phallacy 2

I need a man to feel whole.

Truth

You don't need a man as much as a man needs you. Women are the self-sufficient sex. Men are the dependent sex. Women reproduce the species; they create life within themselves (or the Mother Goddess does, through them). Men know this and in their inadequacy have created a world which cripples and demeans every female accomplishment—from the glory of childbirth itself to women's work in every creative and professional field. You may not be able to change the world—*yet*—but you don't have to buy this lie. You are powerful, strong, self-sufficient. The more you know this, the happier you'll be with or without a man.

Phallacy 3

If you use your power to support a man, he'll always support you.

Truth

Alas, not true. It's wonderful to stand by your man, to give to the one you love, but you must never forget yourself, and your children, since he may. Being a man, he takes for granted that his needs come first. Being a woman, you take that for granted too. Don't. Protect yourself—not with feminist rhetoric or argument, but with actions. A bank account and real estate in your own name, money put aside for your kids' education that he can't touch (or give to the next—younger—wife and *her* spawn), a profession of your own to rely on. Above all, empower yourself, and then help empower him if it pleases you to do so.

Phallacy 4

Men love it when you tell the truth about your relationship.

Truth

They hate it. Their truth and your truth are, anyway, different. Their truth is about their priorities (conquest, winning, fucking). *Our* truth is about *our* priorities (nurturing, creativity, love). Our priorities make *life* possible. Their priorities make their winning possible. They see our priorities as trivial, but they couldn't live without them. They are in denial about their human dependencies, and our priorities enable them to keep up their denial. How can you talk about this? It's like one person talking Greek and the other Swahili. Cross-babble.

Don't talk about the relationship—*do* something. Love it or leave it. Make your needs clear. Seize legitimate power. Always speak of how you feel, or what you need, and *never* accuse. Be gentle but firm. Know what you want and ask for it. If he says no once too often, then consider what your options are. If you are masochistic, get straight with yourself. This world is too cruel for you to compound the felony by being cruel to yourself. Speak gently to him and even more gently to yourself. Love yourself. Men are mimics. If you love yourself, they love you too.

Phallacy 5

Men love women who never oppose them and cater to their every whim.

Truth

Marabel Morgan and Anita Bryant spread this big lie a decade and a half ago and look where it got them. The truth is men feel *insecure* with women who humor them constantly, succumb to all their whims, and never tell them what to do. They don't want to be torn down, but they do want to be *guided*. They know they are bad boys, and a woman who caters to every whim only makes them feel *more* guilty. If you want a man to love you, make him feel big, but also give him firm but gentle guidance. He counts on you to save his life. He knows he's not the knight on the white charger or Prince Charming—why don't you?

Phallacy 6

Men want to be knights on white chargers and rescue you.

Truth

This is true. Which is not a contradiction of number 5. They want to *seem* to rescue you, though they know in the dead of (k)night that *you* are, in reality, rescuing them. Let your knight have his fantasy. Indulge it. Water it. Use it in the bedroom to make the sex hotter. But know it in your heart for the fantasy it is. Chances are, if you're cruising down the Amazon and you are shipwrecked in alligator-infested waters, you'll save him and he'll take the credit.

Phallacy 7

Men hate feminists.

Truth

The truth is: They hate women who *babble* about feminism without doing anything but blame them, but they *love* women who know how strong they are, while paying lip-service to how necessary men are. Is this dishonest? Yes and no. It's dishonest if you feel you always have to tell the truth to men—which is the biggest mistake you can ever make if you want them to fuck you. If you don't need this—you are happily celibate or happily gay—then read no further. You have it figured out.

Phallacy 8

Men love babies and all ache to be devoted daddies.

Truth

Some do, some don't. Most—like you—are ambivalent about parenthood, which is only human, after all. You, however, have hormones rushing through your body that make you—or most of you—gooey about babies in a way most men are not. During your menstruating years, your body reminds you every month of your mortality and your generativity—his body does not. His body reminds him that his penis is ever present, vulnerable, insistent, and lonely. It will get him to say almost anything to you in order to seem invincible, hard, and not-lonely. And afterward it will make him say anything at all to get away. As you long to merge with another, he dreads it. Your primary attachment was to a human being of the same sex, his was to a human being of the opposite. Thus he dreads union even as he seeks it. Your longing for union is unambivalent. You are not afraid to be engulfed by your mother; you expect, in fact, to *become* her. Add that to the hormonal differences between the sexes and you have one sex longing to merge and the other sex both wanting it and dreading it. Men are passionate and claustrophobic at the same time; they advance and retreat simultaneously. This is God's little joke on the human race. Some psychologists theorize that if men took care of babies, this would change. We're willing to try this, but a lot of men aren't. Babies seem to make them nervous. Of course there are those paragons who write articles for the men's column of the *New York Times*. They don't count. Who knows what they *do* after having dispatched the column? Besides, they are no more Everyman than Katharine Hepburn is Everywoman. If you have a man like that, chances are you aren't reading this. Perhaps your daughter will have a man like that—but it's too late for you. In the whiplash generation babies exacerbate male claustrophobia—which is why at just the moment you are at your nestingest, he is at his antsiest. If you understand this and don't take it personally, you'll be a lot happier.

Phallacy 9

Men like lusty women.

Truth

For most men, the ideal woman would be lusty on cue. His cue. And she would switch off as fast as a peep show switches off or you can snap the centerfold shut. Have you ever noticed the way the lustiest man will drool over the centerfold in *Playboy* while ignoring the real live woman in his bed? Is this a paradox? Not exactly. The centerfold (like the peep show) is safer. It's on *his* timetable. A real live woman is not. Better still—two women. One lusty and intermittently available. One nonsexual and mommyish and eternally available (for nurturing). To the male mind, that is heaven (i.e., utter safety)—which brings us back to phallacy number 1.

Phallacy 10

Men are rational, women irrational.

Truth

If consistency is rationality, women are more rational. They long for integration, honesty, union. They may suffer from PMS, postpartum depression, and premenopausal dread, but they are more usually unambivalent about jumping into life. Men know this and long for strong women to lead them. Strong women who strategically pretend to be weak.

Phallacy 11

Men hate women who have more money than they do.

Truth

Men really hate women who control them. They are perfectly happy to have women with money as long as they (the men) control the money—or seem to. Remember the Napoleonic Code? Remember all those heiresses married for their money in the days when a woman's money automatically became her husband's? What men hate is women having the power to control them. And money, in our society, is the ultimate representation of power. If you make more or have more money than your man, you will have to find real—or imaginary—ways of giving him control—enough control to right the balance—and he still may never forgive you.

Phallacy 12

Men like beautiful women with perfect features and perfect bodies.

Truth

Actually, men like them better at a distance than up close, where they make them a bit nervous—except for display.

Reading this now, it seems like a cry of pain disguised as advice to the lovelorn. The lovelorn was me—whether I admitted it or not.

I was dating, trying for the first time in my life to understand the opposite sex. I had to. I felt my survival was at stake. Always, there had been dozens of men to choose from. Now I was in my forties and the men were mostly married or dead. Others only dated women under thirty. The rest were gay—great for friendship, but generally not available for sex. I'd either have to give up men—not a bad idea perhaps, but I figured I could always do that *later*—or learn, at long last, how they *worked*. This unfinished advice book must have been my attempt to codify my knowledge. And I still believe in every one of these "rules of love." After several years of midlife marriage, I believe them *more*.

We could raise the question of why I thought—at fortysomething—that I needed a man. I like my own company; I can earn my own living; I have never had trouble finding lovers. Why, then, did I want a partner at all?

I have puzzled over this question and have never come up with a rational answer. Perhaps the answer *isn't* rational. Perhaps it is only the same reason why geese mate and rhesus monkeys prefer real mothers to heated cloth-and-wire armatures. Perhaps it is only a matter of warmth. Or perhaps it is the sad fact that women are still so discriminated against in a man's world that it is better to have one particular ally rather than face the whole discriminatory world alone.

What a wealth of warmth and protection there seems to be in that phrase "my husband"! What certainty, security, solidarity! Perhaps that's why we marry even though we know that marriage can mean having one's money stolen, having one's children used as hostages, or facing physical abuse. At the very least, marriage means

> the part of mediator, I tell you, between Monsieur and the rest of humanity. . . . Marriage means . . . means: "Tie my tie for me! . . . Get rid of the maid! . . . Cut my toe-nails! . . . Get up and make me some chamomile! . . . " It means: "Give me my new suit, and pack my suitcase so that I can hurry to join her!" Steward, sick-nurse, children's nurse—enough, enough, enough, enough!

Perhaps that was why Colette's character Renée concluded in *The Vagabond*: "I'm no longer young enough, or enthusiastic enough, or generous enough to go in for marriage again, or married life, if you prefer. Let me stay alone in my closed bedroom, bedecked and idle, waiting for the man who has chosen me to be his harem. . . . I want nothing from love, in short, but love."

After three marriages, I certainly agreed with her. What perversity still made me seek the Perfect Man—whom I knew did not exist?

After my blue-collar phase, I began to mingle with the masculine side of what was considered the upper crust of Manhattan. If this was the upper crust, where was the *under*crust? These men were as Byzantine as courtiers in old Constantinople.

I remember first dates that seemed like co-op board interviews or questionnaires about credit rating from Dun & Bradstreet. I remember men who were "almost divorced." I remember men with toupees who drove Bentleys to make up for their lack of hair. I even went out with a still-practicing rabbi and a lapsed priest. I probably would have tried an ayatollah had one found me kosher enough to date.

Some men clearly had been passed around the singles circuit. Everyone had riffled through them. The shopworn men tended to be perfect on paper yet have some fatal flaw when you got to know them. The fatal flaw was rarely obvious on first look. He was only missing a heart, say, or a cock.

One of these paragons was tall, dark, and blue eyed and lived half the week in another country. On the three days he allotted to New York, he had to get plenty of dating in before the Concorde left—so you always felt you were being juggled or squeezed. He would vanish at eight A.M. on Monday and not call for three weeks. You had just about forgotten him when he seemed suddenly to remember your existence. He seemed to rotate women on a schedule as precise as a meal plan in a health spa. It seemed you should get a bonus for fucking him—frequent-flyer miles perhaps.

But his weekends were often cut in pieces like a cherry pie. Perhaps he was afraid a single cherry would ooze out. Oh, he was smart and attractive all right, and he unfailingly carried condoms. More amazingly, he *used* them. Afterward, he unfailingly disappeared.

But at least he was actually *single*. And he *seemed* to be straight—though who can tell these days? I dated him on and off for a year, but wisely never gave up my other beaux.

The most depressing thing about being single is the glut of married men. That any woman gets married again after eight years of single-dom in New York—or anywhere—must be attributable to "the triumph of hope over experience" (as Ken and I put it on our wedding announcements). Either that or amnesia.

Married men are, of course, the best lovers—unless you happen to be married to them. They *always* have time for you. Besides, they tend to be around just about enough for a full-time writer. With married men, you have weekends, holidays, New Year's Eve to write. When the whole world is pretending to be delirious, you can be really delirious, writing. It may not be for everyone, but for writers in mid-career, it's perfect. When your child is with your ex, you have the whole blessed weekend free to work. How many married women long for that?

Where did I meet these men? Just about everywhere. If you are genuinely friendly, it's not difficult to meet men. Most men are so terrorized by their mothers, sisters, wives, and daughters that a woman who's superficially nice to them and laughs at their jokes turns out to be rarer than the unicorn. The secret of meeting men is *liking* men. And having a little *rachmones** for them.

I met them on the Concorde in the days when I still thought I could afford to fly it. I met them at conferences, at openings, at parties. The world is full of married men, as Jackie Collins wrote. You could modify that: *The world is full of lonely married men.*

For they do seem to be genuinely lonely and genuinely grateful for a little listening and a little tenderness. They don't come to you for sex alone, but for affection and a listening ear—something they apparently never get at home. As a mistress, I am my best self: charming, tender, funny. When you live apart from a man, it's easy to be nice to him. You have your own bathroom, bedroom, closet, and kitchen. You can sleep all day and write all night. You can have weekend dates with your children or with yourself. You can soak in a bath, read poems, eat yogurt for supper. You and your daughter can give each other pedicures. All the female nurturing things that men seem to find silly (unless they are the beneficiaries of them) can become the mainstays of your life.

Since I disliked dating, I slid easily into relationships with married men. (Besides, the "eligibles" were always so arrogant. They were sure you were out to nab them. As a result, the more they liked you, the more they ran.)

---

* Compassion.

My analyst warned me that I liked married men *too* much. She claimed I was afraid of marriage. After my three marital outings, why *shouldn't* I be afraid of marriage? Marriage had usually been a bad bargain for me. I had married for love and wound up fighting for my child in court. Wouldn't I have been better off never to have married?

Perhaps I was just a terrible chooser of men. If a nice man was pursuing me, I'd inevitably choose the elusive cad. Why not just admit that marriage was not for me and give up?

My shrink was very pro-marriage. Famous for getting her patients hitched, she looked askance at the married men in my life.

I have burned my little black book. In its place, I plan to create the composite married man.

You meet at a screening, a publishing party, an art opening, or a political event. He meets your gaze more intensely than others do. He has read your books and claims to love them (perhaps his wife loves them). He looks at you with that shy, foot-scuffling teenage look.

The conversation starts and doesn't stop. At some point you wonder if he is prolonging it, or if you are. For a moment, you look in his eyes and see the little boy he once was. He says something intimate about your perfume or your hair. He asks if he can drive you home. In the car, you become aware of something drawing you toward him—a quasimagnetic force that, however, you do not act on. At your door, you proffer your telephone number and no kisses. He touches your hand a little too intimately or he touches your hair with an almost proprietary pat. He doesn't want to let you go, but you make it clear you're going. He looks like a beloved dog left in a kennel before a vacation.

In the morning before ten, you get a call. He invites you to lunch, very soon—perhaps that day. You know he is married because he doesn't invite you for dinner. And also because he is openly yearning. Single men never openly yearn.

At lunch—which is at a charming place a little off the beaten track—you confirm that he is married. Not because he says so but because he *omits* so much about his life.

He says things like "I went to the movies" or "I went to Europe," but from the description you know he was not alone. Men don't usually stay alone at the Splendido in Portofino or at the Hotel du Cap or the Eden Roc. An empty bed with pure white linen sheets may be *your* idea of heaven, but it's usually not his.

It's safe to ask about his children. That way you can confirm his marital state. If he's divorced, he will mention the mother of his children—usually negatively. But if he's married, it will appear he had them all by himself.

If you're still in doubt, you can always ask point-blank: "Are you married or divorced?" He will usually say something disingenuous like, "In between" or "I'm trying to find out" or "We have an open marriage." It may be open for *him*, but it's probably not for her.

One married man once even told me, "We're former hippies and we've had an open marriage since the sixties." Later I learned that this *had* been true twenty years before, but was not now—which probably accounted for their still being married. Another said, "My wife doesn't *want* me around, she's *happy* to get rid of me." Another said, "She's at our house in Barbados with the kids." Another said, "She's on a business trip to California." The implication was *out of sight, out of mind*. Men have an ability to compartmentalize their feelings that women cannot even comprehend.

The lovemaking takes a while to start. He seems endlessly patient, more interested in your mind than your body. He calls you several times a day, but is oddly silent after sundown and on weekends. You always call him at the office. You don't even *have* another phone number for him. And this omission is carefully not mentioned.

Do you really want another number? You have plenty of work to do. You like going to bed alone, reading as late as you wish at night, having your own clean kitchen, bathroom, car. You slide into the clean white envelope of sheets like a bread-and-butter note. You remember the chaos of dirty socks, towels, and empty soda cans—and vow, *Never again*. Yet you feel aroused, alive, female. It's nice to have a man who doesn't live in. It's nice to have a man and not have a man at the same time. You feel serene. Perhaps you will just keep it this way forever—with all the power on your side.

But just as you back away, he becomes crazed to possess you. This is the way the male of the species is built.

The place is set. Your house on a weekend that your kid's with her father, an inn in Vermont (on a weekend the wife is away), an island in the sun (on a week the wife is in Europe or Asia). If he suggests his house, don't go; and reconsider the affair. A man who has no scruples about bringing another woman to his wife's bed is not to be trusted— even as a sometime lover. Besides, you want a part-time man, not another woman's head on a platter. She's the wife so you can get to be the mistress. Being the mistress has its own particular charms.

He arrives that day, looking like a shy petitioner. He may have flowers, wine, CDs, or a red silk nightie. (If he plans to wear it himself, reconsider.) He may have all of these. But no jewelry yet. He is wondering if you're a good investment. (Are you succumbing too soon? Should you have made the chase longer? Will you get better jewelry if you don't succumb? I don't know—but perhaps that's why I have no good jewelry.)

And so to bed. This is when the power shifts. If he's good for you in bed, you're now in trouble. If you're good for *him*, he's now in trouble. Bed is the fulcrum of the power shift. Bed is the seesaw between *before* and *after*. What happens next is up to you.

If you get grabby, you'll push him away. When he calls on Monday with sexy romantic praise, stretch it out. This could be the most fun you ever have in your life. No one ever understood him better. He even uses the word "love." That's another reason you *know* he's married. He is vaccinated. He can say whatever he wants and not catch anything.

Men are very simple creatures. Feed 'em, fuck 'em, but withhold the keys to the castle. Territorial to the core, they're sweeter when they don't park their shoes under your bed.

These affairs can go on for years and still give you time for the whole rest of your life. They are not to be sneezed at. They are not necessarily to be turned to marriage. One married man took a leave of absence from his marriage and rented a country house close to mine. But he still went home on weekends. When the crunch came and he wanted to be invited to move in, I reminded him of how much his wife loved him. I don't think he expected this. But I liked my freedom and thought the relationship might become strained if I had his problems all the time.

Can this really be love?

Why not? Can't women love without giving up their lives? Men have done it for all of time.

We tend to think that unless we give up everything, we are not really in love. But this is *not* a model that can work after fifty. And why should it? After fifty, our lives belong to us, not to the species. Our lives are more important to us than they are to the male world—at last.

But I was still in my forties then, so I was forced to wonder, *Will I marry this man if he leaves his wife?*

I decided I would not. So my conscience told me to send him home to his wife. She wanted him in a way I did not. It was only fair to send him home.

Other affairs never end. They go on intermittently through the years—even after one (or both) of you have reunited with a spouse or married someone else. The affair becomes a private place that has nothing and everything to do with the rest of your life. It has no pain, only pleasure, because it is, by its nature, impermanent. The ultimate fantasy is that of lovers who meet once a year (as in *Same Time Next Year*) finding a little oasis out of time—from time to time.

But sooner or later, even the best affairs dwindle. Perhaps the you that needed that particular oasis is outpaced by another you. Perhaps you find refuge in another relationship, which seems fulfilling enough in itself. Perhaps you get too old and tired for the necessary deceptions. Or you decide you want your life to be clean and honest.

It was really the affair that took you to this point. You will always be grateful. And so will he. You meet your former lover at a party or on a plane and he looks at you with his little-boy look. You have touched him in his most playful place and he is grateful to have been known. Being known breaks the loneliness of being human. You are grateful for it too.

You hug tightly and part—without kisses.

All good boys are also bad boys. And we love them for being both. How boring to have the perfect man—if such a prodigy exists. How boring to be always *good*.

Nice women are drawn to rule-breaking men because our female-goodness training is so absolute that we deeply need to find the suppressed part of ourselves: rebellion. We can't always break free alone, we need a man to cut the ribbon with—if not for—us. What ribbon? The blood-red ribbon that still binds us to our mothers and our fathers.

Think of all the great feminists who ran off with bad boys! Mary Wollstonecraft ran off with Gilbert Imlay—a bad-boy revolutionary who left her broke and pregnant. Did she rail at this? On the contrary, she wrote, "Ah! my friend, you know not the ineffable delight, the exquisite pleasure, which arises from an unison of affection and desire, when the whole soul and senses are abandoned to a lively imagination."

George Sand married a bad boy in Casimir Dudevant and chose a bad-boy lover in Alfred de Musset (if not in the far-too-moral Frédéric Chopin). Before them, there had been plenty of bad boys, including one, Stéphane de Grandsagne, who was the father of her only daughter, Solange. Her first lover, Aurélien de Sèze, had a name that began with the same three letters as her own name, Aurore. After these two, there were plenty of other bad boys who excited her passion and peopled her books.

Passion and poetry were clearly allied for Sand. Bad boys were her muses. Happily, she survived them all, winding up a contented grandmother who never ceased to write. Even in the midst of an affair, even in the midst of travel, she wrote five to eight hours a night. When she locked the door to de Musset to produce her nightly quota of pages, he took up with the dancing girls of the Fenice, Venice's beautiful opera house. This did not stop Sand's writing—though it may have cracked a piece of her heart. Tender and maternal as she was with all her men, she knew that work, not love, kept her alive. She is the first of our modern breed of writer-mother-lovers.

Perhaps Elizabeth Barrett Browning cannot be said to have chosen an archetypal bad boy in Robert Browning, but certainly he was her liberator from home and he became her muse. "How do I love thee? Let me count the ways" highlights the tradition of women poets carried away by liberating love. The tradition continues in this century with Anna Akhmatova and Edna St. Vincent Millay. And who was Sylvia Plath if not a good girl in love with the archetypal bad boy? She paid with her life for her poet's *Liebestod*.

Mary Godwin Shelley (Mary Wollstonecraft's daughter with William Godwin), the writer who invented that evergreen genre the horror novel, loved a bad boy in Percy Bysshe Shelley. He was a revolutionary, a traitor to his class, a sexual rebel, and that was why, being her mother's daughter, she chose him at the young age of sixteen. He honored her dead mother as she did, so there were thrilling seduction scenes in the cemetery, with her mother's headstone as a sort of magic amulet. (But then dead mothers are rather easier for teenage girls to honor than living ones.)

The Brontës—Emily, Charlotte, and Anne—all had a weakness for bad boys, if only in their fiction and poetry. Heathcliff and Rochester have given birth to thousands of bad-boy heroes in lesser novels and movies (written by people who never even read the Brontës but received the archetype through the osmosis of pop culture). The yearning voice of Emily Brontë's love poems has given birth to the generic voice that still pervades much twentieth-century women's poetry.

Young women *want* to love in a self-annihilating way. "All my life's bliss is in the grave with thee" is a cry we echo in adolescence. It is only mature womanhood that finally teaches the value of intimate female friendships, intellectual friendships, and giving service to lives beyond our own.

At sixteen, we find Heathcliff and Rochester stronger lures than anything. We cannot wait to give up all for love. There must be an evolutionary reason for this. Is it because Heathcliff and Rochester help us sever ties with home and release us to pursue our own life's adventures? Is it because they jolt us out of childhood? Is it because they present a greater force than the passion to stay at home with Mom? I think all are true. Young women dream of romance and passion as men dream of conquest, because those dreams are necessary goads to leaving home and growing up. How else can we make sense of the fact that the fiercest feminists have also been the fiercest lovers?

Even if sexual passion did not ensure the continuation of the human race, it would be necessary to break the bonds of the adolescent girl to her mother so that she could eventually *become* her mother. Passion is a great catalyst for growing up.

Many women who fulfill their artistic and intellectual powers are also father-ridden. Mary Godwin Shelley was a perfect example of this. Her problem was a mythic mother, an all-too-real father. He was brilliant but emotionally weak, so he married a harridan—as emotionally weak men often do. Percy Shelley became mother, father, and escape for Mary. There was no way for her to resist him—particularly when he swore he would take his own life unless he could have her.

The Oedipal taboo demands a stranger (seemingly *unlike* Daddy), who arouses passion that overrides all practical considerations. And the bad boy is perfect for this. He must come across the moors with a burst of furious hoofbeats; he must love one's creative work and carry one away to Italy or England or the moon; he must be a different color, race, nationality, class; he must speak a different language; he must dance to a different drummer. Otherwise the Oedipal pull is too strong to let us leave Daddy and home at all.

Why leave, when our first loves are there? Because *unless* we leave, we cannot come home with the treasures of art.

When we look at the lives of women creators like Mary Wollstonecraft, George Sand, Sylvia Plath, Colette, Edna St. Vincent Millay, Anna Akhmatova, Mary McCarthy, and so many others, we should perhaps not regret that they chronically loved Mr. Wrong. Loving the wrong man is sometimes the only thing a woman creator can do when she is young and needs to break away from home. Loving a bad boy means loving the bad boy in herself, asserting her freedom, the wildness of her soul. The bad boy *is* the rebel part of herself that her female upbringing has usually tried to quash. Only when she integrates the bad boy into her *own* personality can she give up his rough love. If she survives it, she is stronger for it. It is her coming of age, her marriage of strength and tenderness, her independence.

After fifty, none of this is necessary. We discover we can *be* the bad boy and the good girl both at once. After fifty, we can assert the bad boy's power, together with our maternal warmth. We no longer need the bad boy at our side to claim our virility. Nor do we need our mothers to be motherly ourselves. We are complete androgynous humans now—fierce and tender both at the same time.

In striving to fulfill our identities as women, it's important not to confound the various passages of life with each other. What we may need in girlhood or adolescence are not the same qualities we need in maturity. The task of adolescence is to leave home. And women in a sexist society have chronically found this hard to do. Our biology has reinforced the very dependence which our minds have been able to fly beyond. Patriarchal practices like arranged marriages, the denial of abortion, and female sexual mutilation have encouraged us to glorify not leaving as a self-protective strategy.

No wonder our creative heroines *had* to find strategies for leaving. Those who were heterosexual devised the strategy of falling for bad boys as a primal means of separation. We make a mistake in thinking they were only victims. They were adventurers first. That they became victims was not their *intent*. Sylvia Plath was not merely a masochist but a bold adventurer who perhaps got more than she bargained for.

As I get older, I come to understand that the seemingly self-destructive obsessions of my various younger lives were not *only* self-destructive. They were also self-creative. All through the stages of our lives, we go through transformations that may only manifest themselves when they are safely over. The rebels and bad boys I loved were the harbingers of my loving those very qualities in myself. I loved and left the bad boys, but I thank them for helping make me the strong survivor I am today.

12

BECOMING VENETIAN

The delusion that art and nature were one in Italy irritated Byron, who had been one of the principal victims of it, when he sensed it in others. Thomas Moore tells this revealing story of his meeting his great friend in Venice after a long separation. "We stood out on the balcony in order that, before daylight had quite gone, I might have some glimpse of the scene which the grand canal presented. Happening to remark in looking at the clouds, which were still bright in the west, that 'what had struck me in Italian sunsets was that peculiar rosy hue'—I had hardly pronounced the word 'rosy' when Lord Byron, clapping his hand on my mouth, said with a laugh, 'Come, damn it, Tom, don't be poetical.'"

—Luigi Barzini, *The Italians*

Water equals time and provides beauty with its double. Part water, we serve beauty in the same fashion. By rubbing water, this city improves time's looks, beautifies the future.

—Joseph Brodsky, *Watermark*

In the middle of these years of shipwreck, these years of upheaval, I fell in love with a city: Venice, *Venezia, La Serenissima, Venise, Venedig*. I thought this magic island would save my life. I believed the literary myths that rose around it like its famous fog. I returned again and again in search of love, in search of myself.

For writers who use the English language, Italy has become more myth than reality.

It's all the fault of a few nineteenth-century poets: first, the Brownings—Mr. and Mrs.—who brought the hordes to Florence in search of Fra Lippi and transforming love (which gets better after death), only to find car fumes, melting gelato, mobbed museums, cynical leather merchants, and cheating goldsmiths on the Ponte Vecchio; second, Lord Byron, who swam the Grand Canal with his manservant rowing behind him (carrying his romantic cloak and open britches), who ennobled the Palazzo Mocenigo by writing verses of the divine *Don Juan* there, but who was beastly to the women in his life and left his beloved daughter, Allegra, to die in a convent rather than give her to her mother; third, Percy Bysshe Shelley, who left his heart on the beach at Lerici, to be plucked out of the flames that consumed the rest of him; and last, but in no way least, Mary Wollstonecraft Godwin Shelley, who conceived her manlike monster in the Alps, then came to Italy, only to see her husband drown, fulfilling her novel's prophecy.

Forget, for a moment, George Sand and Alfred de Musset (deceiving each other in Venice), Henry James, John Singer Sargent, John Ruskin, Vita Sackville-West, Nathaniel Hawthorne, Baron Corvo, Igor Stravinsky, Ezra Pound, and all the besotted others. Byron and Browning and the Shelleys *alone* are enough for the touristic blight of ruinously expensive Italy. The poets came and wrote; then came the hordes. Who says that poetry has no economic clout?

The spell these poets cast over sanctified places on this beautiful, but slightly shopworn boot bewitched all who were bewitched by books. We went to Italy seeking love and poetry—and love and poetry were interchangeable to us.

The first time I came to Venice, I was nineteen and arrived alone on the train from Florence (where I was in that summer program, studying Italians). The college program was located in the thirteenth-century Torre di Bellosguardo (now become an atmospheric though somewhat ramshackle country inn overlooking Florence from that same hill to which Vita and Virginia eloped). Everything in Italy is overlaid with sexual-poetic allusion—for Italy is, above all, the country of poetic elopement—at least to the Americans and English. To Italians, it is another country altogether.

I stood at the edge of Santa Lucia Station clutching a small, blue-covered copy of *Don Juan*. The marble steps of the station loomed longer and steeper than they are. I did not see the dead kittens floating nor the empty condoms and Fanta bottles. I saw only poetry and love. Poets are the best publicists of all.

I took the vaporetto to San Marco, marveling at the palaces on the Grand Canal. When I saw a plaque which read *"Qui abita Lord*

Byron" (Lord Byron lived here) on the wall of the Palazzo Mocenigo, I nearly swooned. I was in the presence of Literature—that old fraud, that intellectual gigolo. As Mary Shelley said of her honeymoon flight abroad, "It was romantic beyond romance."

And so I wandered through teeming San Marco, through the Doge's Palace in this living museum of a city.

A handsome young Chinese doctor (not the one I later married) bought me violets and an ice cream cone and spoke with me of Byron. A coarse American college boy asked me to share his dingy room in a flea bag near the station. A number of Italians pinched my butt. I floated on, protected by poetry.

Nothing altered the spell. I was transfixed, hypnotized. Books were my addictive substance then. I carried them in my heart and head.

I walked into a house with Ruskin's name on the side and was greeted with a torrent of abuse—it was *not* a museum. I ate touristic mini-pizzas and drank sour wine. It was all manna to me.

The crumbling red-tiled roofs, the bells, the seagulls, the golden ball of *La Dogana* (the customs house, which enriched Venice by search and seizure), the green conical hat of the *campanile* of San Giorgio Maggiore, facing the Basin of St. Mark's and its *campanile*, the way the two *campanili* line up in the channel to make a clear marker for sailboats winging into the harbor, the way the cruise ships slide down the Giudecca Canal as if on invisible rails—all this enchanted me, cast a spell that brought me back and back. I went to Venice with women friends, eventually with Allan, with Jon, with Will, and many times alone. I stayed everywhere—from the Ostello della Gioventù, to cheap hotels, to moderate *pensioni,* to the most ludicrously expensive palaces like the Gritti or Cipriani. Later I began to rent houses—as far from the tourists as I could find. I flattered myself that I was, if not a native, then a habitué.

Often I would arrive in Venice and wonder what on earth had brought me back. It was languid; it tended to hold and entrap me; but the *ensorcellement* (as Anaïs Nin calls it) was *not* always pleasant. I felt like a fly trapped in a spider's web, like a sailor dragged down by a fantastic octopus. I was never sure what the city wanted of me.

The blue summer skies and the glittering lagoon can be deceptive. The tourists troop through like bedraggled sunburned beggars, eager to get home and say they've seen it. But when you live in Venice for a while, winter or summer, you discover the city has thousands of secrets and that it lets you in on them only in time.

The summer of 1983, I had been invited to the Soviet Union to attend a conference of writers. It was that lovely man the late Harrison Salisbury who invited me. The company included Studs Terkel, Susan Sontag, Robert Bly, Gwendolyn Brooks, Irving and Jean Stone. Voznesensky was promised, but did not appear. Many appa- ratchiks did. We went by rail from Moscow to Kiev. I was horrified at the way Gwendolyn Brooks's black face provoked frank stares in Moscow and Kiev. She was my roommate on the train and we stayed up all night, talking poetry and motherhood.

Why did Venice follow this trip? It was because of Carly Simon. Otherwise I might just have gone straight back to Connecticut, where Will was house-sitting for me.

"Let's meet in Venice on August first at the Cipriani," Carly Simon had proposed some months before at a dishy lunch we were having in the Village. We were boastfully comparing young lovers. We would bring them both to Venice and see what happened. (Did we plan to swap? Only in fantasy.) So I booked the Cipriani (which I never knew existed before Carly mentioned it). And after Moscow, I met Will at the airport in Milan. We ran to a hotel room to plight our troth—if that's what it's called—and then we flew into Venice at dusk. The sight of the city when you are in love is expansive, not entrapping.

I had money then—or thought it belonged to me rather than the IRS—so we took a suite by the pool at the Cipriani. We never left it during the day. All morning and afternoon we stayed in bed, making love and ordering room service; all night we wandered the streets.

Carly never showed up with her then-lover, Al Corley. It had been one of those exuberant invitations about which the inviter has imme- diate amnesia. But we missed no one. At night, Will taught me to swim in the huge abandoned pool (built oversized because someone had confused meters with feet). We explored the little *calli* of the Giudecca in the darkness. We drank in cafés, in our room, in bed, by the pool. We made love as if we had invented it, thinking we had. In that we were like all lovers.

Venice became our special place. Every summer, we would come to a rented flat or house or *piano nobile* with Molly and Margaret. We would slide into the adagio rhythms of the lagoon. Will would go out to get fresh bread in the morning. We'd lazily breakfast. Then I would write. Then we'd all troop out to lunch in a local trattoria.

From the age of five on, Molly summered in Venice. We'd swim at the Cipriani most of the late afternoon, then shower, take the vaporetto home, then change and go out for dinner—a family of four.

The day revolved around writing, strolling, swimming, meals. The tensions of New York leaked away. I would keep notes, dream up poems, begin stories I thought I had to write. Sometimes they became books and sometimes they did not. But the languid pace of life promoted this flowering. And the watery world baptized it. I would always come home with my head full of exotic blooms.

How I *dreamed* in Venice—that boat floating on the Adriatic Sea! It was like sleeping on a schooner, with water lapping and the rocking of the tides. Sometimes I thought I came to Venice just to sleep.

It was during those summers that I began to research the ghetto of Venice and fall under the spell of the sixteenth century.

Will and I always arrived laden with books to read together. We would read aloud, marking and annotating pages. From the earliest days, we were introduced to Venetians who showed us around, opened the museums and libraries to us. We began to scout the city to see if it had a story it wanted to tell me—or tell *through* me.

The ghetto of Venice caught us. To show his solidarity with me, Will began wearing a Star of David embedded in Venetian glass. We also began reading histories of the Venetian Jews.

Thanks to Cecil Roth, Riccardo Callimani, and the stones themselves, sixteenth-century Venice began to come alive for me. It was an island refuge, infiltrated by all the Jews seeking asylum there. Sephardim from Spain, Ashkenazim from Germany, Levantine Jews from the Near East, met and mingled in Venice with Christians and Muslims, creating the magic of Venetian culture.

I immediately saw an analogy between that island Venice and that island Manhattan. Venice in the sixteenth century *was* Manhattan in the early twentieth century: teeming with Jews driven out of Europe and the Middle East, destined to enrich the Christian world and to change it forever.

The Jews came to Venice because Venice took them in, and they soon became dealers in old clothes, antiquities, books. They specialized in stagecraft, printing, bookbinding, art, antiquities—as now. They established synagogues, theaters, publishing houses, trading companies. They practiced the arts. Focusing their energies on the few things that were not forbidden them, they became a *force*. And they prospered. And Venice prospered. They brought another sort of yeast to the great sugared cake of the Serenissima.

During the long lazy sojourns in Venice, a story began to be whispered through the stones. A Jewish girl, the *real* Jessica, is imprisoned in the ghetto by her father, Shylock (or Shallach, as the name must have been before it was Anglicized).

On quite an ordinary daily excursion, our Jessica encounters a young Englishman in the ghetto—where he has come to hear the famous rabbis preach and learn new stagecraft (for which the Jews of Venice are famous in the sixteenth century). He is only twenty-eight, a poet, actor, playwright, who has come to Venice with his lascivious bisexual patron, the Earl of Southampton. The plague has closed the London theaters and there is time to travel with his lord (who is madly in love with him and also, in the way of mad lovers, wants to be his master).

Will—for that, ironically, is the young man's name—and Jessica fall in love at first sight, as all fairy tale lovers must, and their love inspires them to flee the ghetto, flee Southampton, Shallach, and all cynicism—since love is born to defeat cynicism.

Something along these lines was cooking in my head as I finished another novel, *Parachutes & Kisses*. That winter an unexpected invitation came for me to be a judge in the Venice Film Festival. Knowing I needed to push this novel toward the light, I immediately accepted—bringing along my own Will as *cavaliere servente*.

The film festival was a madhouse. Yevgeny Yevtushenko had come from Moscow, with a British wife he was destined soon to part from, and the manners of a mogul. Tall, theatrical, accustomed to filling stadia with his worshippers, he was spoiling for a fight. Pipe-smoking, brooding Günter Grass arrived from Germany in a similar mood, but he was too clever and thoughtful to show it. Balthus would have rather been painting. He stayed at the Gritti, with his beautiful Japanese wife and daughters, and languidly seemed to take the trip strictly as a boondoggle—which was wise. We saw him rarely, and never at screenings. The brothers Taviani—Paolo and Vittorio—were modest, humorous, and terminally nervous. They were about to showcase *Caos,* their brilliant Pirandello movie. Michelangelo Antonioni was not physically well, but he was passionately serious and he saw every film.

All day, the jury watched movie after movie—the best, the worst, the mediocre. Socialist-realist movies from the Eastern Bloc, Indian movies from New Delhi's celluloid mills, Chinese movies produced by Hong Kong moguls, Japanese art or exploitation movies, movies to shock and movies to numb, more movies than you ever dreamed were made on the planet in a single year.

It grew boring. Nothing is more boring than mediocre movies. And as the days passed, you could see the storm clouds looming over the lagoon.

When Claudia Cardinale arrived with her Sicilian husband-producer, the stage was set for the showdown, the battle at the O.K. Corral. Cardinale was playing Clara Petacci, Mussolini's last mistress, in an awful film based not so much on history as on soap opera. The Russian at once saw something to protest. And the German saw a Russian he could best. And the commotion began.

How it started is a mystery. Conferences and seminars do tend to spontaneously combust after five days or so. Perhaps it is the discipline they impose on undisciplined people. Or perhaps it is that artists are unaccustomed to living communally and can only manage it for brief periods. Perhaps all that community requires a safety valve and the explosion must, inevitably, come.

First, the jury was debating the "morality" of watching a film depicting Mussolini as a lover, then there were verbal skirmishes at lunch and tea, and suddenly Yevgeny was holding a press conference and the Italian papers had something to write! The festival might be a bore, but the judges were not. *Pow! Bam! Socko! Smash!*

"It is an outrage to glorify Fascists as lovers"—or some such. The hoopla fed on itself, as press creations tend to do. The media love nothing more than caricaturish controversy. The French and English vied in absurdity. The Italians leapt in gleefully. The American papers picked it up from there.

We were all duly interviewed and quoted, of course. We were all obliged to take positions over this harmless melodrama. (Anita Hill has said that once you become a public figure, you are expected to have opinions on everything. "I reserve the right not to comment," she said. If only I—and the rest of the jury—had been as wise as she!)

Claudia Cardinale was photographed looking lovely in her outrage. Her husband-producer (or producer-husband) vowed dark *vendette*.

And so the festival got the media event it wanted and everyone got publicity—whether they wanted it or not. And the city of Venice got its money's worth from the celebrities it paid to fly and feed. And Liv Ullmann winged in at the last to present the Golden Lion—rampant once again on a field of flacks.

The wonder of this festival and its spontaneous combustion got me thinking of my Venice novel again. Every writer longs to write a *Connecticut Yankee in King Arthur's Court* sort of tale. Every writer wants to travel back in time as long as the future safely waits to be returned to.

What if *my* Jessica were not Jewish but, when we first met her, Christian? What if she were a Radcliffe-educated reluctant debutante who came from a dusty old WASP family on the Upper East Side, and went to the Royal Academy of Dramatic Art in London instead of making a proper marriage, and was, despite family disapproval, determined to be an actress. What if she had adored Shakespeare's poetry all her life, and, one day in Venice, after judging a film festival, she slipped through a crack in time, and found herself a sixteenth-century Jewess in the ghetto, falling in love with a poetic English lad called Will?

What if is always the beginning of a story.

I had my tale. Or it had me.

I began frantically scribbling notes. Here was a chance to bake a cake made of all I knew about Venice, Shakespeare, Elizabethans, and Jews.

I made the tale properly Shakespearean and bloody. Poniards, poisons, daggers, dirks, *stiletti* were obligatory. I wanted to hear Elizabethan word-music in my ears, so I listened repeatedly to Sir John Gielgud reading the sonnets until I could not stop hearing it. I searched out every production of *The Merchant of Venice* playing that year. I watched old films and videotapes of the play. I read it aloud to myself. Then I read everything about it I could find. "Shakespeare is a happy hunting ground for minds that have lost their balance," Joyce said (through Stephen Daedalus). I did not want to prove him right, but I did want to travel back in time. So I returned to the ghetto in rainy autumn and brooded. Again, I heard the whispers of the stones. Again, I saw young Shakespeare and a Dark Lady walking in the rain.

The secret of making Shakespeare work in the present is not obscuring its basic truths about character with Elizabethan flourishes and folderol. Shakespeare's audiences saw through these, of course, because they were used to his conventions of language and stagecraft. We must make the plays as transparent as they were to the Elizabethans. A good adaptation must remove the barrier that separates Elizabethan England from us.

But *The Merchant* is a very tough play to make modern because Shakespeare's attitude toward Shylock is so distasteful on grounds of anti-Semitism and yet so intrinsic to the play. Shakespeare sees Shylock as a human being like himself, but the old prejudice of Elizabethans toward Jews (in their very Jew-hating time) clings. Even the character of Jessica is weaker than that of Portia. And Jessica's renunciation of her father is cruel. So is her theft of his precious ring (given to him by her dead mother). Shylock's comparison of daughters and ducats can be read coldly as a slur on Jews, but can also be played hotly, illuminating a father's rage and a father's love. (Laurence Olivier and Dustin Hoffman did it.)

I wanted *Serenissima* to solve the dilemma of Jessica once and for all, show why Jessica betrayed her father—not only for love and free-dom, but also for *poetry*. I also wanted to unravel the mystery of the Dark Lady of the sonnets. I thought to kill two birds with one stone, making her that *same* Jewess in the ghetto who inspired the character of Jessica.

It was my usual tall order for myself. The book was to be literary, yet somehow also enlightening to twentieth-century women, yet also a good yarn compelling the reader to turn the page, yet also a brief for poetry's centrality to our lives.

Though *Serenissima* still bewitches me with its *potential*, I suspect I partly missed with this novel because I did not yet entirely under-stand my own relation to the city of Venice. Also, I tried to do too many things in one slim book. *Serenissima* should have been longer and richer, like *Fanny*. It should have had more characters, more crosscurrents and subplots. It should also have been edited less.

Self-conscious about my own tendency toward excess, I hired a freelance editor to trim my sails. We both encouraged each other to trim too much, cutting rather than expanding the novel. V. S. Pritchett says that the strengths and weaknesses of a writer are so interwoven that you cannot give up one without giving up the other.

Venice, like New York, was an ancestral city to me, a city that drew me back to the roots of my Jewishness. But it was more: Its myth is that of the magic island where problems are resolved, puzzles solve themselves, or at least dissolve themselves in water.

The Merchant of Venice is only *one* of Shakespeare's many ver-sions of that tale. But it, too, is not quite a success—despite Shylock's fierce lines on being a Jew, despite the magic starry sky of Belmont, despite Jessica's dark perplexed beauty and Portia's prissy summation of justice as a sort of noblesse oblige given to poor wretches like the Jews as long as they convert on bended knee, renounce their blood, their food, their ducats, their daughters, and the Jewishness of their grandchildren.

So *The Merchant* does not quite work either, it must be said. Perhaps it is the hate at its heart that brings it down. Hate rarely makes for good literature. But that other magic island play, *The Tempest,* resolves all its puzzles beautifully, and works, it must be said, like mad.

There is real love between the lovers, real repentance on the part of the sorcerer king, Prospero, real freedom for the chained spirits, Caliban and Ariel, real freedom for the poet as he takes his leave. The magic island *could* be Venice here (it is an island off the north of Italy after all), but clearly it is not. It *cannot* be, for Venice is above all the island of the dead, as Thomas Mann knew better than anyone. Venice is the place that traps tortured spirits. It is the flypaper island. It must constantly have new blood to replenish the old. Venice herself is no more, no less, than a vampire.

I knew a Danish pianist who came back to Venice to play in a shoddy bar year after year. In the winter and spring, he was employed by a sheik in Sharja for many, many ducats. But each summer and fall, he was compelled to return to Venice as if the ghost of his former self were summoning him there.

This melancholy Dane had done research about his ghost, who seemed to be a thirteenth-century baker. At night, his room would sometimes fill with a floury fragrance or the warm odor of baking bread. Pans and racks would crash and clatter. When he awoke, a fine white dust would cover everything. He would jolt open his eyes, unsurprised.

He was a blue-eyed, blond man, of slight build and weight, with that skull-beneath-the-skin face sometimes seen in Scandinavians. In motion at the piano he looked young, but when you drew near, you saw he was anywhere from fifty to infinity. His face was crazed with tiny lines. He was, like me, addicted to Venice, though you could see it was not good for his health.

Of course there had to be some lover there—some impossible lover, like my Piero, who came and fled unpredictably. The lover surely had the same unconscious childlike cruelty as Von Aschenbach's Tadzio. All Venetian lovers do.

Perhaps Piero was this Dane's lover as well as mine. Perhaps he was also Tadzio's lover. And Alfred de Musset's. And Byron's. And Shakespeare's. Who can tell? In Venice it is possible to lead multiple lives in multiple times. The multiple doorways make it possible. The fog and the shadows cover all. The *aqua alta* rises inexorably, covering the ground floors.

We talked many nights, the Danish pianist and I, and though I do not remember his name, I know that his story had something to do with mine. Eventually people who cannot get free of Venice die there. The lagoon needs their ghosts to lure back other ghosts-to-be.

Here was another problem with my Venice novel: It did not tell the ultimate truth about Venice. That was not because I was not doing my best. I was. But I did not yet *know* the ultimate truth about Venice. Venice is not sunny. Venice is a grave.

The snatched lovemaking between breakfast and lunch, the fierce passion from five to seven, are ways to bring you back and back and back to Venice. But the lovemaking does not produce life. It produces only ghosts, seductive ghosts, ghosts with incredible magnetic and sexual force, ghosts who can rattle pots in the greatest orgasm known on terra firma. In truth, it is not terra firma. It is the sea, and the barque of death floats west to the setting sun.

Not long ago (in the middle of this book), I went to Venice again with my daughter. We walked and talked and reminisced about other summers, when she was a little girl and I was single. But when I went to visit my old friends, she refused to come, preferring to stay at the Gritti, watching CNN and ordering room service. So I went alone.

My friends clutched me back the way island people clutch newcomers—out of a terrified boredom. They made me lunches, dinners, teas, and told me of special properties for sale in Venice. Messages were left for me at the hotel desk by old lovers, but when I phoned, they were never home. When I returned, there were *new* messages, which also proved unreturnable. There were messages from people I did not know. Was a thirteenth-century baker among them?

My Danish friend was gone. I thought I saw Piero in his motorboat, puttering along the Grand Canal alone, but then it seemed not to be him. I tried to call him, but a secretary said he was *"fuori Venezia."** The sky lowered and darkened. Windows flew open in my old room (Hemingway's, I was told) at the Gritti. Footsteps creaked

---

* Away from Venice.

the ceiling all night, but when I complained I was told by the concierge that nobody had the room upstairs.

Eventually, on the fifth day, I found myself in a green garden (reputed to have been a cemetery once) in Dorsoduro. Statuary of cloaked, hatted figures with veiled faces lurked in the velvety shadows. The hedges were mossy dappled green, and here and there, a brilliant fuchsia or cyclamen burst out of the greenery like a flower pot on a grave.

I was sitting in the center of a group of women. One was an Austrian artist who had lived here for nearly thirty years (drawn by Italian lovers and the light). She had now given up men (of all nationalities). Another, a plump American divorcée, had finally sold her New York place and settled here. Another, a rich English widow, had bought a palazzo on the Grand Canal and was renovating. Another was the voluminous duchess who kept my Piero, her Piero, anyone's Piero. He was sailing in the Mediterranean. No one knew where.

We talked of diets, exercise classes, food, wayward children, wayward servants, wayward men. They all urged me to give up New York, my husband, my family, and move here for good. The pace of life was easier, they said, and I could write here.

But I could only write about the past, I thought, and eventually I could not write at all because grass would cover my fingers. The graveyard was creeping up on me, and Venice made that process sweet. The barque that rows toward the sunset was waiting at the edge of the canal. The lapping, seductive sound the water made was the sound of Venice: *vieni, vieni.*

The death it offered was not *la petite morte.* It was the grand one. And it was inexorable.

Venetian lovers, whoever they were, whatever sex, were just her handmaidens, her flacks, her walkers. They lured robust people here. But we could only stay of our own free will—which is the way death wants us. She gets us ready in Venice, step by step, oar by oar, orgasm by orgasm.

I remembered the first time I was drawn to Piero, eight or nine years before. We were on his sailboat in the Basin of St. Mark's on a balmy night in mid-July. It was the Feast of the *Redentore,* commemorating the liberation of La Serenissima from some plague of half a millennium ago. A bridge of boats was built from the Piazza del Giglio in San Marco to Santa Maria della Salute in Dorsoduro to Palladio's magnificent church of the *Redentore* on Giudecca. The whole city was walking on the water, so it seemed. Those who were not strolling the bridges, carrying candles, food, *prosecco*, were reclining in their flower-strewn boats, drinking the fruit of the vine. The music˜of Vivaldi, Monteverdi, and Albinone wafted across the waters. The great ones—the future *tangentopolisti** who now crowd the jails—were ensconced on a sort of floating royal box, a reviewing stand on pontoons that also blasted Venetian music over the waters. Television crews bobbed in little motorboats to broadcast this *festa* to the ogling rest of Italy, which still regards Venice as an oddity—half Italian, half otherness.

Piero's sumptuous duchess was cooking crayfish, squid, and black risotto made with the ink of Venetian *seppie*. I was watching with amazement both at her culinary skill and at her imperturbability. Piero slid close to me.

He breathed on my neck, ran one finger down my forearm in a possessive, premonitory way. He took me with his eyes.

I was lost in that faun-brown gaze, smelled the fire beneath his brown skin, his curly golden satyr hair. His sweat was goatish and delicious—or was it my own? We seemed to have the same smell.

"I am sorry I am not so free," he said, indicating the duchess. What he meant was the opposite—as often is the case: *I am glad I am not so free. She is my inoculation, my protection, my invisible shield. But I shall be glad to bring you back to Venice again and again for little licks and tastes of my magic staff.*

So it began. It brewed in the lagoon a full year, was consummated on a full-moon night a year later, went on intermittently for years, and ended forever when I fled Venice in a panic, not even having seen him.

The wind blew hard from the canal. Windows, pots, and pianos rattled, crashed, played jagged melodies, and blew a cloud of flour dust over everything. I looked in the mirror. I was white as a ghost.

"Woman whom I call Mother—if indeed that is your name," my now fifteen-year-old daughter said, "we *have* to get out of here. Something terrible is going to happen."

In an hour flat, we were packed and had water-taxied to the car-rental depot with all our luggage. As we drove furiously across the causeway to terra firma, a savage storm chased us, rocking our station wagon, darkening our windows.

We had left just in time. Ghosts were whirling and shrieking in the air above the lagoon. The ladies of the cemetery garden were calling, "*Non scappi!*" (Don't run away!)

---

* Profiteers of political corruption.

But I had my pedal to the metal and Milan in view. Back to life, to the rush and ugliness of traffic, to the worldliness of business, to telephones that do not reach the dead.

Even Browning left, and Byron and the Shelleys too. George Sand abandoned Venice when her book was done. Only Aschenbach stayed on. And Pound. And Stravinsky. They are buried here.

Once across the causeway, the ladies of the dark garden could not get me.

"Mommy," said Molly, "I've never been so glad to get out of there. I used to *love* Venice when I was little—what happened?"

"You were young enough for Venice then," I said, driving madly to the mainland.

"I don't get it, Mom."

"We're not ready to be Venetian yet," I said.

But in my mind's eye I saw the waters closing over the place, the golden mosaics floating and falling apart, the Byzantine saints slowly going to pieces.

This doomed Atlantis would sink under the warming waters one day and no one would be the wiser. Archaeologists of 5040 would dig it up, marveling at death's handiwork.

I thought of the day we buried our artist friend Vesty Entwhistle in the green garden graveyard of San Michele, the cemetery island, and how we dropped golden tiles into the earth over her because she had worked such golden squares into her mosaics. Another life to feed the teeming ghosts. *La Serenissima* triumphs whenever anyone is buried there.

Twelve years later, the skull-faced diggers disinter the bones of all those who are not sufficiently famous to draw new tourists. They cast such unworthy bones into the common ossuary—a bone island I have only heard whispered of. For the first twelve years, you have your taste of immortality. And then, if you are no longer famous, off you go—skull, pelvis, spinal vertebrae, tibia, fibula, all. Whose immortality is actually much longer than that? Immortality, after all, is your memory in minds that loved yours.

I no longer want to die in Venice. And so, of course, I cannot live there.

I suppose I am too old to risk being Venetian now.

13

THE PICARESQUE LIFE

Past fifty, we learn with surprise and a sense
of suicidal absolution,
that what we intended and failed,
could never have happened.

—Robert Lowell, "For Sheridan"

Whatever gains I ever made were always due to love and nothing
else.

—Saul Bellow, *Henderson the Rain King*

What is one's personality, detached from that of the friends with
whom fate happens to have linked one? I cannot think of myself
apart from the influence of the two or three greatest friendships of
my life, and any account of my growth must be that of their stim-
ulating and enlightening influence.

—Edith Wharton, *A Backward Glance*

For any writer, the most ineffable of all truths about herself is the
inner story, the story she writes without knowing why, the automatic,
instinctive story her unconscious feeds her intravenously. My story is
picaresque.

I discovered this only after having written six novels—all of them
novels of some road or other (the road to Vienna and back, to
California and back, to eighteenth-century London and back, to
divorce and back, to sixteenth-century Venice and back, to alcoholism
and back, etc). In each one, a troubled heroine smilingly triumphs

over adversity after encountering a lot of ruts and ditches, bastards and badboys, on the bumpy road of life.

Born into a melancholy, hyperintellectual, phobic, paranoiac, Russian-Jewish family, I *needed* such a tale. And such an ending. So did my readers.

In midlife, I was drawn to memoir because I needed to understand myself before it was too late. And what better way to understand yourself than to look at the myths by which you have lived your life?

My generation grew up with an imposed myth: the myth of happily ever after—always implying a man—a prince who someday comes (and makes you do the same).

Whether we wrote this myth or its opposite—there is no prince, and even if there is, he never comes, and even if he comes, he never makes you come—we were still seeing our lives in *terms* of this myth. Pro-prince or anti-prince, the terms of the debate were defined—and not by us. We tried to write other myths—someday my princess will come, or I am my own princess, so there—but they were all derivative. The armature of plot was the same. We were *reacting*, not creating. We had not expanded the terms in which we saw our lives.

Is there only one story? The prince comes or does not come? The princess *replaces* the prince? Solitude replaces them both?

Couldn't we find a story that has nothing to do with that, a story in which neither relationship nor renunciation of relationship was the be-all and end-all?

Apparently not. Our writers and philosophers thrashed through this territory and came up with new versions, not newly created myths.

Even our hypothesizers of cronehood and older womanhood had no new wrinkles on this old theme. Gail Sheehy said: You can still attract men after men-o-pause; Germaine Greer said: Who wants to anyway? But relationship was still the theme. Even Gloria Steinem admitted that she couldn't live just for The Movement. And Betty Friedan said that though old age was great, she wasn't giving up dancing. The women who had given up men had always liked women better *anyway*, or now discovered more kindness there, not realizing that after fifty, there's more kindness *everywhere* and even relationships with men, if you can find any, are kinder.

Perhaps in letting my unconscious dictate a picaresque model, I was reaching for a woman's life as rich, heroic, and many-splendored as an old-fashioned hero's life (even men rarely have such lives anymore), but my heroines also kept getting bogged down in relationships. Isadora learns about life after being ditched by a heartless bastard; Fanny learns heroism by rescuing her daughter; and Leila gets sober by sobering her impossible boyfriend.

Where is the woman who *self*-starts, who doesn't merely *react*, who lives her life for an ideal *apart* from relationship? Can we even *imagine* such a woman? And if we did imagine her, would our readers identify with her?

Last summer I found myself reliving my picaresque life—but this time with a difference.

My daughter and I had rented, sight unseen, a house on a hill of olive and cypress trees, in Tuscany, near Lucca. We were to arrive at the end of July, after two weeks of a teaching stint in Salzburg, and several days in Venice, Milan, Portofino. Two of Molly's friends were to join us, then Margaret, then my best friend. My husband was coming later, and eventually other friends.

We had rented near Lucca, not Venice (where I had spent so many years), because our friends Ken and Barbara Follett had rented there the previous year and had invited us to be houseguests in their grand villa. They never budged in August without their mingled brood of children, godchildren, nephews, in-laws, and children's friends. They also became a traveling Labour party conference, with people like Neil and Glenys Kinnock popping down for pasta, vino, and polemic.

We loved the sweetness of the countryside and the fact that it was not yet a ruined museum of death like Venice. We also liked the fact that Molly, my lonely-only, was with a crowd of kids. We loved Ken and Barbara, who are not only smart and talented but extremely kind and loyal.

Hot with the dust of the road, in a rented Opel wagon with a faulty shift and so-so brakes, Molly and I had made our way to Lucca. We had spent two days with the Folletts in their rented splendor in a nearby village. We had picked up Margaret and all her luggage at the Pisa airport and now we were bound for our Tuscan farmhouse with expectations higher than Miss Havisham's expectations of marriage. (Surely she'd be called Ms. Havisham today and would be in a twelve-step program to cure codependency.)

From the beautiful walled city, we headed north on an old road and began counting villages and vineyards, wine factories and farmhouses.

Turning right at what seemed to be a Tuscan Dogpatch on a road that kept falling away at curves over a dried-up river (some no-account tributary of the Arno or Po called the Serchio), we started up a rutted muddy road, made of loose rocks and irregular irrigation ditches, and promptly ran into a ditch. The Opel wagon stalled, started up again, hunkered down with a weary crunch. We three got out and pushed it back on the road—only to drive into the next ditch—and the next.

An enormously fat fireman, still wearing his rubber gear and hat, ran out onto the cinder-block porch of Dogpatch Manse and started screaming in his pure Tuscan dialect, *"Questa macchina non va su quella strada,"* which we had figured out anyway.

Behind him came Signora Fireman with *la bambina*—who was howling because we'd awakened her.

We puttered up the hill, stalled again, got out of the car, and were riveted by a precipice, nicely spaced with olive trees, beneath us.

I froze. A phobic driver at the best of times, I backed down the hill, hit a cinder block, and banged the rental car into submission. Then I sputtered into the by now very familiar ditch.

The fireman and his wife and baby were laughing.

But Molly persevered.

"I'm going up the hill to check it out, Mom," she said, getting out of the car. I saw her broad shoulders and mane of red hair disappear around the curve of the rocky road. Ever since she grew four inches taller than I, she has been hard to dictate to. "Molly," I screamed.

"Cool it, Mom!" she screamed back, like any picaresque heroine.

Presently, she rode back down the hill in a Land-Rover, driven by a robust gentleman, the owner of the house. Molly was grinning. He looked perplexed.

"How curious," he said. "Nobody has problems with this hill. C'mon, jump in, luv!"

"The rental agent never said we needed a jeep," I said glumly, with what I hoped was an edge of menace. I already had thoughts of papers being filed for "non-disclosure," but who would *dare* sue in Italy? It would take the rest of your life. I leapt in the Land-Rover, and rode up the rutted hairpin hill to the Englishman's castle at the top.

It was a beamed Tuscan farmhouse with a view of heaven—*all' Italiana*. I stared in awe. Then our landlord went down to rescue Margaret and our luggage.

"Hello, dearie!" said the lady of the house, as Molly and I trudged up the three flights of slate stairs to the Chiantishire dreamhouse.

Soon hubby returned driving our wagon—with Margaret in it—up the hill.

"Even with this car, it's a piece of cake," says he.

"Nobody ever complained about the road before," says the wife, looking like Mistress Quickly in her stretch bathing suit covered with cabbage roses. She had a double chin and a pouchy belly that none of the fitter menopause cheerleaders would approve of—nor would Lotte Berk and her fashionably anorexic East Siders. But she was comfortable with herself.

I start toward the house to take possession of what my shekels have leased.

"No you don't," says Missus. "Not in my kitchen till the maid's mopped the floor. Not for love nor money, house proud little me."

Her husband restrained me with a glass of white wine and bubbly water, and we sat down to a nice chat about how the real estate agent had rooked us both, overcharged me (six months in advance) and not paid *them,* but they hoped we liked the place anyway.

"Beautiful," I said, and it was true.

Mr. and Mrs. couldn't have been more solicitous as we sat out there two more hours in the sun, with Margaret making conversation about the Queen, the Queen Mum, Princess Di, flaunting her membership in the Daughters of Scotia, and describing in detail the home of one of her aunts who lived in the heather and gorse country of the highlands and how her Scottish uncle passed away and when and where he was buried and what they all ate for tea after.

Conversation. It fills a lot of life's little gaps.

Eventually, toasted by the Tuscan sun, and addled by its grapes, we were ready to inspect the house.

"We built it out of a ruin," said the husband.

And indeed, you could still see the chrysalis from which this butterfly had sprung. A shepherd's cottage on a hillside had become a bastion of Britishness, complete with Sky TV, MTV, CNN, shelves of videos, and road atlases, but few books except cookery and home repair (and the usual shelf of abandoned bestsellers left by the motley renters). There were celebrity ghostwritten tell-alls, books by generals and surgeons general, novels by fading movie stars, former cabinet ministers, and television evangelists. (Some were even current.) But the house was not less lit'ry for all that, since John Mortimer had rented it one year to write a book on Tuscany.

"I told you you should have studied *Summer's Lease*," my husband heckled on the phone from New York.

"Who can *read* in New York?" I countered. "You have to go to Tuscany for that."

In due time we were admitted to Weetabix Wonderland, with its astonishing views from all over the house. Cypress trees stepped down the hill, dark and spearlike against the leafy chestnuts and the silvery olive trees. Fuchsia and wisteria grew in profusion everywhere. Swallows careened from hilltop to hilltop against a broad expanse of pure blue sky. Who *wouldn't* have moved here from London? It was an English poet's dream of Italy.

The beds were lumpy, and the pillows were apparently made of the local Carrara marble. There were four double bedrooms, not seven as promised, and the term "double" was a reach. Fifteen people could sleep in this house only if they were very rowdy people and if some of them were sleeping on the terrace, under the pergola, or in the pool.

No matter. We were here to stay. Molly's friends were flying over. I had already paid in full, and this homey couple needed to winter over on Weetabix with my *soldi*.

"Don't you just *love* this house, Mommy?" says Molly, who really *does* love it.

"It's cozy, not spooky, Mom," she says. She is remembering the place we used to call Palazzo Erica in Venice—that crumbling *piano nobile*, with its secret tunnel to Piero's palazzo.

Palazzo Erica had one main thing to recommend it—the proximity of Piero, and the tiny studio off the walled rose garden where we could tryst while the family was ensconced upstairs. With a teenager in tow, I would never risk that. Suddenly my teenager has made me into a model matron, and I don't know whether I like it or resent it. Children want nothing but *everything*—heart, soul, genitals, MTV, and CNN. (And we mostly want to give it to them, too.)

"I saw this article in *Elle Décor*, Mom, or maybe it was another magazine, which says that you should always move the furniture around in a rented house. You should give it your own personality, it says."

Molly is on doily patrol, snatching doilies from under every plant, every arrangement of dried flowers, banishing all doilies (do they still call them antimacassars?) to the cupboard drawers.

Then she is lining up apples on a beam as she saw in her decorating magazine. Then she is pushing the huge ugly dining room table against a wall to make a desk for me.

"You can write here, Mom, I know it!" she says, having suddenly become my co-conspirator, not my saboteur. She has fish of her own to fry—a villa full of English and South African boys over at Vorno, friends coming, her stepfather's promise to teach her to drive in Italy. ("If you can drive in Italy, you can drive *any*where," she proudly tells her friend on the phone.) She *wants* Mommy writing now and out of her hair. She's become expert at using my perennial deadlines as a way of getting rid of me, yet also having me there when needed. The writer's child is infinitely resourceful, the writer's best creation for sure.

Molly is the picaresque heroine now, and I am Sancho Panza.

She is fixing up her house for her friends, trying on bathing suits to wear around the pool with the boys, thinking about the boy she met last year in Lucca. Will she have a life not centered on relationships? I doubt it. Already, she takes her happiness or sadness from passionate friendships; she fantasizes about boys; she wants a cozy house to bring her loved ones to.

But she navigates the road like any picaresque heroine and she can find airports and *autostrade* unhesitantly. She zips through Italian supermarkets in under an hour. She's plotted the way to the other villa—where the boys are.

She's on her own picaresque journey now, but already the point of her quest is to make a new home. She has taken all my deficiencies and made them into virtues: I get lost, so she does not; I am passionate and romantic, so she is pragmatic and cynical; I have lived for writing, so she lives for living. I like her much better than I like myself.

A few days later I have rented a jeep, mastered the road, got used to the beds, adopted a couple of semiferal cats, stocked the house with food, picked up the first of Molly's friends, and I am sitting in the moonlight watching the full moon rise, skewered by a dark cypress. Swallows still careen from hill to hill. The olive leaves flicker silver in the moonlight. The supposedly half-wild black cat with the cropped tail pounces up on my lap, butts my belly with her pointed muzzle, then puts her head on my lap for stroking and starts purring like a coffee grinder.

I am sitting at the outdoor dining table with my pad and pen. The full moon seems to be trying to disembowel itself on the *cipressi* but soon it rises above their apical points and makes a slow, silvery arc across the sky. I sit, enthralled, the cricket serenade ringing in my ears, as the moon moves to the opposite hill. I glance at my watch and note that three hours have passed. I have not written a line. Time always plays tricks like this in Italy. The rutted road, the Dogpatch at the bottom, the rocky beds, are all forgotten as the moon guides my eye through eternity.

In love with the landscape again, with the pleasures of blackish green, silver green, and the differing deep purples of the grapes and berries, I know why Italy always lured the poets. Death is not too great a price to pay for this beauty. I go to sleep with the full moon shining in my window and all the men I've loved on my dream dance card and invited to visit my bed. I miss my husband, but I know that it's important for us to spend some weeks apart every summer. It's a way of remembering who we are without each other. It enables us to have lives and fantasies that are not always interlocked.

The next morning, I am expecting my best friend to arrive from New York. Suddenly a panicked call comes from the Rome airport.

"I missed the plane to Pisa and I've rented a little disco-dude car to drive to Lucca. The only problem is, I'm so weak, I don't think I can make it. . . ."

"What's the matter?"

"I'm bleeding," she says worryingly. And then an explosion of static and we are cut off by the sadists who run—or fail to run—the Italian phone company. I pace around the pool waiting for the phone to ring again. I pull the phone outside by the pool and stare at it, hoping to make it ring. I putter in the hot sun, watering geraniums, slathering on sunblock. I pace and think. Since Gerri's husband died, I have felt responsible for her, yet there's no way I can reach her if she doesn't call back. I imagine her driving down the *autostrada* in the baking sun—even though she's too weak to drive. She will have rented an inexpensive car with no air-conditioning. Even sick, she could not be persuaded to hire a limousine and driver—since Gerri prides herself on her self-sufficiency. The "disco-dude car" probably has iffy brakes and a gearshift on the dashboard.

And then I look out over the Tuscan hills with their black *cipressi* and a feeling of peace comes over me.

Of course she's all right, I tell myself.

And I take a deep breath and begin scribbling in my notebook everything I remember about my years of friendship with Gerri.

We call each other best friends.

It is like being twelve, but strangely it is not. We share illnesses, breast lumps, houses, neurotic fears about our children, real fears about our children. We tell horrible secrets about our husbands, ex-husbands, dead husbands. We know the size of their cocks and how much money they make/made and whether they are/were glum or playful in bed and whether they snore/snored, whore/whored, and whether they remind/reminded us of long-dead/still-alive grandfathers, fathers, uncles, or brothers.

I have no brothers. She had two. One, funny and beautiful, died of AIDS. And she was the one elected to help him die. Her older brother alone remains. Gerri is a middle child like me.

But I had two sisters who often envied me, and she was always my good sister, who knew I had problems too. There's still sibling rivalry, but it rarely goes entirely unchecked. Not that we don't scream and fight and say horrible things to each other. In seventeen years, you'd have to say horrible things. But the other one always looks beyond the screaming. How we know to do that, I cannot say. I cannot always do it with my real sisters. Though lately, propelled by our sense of midlife mortality, we are building new bridges to each other.

Gerri and I met on a Sunday afternoon in the seventies. I was wearing an ivory crocheted string bathing suit with more holes than string and she was wearing a tank suit—probably Speedo. (She is a jock and I am not. She can never believe the blank looks I give her when she mentions famous ball players. Her whole family is composed of jocks. When they aren't throwing balls or watching people throw balls, they invest money: a world that baffles me as much as sports.)

When I met Gerri, the first thing I noticed were her enormous gray-green twinkly eyes, her curly red-brown hair, which surrounded her face like a coppery halo, her high cheekbones, her full mouth, which looked like an edible plum.

In a lot of ways we were opposites. She had three children and I then had none. She had always wanted to be a mother and was perplexed after motherhood stopped being a full-time job. I had never wanted to be a mother, but took her word that it was great. She was verbally quick and clever, but didn't feel my need to get everything down on paper. She was an athlete and I was a desk person. I could hardly believe she was Jewish. She skied like a WASP.

Pretty soon we discovered that we were almost the same age, that we had both gone to the same summer school in Florence, that we both loved Italy, ribald jokes, and vodka and orange juice on summer afternoons by the pool. We swam through pools of vodka like John Cheever's swimmer. We lived down the street from each other in Connecticut (where I lived all the time in those days). She was a weekend Connecticut person then.

I was living with Jon, and our relationship was then entirely blissful. We hadn't committed wedlock yet. We wrote all day at home, practiced yoga, took care of our two dogs and each other. She was married to David, a gorgeous hunk with muscles like Michelangelo's David, green eyes (one of which wandered—though not in the biblical sense), and she had three fabulous children: an athletic (and poetic) little girl named Jen and two raving boy jocks called Andy and Bob. They were the best kids I ever met: rambunctious, loving, smart.

We adopted each other at once.

Regarding my friend as an expert on motherhood, I asked her if I ought to have a baby. (Of course I already knew the answer. We never ask for advice otherwise.)

Unhesitatingly she said: "You'll never regret it." Thus she became Molly's godmother—Jewish style—whatever that means. (I think it means trustee.)

When I was pregnant with Molly the following summer, she helped make the pregnancy into one long celebration. I remember days by her pool, with families mingled, and nights in my hot tub, when all four of us took sidelong glances at one another's naked bodies and decided our friendship was more important.

When Molly was born, Gerri and I bonded more closely. I understood now how she had spent what she considered the best days of her life. At that point, I was terrified of caring for an infant. I tried to imagine I *was* Gerri, but I was not. I could not always give that unbroken concentration children demand, but at least I had a model for it.

My own mind was chronically divided. When I was singing to my child, I heard the siren song of my book. When I was immersed in my book, I missed my child. Only occasionally did I fall into that rapt listening that is the principal gift of motherhood.

From the start, Gerri and I respected in each other talents the other had yearned for. She loved books and would have loved to make them. I read chapters of *Fanny* to her, and she encouraged me to keep going. Later, she invested the money it took to workshop the musical version. Whenever my work was endangered, she was there to rescue it.

I loved children and would have loved more of them. I adopted hers.

I got divorced; she never did. She turned fifty first. She lost a sibling first, a father first. She nursed me through divorce. I nursed her through her bereavements, crying with her for years after some of her other friends thought the crying should be over.

I went through terrible times with men, and she was always there. After her husband died, she was the only person besides Molly and Ken who could interrupt me when I was writing.

She felt stalked by death. I felt stalked by upheaval and abandonment. Sometimes the abandonment was at least partly of my own making, but I could not say the same of hers. I needed solitude just as much as she hated and feared it. Sometimes I drove men away so I could write. But she clung to her marriage, *making* it good even when it had the potential for going bad.

We shared an analyst—our own Mother Sugar—a sumptuous mama doll full of soothing bromides and fierce insights; she had tiny feet and flowing robes like a Delphic oracle. She was the high priestess of self-esteem and getting married. She also had an aversion to saying good-bye to patients.

With her Botero body and her tiny legs and feet, her serene, beautiful, aging face, she would cry when you told her sad stories about your life, met a special man, or made a "breakthrough."

"I'm so proud of you" she would say. She was the good mother nobody ever thought they had. She was perfect at everything but letting you go.

Who, anyway, can wholly be the mother you need? You can't even be your *own* mother. And with your own child, you find yourself doing all those terrible things your parents did. Sometimes I find myself screaming at Molly in my mother's voice.

"You sound like Grandma," she says. "This is *child* abuse. I'm going now."

Did I *really* say that she ought to be grateful for school because children in Bosnia can't go to school? Did I *really* tell her that Benetton, the Gap, and Calvin Klein were not spiritual destinations? Did I *really* say that at fifteen I was not allowed to buy custom-blended makeup? Did I *really* say that she was a spoiled brat?

Apparently, I did. The term "child abuse" did not exist in my time. Nor did "date rape," "incest survivor," and "politically correct." How did we manage with only "Freudian slip," "making out," and "Momism"? We must have been verbally challenged. How did I ever stop my mother from yelling at me without the term "child abuse"?

Gerri and I had similar mothers: another bond. Both were loving but unpredictable wild creatures. Both could go off into the ozone. And suddenly come back. Both of us had to learn to live with this. Since we are both middle children, looking for our place in the family constellation, each of us found it by being the family clown. And neither of us has ever abandoned the *"Ridi, Pagliaccio"* role. We both laugh to hide the pain.

And what is laughter anyway? Changing the angle of vision. That is what you love a friend for: the ability to change your angle of vision, bring back your best self when you feel worst, remind you of your strengths when you feel weak. And speak the truth—but without malice. Loving candor is the secret of friendship.

Our friendship began during the long green Connecticut summers and flourished like a big healthy weed. I was, I thought, only a passable mother (despite the fact that I won something called the Mother of the Year Award given by the Federation of Florists in 1982). But Gerri was one of the great mothers of all time. I was awed when I saw the way she could talk to a baby. I was so spastic with Molly at first. I was afraid that the key to the mystery of motherhood would be forever denied me. Molly was a robust baby, but I was always sure she would choke on a piece of bread or get a concussion tumbling from her crib. At about eleven months, she turned somersaults in her walker and flew down a stair onto her head on a tile floor. In a panic, I dialed the pediatrician.

"Does she have memory loss?" the pediatrician queried.

Forgetting Molly was under a year, I quizzed her. She was crying. Was she remembering her birth trauma or was she brain dead? She cried more. Then she perked up and began to laugh.

"How do I *tell* if she has memory loss?" I asked the doctor.

"Make her count backwards."

"She can't even count forward."

"Oh. Who is this?"

"Molly—Molly Jong-Fast."

"Oh, yes, that one, the redhead. I'm sure she'll be okay."

How could I be a mother *and* a writer? I was always sure I couldn't be. The moment I stopped watching the baby, the baby would die. And the moment I stopped watching the book, the book would die. That was the way I lived the first decade of my daughter's life—both married and divorced. I was always sure I would be punished for my writing by having my beautiful daughter snatched away. When Jon began his crazy custody suit, I panicked.

I see the same fantasy of retribution in many women's novels. Usually it has to do with sex. In *August Is a Wicked Month,* Edna O'Brien's heroine goes to the South of France for her first holiday in years, and suddenly her son is killed. The son is on holiday with his father, but in women's fantasies, no one but a mother will do. In *The Good Mother* by Sue Miller, a similar archetype surfaces. The heroine reaches out for pleasure and thereby loses her daughter. The myth is deeply buried in our psyches. We cannot call it merely paranoiac because we are the generation for whom it often came true. We *were* punished for our independence and success with custody suits.

I half believed that ordinary things—like diagnosing a baby with fever—were beyond me. I was only put on earth to write, not to live, I thought. Gerri's greatest gift to me was giving me the courage to seize my life.

Gerri grew up in New Jersey, after all, so she knew things that a kid who grew up in Manhattan would never know—like driving at sixteen, buying wholesale, and how to be a *real* mother.

"Writing is *easy* compared to taking care of a baby all day," I used to tell Gerri—who didn't think so. Soon after we met, she rented a little office and went to it every day, hoping to become a writer. I got pregnant with Molly. These were our tributes to each other.

She never became my competitor, nor I hers. An amateur mother with only one child, I never took even a month off from writing. And it was already too late for me to have three kids. For me, then, she was a road not taken—an earth mother like my older sister. She was proof that plenty of funny, literate, intelligent women might choose to focus their lives on motherhood.

Her life was a balance wheel to mine. From her I learned that feminism *had* to include women like her. From her I learned that just because a woman chooses to be a homemaker, it doesn't mean she wants an all-male Congress, or an all-male Supreme Court. My grandmother could have taught me that, but my grandfather had trained me not to listen to her.

In the mid-seventies, when Gerri and I became friends, the women's movement was in the midst of this very crisis. The heady enthusiasms of the late sixties and early seventies had inevitably waned and it was time for the movement to embrace the average woman with children rather than alienate her. The failure of Betty Friedan and Gloria Steinem to forge an alliance was symptomatic of the problem. Women who had rejected family life despised women who had embraced family life. Perhaps the hatred was partly sour grapes. The urge to have children is so strong that you renounce it in yourself only at great cost.

My best friend understood all this long before I did.

"How can I identify with a movement that says I have to be childless or a lesbian in order to be a feminist?"

"You're exaggerating the problem," I told her. "You're part of the constituency too."

But she *felt* excluded. And so did many women. I meet them everywhere—these passionate feminists who love men and children. Until we openly acknowledge the mistakes feminism made before the backlash decade, we cannot prevent backlash from happening again.

As women we still need practice in making alliances with other women. We still tend to see other women as competitors to be eliminated. We still act out *All About Eve*. Younger women plot to replace older women; older women find it hard to praise younger women. Men are led up the success ladder by male mentors, while we find ways to put down members of our own sex. We are not even allowed to admit to this sabotage because it is officially nonexistent. But we have all experienced it. And the more we keep silent about it, the more we prolong its power over us.

*   *   *

David's death. How did I hear of David's death?

It was March—that wet gray month that brings my birthday, Passover, Easter. Usually I feel reborn in March as the days grow longer and lighter and my birthday approaches. But this particular March was to have a winter sky that would not lift. Halfway into the month, I was on the phone with my old friend Arvin Brown, discussing casting for a workshop of my musical of *Fanny Hackabout-Jones*, when suddenly another call came through.

"Can I put you on hold for a sec?" he asked.

"Sure." Then I waited for what seemed a very long time.

Arvin's voice came back—utterly changed.

"I just heard a horrible thing," he said in a low, hesitant tone, "and I don't even know if it's true."

"What?"

"David was killed."

"How? Where?" I asked.

"That's all I know," Arvin said.

I told him I'd call him back and pressed the button that speed-dials Gerri in Colorado.

"What's happened?"

"David is dead," she said as if from some space in the sky where the phone lines stop.

"David was in an avalanche . . . Jesus God . . . ," she said. There was finality in her voice as if she always expected this to happen.

"Good God!" Arvin exclaimed when I called him back. "Good God," he said again, hanging on the line as if waiting to be told it wasn't true.

Arvin was David's best friend, and knowing that, some acquaintances who had another friend on the same heliskiing trip had called him with the horrible news. The word was crisscrossing the country by optical fiber.

The way a tragedy first makes itself known to a group of friends: like poison seeping into the groundwater. On a certain day everyone knows. The well is poisoned. The calls come from all over, first informing, then verifying, then sharing feelings. Each of us shivers in the punishing wind of mortality. It is our Big Chill moment. Beautiful David is dead.

We were all just about the same age as David—David who snow-shoed up Ajax just to warm up for a day of downhill skiing. We never dreamed we would outlive him. David was rock solid, fearless, with a perfect body. David should have buried us all. Now he no longer *had* a body.

It was staggering and unbelievable. The fact could not quite penetrate anyone's understanding.

Day by day the puzzle began to unpuzzle. But it was still beyond our comprehension. Factoids accreted like crystals on an orange stick thrust into sugary water.

He made one last run down the virgin snowbowl. He was too tired to carry the emergency backpack, so he passed it to another skier—who lived. The ground vibrated, but no sound was heard. The guide yelled "*Slide!*" and the first few skiers on the glacier missed the onslaught of snow traveling a hundred miles an hour with the weight of wet cement.

Somehow the guide swam her way back up and out of the snow, but David was crushed on impact, carried by that tidal wave of snow, and slammed into a tree. He hung upside down, entangled in its branches, his transmitter emitting its dismal signal. Nine people died. David was the only one not decapitated or dismembered. Most of the victims were held together only by their ski suits.

What was once David came home—or at least to Frank E. Campbell's funeral home. The message was: Flesh is an illusion. Spirit alone is real.

"It was murder," says my broken friend. "They taught the *guide* to swim through the snow, but not the paying customers. His face looked like he was saying '*Shit!*' His beautiful back was broken, his lungs crushed, his aorta burst. His chest felt spongy to the touch—his strong beautiful chest. He must have died on impact. He didn't even know what hit him." She sobs in my arms as if all the tears in the world are hers. And they are. Inexhaustible, these tears.

"At least he died instantly," I offer, feeling so damned useless. "He didn't suffer."

"He *knew*," she says. "He knew."

The funeral takes place where we buried her younger brother and her father.

We all stagger through the motions like sleepwalkers.

I am in charge of poetry and underwear for this melancholy occasion. I take Jenny to buy a black bra. She doesn't have one, being just a kid. "I miss my dad," she says, stricken. We discuss what we are going to wear to the funeral and then I go home. I lock myself in my study in New York, pull the plug on the phone, and try to take my anarchic feelings and see if they will condense into a poem.

THE COLOR OF SNOW

For David Karetsky (April 14, 1940–March 12, 1991)
Killed in an Avalanche

Putting the skis down
in the white snow,
the wind singing,
the blizzard of time
going past your eyes,

it is a little
like being snowed in
in the Connecticut house
on a day when the world
goes away

and only the white dog
follows you out
to make fresh tracks
in the long blue shadow
of the mountain.

We are all halfway there,
preferring not
to think about it.
You went down the mountain
first,
in a blaze of light,
reminding us
to seize our lives,
to live with the wind
whistling in our ears,

and the light bedazzling
the tips of our skis

and the people we love
waiting in the lodge below
scribbling lines
on paper the color
of snow,

knowing there is no
holding on
but only the wind singing
and these lines of light
shining
in the fresh snow.

At the end of the service at Frank E. Campbell, after the kids and
Gerri and other family members spoke, I read that poem—"the David
poem," I call it in my head. Crowds of people flowed into the streets.
The funeral directors were unprepared with chairs. Even the famous—
sometimes especially the famous—have few to mourn them but curiosity seekers. When their moment of heat has passed, nobody comes—
not even a friend. But David had friends none of us even knew about.
There were kids he'd taught, adults he'd helped, associates from years
ago, college friends, and business associates he hadn't seen in years.
They all stopped by to say why they were there.

My friend made a beautiful speech neither of us remembers. She
and her children stood with their arms round each other, swaying
slightly. Everyone was trying to find some humor in the unrelieved
darkness, but we all knew we were next.

This was the death that made me know I was mortal.

I knew David had wanted to take the kids on this last trip and had
been stopped by Gerri. I knew he wanted to take her and she had
refused. She had been there once before and had felt death in the air.
All I could think was he had never wanted to grow old. Some blind
foreknowledge had restrained her, and now she knew the guilt of
being alive.

I only saw the outside of the grieving, so it is hardly mine to claim

with words. I noticed Gerri's reluctance to let go of him—as if letting
him go would kill him permanently, as if she were the keeper of his
sacred memory and if she stopped focusing on him for one second, he
would slip away.

Emily Brontë knew this. It comes to us all in grief. We *want* to forget in order to live, but we are afraid forgetting will make the dead die
again. And this death will be final.

Cold in the earth, and the deep snow piled above thee!
Far, far removed, cold in the dreary grave!
Have I forgot, my Only Love, to love thee,
Severed at last by Time's all-severing wave?

The first few nights, Gerri and the kids slept in a love pile, like
puppies or kittens. Then they all had to cope with their own grief—
each in a different way.

The clothes came home, then the skis, then the "personal effects."
Legal things had to be dealt with: money, reams of useless paper. My
friend staggered through it, not wanting to live. Sometimes the mornings were okay, but the nights were always bad. Sleep had also been
murdered. She could not lose herself in sleep for fear of losing David,
whose tenuous connection to life was now her memory.

What I remember most was how everyone wanted her to perk up,
bury the dead, remarry. But she needed to mourn. Her need was made
more painful by the denial of death that pervades our culture. She had
to scream and rage and rend her hair. Both New Yorkers and
Aspenites found this uncool.

"Dust yourself off and go on," said the collective voice of collective wisdom. "Haven't you been grieving an awfully long time?"
Implicit in this question was the idea that any mate was replaceable.
Get another one—like you'd "get" a new dog. But even a dog can't
be "replaced" till you have mourned enough. The new puppy can
never be loved until you've cried enough over the old one to float it
out to sea with your tears. The new puppy waits with watery eyes
until you do this right. Only then can you embrace her with an open
heart.

People whispered to me that two years were *enough*. How they
dared to judge another's grief I did not know. Maybe no one's

absence ever was allowed to hurt them very much—or else they believed you had to deny feelings to be hip. It was like fixing your eyes and chin, like staying fit; messy emotions were as unwanted as messy flesh.

I had never been widowed, but I knew how destroyed I'd been when Jon moved out. It had felt like widowhood to me. Awash in fluids and feelings I had never let myself know before, I didn't *want* to be comforted at first. The studs couldn't quite distract me, nor the old boyfriends, nor the medical student, nor Will. Sex was a temporary anodyne, but I still had to live till my flayed skin grew back. That took seven years. And I *did* marry again, exactly seven years later.

Barbara Follett suddenly rings. (I have been writing these notes in my journal, and when I look at the clock, I see that five hours have vanished.)

"I'm racing down to Lucca to get Gerri. She's lost your phone number and just found mine. She's *lost* the directions to your house."

"How is she?" I ask.

"Weak with the flu and cystitis, it seems, but she'll be okay, I think. I need the doctor's number."

I give it to her and sit immobilized by the phone again. I think it's funny that I no longer wait by the phone for men to call, but for my women friends to rescue one another. A startling ring, a very harried Gerri. "I'm in a hotel lobby in Lucca. Barbara just gave me your phone number. I had left it *and* the directions on the rental car desk in Rome. I was terrified. Then I found the Folletts' number on a scrap of paper."

"Don't explain! Barbara's coming to take you to the doctor."

About an hour later, a caravan of cars arrives, rearranging the rocks on our road.

A taxi driver leads (with Barbara and Gerri in the back), then a Follett godchild, driving Gerri's car, then the Follett caretaker, driving Ken Follett's car, with London plates.

Dazed by the sunlight and the view, Gerri collapses in my arms. I lead her to bed, bring plenty of water, mint tea, and her medicine. She looks weak and tired. Margaret and I transfer her bloody clothes into a basin of cold water.

"I'll wash them," I say.

"For God's sake, *don't*," she says.

"It's only blood," I say. "How can we be afraid of blood after all these years of menstruation and motherhood?"

She shuts her weary eyes.

"Just try to sleep," I say.

And she passes out.

Later the moon rises—a bit fuller this night. I sit watching it while the five other women of the house are fast asleep.

What do I want of this old moon? I want her to release me. I no longer want this picaresque life dictated by the blood of women, by the pull of the tides, by the pull of the moon. I want sex to let me go. And I want to let go of that place inside myself that hooks onto men and makes them the center of every adventure.

I'm ready to impersonate Erica Orlando now (and I don't mean Disney World). I'm ready to become an androgynous creature, flipping from century to century, in a wardrobe full of petticoats and riding britches, redingotes and shawls, tricorns and bonnets, fichus and cravats, periwigs and perukes. I'm ready to walk along the road unrecognized as a sexual being, singing my songs from under a veil, a mask, a hood—like those ambiguous statues in my friend's Venetian garden. It would be liberating to be as genderless as death—taking on the properties of man or woman as suits my immediate seduction.

It is not that I no longer love men, but that I want to experience being untouched by sex so that I can *really* know love—the love that gathers everything up into its arms at journey's end.

In the last few days I have been rereading a book I loved in my twenties—*Henderson the Rain King* by Saul Bellow. Again, a picaresque adventure. And one in which the hero, because his heart forever pounds *I want! I want!*, goes off to Africa for reasons even he knows not of. There he meets various tribesmen, who take him on a spiritual journey through which he redeems his own soul. At the end of his story, he credits love with having given him every spiritual advance he ever made in his life. And by love he seems to mean the love of women and of children. He has not had any men friends before he came to Africa. It is the African men who teach him to trust other men. His life with men—from his father onward—has mostly been a battleground. And women have been *love*. Women have supplied the missing half.

Perhaps Henderson the Rain King can attribute the grace of his life to love, but for women, sexual love is a more perilous matter. Centuries of death in childbed, deaths of children, the myriad broken promises of men, have taught us that we cannot trust carnal love above our own survival.

For women, sexual love may be a luxury to come home to at journey's end. For men, however, it is a necessity on their picaresque path. Henderson comes home for love; Ulysses and Tom Jones do the same. But for women this sort of love is the great La Brea Tar Pit—a gummy pool that may eat everything except our bones.

At this time in history, perhaps we cannot afford such surrendering love. Perhaps it takes too much away from us. As women of the whiplash generation, our dilemma has always been how to love yet love ourselves at the same time.

Part of us wants to love like the goddesses—coldly and capriciously. Part of us owes allegiance to Kali, eating her lover and attaching his skull to her waist. Part of us wants to love like Juno, scooping up mortal men, toying with them, then letting them go, turning them, in parting, into caves for the sea to crash through, great phallic stones, or even, if we are merciful, swine. Part of us wants to be Athena and Diana—who need no lovers, who have intellect and marksmanship instead.

The moon herself, with her big hollow head, counsels coldness. *The end of the picaresque is reason*, says she. *And reason always rules out love.*

But is she right? Eventually, we may come to another sort of love. Primed for it by sexual love, motherly love, attachment love, we may come to the love that connects us to eternity. In order to come to it, we must first begin to *believe* in it. This happens grudgingly at first, then tentatively, then passionately. We must come to believe that carnal love is not enough. And then the ocean of spirit in which we swim will become manifest.

It takes certain disciplines to break through our habitual blindness to all but matter. Abstinence from alcohol or drugs may be necessary for some; abstinence from food or material things may be necessary for others. Renunciation helps us see the path more clearly, but the issue is neither drink nor food. These abstentions merely reveal the path that was always there.

*   *   *

A week later Gerri is wholly recovered. She and I walk down the rocky path from our house and up the country road toward (I swear it) Dante's Restaurant. The path has become less rocky and precipitous with each day and the Tuscan countryside is ripening as August approaches. There are hanging plum tomatoes, bunches of purple grapes, single yellow tree roses with heavy fragrant heads.

We are talking about love, as usual, and surrender.

"It's not the not-drinking," says Gerri, "but the giving up of the struggle—seeing yourself not as a rock in nature's path, but as the path itself."

Struck by the beauty of her phrase, I remember the clarity I had when I was sober: a calm clarity that inspired everyone around me, but my best friend in particular.

Why had I lost my sobriety? It was not that I drank a lot, or uncontrollably. Drink is not my *only* addictive substance. Work can be. Or food. Or worry. Or prescription drugs. Or spending money. Or never saying no. Or men. My addictions shapeshift to deceive me. They sneak up on me—cunning, powerful, bearing their own denials.

But I had had real serenity once and had passed it along to my best friend when she was grieving for her beautiful husband, senselessly dead in an avalanche. I was the rock for her to cling to as the snow flowed around her with its terrible secret. Now she was passing that steadiness back to me. If we are all made of God, it is our friends who remind us. We pass the gift of God to them. They pass it back to us when we need it most.

The picaresque path can probably also be a metaphor for the passage of the soul back to its creator. The thieves along the way—the thieves of money, of love, of magic, of time—are merely human obstacles to keep the traveler from perceiving that she herself *is* the path.

The path is as steep and as precipitous as we make it, as level and rolling as we can grade it, as steady as we are steady, as passable or impassable as our own will to pass.

In a true picaresque, the hero stops struggling and *becomes* the path.

At fifty, we need this knowledge most of all.

In Tuscany Gerri and I slept late and shared our dreams when we awakened. There were dreams of old lives, old loves, and fields of bluish snow. Dismembered bodies and dismembered cars littered the slopes. At times our dreams infected each other's sleep. We read to each other from books of poetry and meditation. We analyzed each other's troubles, as we always do. We laughed about everything.

We also fought about everything—like real sisters. We fought about money, bedrooms, whose car to take. Every one of these fights was actually about something else—usually abandonment. I wanted to be first on her list and she wanted to be first on mine. I wanted all her attention, all her love, all her care. I wanted her to be my mommy, my daddy, my sister. She wanted the same from me. She wanted to be fed, cared for, nurtured without limit. She wanted backrubs, poems, pastas, and to be left alone when she needed to be left alone. She wanted to come before my writing, my child, my man. And I wanted no less from her.

She was sick at first, so I took care of her. Then I was jealous of the attention, and she took care of me. We had gone down into the primal cave of our friendship. We had felt loved enough to rage and fight, to show the inside of our naked throats and our bared fangs, and the friendship took another leap toward intimacy. Without rage, intimacy can't be. I had learned this from my marriage—the fourth one—the one that just might last.

The rental is over today. Everyone left at dawn but me and Ken. Molly is fifteen and two days. Early this morning, she thanked me for "the greatest summer of my life!" Then she flew home to her father with Margaret and her friends. Gerri has flown home too. I am alone on the Tuscan hill at seven o'clock in the morning, watching the morning star fade into the pink of the rising sun.

The cock crows. The cicadas warm up for a hot day.

The cypresses are still black, the olive trees still dull silver, the chestnuts still green.

The black cat we have been feeding all month prowls the stone terrace, hissing at the brown and white cat who has come around to share the bounty. They live on this hill, are fed by the fireman and his wife, our landlords, and another English family, but they belong to no one. This is *their* hill, not ours. Territoriality rules the animal kingdom to which we so reluctantly belong.

Our bags are packed. We are leaving wine and olive oil and stacks of books for the next transients to inhabit this little shelf before heaven. The road is still impassable, but not for us.

None of this is ours. We rented it for a month and are moving on. The olive trees, the cypresses, the walnut trees (with their still-green fruit), are not ours, nor will we be here for the harvest. I will take my poems and photographs, the chapters I wrote here, and go on to the next destination.

All the things that maddened me—the maid who would not wash dishes, but only towels for the next renters, the owner who lurked, pretending to be fixing the pool filter, but really spying on my daughter and her friends sunbathing, the oven that would not light, the wasps that swarmed whenever we cut a peach or a melon, or opened a Coke, the fighting semiferal cats—all these finally delighted Molly and have filled her memory bank with shiny coins.

"We always spent summers in Italy," she will say, "so my mom could write."

And all the push-pull of mother and daughter will be forgotten as the memories pile up.

Of course we have screamed at each other in cars over road maps, in the kitchen over dirty dishes, in stores over the prices of things. Of course she has pushed me to the limit with her endless needs, and I have maddened her with mine—particularly my need for the silence that teenagers find so utterly incomprehensible.

Sometimes I feel too old to keep up with a fifteen-year-old. Sometimes I feel so young that only her existence makes me pretend to be a grown-up.

How did I *get* to be a grown-up? At times I find myself still sitting on the hillside, plotting revenge against the adult world. I still say "Mom" when I am scared—though I never called my mother that and "Mom" is anyway too unsteady to help me now. In truth, she was always shaky—though she loved me. And Molly really needs to know things I have forgotten I know. Like when it's okay to call a boy or how to memorize dumb stuff for SATs, like when to try scary new things and when to pass them up for the sake of self-preservation. I wake up and remember to be an adult for her. She summons me to shed my baby ways.

I have plans and plans. Finish with my *Fear of Fifty* and jump back into my novel of the future, give myself the gift of writing poems again, write some short stories, finish my musical, complete my book of meditations, affirm my life every morning and let myself have a good day, free myself each night to dream the necessary dreams, find pleasure in serving those I love, give up guilt at refusing when they demand my self-annihilation, find joy in teaching, joy in talking to loving readers (who think I have answers when all I have are a few pointed questions), give myself time every day to walk or go to a museum, be generous because it reminds me how much abundance I have been given, be loving because it reminds me not to feel jealous of those who only *seem* to have more, seize my life, release my anger, bless the known and the unknown world, bless the hill of olives, bless the pinecones falling from the umbrella pines, bless the still-green walnuts, bless the rosy glow of the sun, which I may not get to see another summer, or even another day.

If, every day, I dare to remember that I am here on loan, that this house, this hillside, these minutes are all leased to me, not given, I will never despair. Despair is for those who expect to live forever.

I no longer do.

14

HOW TO GET MARRIED

The real marriage of true minds is for any two people to possess a sense of humour or irony pitched in exactly the same key, so that their joint glances at any subject cross like interarching searchlights.

—Edith Wharton, *A Backward Glance*

But I had been in love pretty often and I didn't think it stood the wear and tear.

—Enid Bagnold, *Autobiography*

I met my husband on a street corner, nearly running him down with my car. I was picking him up for a blind date (arranged by a mutual friend who is a humorist) and I certainly knew I didn't want to be trapped in a blind date's car.

At dinner, he inhaled his food in less than two minutes flat, and talked at the same time. I was trying to remember the Heimlich maneuver—though perhaps he would have preferred another maneuver. I must have liked him because I let him monologue all night. Usually *I* monologue.

At that point I still had various snake-hipped studs on various continents, and I didn't think I *needed* a husband, though I certainly needed a friend. I'm embarrassed to admit this, but I married him five months later. We sailed the Mediterranean for our honeymoon. Then we got to know each other. I now recommend longer courtships.

Even now, we have laryngitis from screaming at each other: the dirty little secret of a durable marriage.

I'll never divorce him—how can I, he's a divorce lawyer—but I may just shoot him. This is the way two people know they're mated.

He seems to want the best for me (and I for him). His prison record cannot be found in any computer. He has—gasp—"good character," as my mother might have said if she'd ever said such things. I hate to write anything good about this marriage, because it's a known rule of life that just as a "happy couples" piece in any magazine causes immediate divorce, writing good things about your mate in a book causes marital problems. (So does writing bad things.)

Somehow, after our first date, Ken and I found ourselves talking to each other wherever in the world we were. I went to California to see my agent, who was living there briefly, and without really meaning to, I called Ken. I went to Italy, supposedly to attend an Umbrian cooking school, but really to see an unavailable lover who moved heaven and earth not to see me for more than one night—and I called Ken. I waited for the unreliable Umbrian phone to ring and it was always Ken. I debated about going to Venice to see the other one and instead made a date in Paris with Ken. My clever husband-to-be had actually wired me a ticket to Paris, whereupon I amazed myself by flying to meet an available man when I had an unavailable man waiting in Italy. Something must have changed in my tiny masochistic mind, or else I was—horrors!—in *love*.

But I didn't want to be in love. I only wanted to be in *like*. Love had never proved anything but trouble. As Enid Bagnold said, it didn't stand the wear and tear. So when I met Ken, I decided I was through with love. In the past, I had usually gotten married with my fingers crossed.

The first night I met Ken, I was just back from that wedding in St. Moritz where my best (male) friend, the beautiful Roman, had married a clever, beautiful blonde princess—with the *von* and *zu* to prove it. She was twentysomething. I was fortysomething. He was thirtysomething. Somehow that made me happy to meet a man my own age. And I liked the way Ken looked: like a bear stumbling into a campsite in Yellowstone.

A big, tall, disheveled-looking man with a black mustache and beard, a full head of black hair (going silver at the edges), and a

three-piece suit with a red bow-tie, Ken had the feel of a friendly animal sniffing the air. His eyes were brown and warm. He seemed to
have to collapse his legs (like folding umbrella spines) in order to get
into my car. He turned and smiled at me like a cat staring at a saucer
of cream.

"Helllllo," he said, clearly relieved. Was he expecting Vampira or
Boadicea or a spear-carrying Amazon queen with one breast?

My friend the humorist, Lewis Frumkes, had told me he was
about my age. And smart. And nice. "A rare combination," Lewis
said. "Usually they're smart or nice, but not both."

"He's not, I hope, an eligible single man?"

Lewis was baffled by this phrase—as well he might be. How
could he know I hated "eligible single men"—who usually proved to
be work-addicted and sexophobic and wanted you to settle the pre-
nup on the first date? I'd long ago decided that faithless Italians,
unemployed actors, underaged WASP heirs, and married men were
sexier.

My analyst analyzed this as an allergy to marriage—which was
really an Oedipal crush on my adoring father. She was big on advice
though she always protested she gave none. It was clear whom she
approved of and whom she did not.

"Where is he *now?*" she always said when you made a reference
to a man who was rich or famous, or both, whom you'd dated, even
briefly, in the past. Her ears perked up like those of an Edith Wharton
matron.

She looked at me as if my itinerant actors and straying husbands
were *trayfe.*

She wanted me married, and *getting* credit cards rather than dis-
pensing them. She thought I flung myself like pearls before pigs. She
thought I valued myself too little. Maybe I did. But I liked sex, and
most of the so-called eligible men were scared to death of it.

"If I were single, would *I* be eligible?" Lewis asked.

"Definitely *not,*" I said, laughing.

He looked perplexed, not knowing whether this was an insult or a
compliment.

"I told Lewis I didn't *want* to meet a celebrity," Ken said. "But
then *he* said: 'She's not like that.'"

"You mean you were *judging* me before you met me?"

"Everyone's always judging everyone," he said, pushing the car seat back and extending his legs. "Every time I negotiate with other lawyers, it's a cock-measuring contest. You know that. Your books are all *about* that."

"So why were you reluctant to meet me?"

"Probably fear. I thought you'd be a man-eater. It's clear you're not."

Was *this* an insult or a compliment? Who could say? I knew at once he was honest and extremely nervous. He couldn't sit still. Like Tigger, he seemed bigger because of the bounces.

I parked the car in a garage off lower Fifth Avenue and we walked to a horrendously overpriced downtown restaurant—about to be a casualty of the late-eighties bust.

He refused the first table, and the second. We sat down at the third. A native New Yorker, I figured.

"No—Great Neck," he said, "but Central Park West when I was a baby. I remember throwing ration coupons—red points—out the window, or *they* remember it. I was a wartime baby."

So was I, I thought. Should I say it? Or was I expected to lie about my age? In my forties I still hadn't made up my mind. My analyst believed in not telling. I disagreed. Who am I if not a person born in the middle of World War II? My age is part of who I am. But women, even desirable women, are always afraid of seeming undesirable. Honesty takes a long time. Undecided about how honest to be, I let him talk. I didn't do my usual rambunctious audition piece, nor did I sing for my supper. Our first date had no trace of the New York verbal duel of *Can you top this?*

Ken told me the story of his life, from the ration coupons on. He sketched in his parents, his schools, his first jobs—journalism, film— becoming a lawyer. He told me of two ex-wives, an adored stepdaughter, a long relationship that had just ended, a love for airplanes and rare-book collecting. It all tumbled out of his mouth with much self-deprecation. And much bravado. Not unlike my own.

He was not hiding from me. A lot of the men I knew were hiding and didn't even know it.

I was bemused by his being a pilot. The novel I'd delivered to a publisher that very afternoon (and had spent the last three years struggling with) ended with Isadora Wing marrying an amateur pilot, her fourth husband. It was total invention. I had never even *dated* an amateur pilot. Isadora simply *needed* to marry a pilot and take flying lessons to overcome her fear of flying forever.

Any Woman's Blues opened with her death. She had left a last manuscript to be published posthumously. This tome fell into the hands of an utterly humorless feminist hackademic who took all Isadora's jokes literally and objected to them politically. But Isadora was really not dead. She had merely disappeared into the South Pacific like Amelia Earhart. But unlike Amelia, she was able to save herself. She returned to Connecticut to become a poet again—disappeared to the world, that is, but not to herself.

My unconscious had devised this automyth of aerial-poetic rebirth because I tend to make metaphors of the conflicts I am living. When I began *Any Woman's Blues* I felt dead. Disgusted with my public persona, I never wanted to write another Isadora book, so I wantonly killed off my most famous heroine. But as I wrote, she came back to life, thus so did I. We are saved by our own creations.

And here I was, meeting an amateur pilot on the same day I delivered the book. All authors know that any book is a casting of runes, a reading of cards, a map of the palm and heart. We make up the ocean—then fall in. But we also write the life raft. And we can blow healing breath into our creatures' mouths.

For all my attempts to kill my alter ego, Isadora, she remained stubbornly unkillable. So was I. Now all I had to do was learn to fly.

I could be friends with this man, I thought, as he talked about why he loved flying.

"It's freedom," he said, "a defiance of limits."

"How did you get to be so honest?" I asked.

"What's the alternative?" he asked. "It's now or never."

The first date was on a Wednesday night. I dropped him off at his apartment in the East Sixties and sped home to Connecticut—where Molly and Margaret and Poochini were ensconced for spring vacation.

He called the next morning at ten. He was not playing games.

"I had a great time with you."

"So did I," I said.

Then, panicked at having given away *that* much, I shut up. I had learned from my various noncommittal swains not to gush. It was dangerously uncool.

"How about next Saturday?" he asked.

"How about it?"

"Will you go out with me?"

"I don't go out Saturday nights," I said matter-of-factly. "I'm in the country on the weekends. . . . I write—"

"So I'll come to the country—"

"No you *won't*," I said.

"Why not?"

"I don't invite new men to my house. . . . It's against my religion."

"So—convert."

"Not so fast," I said.

There was an awkward pause while we both contemplated our first power struggle.

"I'll *meet* you in New York," I finally said.

"Great! Take the train in and I'll pick you up at Grand Central. Then I can drive you home."

"No," I said fiercely (I never wanted to be without a car with a new man). "I'll drive in and meet you."

"Don't do that. Where will you *park?*"

"I'll park at my garage—or I'll get a driver. That's it—I'll get a driver so I can zoom back and see my kid in the morning."

"*I'll* drive you back—I love to drive."

"No you won't," I said.

"Okay—however you like. Just as long as you show up."

"Why shouldn't I show up?"

"You might panic," he said. "People do."

Did I think about him much after that call? No. I knew better than to start thinking about any man at that point.

My days were consumed with figuring out when to call Venice, which weekends my current married boyfriend's wife was away, and endlessly revising *Any Woman's Blues*—even though I'd handed it in. (I am one of those writers whose editors have to snatch the manuscript out of their hands.) I was also working on the musical of *Fanny Hackabout-Jones,* researching a book on Henry Miller, and making notes for a new novel. In the middle of all this, one of my more reticent suitors showed up, after an absence of four months.

He sent me a birthday present—an Indian miniature of a dancing goddess—and he followed with a call. What was I doing for my birthday? he wanted to know. It was as if he had intuited I was unavailable. Otherwise he wouldn't have asked.

I told him that Ken and Barbara Follett were coming to Connecticut for my birthday (which fell on Easter Sunday that year). He asked if he could join us. I said I'd call them and see how they felt.

"Which guy is *this*?" Follett wanted to know, having seen me six months before in Venice with Piero. And then he laughed. "Of course, invite him too. I'd like to see how he compares with the other."

"Do we *know* this one?" Barbara asked. For the past few years, I had been schlepping through London with all manner of escorts—married and single. My friends were always intrigued but also fiercely protective of me. Barbara once asked one of my swains point-blank: "Are you *married*?" He was a handsome Portuguese historian I'd met at a conference in Rome. He had no *idea* what to say to such a query.

"I suppose I am," he said sheepishly.

Barbara gave him a withering look.

"Let's have a look at this one," said Barbara on the phone. "Let's see how he paints Easter eggs anyway."

That weekend, we really *were* painting Easter eggs in Connecticut. We sat at the big round dining room table with Molly, doing self-portraits in oils on boiled eggs.

"How you see yourself says something about who you are," said Barbara, who is an expert palm-reader, face-reader, people-reader.

"And which animal you are. Ken's a wolf—aren't you, Wolfie? And Molly's an elephant—the big domed forehead. And Erica's a bichon frise like Poochini."

We all painted ourselves on eggs—even the reluctant suitor. His was a noncommittal face. Barbara's confrontational manner cowed him somewhat. I was glad.

He and I slept together that night, but we did not even touch. I dreamed of flying in a little plane with Isadora Wing and Piero and a big black bear. Piero was rattled, but the bear was not. "*Don't panic, ladies and gentlemen,*" he said. And suddenly Ken and Barbara Follett were in the plane too, and Molly, and all the Follett kids.

"Have you ever tried wing-walking?" I asked the bear.

"I'm a conservative pilot," he said. "I don't want to die just yet. I have a lot to live for."

On my birthday, Easter Sunday, the bear called from Toronto.

"How's your weekend?" I asked.

"Awful," he said. "I guess you can't relive the past."

I was puzzled.

"I came up to spend my birthday with my former girlfriend."

I swallowed, but my mouth remained dry anyway.

"Your birthday? *When* is your birthday?"

"Today—March twenty-sixth."

"My God," I gulped. "So is mine."

A long silence. But he didn't seem surprised.

"Will I see you next week?" he wanted to know.

"Saturday?"

"Yes—the night you write."

"Yes," I said. "I'm making an exception in your case."

It annoyed me that he had *my* birthday. First of all, *nobody* else should have my birthday. Secondly, it seemed another goddamned omen. Something was closing in on me and I didn't like it. As Anita Loos said, *Fate keeps on happening.*

How *dare* this man have my birthday? Did he respect *nothing*? Did he want to horn in on everything I had? My birthday was *mine*.

That Saturday night, I picked him up in my car—with a driver hired for the occasion—and we went downtown to the Public Theater to see a musical that was half in Yiddish, half in English. His choice. From the way he kept looking at me, I knew this was a *test*. He wanted to know if I laughed at the appropriate moments, if I understood the Yiddish, if I was *Yidderate*. Ahh—I got it. This was some kind of ordeal: the theme of the three caskets, the glass mountain to climb, kissing the sleeping prince to see if the spell could be broken. How *dare* he be testing me? I thought. I ought to be testing *him*.

"Well, did I pass?" I asked as we got into my car.

"What on earth do you mean?"

"Look—I know an audition when I see one. I'm not stupid."

He looked at me mockingly.

"Where did you learn Yiddish?" he asked.

"The same place you learned it," I said. "Besides, I don't know much."

"You laughed in all the right places," he said.

"As defined by you," I said. "God—you're a cocky son of a bitch."

"You love it," he said.

After that, we started going out for dinner every night.

"I've met this really nice man," I told my therapy group.

"Yeah, yeah," they said. "If he was *really* nice, you wouldn't be able to like him. . . ."

"Oh yeah?" I said.

"Yeah, yeah, yeah," they said.

Ken and I were in the habit of closing restaurants. We would sit and eat and drink and talk and then suddenly people would be sweeping or mopping up around us.

What did we talk about? I cannot remember. But we couldn't stop. I used to gaze at him at the table and think: I'm never going to sleep with him. I was so sick of things that started with sex and then fizzled. We would be friends, I told myself—friends, not lovers. Then nothing could ever go wrong. Friendship was best, after all. Friendship had a *chance* of lasting.

So we had dinner together every night and didn't sleep together.

It became a game to see how long I could string this out. Sex proved nothing, I told myself. It only muddied the waters. I had been sexually enthralled by many men, and when I broke the addiction, what remained was usually not worth bothering with. This time I was going to *like* the man first. I was *not* going to marry the man today and change him subsequently.

Meanwhile, there was Piero. His love was imperishable because his life was promised to another. He had come to visit me in Connecticut not long before I met Ken, and he was somewhat less impressive taken out of the watery world of Venice. Like Ondine on land, he needed his iridescent scales to dazzle. I had seen him briefly after the wedding in St. Moritz and the magic was partly restored. But I think the truth was I was growing tired of his predictable elusiveness. If I made myself convenient, he would conveniently appear—for a while. The sex, of course, had never stopped being delirious, but even delirium has its limits. Without masochism to fuel it, it grows cold. Like the men who pursued ardently and then ran away, like the eligibles who quizzed you on your property and investments, even the great studs became boring, after a while. They had figured out a new gig—that was all: the gigolo gig. They knew how to make you come and come and come and come and come. And so what? As soon as you saw the cynicism underneath, the swooning ceased to be so important. Manipulation rather than revelation.

In Los Angeles for a few days to see my literary agent and pitch my new novel to a handpicked selection of baby moguls (who had read *Fear of Flying* in *grade* school), I stayed at an actress friend's apartment in West Hollywood. Every morning, up three hours before I needed to be, I found myself calling Ken even without really planning to. I found myself describing to him the scene in which I am tap-dancing the plot of my new novel to a room full of Armani-clad twentysomethings who used to shanghai my first novel from their parents' bookshelves and jerk off into it in the bathroom. I am trying to tell them why this novel about a middle-aged woman artist in thrall to a gorgeous young stud will make a *great* movie. But there's no way they're going to buy it. For them, I'm a curiosity, an antique from an age shrouded in the mists of history: the seventies.

"My mother loves your books," one of them says. And it rises to a chorus of: *Mine too, Mine too, Mine too.*

They're going to go back to their offices and call their mothers with pride. "Guess who I met?" they'll say. But do they want to make movies their mothers might like? Absolutely not. Their mothers are, by definition, *old*.

"I've gone from being too young for everything to too *old* for everything," I tell Ken on the phone. "When I was in Hollywood in the seventies, I was newly famous and a fool for any con-man. All the people in charge were *older*. Now all the people in charge are *younger*—but they're still all guys."

Why am I telling him all this? I wonder. Because he understands? Because he *gets* it? Because we can talk as if we've been talking all our lives?

Nevertheless, I mistrust it. When is he going to turn into a monster or a wimp? When is he going to flee from intimacy? When is he going to reveal the Mr. Hyde behind the Dr. Jekyll?

During my week in Los Angeles, I keep remembering Hannah Pakula's immortal line about moving back East: "Hollywood is no place for a woman over forty with a library card." Hollywood always makes me feel that I'll never be rich enough or thin enough or young enough. Even when I *was* young enough, I felt too old for Hollywood. So I am all the more delighted when the very epitome of older women who have conquered Hollywood comes to my table at Morton's— where I am having dinner with my agent—full of excitement about my books. She invites me to lunch at her house the next day and I discover that the very grand, the very glamorous Joan Collins is really a cuddly Jewish earth mother under all that paint.

We sit in her white living room trading stories about younger men. She has just about survived her palimony ordeal with that very snake-hipped and slithery Peter Whatever-his-name-was.

"I never *knew* he was lying," she says, "or fucking my friends. He was *so* romantic. That's what we miss—men who aren't afraid to be romantic with us."

I fly back to New York, and Ken is waiting at the airport.

"I thought you needed someone to meet you," he said, shooing away the hired driver.

Shortly after this, he took me flying for the first time. His plane was a Cessna 210 that he parked at Teterboro airport in New Jersey. He taught me to do the walk-around, checking the fuel, the landing gear, the flaps, had me read off the checklist for take-off, and then he became totally calm and concentrated when he took off. Flying was an altered state of consciousness for him. He was never so happy as when airborne. As we ascended over the gas drums and industrial wastes of New Jersey, the problems of the earth fell away. The air was full of little planes—each tethered to the ground by a constant stream of radio communication. The air was the last place left where freedom was more than a word.

We flew north up the Hudson with its purple palisades, then turned east over Long Island Sound and made a quick tour of the end of the island with its foaming surf and green potato fields. We listened to the weather as reported by other pilots and we rode thermal bumps clearing the tops of clouds. No wonder I had invented a pilot husband for Isadora! This was the freedom I had sought my whole life. But how had a fictional character managed to summon a real man? I must have written a powerful spell.

We landed.

"You weren't afraid at all," he said.

And it was true.

After that first flight, we drove back to my brownstone, where Molly was waiting, having just returned from her father's house. This was the first time Ken had met her. She was diligently completing her homework at the dining room table.

"What are you going to be when you grow up?" he (uninspiredly) asked.

"A civil litigator," she said brightly.

And he fell in love with her on the spot.

Alarm bells went off again. This guy is *not* kidding, I thought. What was I going to do?

Leave for Italy, as soon as possible, that's what. Fortunately I had a friend who had invited me on a junket to a cooking school in Umbria. We were all supposed to meet in Rome, journey to the Umbrian hills for a week of learning how to taste olive oil, knead pasta dough, and simmer *sugo*. I had committed myself to this trip long before I met Ken, but no sooner did I arrive in Rome than I felt bereft of him. I also missed Molly. It seemed there was no reason for me to be here. I had long since given up even the *pretense* of cooking.

We were all put up in a charming inn located in a former stable. The rooms were made of stone, were dank and damp, and had no telephones. The Umbrian countryside was a riot of wildflowers—poppies, irises, hyacinths—but the rain came down unceasingly. I put in the usual call to Piero and he was, as usual, hard to reach. Then he called back (while I was elbow deep in pasta dough) and said he couldn't come. Then he put me on the phone with his stepson—which I later learned was supposed to be a cue to me that he *was* coming, but didn't want it generally known by his family.

Assuming he *wasn't* coming, I made plans to go home at once. But when he called and said "*Non scappi*," I was hooked again by his voice.

Ken, meanwhile, called from New York and asked me to meet him in Paris. I waffled. Then Piero showed up as if out of nowhere. We spent a blissful night together in the stone stable. We made love with our usual miraculous ease, and slept in each other's arms all night. The next day, we explored the wet Umbrian countryside and wound up in Todi, eating at Ristorante Umbria. As we were laughing and touching, eating and drinking, I asked him why he stayed with a woman he didn't love.

"She's my antibiotic," he said. "Without her, I would have been married twenty times."

I have my answer, I thought to myself. She's the antibiotic and I am the disease.

He drove me back to my cooking school and we kissed and said good-bye. When I returned to my room, there were three messages from Ken, the last one informing me that a ticket to Paris would be waiting for me at the Rome airport.

He called later to say, "Don't feel obligated to come, but it would be great if you did."

The day finally dawned when I was supposed to go home, and I taxied to the Rome airport not sure where I would end up that afternoon.

If I went to Venice, I would wait and wait to be able to fit in hours with Piero. If I went to Paris, something else would happen.

At the airport, I went to the Air France counter and found my ticket. I checked the schedules. The next flight to Venice left in an hour, the next flight to Paris in an hour and a half. I wandered through the terminal in a panic, pushing my luggage in circles. My eyes glazed over. I bumped into people and walls. It seemed to me that this decision was pivotal in my life. I thought of beautiful Venice and beautiful Piero and the few magic days we'd spent after the wedding in St. Moritz. I could recapture that. Or could I? You never step twice into the same bedroom. Once you begin to see the *routine* of bliss, is it still bliss? Even voluptuaries can become chained to their clocks. Ah— time to have my nightly immersion in Chaos and Old Night. The chthonic deities won't be put on a schedule. Once you routinize them, they tend to drift away. And Pan? He gallops back into the primal wood.

And if I went to Paris? Well, something new would happen. Another door would open. Or close. I was in a sweat just thinking about it. I was afraid I was giving up my freedom, my life.

I flew to Paris. When I went to pick up my luggage, I saw, through the glass barrier, this big bear of a man, waving madly at me, smiling. He had such an open face. When I met him outside the barrier, he couldn't stop saying how glad he was I'd come. When we got into the car he'd rented, he kept looking at me so hard that he continually drove up on the sidewalk. He never stopped saying "I'm so glad you came. I'm so glad you came."

We checked into his favorite hotel, a little *relais* in a park in the center of the sixteenth arrondissement. Formerly a *maison de passe*, it had tiny rooms full of dreadful rococo furniture, but our suite looked out on a green garden.

"I need a bath," I said. A bath tends to be my solution to everything.

Ken fussed around, running the bathwater, pouring in the piney green Vitabath, trying to help me unpack, bouncing around the tiny suite until I screamed, "Please sit still! You're driving me crazy!" He was so eager to please, it made me nervous.

Finally alone in the bath, I soaked and thought. What on earth was I doing here?

A knock at the door.

"Do you want some tea or coffee?" he asked. "Shall I order something?"

I was annoyed to be interrupted in my stew. But I yelled, "Coffee."

When I got out of the tub, we sat down in the living room of the suite and drank the coffee.

"I love how comfortable you are with your body," he said. "You just walk around the room dressed, half-dressed, undressed, and you're happy in your skin. I've never been with a woman like that."

"What do you mean?"

"Usually they lock the door and put on makeup. Women are so afraid to be seen in their own faces."

We talked. We went out for dinner at a local brasserie. We talked and talked and talked some more. I thought about how different my evening would have been if I'd gone to Venice. There would be lots of time spent phoning, arranging, canceling, arranging again. Then there'd be hot sex—and then good-bye. This was the opposite. We were at the beginning, not at the end of something. We walked and walked the streets of Paris. We talked. When we got back to the hotel, we talked some more. At some point, I thought, we're going to have to get sex out of the way, and then what? It was a Rubicon to cross, possibly a Waterloo.

"I haven't worn a condom in years," he said, faking jollity and humor to cover his panic when the matter of sex arose. "I've been living with someone forever." And indeed, the whole duty to apply the obligatory condom caused instant detumescence.

"So much for political correctness," he said. I pretended to laugh. But I was in despair and so was he. When I awoke next morning with his erection pressing against me, I promptly gave myself a full-scale guilt attack about Piero to avoid even the possibility of sex. *Poor Piero*, I thought. How could I *do* this to *him*? How could I abandon him for another man?

Poor Piero? Poor Piero must have had a succession of other women all the time I knew him, and I'd never forced *him* to wear a condom. (We have one set of rules for bad boys and another set of rules for good.)

What did I want? Did I want to go back to the gigolo gig? After all, it was heresy in my generation for first sex to be anything *but* magic, zipless, a marvel of chemistry. We had stopped believing in God and in her place we had substituted great instantaneous sex. When that proved problematic, we declared God dead. The Land of Fuck was our sacred country, and when it proved difficult of access, we declared ourselves marooned.

In the morning, thank heavens, Ken had a meeting. And I stayed home to write. I brooded a while, then called Picro in Venice. He seemed remarkably nonchalant that I hadn't come, and he muttered of projects he had to work on with his lady and how pressed he was for time. (He expected to see me that summer when I was due to rent my usual ramshackle palazzo.)

When Ken came back, I was delighted to see him. He had this sunny smile that made you glad to be alive. He handed me a smallish packet. I opened it. It was a first edition of *La Fin de Chéri* by Colette.

"I wanted you to have something to remember this weekend by," he said, "in case it's our last."

"How did you know that's one of my favorite books!" I exclaimed.

"I don't know. It just seemed to be calling to me from the shelf."

How could he know that I measured all the stages of my life against Colette's progress? I had had my Willy, my Chéri—was he to be that impossible man who also becomes a *friend*? Colette saw that as the ultimate stage of a woman's life. He had bought this book, thinking of it as a parting keepsake. He knew it was salvage time.

But what salvage! Somehow he had picked the only book that would have opened my heart.

Even now it amazes me that we persevered.

Because the truth is that what I found with Ken was the one thing I did not catalogue in my sex chapter: empathy. I thought I knew everything, but I did not know this. Men are as oppressed by macho mythology as women are. They are *terrified* of having to be studs. In the name of liberation we have reduced them to studs or nothing. We have insisted on gigolos and then cried that gigolos were all we got. "Chemistry" has become the new tyranny for our supposedly sexually liberated generation. But chemistry can be blocked by closeness.

What I learned with Ken is that some of us fear love even more than we desire it and we have learned to use sex as a way to banish love.

An odd alignment of the stars led Joan Collins to be in Paris at the same time we were. She invited us to come and see her filming an interview for French TV. Afterward we were all to go to Brasserie Lipp for dinner.

The show Joan was doing required her to be interviewed wearing a fabulous pink Chanel suit, in a setting of Didier Aaron antiques. For some reason, she was speaking of antiques and how much fun it would be to buy them. I sat and watched her consummate professionalism. Here was a woman who had beaten the system, survived all her husbands, rescued her children, thumbed her nose at a world that laughed at older women (and treated actresses as disposable commodities). She had wound up with the best revenge: living well. In a sane world, she'd be a role model, not a target for other women to attack. But feminists were as hard on her as male chauvinists. Why? Because she wore makeup? Because she dared to play a sexy older woman? Because, like the actress she was, she knew how to make an entrance?

After the taping, Joan, her friend Robin, Ken, and I were walking toward the Hotel Bristol for tea. An American couple spotted us— Joan and I walking ahead of the men. The woman stopped and exclaimed, "There's Joan Collins!"

"Which one?" the husband asked.

Such is fame.

That night at Lipp, we made a merry entourage. After her ordeal by press, Joan did not want to be photographed with her boyfriend, Robin Hurlstone, so she asked Ken to be her beard. She talked to him and I talked to Robin and the paparazzi were suitably confused as we entered. Now they were massing in the street outside the restaurant. (No wonder the paparazzi hate the celebrities on whom they feed. They are always outside waiting in the cold while the prey is warm inside, eating.)

Being around celebrities of Joan's wattage always makes me grateful to be merely a writer. I may be recognized for brief periods when I am promoting a book, but the rest of the time I am invisible, making notes.

Somewhere in the middle of that very merry (though rather too public) dinner, Joan, her secretary, and I all went downstairs to the tiny bathroom.

"He's *rather* dishy," said Joan of Ken. "And he does seem clever enough for you." She rolled her enormous eyes.

Since I was trying to do *anything* in my power to get away from Ken at that point, it gave me pause that Joan found him "dishy." I kept thinking of leaving Paris and flying to Venice, but then I'd remember I had nothing to fly there for.

It is hard to open yourself to someone who might really love you. I kept trying to drive Ken away and he kept passing the test by staying.

He was forever trying to *do* things for me—from running my bath to feeding me snacks. I remember the two of us bouncing around that tiny suite like boxers in a ring.

"Don't you believe that anyone will ever love you unless you *do* and *do* and *do* for them!" I screamed at him in exasperation.

That stopped him.

"No," he said.

"Well—you *are* lovable," I shouted. "The trouble is—*you* don't believe it."

He started to cry. He lay back on the bed with tears streaming down his face. I threw my arms around him.

"You *are* lovable, you *are*," I said. And, both of us weeping, we made love that night for the first time.

That was how our relationship began. If I were a bookie, I wouldn't have bet on it.

A few weeks later, back in the States, he took me to his house in Vermont for a weekend. It was too stormy to fly, so we drove up Route 91 to Brattleboro and then made our way into the Green Mountains. In Putney, we stopped for dinner. The conversation between us flowed as always and I grew terrified of how close we were getting.

"I've been waiting for you all my life," he said.

"I'm terrified," I said, finally knowing it.

"Of what?"

"If I love you, I'll try to please you all the time and then I won't be able to write," I said. "I have to be free to be honest in my writing, and that has to come before everything. I can't be protecting a man."

"Write whatever you need to write about me, about everything," he said. "I'll never fault you for that. That's why I love you."

"You say that *now*—but it will change. It always changes. Men say one thing when they pursue you and another thing when they trap you. You probably believe what you're saying now, but it will change, I promise you."

"No, it won't," he said. "Besides, I'm not *men*." He grabbed a napkin. "*I release you—from everything*," he wrote on it. And then: "*Write whatever you like, always.*" And he added his signature and the date.

I still have this document in a safe.

But the truth was that I was more afraid of myself than I was of him. If I loved him, would I censor my writing to please him? If I married him, would I force my writing to be married as well?

This was my dilemma at first—for we did get married, three months later, in Vermont. I had to fight my own tendency to try to please by censoring the truth.

"If you censor anything," he said, "you'll eventually get mad and leave me. And I'd rather have you tell the truth and *stay*."

It was my particular craziness to think I always had to choose between my writing and life. Perhaps it is every writer's craziness. I was still fighting my mother's and grandmother's war.

Before we got married, our parents made a little dinner at a country inn. Ken then drove his parents back to the Sugarbush Inn and I drove Molly. Somewhere I took a wrong turn and started over the mountains toward New York. The rain was sheeting down. I drove and drove.

Molly was razzing me as usual about my rotten sense of direction.

"You know, Mom," she said, "you don't *have* to get married unless you *want* to."

At that moment, Ken and his father drove up behind us.

It was only after we got married that we discovered all the reasons our marriage was inevitable. His natural Prozac offsets my habitual gloom. He has my father's mad tenacity. He never gives up a fight. He is possessed by the Mad Joke Demon. He wakes up laughing in the middle of the night. He needs to love me more than he needs to push me away. I need to love him more than I need to feel abandoned and deprived.

Why did we get married instead of just living together? Because we needed to know that when the tough stuff came we would stay and work it out. And there have been all kinds of tough stuff. Sexual problems, money problems, the unique difficulties of stepfamilies. Sometimes we fight like hellcats and make love like lovers. Sometimes we turn our backs on each other. Even when we are screaming and throwing things, we are friends. Who is the man and who is the woman? Sometimes neither of us knows. The marriage is androgynous—like the closest friendships. It will keep.

We both accept the fact that, in trying to have a marriage of equals, we are making history (like the rest of our pioneer generation). We both accept the fact that we do not own each other. We are both able to say anything to each other—and we have had fights so black that it seemed the sun would never rise again.

But at the bottom of all the gloom, there is a sense that we are responsible for each other—if not for each other's happiness. There is empathy, admiration, respect for the other's intelligence, and honesty. I cannot imagine writing a book as naked as this if not for this marriage.

Seeing me stuck, Ken will say, "So what if they attack you or make fun of you—you've lived through *that* before. It doesn't erase your words."

And I realize that I've lived through everything and have come out the other end, laughing and reading aloud to my best friend in bed.

15

MEN ARE NOT THE PROBLEM

Women are the cowards they are because they have been semi-slaves for so long. The number of women prepared to stand up for what they really think, feel, experience with a man they are in love with is still small. Most women will still run like little dogs with stones thrown at them when a man says: You are unfeminine, aggressive, you are un-manning me.

> —Doris Lessing, Introduction to *The Golden Notebook*

Men and women are two locked caskets, of which each contains the key to the other.

> —Isak Dinesen, *Seven Gothic Tales*

Raised as the meat in the sandwich between two sisters, I have always been aware of the ruthlessness of women, the fierce competitiveness possible between sisters. As a little girl, I wanted to join the Brownies or Girl Scouts and didn't dare to because my older sister considered Girl Scouts goody-goody and pathetically square. At Barnard, anointed with an appointment to the Honor Board (something that gave you the dubious privilege of wearing a black gown and monitoring final exams), I hid this from my older sister, also a Barnard alumna, knowing she would mock me. She was the rebel and I was the goody-two-shoes, while my younger sister, Claudia, was, I thought, my charge, my responsibility, my cross to bear. I used to lie in bed wondering whether the nail scissors in my mother's bathroom would mysteriously fly out of the nail kit and stab my baby sister in the heart. Then I would think up elaborate schemes for preventing them from doing so—undoing my own wish.

So I know how mean women can be to other women. I know it from my own repressed wishes. Men in my life have usually been kinder and less critical. Even my literary career has been encouraged by kind men—from James Clifford to Louis Untermeyer, from John Updike to Henry Miller to Anthony Burgess. Sometimes these very men, famed as sexists, would exhibit more good-natured approbation of the female imagination than many women. Many women, in fact, seemed to demand that literature *not* be playful, that heroines adhere to some party line or other. Writing fiction and poetry, I often felt I could do no right because versimilitude was not the goal but a political correctness so Byzantine that it seemed as if no one could measure up—not even the lawgivers. If I wrote about a woman in thrall to a man, I was considered wrong to do so—as if my fiction might *create* fact, as if the mirror held up to nature were a sword instead. If I wrote about loving to nurse a baby, I was considered counterrevolutionary, a bad sister—as if the breast were not our symbol. If I wrote that women could be unkind, I was considered a traitor—as if it were not *worse* treachery to pretend that all women were always kind. I was not *allowed* to play on the page. Everything was seen as a political prescription and therefore dangerous. I discovered (as many women writers have discovered) that the rules were much more stringent coming from women than from men.

I had a bitter taste of this in 1979, when, a new mother, who had just stopped nursing, I read a group of poems about pregnancy and birth at a women's poetry festival in San Francisco. I began with this one:

ON THE FIRST NIGHT

On the first night
of the full moon,
the primeval sack of ocean
broke,
& I gave birth to you
little woman,
little carrot top,
little turned-up nose,
pushing you out of myself

as my mother
pushed
me out of herself,
as her mother did,
& her mother's mother before her,
all of us born
of woman.

I am the second daughter
of a second daughter,
but you shall be the first.
You shall see the phrase
"second sex"
only in puzzlement,
wondering how anyone,
except a madman,
could call you "second"
when you are so splendidly first,
conferring even on your mother
firstness, vastness, fullness
as the moon at its fullest
lights up the sky.

Now the moon is full again
& you are four weeks old.
Little lion, lioness,
yowling for my breasts,
growling at the moon,
how I love your lustiness,
your red face demanding,
your hungry mouth howling,
your screams, your cries
which all spell life
in large letters
the color of blood.

You are born a woman
for the sheer glory of it,
little redhead, beautiful screamer.

You are no second sex,
but the first of the first;
& when the moon's phases
fill out the cycle
of your life,
you will crow
for the joy
of being a woman,
telling the pallid moon
to go drown herself
in the blue ocean,
& glorying, glorying, glorying
in the rosy wonder
of your sunshining wondrous
self.

When I finished, I realized many in the audience were hissing.

Having become converted to the transformative power of motherhood, I had come to understand that it was part of female heroinism:
that once becoming a mother, a woman might be radicalized in her
feminism. She had a greater stake in saving the earth from male politi-
cians. She had a greater stake in education and health, in the environment, in all social policy. She finally understood the way our society
makes children and mothers the lowest of priorities.

But the women at that festival—many of them fans of *Fear of
Flying*, *How to Save Your Own Life*, and the early poetry books—
seemed to feel *betrayed* by this and other poems about motherhood.
They hooted and booed the *Ordinary Miracles* sequence, though
many of them had children in their arms. At the time, I was devas-
tated. Hadn't I sought to be a writer and a mother? Hadn't I tried to
support other women creators? Wasn't I trying to show that mothers
could also be passionate creators? The criticism by women hurt far
more than any criticism by men. It seemed written on my skin by my
mother and sisters, who had long resented me for my success.

But my whiplash generation had grown up with notions of compulsory motherhood. We were called names like *elderly prima gravida*
and worse. Liberation meant no more compulsion. Maybe the booing
women in that audience were feeling that I was adding my weight to
compulsory maternity—though of course I was not. A late, reluctant

mother, an elderly prima gravida, it had taken all my strength and courage to decide to have a baby. And then it surprised me that I was transformed by pregnancy and that I fell in love with the baby. I was hardly mellowed by the maternal transformation. If anything, my feminism grew more fierce.

But I could not verbalize all this that day in San Francisco. I didn't yet understand it myself.

This experience, and others like it, taught me that it is crucial for women to learn to be allies. We are deliberately trained not to be good at forging alliances. Even with all the team sports now available to teenage girls, they plot against each other as girls of my generation did. They compete about clothes, guys, status, money, and they still call each other names.

Once I walked into my daughter's room, to overhear her and two girlfriends calling another girl a "slut."

"Don't ever call a girl a slut," I said. "It's a sexist term."

Molly: "But she *is* a slut, Mommy."

Mommy: "It's a way of putting down women for being sexual."

Molly (to friends): "This is because my mom is the sex-writer of the Western world. She's been married *a lot.*"

"Four husbands is not a lot, considering how old I am," I say, quoting Barbara Follett, who has also been married four times.

Molly's friends titter.

I close the door.

Separatism between the sexes does not automatically mean feminism and feminism does not automatically mean man-hating. Plenty of mothers and wives who wanted to be involved with organized feminism in the seventies reported the kind of painful rejection I had experienced. Feminist ideas were never more powerful to my generation than they were then. But a chronic shortsightedness made it hard for some feminist organizations to strike while the iron was hot. If you practiced a "bourgeois lifestyle," you were treated as an outcast. You got the feeling that unless you had the trappings of radical lesbianism about you, you would be shunned. And trappings they were. There was a style prevalent then to which you were expected to conform: overalls, workboots, no makeup. It was important to *look* like you'd stepped right off the commune. Lipstick and eyeshadow were not only counterrevolutionary, they would be mentioned in reviews of your books. Nobody was more sexist than these feminists.

How could our generation suddenly forswear the values with which it had been raised? It couldn't. So some of us became extremists, as all frightened people do. As usual in revolutions, the zealots drove out the moderates. And the haters of feminism exploited the split for their own ends. Thus, a whole generation of daughters grew up turned off by the term "feminist."

The truth was, we were all discriminated against simply for being female—why did we fail to see this? Women rejecting each other for their political impurity would never solidify and expand feminism. We needed all *kinds* of feminists. We still do.

Who is in more trouble during a holocaust—the few who join the resistance and devote their lives to the struggle or the many who think it will blow over and life will be normal again?

Married women with children must be recruited, because they are in danger of deceiving themselves about the "protection" they receive from men. It may take unfair divorces, the molestation or kidnapping of their children, or brutal abuse to wake them up. The daily, ordinary domestic atrocities that occur in male-female marriage may create rage, but they cannot build a movement. That is the role of feminism.

All women have common cause. Separatism is bad for our movement. Separatist tendencies of the seventies set our progress back and helped open the door to backlash.

No wonder the word "feminism" was feared. It had been much too narrowly defined. I define a feminist as a *self-empowering woman* who wishes the same for her sisters. I do not think the term implies a certain sexual orientation, a certain style of dress, or membership in a certain political party. A feminist is merely a woman who refuses to accept the notion that women's power must come through men.

The resurgence of woman-hating in the eighties was partly a product of right-wing political power. But it was also at least partly a reaction to women-against-women politics. Imagine what we could have done to counter the backlash had we been *united* rather than *divided*? We only woke up and began the process of building solidarity when the reaction against feminism had been entrenched for over a decade.

Why are women so ungenerous to other women? Is it because we have been tokens for so long? Or is there a deeper animosity we owe it to ourselves to explore?

A publisher who specializes in excellent volumes of poetry recently wrote to me in despair that every major woman poet he had contacted had refused to "blurb" a book by a gifted new young woman poet he was publishing. He couldn't understand why women were so loath to help each other—even in the supposed "Year of the Woman"—and he begged me to read the book. I read it, was moved by it, and "blurbed" it. But the notion flitted through my mind that somehow, by helping this poet, I might be hurting my own chances for something or other—*what* I did not know. If there was room for only one woman poet, another space would be filled.

"Fuck it," I said to myself. And I mailed off the blurb. But my reaction is telling. If I still feel I am in competition with other women, how do less well known women feel? *Terrible,* I have to assume.

I have had to train myself to pay as much attention to women at parties as to men. I have had to nurture my relationships with my sisters and try to root out the hostility and envy. Gradually my younger sister and I are building a new, adult relationship. I long to do that with my older sister as well. I have had to labor on my friendship with my best friend and make it work against all odds. I have had to force myself not to be dismissive of other women's creativity. We have been semislaves for so long (as Doris Lessing says) that we must *cultivate* freedom within ourselves. It doesn't come naturally. Not yet.

In writing about the drama of childhood development, Alice Miller has created, among other things, a theory of freedom. In order to embrace freedom, a child must be sufficiently nurtured, sufficiently loved. Security and abundance are the grounds for freedom. She shows how abusive child rearing is communicated from one generation to the next and how fascism profits from generations of abused children. Women have been abused for centuries, so it should surprise no one that we are so good at abusing each other. Until we learn how to stop doing that, we cannot make our revolution stick.

Many women are damaged in childhood, unprotected, unrespected, and treated with dishonesty. Is it any wonder that we build up vast defenses against other women, since the perpetrators of childhood abuse have so often been women? Is it any wonder that we return intimidation with intimidation, or that we reserve our greatest fury for others who remind us of our own weaknesses—namely other women?

Men, on the other hand, however intellectually condescending, clubbish, loutishly lewd, are rarely as calculatingly cruel as women. They tend, rather, to advance us when we are young and cute (and look like darling daughters) and ignore us when we are older and more sure of our opinions (and look like scary mothers), but they don't really *know* what they're doing. They are too busy bonding with other men and creating male pecking orders* to pay attention to us. If we were skilled at compromise and alliance-building, we could transform society. The trouble is: We are not yet good at this. We are still quarreling among ourselves. This is the crisis feminism faces today.

Reading younger feminists like Naomi Wolf and Katie Roiphe has been instructive. Here are two women raised by brilliant and accomplished feminist mothers in a time when women could go to Princeton and Yale and become Rhodes scholars, and both have found themselves uncomfortable, in different ways, with programmatic contemporary feminism. What have they been uncomfortable with? Put simply: with feminism's failure to take into account female sexual desire and female ambivalence about power. Katie Roiphe reacts to the Take Back the Night Marches on her Princeton campus with a plea for seeing sexuality as a human trait rather than something imposed on women by raving rapists. Naomi Wolf dares to explode the myth of "victim feminism" and pleads for allowing women to be as full of good and bad desires as men, as avid for sexual fulfillment and power as men, but held back by the twin myths of good-girlism and sentimental sisterhood. Though she is perhaps too sanguine about women quickly overcoming their fear of power, Wolf fills me with hope because I see her analysis as having shattered the false categories that imprisoned my generation. Women do not have to agree about *everything* to join in alliance with each other to promote female power. Women do not have to cast out their inner bad girl to assert their right to power. Women do not have to cast out their sexuality to be "good sisters."

The fact that younger feminists are coming along to enliven the women's movement with this debate is thrilling. (Susie Bright is another young voice of fierce feminism and lusty political incorrectness.) These feminists and their many contemporaries give me hope

---

* One wit calls them scrotum poles.

for a new movement that can truly become a mass movement. I know the obstacles Roiphe, Wolf, and Bright will have to face in maturing as writers. Most of the obstacles will come from other women, who—having starved themselves of self-expression for years—may react with rage that attractive, privileged young women dare to take on the world of intellectual discourse in such a free and contentious fashion. Already these young writers have been strongly denounced for their sexual openness.

Which brings me to the question of older women and younger women and the rivalry between us. When I was young and the flavor of the month—as Wolf, Roiphe, and Bright are today—I was appalled by the jealous hatred and hostility I faced from older women. This was not something I expected. And it hurt more than the criticism I received from men, which I more or less expected. It is hard even now to remember the hatred that came on the heels of *Fear of Flying*. Women journalists who confessed deep identification in private would attack in public, often using the very confidences they had extracted from me, citing their feminine identification. The sense of betrayal was extreme. I felt more silenced by these bitter personal attacks than I ever did by male critics.

I came gradually to understand that this tendency to draw blood was not in itself a female characteristic but the characteristic of a female who had been deprived of important body and personality parts. Her feet had been bound, her clitoris excised, and what she was left with were nails and teeth. These were not natural women, they were women with parts missing. *Female eunuch* was the phrase Germaine Greer coined for such creatures, intuitively understanding that full female sexuality implied full female revolution. But women trained in puritanism and second-classness were hardly ready for full female revolution. Pitted against each other in rivalry, they could not even *imagine* a society in which older women emotionally supported younger women, in which women's sexuality was prized, in which women's excellence was celebrated. The capo system had for centuries split women off from each other and made them enemies of each other and of female progress.

I have often had the experience of welcoming a young woman journalist who has been inspired or moved by my books and who later sends me a tearsheet from her paper with a sad apology about how she was forced to censor her own feelings, turn her agreement to disagreement, provide more "edge" (i.e., nasty swipes and character assassinations—whether true or not). Often the commissioning editor demanding this clitoridectomy is a woman—a woman well-pummeled by the system—a woman who has kept her job by seeming to have the opinions of her male bosses and who therefore enforces these opinions more stringently than they might themselves.

We must learn to be whole creatures in order to make women's freedom a natural part of our society. It is up to us to claim that territory. Men *cannot* do it for us. It is not their mountain to climb. We must learn to love and support each other *without demanding ideological conformity*. We must learn to agree to disagree, to struggle like grown-ups and fight fair, to allow many kinds of feminism into the big tent, not to let ourselves be splintered into smaller and smaller and less and less powerful groups. That way lies the triumph of sexism—with our own complicity. Feminism cannot afford a "Big Lie," and it has had one for the last couple of decades—which is partly why the word has become discredited. Women are *not* merely kind and sweet, victims of a sexual rapaciousness we want no part of, nor are we defanged, declawed, neutered creatures. In the name of a false feminism, we have been asked to *pretend* to be. And those of us who wrote about women in a different way were declared "bad sisters" and excluded from the circus tent.

Since this has been my fate as a writer in my own country (though much less so abroad), I feel I have the right to talk about it. It has resulted for me in periods of excruciating blockage in which I tried to write and couldn't because I knew that *anything* I said would be wrong. I realized gradually that women had managed to do to me what men no longer had the power to do: make me feel utterly and absolutely in the wrong, make me hate my own creativity, distrust my own impressions, second-guess myself until nothing I said could be clear enough to understand. I would sit down to write and be so seized with self-hatred that I could not function. Every time I put pen to paper I would see a chorus of jeering women telling me that everything I said was not worth saying.

When women have so absorbed the disease of sexism that they themselves can inflict it on each other, we clearly have a perfect, self-replenishing machine for the continuation of sexism. Unable to turn our assertiveness against men, we turn it against each other. Thus we remain stuck in the troubles we have always had. It is imperative we renovate the machine—no, not renovate it, but smash it entirely, so that we allow women to be all they need to be.

The Jungian analyst Clarissa Pinkola Estés has reached a wide audience in part because of her insight into women's wildness:

> A good deal of women's literature on the subject of women's power states that men are afraid of women's power. I always want to exclaim, "Mother of God! So many women themselves are afraid of women's power." For the old feminine attributes and forces are vast, and they *are* formidable. . . . If men are going to ever learn to stand it, then without a doubt women have to learn to stand it.

But we are only at the beginning. And our strictures on each other prove this. Our enforcement of thinness, of nonsexuality, of "good" feminism versus "bad" feminism, are proofs of our being at the beginning, not the end, of a process. That younger feminists are embracing their sexuality is a sign of hope—a sign that women's lives will someday be less constricted, less fearful of the dark side of creativity (to which Eros provides the key). If that happens, we will at last have the full gamut of inspiration so long denied to us. We will have access to *all* parts of ourselves—all the animals within us, from wolf to lamb. When we learn to love all the animals within us, we will know how to make men love them too.

And what about aging? Do men force the fear of aging upon us or are we ourselves terrified because we only know one kind of power—the power of youthful beauty?

Isn't it possible that if we became comfortable with other forms of female power, men might too? In her futurist novel, *He, She and It*, Marge Piercy imagines a cyborg who is taught to love the bodies of older women. A delicious proposal, because it tells us that whatever we may imagine can come true. Women often hate their own bodies. Sometimes I think that the most important thing about having at least one relationship with someone of your own gender—especially if you are a woman—is to confront the female self-hatred and turn it into self-love.

In my forties, I fell in love with a blonde artist who looked like my twin. Ours was a close friendship that sometimes included lovemaking and sometimes did not. But when we turned to each other in desire, it was the lust of doubles seeking to accept their mirror images. It was an affirmation, not only of friendship but of self. In a sane world, love and sex would not divide by gender. We could love like and unlike beings, love them for a variety of reasons. The battered adjectives for homosexuality—queer, lesbian, gay—would disappear and we would only have people making love in different ways, with different body parts. We are too far gone with overpopulation to insist that procreation be an immutable part of desire. Desire needs only itself, not the proof of a baby. We would do well to baby each other instead of making all these unwanted babies that no one has time to nurture or to love.

At this point in my life, I am blessed by my friendships with women. I make no distinction between my gay and straight women friends. I hate the very terms, feeling that any of us could be *anything*—if we were to unlock the full range of possibilities within.

It is not just women who are going through a transformation of roles. Men have been asked to change everything about their lives too. They do increasingly sedentary work, which is difficult for restless creatures, filled with testosterone. They are asked to take care of babies and share responsibilities their mothers never prepared them for. If we are going to ask men to change their usual ways of responding and relating, we should be prepared to do the same. We should remember that loving responses to other women may not come easily at first because of our own ingrained self-hatred. But little by little, we will learn to nurture, not attack, other women. We will not let men separate us from each other or use us as tokens. With practice, this will get easier. When we feel the impulse *not* to share power, not to collaborate, we will remind ourselves that women's power depends, not only on men changing, but on our own inner changes. We will exchange the harem model so long established in our psyches and replace it with a model of mutual nurturing, mutual support. When men begin to see that we cannot be separated, our statistical force in the population will have the power it should have had many decades ago. When we stop beating ourselves and each other, we will be able to join hands to conquer the abusers of women and children.

ALCESTIS ON THE POETRY CIRCUIT

(In memoriam Marina Tsvetayevna, Anna
Wickham, Sylvia Plath, Shakespeare's
sister, etc., etc.)

The best slave
does not need to be beaten.
She beats herself.

Not with a leather whip,
or with stick or twigs,
not with a blackjack
or a billyclub,
but with the fine whip
of her own tongue
& the subtle beating
against her mind of her mind.

For who can hate her half so well
as she hates herself?
& who can match the finesse
of her self-abuse?

Years of training
are required for this.
Twenty years
of subtle self-indulgence,
self-denial;
until the subject
thinks herself a queen
& yet a beggar—
both at the same time.
She must doubt herself
in everything but love.

She must choose passionately
& badly.
She must feel as a lost dog
without her master.

She must refer all moral questions
to her mirror.
She must fall in love with a cossack
or a poet.

She must never go out of the house
unless veiled in paint.
She must wear tight shoes
so she always remembers her bondage.
She must never forget
she is rooted to the ground.

Though she is quick to learn
& admittedly clever,
her natural doubt of herself
should make her so weak
that she dabbles brilliantly
in half a dozen talents
& thus embellishes
but does not change
our life.

If she's an artist
& comes close to genius,
the very fact of her gift
should cause her such pain
that she will take her own life
rather than best us.
& after she dies, we will cry
& make her a saint.

That is the *old* model of women's self-hatred—the one we must
smash. Change does not come through denial but through acceptance.
Those feminists who have complained that we must not write about
women's self-torture, self-loathing, obsessional loves, are slighting a
crucial phase in female evolution. The surrender of our self-loathing,
of the slave in the self, is an essential phase we must go through—a
sort of group exorcism or mass analysis. If we demand that women's

literature be prescriptive rather than descriptive, we will never exorcise the slave. A future of socialist-realist art—happy feminists in blue
overalls waving from shiny tractors, or the contemporary equivalent—
will not take us where we need to go. We need to unlock the staggering power of Eros in the female psyche. We have let Eros mean slavery, but Eros also has the power to set us free. We must demand the
right to depict women's lives as we *know* them, not as we might like
them to be. We must stop applying political prescriptions to creativity.

We have been much freer to grant women of color the right to
depict their lives without political prescription, and their writing
shows a freedom white women's writing often lacks. The lushness,
openness, and moral weight we find in such writers as Zora Neale
Hurston, Gwendolyn Brooks, Toni Morrison, Maya Angelou, Alice
Walker, Terry McMillan, Lucille Clifton, Rita Dove, and so many others have a common source. Black women were at least a century
ahead of white women in banishing the slave in the self. It was a matter of necessity: If both the white world and black men disempower
you, you had better not disempower yourself. "Wild women don't
have the blues," wrote the African-American poet (disguised as blues
woman) Ida Cox. The energy we so admire in African-American
women's writing is the energy that comes when we stop denying reality. There is no shame in this writing, no rearranging of reality to suit
political ends. The chronic racism of our culture selectively permits the
black woman to be in touch with the chthonic impulses beneath the
veneer of civilization. The black woman is *allowed* to be our seer, our
poet laureate, our oracle. I would like to see all women writers—
whatever their ethnicity—claim this power, so that eventually both
color and gender can become insignificant.

I look at my own ethnicity—Jewish—and I see an ambivalent
identification among my colleagues. We seem to have turned our
backs on our great poets like Muriel Rukeyser, mirroring the contempt
intellectual Jewish men have had for their sisters. This is an ambivalence we will have to understand and triumph over if we are going to
claim our right to sing unambivalent songs. We Jewish women writers
have mostly hidden our ethnicity as if it were unimportant. From
Emma Lazarus identifying with the "huddled masses" to Gloria
Steinem reading Alice Walker's poems aloud to express her own sometimes stifled self-expression, we have taken on the role of social workers and freedom fighters, but we have not dared the *first* act of free-

dom—to free ourselves. In her book *What Is Found There: Notebooks on Poetry and Politics,* Adrienne Rich traces her own self-acceptance as poet, as lesbian, as Jew. Jew comes last, an identity we have been taught not to bother with. But perhaps that is why it should come first.

What does it mean to be a woman in a tradition that teaches its men to rejoice in *not* being a woman? What does it mean to have self-abnegation built into the very principles of your religion? Unless we address these questions and stop hiding behind the "huddled masses," we cannot claim our birthright: free expression. What might Jewish-American women's writing be like if it stopped crouching behind social meliorism and dared to wholly express what is in our own hearts?

How ironic that we have celebrated such freedom in African-American women writers while denying it to ourselves! Why are we still pretending assimilation into a white male society that wants us only as cultural caretakers, not as artists? I foresee a flowering of expression by Jewish women writers if we dare to answer that question.

It is odd that so few of our writers have dared to claim their particular female Jewishness. And the ones who *have* begun to explore it—Letty Cottin Pogrebin, Phyllis Chesler, Anne Roiphe, Marge Piercy—have sometimes been denigrated by the same critics who applaud ethnicity in African-American or Asian-American women writers. This difficulty of claiming double identity of woman and Jew troubles me because I see the poets who should have followed in the footsteps of Nelly Sachs and Muriel Rukeyser turning instead to a false solidarity with Jewish men who would never accept their prayerful presence at the Wailing Wall of literature!

Cynthia Ozick and Grace Paley are among the few Jewish women writers who have been permitted to display both feminism and Jewishness and have not been stoned for it. But their feminism is mostly ignored as one of the wellsprings of their talent.

Much remains to be done. We must confess our double self-hatred to ourselves first of all and then to our writing. We must stop wearing leather leggings and chesterfield coats. We must put our immigrant class snobbery behind us and stop pretending we can pass as Jane Austen. We must reclaim Emma Goldman and Muriel Rukeyser and the strength their voices represent.

We ourselves have absorbed not only the misogyny of our culture but also the anti-Semitism. We ourselves equate Jewishness with vulgarity and loudness, and thus we are tempted to soft-pedal it. We leave our Jewishness to be expressed by our musical comedy stars and comediennes. Perhaps the Jewish woman terrifies because she represents strength, sexuality, a loud voice. In fact, we have never needed her courage more. I do not mean that we should balkanize feminists into Jewish-American, African-American, Asian-American, Native-American. In truth, the universality of our experience is far more important than the specifics of our differences. I am only pointing out the oddity of our suppressing our ethnicity while celebrating the ethnicity of other groups. If we really believe that self-knowledge leads to freedom, we should allow ourselves the same exploration of ethnicity.

After fifty, I begin to question my ambivalent relationship to my Jewish identity and the unexamined assimilationism I have written about earlier. It seems astonishing to me that a woman born at the height of the Holocaust should not have been trained to a stronger sense of Judaism. And I also begin to regret not having raised Molly more Jewishly, and not having had more Jewish children to replace those lost among the six million. Lately I have begun to yearn for solidarity with other Jewish feminists, to join the search for nonsexist Jewish rituals, to celebrate my Jewishness without shame, without internalized anti-Semitism, and to embrace my Jewishness as part of my search for truth in my writing. In this, I have been inspired by African-American, Asian-American, and Native American writers who have already overcome the false assimilationist stance. As a secular Jew, I will have to *invent* a heritage as much as rediscover it. For the first time, I am willing. My heart is open.

16

WOMAN ENOUGH: INTERVIEW WITH MY MOTHER

Believe me, the world won't give you any gifts. If you want to
have a life, steal it.

—Lou Andreas-Salome

A prison gets
to be a friend . . .

—Emily Dickinson

Much that you need has been lost. The poems that we know are
merely fragments. . . . We must use what we have to invent what
we desire.

—Adrienne Rich, *What Is Found There*

*The first thing I remember about coming to America was my father
meeting me at the dock. "He's not my father!" I spat out. I hadn't
seen my father since he left for New York when I was two, and I must
have thought he would look like my Uncle Boris—whom I adored.*

*We lived in Bristol with my Auntie Sarah, my mother's sister, and
our two cousins Minnie and Lennie. From time to time, my mother
and aunt would fight bitterly and we would move out to a rooming
house—though less and less after my mother became tubercular and
grew skeletally thin.*

We came to America on a boat swarming with soldiers returning home after the Great War. Even skinny and ravaged, my mother was always a beautiful woman who was noticed and admired by men. She did not notice being noticed.

Crossing to America, I was playing behind the lifeboats (where there was no railing) and I nearly fell into the sea. A soldier scooped me up and saved me. We became the talk of the crossing. I was the little girl who was saved!

The first place we lived was somewhere way up in the East Bronx. We were dressed like nice little English girls with hair bows and we knew how to curtsy and say "Please, Miss So-and-so" or "Thank you, Miss So-and-so." Compared to the kids in the Bronx, we were royalty. So, of course, the teachers, who were creaky old Irish-American women, thought we were just wonderful. They took us around the school as examples of how you should look and dress and act. That did it. The kids waited for us after school and beat us up. We became American fast. No more good little English girls after that. We wore woolen stockings and something called "round combs" just like the tough kids in the Bronx.

Mama missed her garden in Bristol, so Papa moved us out to this deserted suburb, Edgemere, Long Island—a formerly fashionable resort, now down on its luck. The sea was gray and cold. I had a girlfriend there whose father was a musician at the Capitol Theatre and I remember thinking that we were both children of artists who didn't want us. At that time, Papa had a studio on Fourteenth Street at Union Square and he rarely came home. When he did, he and Mama would have hideous fights. There'd be screaming in Russian, and Kitty and I would hide under the kitchen table. Once I remember Papa breaking the glass door with his hands and marching into the sea. He came home with his trousers soaked and his hand still bleeding. Mama was sobbing into the kitchen table.

Later, I remember her having an abortion on that kitchen table—something secret and horrible and also whispered about in Russian. She was rushed to the hospital after that—butchered and bleeding. Kitty and I knew that something awful was happening but we weren't sure what. Only later did we understand. Papa didn't want another child and that was that. He made all the decisions. Mama wasn't merely unhappy, she was absolutely miserable. It never occurred to her she could leave.

But every summer, as long as my grandparents were alive, we went to England. That was the great escape! Papa was making enough money to send us. We'd go to visit my grandparents when they still kept a grocery store in the East End of London. My grandmother had bright blue eyes and my grandfather had a goatee and rode horses. He never bothered to speak to girl-children, thought they weren't worth the trouble. But my grandmother adored us. My grandfather had been a forester in Russia, a timber merchant who bought up stands of trees—though of course Jews weren't allowed to own land. He rode beautifully and when his only son, Jacob, made a fortune—first as a furrier, then as a motion picture exhibitor—he and my grandmother retired to Jacob's horse farm in Surrey, thatched cottages, paddocks, and all. Of course Uncle Jacob dumped his Jewish wife and married a shiksa. Horses and shiksas—proofs of grace for Jewish boychiks. He brought my grandparents to his farm and rescued them from the grocery store. In his old age my grandfather studied to be a rabbi. Naturally, he still didn't talk to girls.

My father must have made a small fortune in the twenties—first ghost-painting for those agents he called "picture-fakers," then painting the heads of the movie stars on posters for Metro-Goldwyn-Mayer. They did piecework then—like the catalogue artists. Some people specialized in heads, some in bodies. He did heads.

The "picture-fakers" were guys who'd set themselves up as artists in resort towns like Palm Beach. They'd have a grand studio, wear a beret, a flowing smock, and chat up the society ladies. They'd pose as the artist, keeping the canvas carefully draped from view. Then Papa would sneak in at night and do the portrait from a photograph, a hank of hair, a swatch of fabric. He did hundreds of those portraits. He once told me he had lost more than $100,000 in the Crash of '29—so he must have been the equivalent of a millionaire then—and all from painting. He had to build his fortune all over again after the Crash.

I could have gone to college anywhere I chose—but since Kitty quit school and went to the National Academy of Design, and since she was always coming home with stories of how splendid it was, how many handsome boys there were, how much fun it was, I decided I wanted to leave school too. Papa let me. He had nothing but contempt for formal education. He was an autodidact himself. At the National Academy of Design, the teachers always twitted the boys:

"*Better watch out for that Mirsky girl—she'll win the Prix de Rome,*" which was the big traveling scholarship. But they never gave it to girls and I knew that. In fact, when I won two bronze medals, I was furious because I knew they were just tokens—not real money prizes. And that was because I was a girl. Why did they say "*Better watch out for that Mirsky girl!*" if not to torment me?

I would never have met your father if not for a friend of Papa's named Rebas, who was a white Russian. He was one of those catalogue artists who specialized in heads, and he and his friend, a certain Mr. Hittleman who played the fiddle, bought a resort in the Catskills and called it Utopia. I was supposed to be there as a sort of children's counselor. I was seventeen. But Mr. Rebas—for some reason—insisted on sleeping in my room. He said it was to protect me. He never laid a hand on me. I think he was gay and I was the beard. Anyway, when your father arrived with his band, it must have seemed as if I was sleeping with the owner of the place. And I wore wonderful clothes— a black velvet cloak that I made myself—and fabulous hats. And I would float through fields of cowflop like an apparition out of Midsummer Night's Dream. So your father was determined to have me. And he was very good-looking. And very aggressive.

He had blue eyes and light brown hair. He was the tummler, the director of the rec hall, the band leader, the main skit writer—he did everything. I thought it was absolutely shocking how bad the skits were—how shameless the jokes. The level of humor was abysmal. Friday nights, they'd joke about the stiff train arriving—the horny husbands from the city.

But my darling sister never saw anything that belonged to me that she didn't want. So as soon as she came up from the city, she made a play for Seymour. If she hadn't made a play for him, I might not have been so sure he was the one—but that settled it. If Kitty wanted him, then I would have him. Such was our sisterhood! I didn't see any point in getting married. I was a free spirit, an artist. Women were supposed to be free. My idol was Edna St. Vincent Millay. And even my mother, who had such a terrible marriage, was most proud of that friend of hers who was a woman dentist. She very much believed in what you would call Women's Lib. She wasn't one of these women to go out and march about it—but she believed in it. When I was having problems with your father before you were born, she said, "Leave him if you want to. I'll help you all I can." She wanted me to have a

*better life than she had had. She didn't want to see me trapped in a
bad marriage.*

*Once, on a trip to Japan with Daddy, I had a dream about my
mother that I'll never forget. Her legs were cut off and bleeding and
she was tied to a column, or the top of a church steeple, and I remember myself crawling on the ground and crying at the sight of her, but
she kept saying: "It's all right, darling, it's not so bad." That epito-
mizes our relationship.*

*My father was no kind of father when Kitty and I were little, but
when your sister Nana was born, he discovered fatherhood like it was
going out of style. He never could get along with my mother, so he
insisted on our all living together—roping us in with this big apartment and making the baby the center of everything. I was the maid,
your father was the butler, Mama was the cook. Papa was the king
and your sister the princess. So—the grandfather you loved so much
was a recent invention. He was no father at all to me. You have such
wonderful memories of him—and to me he was nothing but a bloody
tyrant. He practically cornered the market on male chauvinism! He
treated Mama like she was an idiot—tore her down constantly. I had
to be a fighter to grow up with a father like that. Then, with his
granddaughters, he became a saint! First he ruins my life, then he kid-
naps my children!*

*When you were born, during the war, you practically died. You
were the only baby who survived. I always felt I loved you most
because I had such a struggle to keep you alive.*

It is a beautiful Indian summer day in mid-September—about a
year after I have interviewed my father. We are at my house in
Connecticut. My mother has been talking into a tape recorder at my
urging. She has unwittingly spilled the beans about the feud with Kitty.

"So we all owe her a lot," I say. "Without her, we wouldn't be
here."

"I suppose so," says my mother, not meaning it.

There is another old quarrel between us: She resents my idealiza-
tion of my grandfather, feeling I got the best of him somehow and
never having resolved her bitterness toward him. She wants me to
think of him as she does.

"But he was *different* to me," I protest. "Can't I have my own
view of him?"

Apparently not. Even when I'm fifty, interviewing my mother, hoping to get it straight for an autobiography, she is pissed off at my having my own point of view. Her viewpoint is the only right one.

"Why did you stay with them if you hated it so much?" I ask.

"It was the path of least resistance," says my mother. "Eventually, we got away. And we never let them move back in."

There is the smell of old blood in this feud, and I feel I will never get to the bottom of it. My grandparents are dead, but the feud remains alive. It has sapped all our energy for years and it remains memorialized in the names we call each other. I call my grandparents Mama and Papa—and my parents Eda and Seymour. In adulthood I have tried to call my parents Mother and Dad, but it feels like a secondary accretion—unnatural somehow. My grandparents still rule the roost—even though they are long dead.

My father has been itchy as my mother and I have sat together over the tape recorder. He has felt excluded. Now he wanders in, holding a card on which he has written a longish quote. He reads it aloud to me and my mother, as if it is a poem:

I have come to be who I am,
Old, derelict, unreal to myself,
A victim of the sheer incomprehensible
Randomness of living,
And the atrocious running out of time.

Why am I, I and not another?
Young, not old or unborn—
Rather than the result
of random conjoining—
Made flesh—and deposited in a
Hard world,
To flourish, mate and presently to die.

"Do you know who that is?" he asks.

And before either of us can answer, he replies, "Gore Vidal. A great writer. From his book *1876*."

"He's also had a tough time with the critics," I say, hoping to comfort my father.

"Fuck 'em," my father bravely says. "You beat the odds once, you'll beat 'em again."

"You nearly *died*," my mother says, "being born." Then she pauses and adds gravely: "But I wouldn't let any of my children die."

It has been an extraordinarily mellow day. My mother has painted out on the deck—painted a watercolor of an overflowing barrel of nasturtiums. Ken has made everyone lunch and we have been comfortable in each other's company in a way that would have been impossible before I married him. Yet the divisions remain. I cannot truly imagine the limitations of my mother's or my grandmother's life and I cannot answer the perplexing question of why I have been so much freer than my mother and grandmother. I know there is something in the beating of daughters against maternal limitations that pushes us to find out who we are. I see my own daughter demolishing me, deconstructing me. She has to do this to get free of me. She mocks my absentmindedness, my tendency to worry, my perennial deadlines. She makes fun of my marriages, my friends, my ignoble reputation as a pornographer. She has to do these things to establish her identity in opposition to mine. This is the way she grows. I am the ground from which she pushes off. She has to tear me down to build the edifice of herself. For her, I am only a building site—which is how it should be.

Is love freedom or is it bondage?

This was the argument Ken and I had whenever we discussed getting married. And it is the essential argument, isn't it? "Love versus Freedom," I wrote somewhere in the notes for this memoir: "How to remove the *versus*."

"If we know we love each other, it will be freedom," Ken used to say. "What freedom to know who you are coming home to at night! What freedom not to have to fuss and fret about the basics of your life! What freedom to know that somebody loves you for who you are!"

At first, I fought him on this, thinking *how like a man*. Marriage, to me, had always meant bondage and submission, from which I could never wait to escape. A man might feel grounded in the same marriage a woman experienced as a trap.

But this time I swore it would be different. Our basic rules were different. I got married determined not to be that dread thing—*a wife*.

I insisted on equal partnership, knowing that otherwise it would not work at all.

Yet early on in the marriage I found myself—despite all my self-promises—drifting into the role of wife: focusing on the renovations of the apartment, doing silly little domestic things instead of writing, using the wife role as cop-out from my work, my work which had always involved me in so much controversy and which some part of me longed to retreat from. I could blame Ken for this, but it was not Ken's fault. Rather, it was the wife-tropism in me. Even when I was forty-seven, full of my own power, my own identity, something in me *wanted* to escape from the fray and dwindle into a *wife*. It seemed so comfy, so safe. I was so tired of fighting. I drifted through the days, sleeping and shopping. I did not want to carry on the war.

Many fighting women have related this passage—the desire to subside and hide, the desire to let a man lead. Until I bearded this particular dragon in her cave, how could I even pretend to speak for other women?

I have asked myself again and again how it is possible that the women's revolution has started and stopped so many times in history—beginning with the suddenness of an earthquake and often dying away just as quickly. Women spill oceans of ink, change some laws, change some expectations—and then subside and become their grandmothers again. What is this dialectic that drives them? What is this guilt that causes them to sabotage their own gains? Or maybe it is not guilt. Maybe, as Margaret Mead says in *Blackberry Winter,* "the baby smiles so much." Or maybe it is the emotional strain of having to fight the world every day.

The battle for women's rights has not yet been *won.* Women cannot see how cunning the patriarchal traps are until they season a little. Younger feminists like Naomi Wolf have underestimated how entrenched patriarchal power is and how often women assent to it in their own souls. They are not yet considering the whole arc of a woman's life. We assent to wifedom because we are so used to having someone to blame and so unused to freedom. We prefer self-punishment to the conquest of our fears. We prefer our anger to our freedom.

If women were totally conscious of the part of themselves that gives away power to men, the prediction of victory might prove true. But we are far from this self-knowledge. And we move further and further away as we retreat from the psychoanalytic model of the self. As long as we disclaim the importance of unconscious motivations, of the existence of the unconscious itself, we cannot root out the slave in ourselves. Freedom is hard to love. Freedom takes away all the excuses.

If this were conscious, everything would be easy—and easy to change. But it is deeply buried. We do not usually know that we value the male and devalue the female. We do not usually know that we are divided against ourselves. We do not know that we have internalized Papa as right and Mama as wrong.

Every book I have written has been written on the bleeding corpse of my grandmother. Every book has been written with guilt, powered by pain. Every book has been a baby I did not bear, ten thousand meals I did not cook, ten thousand beds I did not make. I wish, above all, to be undivided, to be whole (this, in fact, is the theme of all my work), but somewhere I remain divided. Like a person who once committed a terrible crime that went unpunished, I always wait for the ax to fall. In this, I suspect I am not unlike other women.

My grandmother died in 1969. Ten years later I wrote this poem, attempting to capture something of the feelings her example raised in me:

WOMAN ENOUGH

Because my grandmother's hours
were apple cakes baking,
& dust motes gathering,
& linens yellowing
& seams and hems
inevitably unraveling—
I almost never keep house—
though really I like houses
& wish I had a clean one.

Because my mother's minutes
were sucked into the roar
of the vacuum cleaner,
because she waltzed with the washer-dryer

& tore her hair waiting for repairmen—
I send out my laundry,
& live in a dusty house,
though I really *like* clean houses
as well as anyone.

I am woman enough
to love the kneading of bread
as much as the feel
of typewriter keys
under my fingers—
springy, springy.
& the smell of clean laundry
& simmering soup
are almost as dear to me
as the smell of paper and ink.

I wish there were not a choice;
I wish I could be two women.
I wish the days could be longer.
But they are short.
So I write while
The dust piles up.

I sit at my typewriter
remembering my grandmother
& all my mothers,
& the minutes they lost
loving houses better than themselves—
& the man I love cleans up the kitchen
grumbling only a little
because he knows
that after all these centuries
it is easier for him
than for me.

Now, decades later, these feelings are even stronger.

Where does this leave the female creator? In a quandary, as usual.
My grandmother sits on my shoulder and I seek to silence her. She is

reminding me of my duties: the school conference, the marketing, the creation of a nest, the care of the private sphere. But I need to work and to say no to my child. My husband has to cook and nurture too. He has to clean up too. Is there an androgynous freedom beyond female and male? Women and men both need it.

A memory from childhood drifts back through the synapses. I am lying in the big bed between my parents. Perhaps I am four or five. I have awakened with a nightmare, and my sleepy father has carried me into bed and placed me between himself and my mother.

Bliss. A foretaste of heaven. A memory of the amniotic ocean—the warmth of my mother's body on one side and of my father's on the other. (Freudians would say I am happy to separate them, and maybe they are right, but let us shelve that question for now.) It suffices to say that I am happy to be here in the primeval cave, bathed in the radiance of paradise.

Back, back in time. I lie looking up and the ceiling seems a kaleidoscope of diced peas and carrots—nursery food—comforting and warm. My parents' mingled smells and mine. Family pheromones. Familiar smells out of which we are born. For the moment, there is no world but this, no siblings, no teachers, no streets, no cars. Eden is here between my sleeping parents and there is no banishment in sight. I deliberately hold myself awake to savor the moment of *paradiso* threading through the *purgatorio* of everyday life, the *inferno* of school and sisters, of competitive sandbox wars, and of the cruelty of other children.

This is where we all begin—in the *paradiso* of childhood. And it is to this place that poetry seeks to return us. The poles of our being—love and death: the parental bed and the grave. Our passage is from one to the other.

My grandmother on my shoulder is upset. She doesn't want me to write these things. She believes the course of wisdom in a woman's life is to keep silent about all the truth she knows. It is dangerous, she has learned, to parade intimate knowledge. The clever woman smiles and keeps mum. My problem is that books don't get written that way. Especially not books containing any crumb of truth.

So we come back, inevitably, to the problem of women writing the truth. We must write the truth in order to validate our own feelings, our own lives, and we have only very recently earned those rights. And only provisionally. Dictators burn books because they know that books help people claim their feelings, and people who claim their feelings are harder to crush.

Patriarchal society has traditionally put a gag on women's public expression of feelings because silence compels obedience. My grandmother thinks she wants to protect me. She doesn't want to see me stoned in the marketplace. She doesn't want me pilloried for my words. She wants me safe so that I can save the next generation. She has a matriarch's interest in keeping our family alive.

Hush, Mama, the world has changed. We are claiming our own voices. We will speak not only for ourselves but also for you. And our daughters, we hope, will never have to kill *their* grandmothers.

I make a foray into the kitchen for butter-applesauce-and-powdered-sugar sandwiches while my older sister holds the fort (and the baby).

"What are you doing?" asks my grandmother.

"Oh, nothing," I say, running back for cover with the sandwiches.

"Children!" calls my grandmother. "Children!"

We pretend not to hear.

"*Children*," she calls. "What are you playing?"

"Oh, nothing," we say, munching our sandwiches in the closet, hiding from imaginary Nazis.

We cannot say that we are playing love and death. We would not even know how to form the words. But we are playing for our lives, playing for time, and playing as a way of learning life.

My older sister, who originated this game, was born in 1937. The world was on the edge of war when she first emerged into it, and she absorbed the threat of danger with our mother's milk. I followed her lead, as second children do. The details obsessed me: the baby bundled in the doll carriage, my mission to the kitchen to snatch the sandwiches, my mad dash back down the hall through imaginary woods, filled with imaginary Nazis, shouldering imaginary machine guns, my sense of my own importance as a survivor, provider, purveyor of food.

"In dreams begin responsibilities," says the poet Delmore Schwartz. In games begins the serious business of our lives. Still the messenger, still the provider, I am still hiding in the scented cave of the linen closet to write, then rushing out to gather sustenance from the world, then running back to feed the baby and myself.

The baby that I feed is sometimes my daughter, sometimes myself, sometimes my books. But the model of frenzied survival is clear. I alternate between periods of calm and periods of maximum stress. World War II still rages in my head.

I try to imagine my grandmother's life compared to my own. Born in the 1880s in Russia, raised in Odessa, she came to England in her teens, married and had two daughters before World War I began. In the twenties, she raised two small children in New York, having survived pogroms, prerevolutionary unrest, the influenza epidemic, tuberculosis, the First World War, displacement, emigration, two new languages, two new lands. And I, the second daughter of a second daughter of a second daughter, bear her burdens in my soul.

I seize them as opportunities. I embrace the courage and tenacity she passed along to me. But I have won the right to speak of it—a right she never dreamed of.

Where do all the memories go?

Now that my mother knows I am writing an autobiography, she brings me notes on little yellow Post-its. The latest Post-it note reads: "DeeDee, Funalike, and the Famous Guy."

"I have only the vaguest recollection," I tell my mother. "Who were they?"

"Oh—they were your imaginary friends," she says. "You used to converse with them for *hours*. You never went *anywhere* without DeeDee, Funalike, and the Famous Guy."

I am standing in the middle of a cemetery. Every day, another person younger than I dies. Every day the obituaries bring news of someone from college or high school or camp who *died* at forty-seven or -eight or -nine or even at fifty. Sometimes I see classmates of mine on TV and they look like old men or old women. And sometimes I meet people and don't remember their names at all. When do I get to be like Aunt Kitty? When do I forget it all?

And now even my beloved imaginary friends from childhood have bitten the dust. All I have are their names on a Post-it note. I remember nothing whatever about them. Who on earth could they have been? Shall we reinvent these friends from the names up?

"The Famous Guy" is, I suspect, some sort of sneaky stand-in for my father. He wears an ice-white tux with a bright blue cornflower boutonniere. His hair is slicked back with Brylcreem and he reeks of ice-blue Aqua Velva. The smell evokes tinkling pianos in the next apartment and midnight-blue limousines with phallic fins. He dances like a dream, gliding over floors of polished anthracite in his polished anthracite shoes. He is desire, love, luck, a trip to the moon on gossamer wings. He can play anything from his fake book—forgotten songs like "So Many Memories" or "The Jersey Bounce," and famous songs like "Love Walked In" and "Smoke Gets in Your Eyes." He can dance the tango, the mambo, the rhumba with an *h,* and when he leaves, he gives you the blues (but you'd rather have the blues than any other guy). He is Daddy and the wild redheaded boy with the Harvard scarf who held the doors of the subway train on Seventy-eighth Street and Central Park West. Once, he sweated into a T-shirt, left it in your hamper, and you pulled it out and never washed it. You have been sleeping with it ever since.

Everyone else you have loved or married is a stand-in for the Famous Guy. His eyes are blue and green and brown and warm gold all at once. He can change heads faster than Princess Langwidere. As you get older, you meet him less and less often. A snatch of melody wafting through a wall, a scent of sweat and sweet cologne, and you seem to see him. Once, you cruised the city in a midnight limousine looking for him, sure that when you found him you would drag him into it and make love right there on the floor, while the chauffeur with the Braille eyes and the crystal skull drove like wet velvet. giving you the chance to do the same. *Oh, Famous Guy—when will you come to live in my life?*

"Never."

Why?

"*You* know."

Because desire is a limousine that never stops moving, a flying carpet gliding over the chimney pots as seen by an airborne Peter Pan, a fragment of song to which you cannot remember the release. *Ah, Famous Guy, come and make love to me right now.*

"I am. I am doing it by dictating these words."

And what about DeeDee? DeeDee is the all-American girl. She's the one who doesn't have Russian grandparents or Balinese batiks over the stair rail. She's the one who has ice-white refrigerator teeth and hair made of blonde Dynel. She has a candy-striped crinoline and over it a blue felt skirt with poodles—poodles chained to other poodles. You had a skirt like that too, but you never looked in it the way DeeDee looked. How was that? *Regular*. DeeDee was a *regular girl* and you would never be regular if you lived to be a hundred and six. You had the poodle skirt and the twin set and the pearls and the circle pin, but you fooled no one. You were definitely *irregular*. And do you know what? You are still irregular—even among writers, you are irregular. You will never be DeeDee. You belong nowhere, have a funny name, are seen always as something you're not. You cannot change your name to DeeDee, whatever you do. You are Erica, Erotica, Eroica—as they called you in high school. Or Isadora, Fanny, Jessica, Leila—as you called yourself in books. But never normal blonde happy DeeDee who marries the captain of the football team and never even *longs* for the Famous Guy, let alone cruises the city, searching for him and inviting him into that long limousine.

DeeDee had a white wedding and two-point-five kids. She never had anything she didn't want and never wanted anything she didn't have. What on earth was she doing playing with you? That's exactly it. She's taken her marbles and gone home, leaving no memory traces. Her mother wouldn't let her. She never belonged in your house in the first place. But you miss her. And she reads your books and tries to tell you in bookstores in shopping plazas that she is just as irregular as you are and that DeeDee doesn't really *exist*. She loves you for *not* being DeeDee, for having exploded DeeDee as a myth, for having taken her clothes and filled her head with wet dreams that never drive away.

Funalike was a name I made up for myself: middle child, me too, having funalike, bouncy, eager to please, a good kid who blended in, was polite, thanked parents for dinner, ate her peas, minded her Qs, and *never* made peepee in the bathwater. Funalike kissed boys she didn't like *that* much, because she didn't want to be considered un-funalike. She ran errands, saved quarters, shouted *Wagon, wagon!* at the Fire Island ferry dock until she had enough money to buy all the Nancy Drew mysteries. And then she read them one by one alike until she knew how a book got made and how you got the reader to turn the page—which was the most funalike Funalike ever had.

Oh, Funalike, will you ever marry the Famous Guy? Only in books, said she, so that DeeDee can marry him too.

The fourth imaginary friend was not my invention but my mother's or my grandmother's or maybe even my great-grandmother's. This was Hashka the Meshugganeh. (She is not on the Post-it—but somehow the other three bring her along with them.)

Who was she? (For she definitely was a she.) She was invoked when somebody got herself up in mad get-up (a frequent occurrence in our house) and somebody *else* said, "You look like Hashka the Meshugganeh." Was she an apparition from some distant shtetl? Was she the madwoman of Grodno or some ragpicker from the outskirts of Odessa? She wore a crazy hat—summer or winter. Her clothes were voluminous and black and hid owls, children, severed body parts. She cackled like a hen, flapped like a swan, and had glittering mad eyes. She told tales of babies made into fruit compote and sausages that sang and puppets that turned into real children.

She was on pretty good terms with the Famous Guy. He came for her nightly in his long limousine. (Nobody in that shtetl had ever even seen a *car,* let alone a limousine.) What he wanted with her, we didn't know, but what *we* thought was her madness evidently beguiled *him.*

They got married and had various daughters. One was DeeDee—who was, of course, perfect. One was Funalike, who *tried* to be, by overachieving and spreading fun, fun, funalike. Another was Erica with the ambiguous last name. She kept changing her last name, in the hopes of capturing memory. But memory is a fickle friend. And, in the end, all that's left of it is what you read in books.

And so we see that the frayed thread of memory is likely to snag on any will-o'-the-wisp. If you have had a childhood in which no one punishes you for your fantasies, in which your mother even delights in remembering the names of your imaginary friends, you may grow up to be that trio of alter egos: DeeDee, Funalike, and just plain Erica. Of all the things I bless my mother for, it is this delight in fantasy, the right to dream, that she passed on to me. It is a gift—the greatest she gave.

It was only after Ken and I had been married for a while that I reached this truce with my mother.

First, I feared I was *becoming* her—a natural enough evolution in a marriage that replayed many elements of my parents' marriage: the closeness, the fierce fighting, the sense of safety. I think it is not unusual for couples to go through a copycat phase of parental marriages, but it is important also to leave that phase behind. Otherwise, the marriage risks becoming permanently desexualized.

As a kid, I felt doomed to loneliness, a misfit, a martyr. Only with my parents, sleeping between them in that magic hollow, did I lose the loneliness. But I was, like all kids, an interloper. I had no partner of my own. For years I acted out variations of Oedipal dreams. My constant traveling, meeting men in distant hotel rooms, was, I realized in my forties, a disguised dream of meeting my father abroad on his endless travels. When I flashed on that—perhaps it happened on that fateful trip to Umbria—the game of hotel sex became suddenly superfluous. I was not going to meet and seduce my father in a foreign hotel. He belonged to my mother. When I gave up the fantasy of springing him loose and having him for myself, I could finally accept having my own partner and stop flying from city to city meeting man after man. (Maybe my choosing married men and then choosing *not* to let them leave their wives was another Oedipal undoing—I would have them and not have them, both at the same time.)

My mother accepted Ken as she had never accepted anyone before. It may have been merely exhaustion. Or it may have been the *mamaloschen*. Or maybe she knew that *I* had acknowledged her marriage at last. I was no longer her rival. I had my own man to love me every day. My mother and I talked in a new way. Perhaps I had learned to listen in a new way. I think we see our parents' lives differently at every stage of our journey, and at fifty, married to a friend and accepting being loved, I could look at my parents as people.

I had never thought my mother would agree to be interviewed, but it turned out I was wrong. I have been wrong about so much in my life—why not this?

My mother is now so frail that though I want to take her in my arms and hug her, I fear she will break. I walk on eggs around her—a funny metaphor to use of mothers. Even while I am interviewing her, I am trying not to offend. The truth is, I only got to this point because, once, when I was in my twenties, I *did* offend. I thumbed my nose at her life. I emancipated myself with *Fear of Flying* and cut free. I wrote a manifesto against my mother. And it was she herself who had given me the courage to do this.

"I feel that I have just read my obituary," she used to say after reading certain poems of mine. As for the novels, she claimed never to have read them, preferring me to be a poet.

"That's not your obituary," I said. "I love you." But she was right and I was wrong. And anyway, what did it have to do with love? You can love and still kill, then mourn. When did love ever preclude murder?

Of course I wrote her obituary, just as she wrote *her* mother's obituary in that ghastly dream, just as Molly is writing mine. Writing your mother's obituary is a sign of being alive. It is the indispensable act. It is the way you steal a life.

And the mother whose heart has been plucked out to make a sacrifice on the altar of poetry or fiction or love or freedom still says, when the grown child stumbles, "Are you hurt, my child?"

17

BIRTHS, DEATHS, ENDINGS

To act and make flower . . .

—Muriel Rukeyser, *The Life of Poetry*

There is a final antidote we must learn: to love them and forgive them. This attitude comes hard and must be reached with anguish.

—Louise Bogan, *Journey Round My Room: The Autobiography of Louise Bogan: A Mosaic*

As I come to the end of this book, something in me panics and wants to block. I stop writing forward. I go back and try to rewrite the old chapters of my life—recast them, hone them, change the episodes, the order, the ending. The truth is: I do not want to finish the book and let it go. It is like letting my life go. It will cease to be mine; it will go out into the world and become like a fire hydrant for any cur to piss on. It will begin its long journey from my will, my brain, my language, into the hearts of those who need it. But, in the interim, like a child, it may have to take a lot of abuse. Sometimes my books are messengers that people want to shoot. And then they linger on, despite the odds.

I look around me in America and madness reigns. The antisex league is in charge. Some feminists of my generation have rallied mightily to the antisex cause. The truth is: Sex *is* terrifying, full of uncontrollable darkness and illogic that it is far easier to suppress. Easier to scream *Rape!* than admit complicity in desire, easier to claim the moral high ground of victimhood than to admit to our own desires to victimize others, easier to project the evil outward than recognize it as a part of the anarchic self.

Shall we burn the flesh rather than allow it to bubble from within? Women are so moved by sexuality, so unable to compartmentalize it, that we are always fair game for mortification of the flesh, and America is still a puritan country. We worship not Mary but Cotton Mather, not the mother but the mad eviscerated Virgin, the preadolescent who pronounces all human effluvia *yucky* and is willing to kill all the *yuckiness* in herself—and in others.

What I have fought for in my life and in my books—irony, the double vision that sees good and evil as flip sides of the same human coin, the integration of body and brain, sensuality and spirituality, honeyed voluptuousness and philosophical rigor—these are the things most endangered today. In Catharine MacKinnon we have a contemporary version of Savonarola—ready to sacrifice art to the flames because it might "harm" women, women who have been harmed for centuries by their deprivation of this very nourishment. But there is no way to argue this in a world that knows no linguistic precision nor irony nor satire, a world where video snippets measured in milliseconds pass for communication.

I have been writing books now for over twenty years, and each time I let go of one it gets harder. I see the publication process as a Shirley Jacksonesque lottery in which every reaction is a hurled stone. Not that *only* stones are tossed. There is great appreciation—even love—from readers. But to get to them, I find I must run a kind of gauntlet. It is precisely this mockery, ridicule, and humiliation that makes women tremble at the presumption of leadership (or authorship). The hatred is so great, the anger so unforgiving, the self-loathing so bottomless. What is the crime? Daring to have opinions? Daring to be exuberant, sexual, funny, opinionated, excessive? If you doubt these things are seen as criminal, look at the things that have been written about women's exuberance, sexuality, humor, and excess! They will shut you up.

The whole point seems to be to shut us up by getting us to shut each other up. When will we stop playing this coward's game?

It is that time of year I most dislike: the parenthesis between Thanksgiving and Christmas. The days are short. Darkness slices into the afternoon. The city doesn't move, mired as it is in false gaiety and empty ritual.

It has been almost a year since Kitty was admitted to the Hebrew Home for the Aged. She is complaining that they are giving her pills to take away her memory, and perhaps that is as good an explanation as any. She is unable to paint. Her social worker explains to me that perhaps it makes her too upset to paint or perhaps she doesn't remember *how* to paint and *that* is upsetting her. Nobody seems to know. If she is no longer painting, then I think she has outlived her time. But I do not say so. I merely make an appointment to meet with her and her "support team" and go back to my struggle with my book.

At the end of November, there is an eclipse of the moon. Ken and I have driven all the way back from Vermont under its full golden disc and, at midnight, we climb up the back stairs of our apartment building to the twenty-ninth floor, exit the stairwell at the roof level, and walk among the stars. The city is still. The roof looks like a lunar landscape. The traffic noises seem suddenly stopped. And we stand alone in the middle of the roof, heads tilted back until they hurt, watching a dark shadow encroach across the face of the moon. It takes an hour and a half for the eclipse to be total. We stand transfixed and shivering, unable to leave until the whole disc is closed in darkness. When a sliver of light emerges on the other side, I say, "I'm glad I saw that."

"So am I," says Ken.

Neither of us could tell you why.

After the eclipse, I find myself unable to sleep. Basil the cat and Poochini the bichon frise have found a warm hollow between me and Ken and are sleeping peacefully. Ken is out cold, his breathing shallow, his bearded baby face serene. I am slightly hungry but too lazy to get up. Suddenly the taste of fresh farmer cheese and homemade plum jam with shriveled skins comes into my mouth—and my grandparents are here.

They used to have this for breakfast: fresh rye bread or challah, fresh farmer cheese, sliced in a crumbly rectangle, cold, sour, and faintly chalky to the tongue, my grandmother's garnet damson plum jam with the shriveled skins left in, and sometimes a stone. The cheese went on the bread, was spread slightly, and the jam was dripped over that. You ate it quickly so as not to make a mess. Tea with milk and honey was the beverage.

My grandparents are sitting at their little breakfast table, feeding themselves and me.

"Patriotism is the memory of foods eaten in childhood," said Lin Yutang.

And suddenly I remember disposing of my grandfather's things after he died. And I realize I will have to do the same for my parents and for Kitty, and Molly will have to do the same for me. And the taste of these foods will be gone—as vanished as the moon during eclipse.

What will bring them back? Nothing.

We are creatures whose memories are too big for everyday use— until they are too small. During this moment of insomnia, my brain aches with the fullness of past, present, and future. But already I feel sleep coming.

I go to visit Kitty at the Hebrew Home for the Aged and find her sitting between two men. One of them introduces himself as a dentist and admires my bicuspids. "The incisor is the strongest tooth in the body—didja know that?" he asks. The other man, a certain Mr. Goldlilly, has his hand on Kitty's thigh. She seems to have forgotten she is a lesbian.

"Darling," she says, "I'm so glad to see you." She looks well— hale, even plump. She calls everybody "darling" to cover the loss of names. (Perhaps this explains the widespread practice of *darlingfication* in the theater too.) Leaving her two male admirers, Kitty walks with me to another lounge area. We sit down, looking out at the river, glinting in the December light.

"I'm so glad to see you," she says.

"Me too," I say. And I am glad to see her.

"What are you doing?" I ask.

"Nothing much. Just living from day to day. But I worry about my apartment."

"Don't worry, Kitty, I'll take care of it."

I don't tell her that we will have to sell it to pay her bills in this glamorous old age spa.

"Why don't you take the apartment, honey, and rent it out? Then I could live with you. All I need is a nice room with north light, a bathroom. I'm not the sort of person who imposes. We could see each other from time to time."

Suddenly, there is a commotion in the unit. Molly and two of her friends come running down the hall. With their long hair, ripped jeans, big workboots, grungy checked shirts, they change the energy in the place. They are all so *tall*. Kitty has been shrinking as they have grown.

A baby-faced white-haired woman wielding a walker has been circling the hall as Kitty and I have talked. Now she stops and asks Molly, "Where is my room? I don't know where my room is." Molly gently takes her to the nurse's station and asks for the location of her room. Then I see her guiding the old woman there.

"Who's that? Who's that?" says Kitty when Molly and her two friends walk over. Molly introduces her friends, Sabrina and Amy.

Kitty says, "Pleased to meet you." Her memory is gone but her charm is intact. She smiles lovingly.

"Darling," Kitty says to Molly, "I can't live here the rest of my life, can I? I want to live with you."

"No, Kitty," says my daughter, "you're much better off here. You were so lonely and scared in your apartment." She is very strong and very direct. She is much braver than I am. "I think Mommy will have to sell your apartment," she says.

"And what about my paintings?"

"I will take care of them," Molly says. "I love your paintings."

In the year that Kitty has been here, my daughter has become a mensch.

"I guess you're right," Kitty tells her.

When I leave to drive Molly, Sabrina, and Amy back to the city, Kitty returns to her two dazed men friends.

"That's my niece," I hear her saying to the dentist and Mr. Goldlilly. But she still does not remember my name.

My mother celebrates her eighty-second birthday on December tenth. Surrounded by her grandchildren, she is laughing and looks almost happy. Seeing my mother relaxed, something in me also relaxes. If she will only embrace her life with joy, then so can I. I feel that all my life I have tortured myself because I feel she has been tortured. All my life, I have suffered because somehow I sense she wants it that way. *Be happy*, I think, watching her among her grandchildren. *Please be happy so I can be.*

Two nights later, a call comes from my father in the emergency room of New York Hospital.

"Mother collapsed," he says. "We're in the emergency room. Don't come."

If I take that at face value, he will be furious, I know. But for once I defy him by taking him at face value. Later, I call him at home to ask him how my mother is.

"She's furious at you," my father says, "for not coming." And he hangs up on me.

I sleep the sleep of a dead person, hoping never to wake and have to face my parents again. I dream I am wandering the Elysian fields among my ancestors, asking each one, "Am I dead yet?"

In my pocket, I have a dried embryo the size of my index finger. It is a child I never had—or else it is me. Its legs have crumbled away. Also its arms. Why did I never have this baby? Why is it crumbling in my pocket?

In the morning, I go to New York Hospital, walking like a zombie in the cold air. I have no makeup on and I wear black leggings, a black turtleneck sweater, and black hooded jacket as if already in mourning. Very well, then, if I am the bad daughter, let me be the bad daughter. I wander the labyrinthine passages below the street level, wondering which corridor will take me to an elevator that will take me to the cardiac unit. Eventually I find it. I ascend to the third floor, make my way into my mother's room, and greet her snarling face.

"Why did you come at all?" she asks.

"Because I love you," I say.

"Hah," she says. "Where were you last night?"

"Daddy told me not to come."

"He's upset," she says. "You can't listen to that."

"I know," I say.

But I am waiting, waiting for some big book of rules for living (or dying), waiting for some huge assurance of love, some final nourishment, some epiphany, some spiritual transcendence. My mother leans back on her pillows, her hair straggling behind her, her eyes at once cold and kind.

"It is not pleasant," she says, "to contemplate your own death."

And I think, if I could take my years and give them to her like some latter-day Alcestis, would I? Would I trade my life—what's left of it—for hers? No. I would not. I would snatch my remaining years with greedy hands. I would finish this book and go on to the next and the next. I would cast off my secret delight in my own paralysis.

Generations of women have sacrificed their lives to become their mothers. But we do not have that luxury anymore. The world has changed too much to let us have the lives our mothers had. And we can no longer afford the guilt we feel at *not* being our mothers. We cannot afford *any* guilt that pulls us back to the past. We have to grow up, whether we want to or not. We have to stop blaming men and mothers and seize every second of our lives with passion. We can no longer afford to waste our creativity. We cannot afford spiritual laziness.

My mother will not give me rules for living—but perhaps I can give them to myself.

"What are you thinking?" she asks.

"That I love you, that I don't want you to die."

"I won't die," she says, suddenly brightening.

The blood fills her face; the tears stream down my cheeks.

When I leave the hospital, I go home and get drunk on red wine for the first time in ages, while waiting for my husband and father to join me for dinner.

"My mother's going to die," I blubber to myself, getting blurrier and blurrier. "If not now, then next time, or the time after. . . ." I am waiting for the wine to give me inspiration, but all it gives is numbness.

By the time we all sit down to dinner, I am thick and headachy and I miss most of the conversation. It happens at the periphery of my awareness. Ken and my father are singing Yiddish music hall songs together as a bonding ritual. I begin drinking coffee to sober up. By the time I am fully awake, my father is ready to go.

In the morning, I get up to have breakfast with Molly as I usually do, and then I go back to bed. Eight o'clock gives way to nine, nine to ten, ten to eleven. I lie in bed as if I am dying—in place of my mother. And of course I *am* dying. We all are, at every moment. But my separation from myself is extreme. I am ferociously angry, depressed and stuck, not wanting to release this book.

What's the point of loving my mother since she is only going to die and what's the point of loving myself since I am only going to die and what's the point of loving this book since it is only going to go out into the maelstrom of publication?

I have forgotten my readers. I have forgotten that my job is to be a voice. I have remembered only my paltry ego and its bruises. I am thinking of endings, not process. Whenever I think of endings, I get stuck.

All last summer, in an effort to lose weight and look young, I took pills to kill my appetite. I lost lots of weight, but also became so speedy I couldn't sit still. When I went off the pills, my personality seemed to fragment. I saw wild animals in the corners of my eyes. I felt a gnawing at my heart and an urge to scream in the streets. When that phase ended, I went into a valley of despair. Divided from myself, I wanted some substance to knit me back together. I drank little—but what did that matter since the little I drank depressed me so? The substance I needed was spirit, not spirits. I needed *myself* to finish this book, and I was finding a million ways to escape from myself.

Gradually, I drag myself out of bed and begin the new day. "I can't drink," I say to myself. "I should remember that." I have coffee, work out on the exercise bike, get dressed, and walk across the street to my office.

"Of course, I can't finish the book if I don't have myself," I say to myself. The soul is awakened through service, and writing is my way of serving. Serving is my way of reattaching mind and spirit. Without spirit, I am dust. I had better keep my head clear of wine and pills so I can write.

This is not a boozy promise to myself. It is a fierce recognition of the truth. I have been distancing myself from the energy that keeps me alive.

The next day, I neither drink nor take pills. My mother comes home from the hospital. The next day, I neither drink nor take pills. My mother goes to the doctor to get her medication adjusted. The next day, I neither drink nor take pills. I go to lunch with friends, giving myself a rare mental health day. If the book is not coming, I'll leave it alone. Let it gather its curious crystals in the darkness.

After lunch, I go to see my mother. She is lying on top of her bed, wearing a yellow silk kimono. Her window opens on Central Park—a human view of the park from the twelfth floor—the tops of trees, the roof of Tavern on the Green, the skyline of Fifth Avenue. Her room is papered with chrome yellow against which pink cabbage roses dance. Scattered among the roses are paintings of babies. The wall contains all the babies, done by her able hand: Molly with her red topknot, me with my flaxen ringlets, Nana with her auburn hair, redheaded baby

Claudia, dark-haired Tony and Peter, and blond Alex—all the children and grandchildren captured in sleep a month or two after their births.

"Why are you here?" my mother asks. "Is there a problem?"

"No, I just want to know what you are doing to take care of yourself."

My mother tells me vaguely of her medication. She seems bored with it all, not paying attention.

"Look," I say, "if you want to die, why not call everyone in and say good-bye? That's an honorable choice. It's your choice. But if you want to live, then take your medicine and try to have another few good years."

"I want to live," she says.

"I love you. I'm not ready to do without a mother yet," I say, and I lean down and take her in my arms as if she is one of those babies on the wall. Her body is slight, bones wrapped in silk, but the smell is all my history. This is the deepest embrace we have had in years.

"Why haven't you finished that book?" she asks.

"I don't know," I say.

"You're afraid of criticism," she says. "But criticism is a sign of life! You know who doesn't get criticized? Nonentities! Only the dead escape criticism."

"That's true," I say.

"We're all going to sleep a very long time," she says. "Don't put yourself to sleep with fear. Do you think I kept you alive when all those babies died so you could sit on your hands and tremble?"

"I suppose not."

"So—go home and finish the book!"

"I will," I say.

"So—what's the last line?"

I stop to think, looking at the wall of babies, myself included. Suddenly a line comes into my head. I speak it in a strong voice. "I am not my mother, and the next half of my life stands before me."